Transitional Justice in the Twe

Dealing w
governmen
Whereas r
the relativ
the end of
was inappr
justice exp
that a sing
conflict or
analyzes h
with comn
ture, whils
national or
also now
emerging a

NAOMI R
California,
Pinochet Ej
and Impun
(1995).

JAVIER M.
for Human
Manager a
Notre Dar
Rights and
Homage to
Vol. X (20

Transitional Justice in the Twenty-First Century

Beyond Truth versus Justice

Edited by

Naomi Roht-Arriaza and Javier Mariezcurrena

CAMBRIDGE
UNIVERSITY PRESS

CAMBRIDGE UNIVERSITY PRESS
Cambridge, New York, Melbourne, Madrid, Cape Town, Singapore, São Paulo, Delhi

Cambridge University Press
The Edinburgh Building, Cambridge CB2 8RU, UK

Published in the United States of America by Cambridge University Press, New York

www.cambridge.org
Information on this title: www.cambridge.org/9780521677509

First published 2006
Reprinted 2008

Printed in the United Kingdom at the University Press, Cambridge

A catalogue record for this publication is available from the British Library

ISBN 978-0-521-86010-9 hardback
ISBN 978-0-521-67750-9 paperback

Contents

Contributors

MARICLAIRE ACOSTA was Deputy Minister for Human Rights and Democracy (2001–03) in the Ministry for Foreign Affairs of Mexico (Secretaría de Relaciones Exteriores). A long-time human rights defender, she presided over the Mexican Section of Amnesty International in the 1970s, and founded two important human rights organizations: the Mexican Academy for Human Rights (Executive Director from 1984 to 1989) and the Mexican Commission for the Defense and Promotion of Human Rights (Chairperson from 1990 to 2001). She has also been a member of the International Advisory Board of the Council for Foreign Relations. She received the Encomienda de Número, Orden del Mérito Civil from the King of Spain in January 2003 for her longtime dedication to the cause of human rights. She works with the Organization of American States.

REED BRODY is Special Counsel for Prosecutions at Human Rights Watch. He was part of the international coalition supporting the Habré prosecution. Prior to his current position, he worked with the International Commission of Jurists and the United Nations Mission to El Salvador, among others.

PATRICK BURGESS is Principal Legal Counsel for the East Timor Commission for Reception, Truth and Reconciliation. He was formerly the Director of Human Rights of the UNTAET and UNMISET missions to East Timor (2000–03).

EDUARDO GONZÁLEZ CUEVA is a Senior Associate at the International Center for Transitional Justice. He worked at the Peruvian Truth and Reconciliation Commission as the Director of the Public Hearings and Victims and Witnesses Protection Units during 2002, and as a member of the Editorial Committee for the Final Report, during 2003.

ESA ENNELIN studied for his Masters thesis at the Department of Social and Political History at the University of Helsinki. He has researched crisis decision-making at the Finnish Institute of International Affairs and worked defending human rights in Mexico. Currently he is working in London at the international human rights organization ARTICLE 19.

PATRICIA GOSSMAN is Project Director for the Afghanistan Justice Project. Ms. Gossman was previously a researcher for Human Rights Watch's Middle Eastern Division.

MARIA JOSÉ GUEMBE, LL.M. University of Notre Dame, is an Argentine attorney. Ms. Guembe previously headed the program on accountability for human rights violations at the Center for Legal and Social Studies (CELS) in Argentina. She now works on human rights issues in Mexico.

SIGALL HOROVITZ is an Attorney-at-Law and member of the New York and Israeli Bars. She works at the International Criminal Tribunal for Rwanda as the Associate Legal Officer directly attached to the Tribunal's President. Previously, she worked at the Special Court for Sierra Leone and at the Israeli Justice Ministry's International Department. She has also conducted research on behalf of the United Nations Office of Legal Affairs and Human Rights Watch.

TIMOTHY LONGMAN is Professor of Political Science and Africana Studies, Vassar College. Since 2001, Dr. Longman has been the Rwanda research director for the Human Rights Center at the University of California, Berkeley. From 2001 to 2003, Dr. Longman was based in Berkeley, directing a number of research projects funded by the MacArthur Foundation and Hewlett Foundation looking at the process of social reconstruction in Rwanda. Dr. Longman was head of the field office for Human Rights Watch and the Federation International des Ligues des Droits de l'Homme (FIDH) in Butare, Rwanda. He continues to work as a consultant to Human Rights Watch, working on Rwanda, Burundi, and Congo.

ELLEN LUTZ is the Executive Director of Cultural Survival. She formerly was the Executive Director of the Center for Human Rights and Conflict Resolution and taught international human rights law at Tufts University's Fletcher School. She has written widely on human rights and conflict resolution, accountability for human rights violations, and human rights in Latin America.

JAVIER MARIEZCURRENA is an attorney in the office of the Argentine Secretariat for Human Rights. He was previously the Transitional Justice Project Manager at the Center for Civil and Human Rights, University of Notre Dame.

HANNY MEGALLY is Director, Middle East and North Africa, International Center for Transitional Justice. Mr. Megally was previously the Executive Director of the Middle East and North Africa Division of Human Rights Watch.

HANIA MUFTI is a researcher on the Middle East for Human Rights Watch.

HELENA OLEA is a JSD candidate at the University of Notre Dame. A Colombian attorney, she previously worked at the Colombian Commission of Jurists.

CAITLIN REIGER is a Senior Associate at the International Center for Transitional Justice. She was previously the Senior Chambers Legal Officer at the Special Court for Sierra Leone. From 2001 to 2002 she was co-director of the East Timor Judicial System Monitoring Programme (JSMP) in Dili, which monitors the operation of the Special Panels for Serious Crimes and the development of the national justice system.

NAOMI ROHT-ARRIAZA is Professor of Law, University of California, Hastings College of the Law. Professor Roht-Arriaza is the editor of *Impunity and Human Rights in International Law and Practice* (1995) and *The Pinochet Effect: Transnational Justice in the Age of Human Rights* (2005), as well as numerous articles on transitional justice.

WILLIAM A. SCHABAS is Professor of Human Rights Law, National University of Ireland, Galway, and Director, Irish Centre for Human Rights. The author was a member of the Sierra Leone Truth and Reconciliation Commission. This article is written in his private capacity and does not necessarily reflect the views of the other commissioners or of the Commission.

KATHRYN SIKKINK is Arleen C. Carlson Professor of Political Science and the McKnight Distinguished University Professor at the University of Minnesota. She is a fellow of the Council on Foreign Relations and the American Association for Arts and Sciences, a member of the editorial board of the American Political Science Review and International Studies Quarterly, and the chair of the editorial board of the journal International Organization.

ERIC STOVER is the Director of the Human Rights Center and Adjunct Professor, School of Public Health, University of California, Berkeley. He was the Executive Director of Physicians for Human Rights (PHR) until December 1995. Since 1993, he has served on several medicolegal investigations as an "Expert on Mission" to the International Criminal Tribunal for the former Yugoslavia in The Hague. In March and April 1995, he conducted a survey of mass graves throughout Rwanda for the International Criminal Tribunal for Rwanda. In June 1984, Mr. Stover testified for the prosecution at the trial of leaders of the military junta which ruled Argentina from 1976 to 1983.

CARRIE BOOTH WALLING is a PhD candidate in Political Science, University of Minnesota.

Acknowledgments

This volume has been a collaborative effort from the beginning. The project originated as part of a larger Transitional Justice project at the Center for Civil and Human Rights at the University of Notre Dame. That project also includes a number of other publications, a documentation center, and a fellowship program. Many thanks are owed to the Center and its staff for conceiving of the project and making it happen. Thanks especially to Juan Méndez, then-Director of the Center, for his support, help and inspiration, and to the Ford Foundation, and especially Larry Cox, for funding support. Thanks also to the Center's Advisory Board for convincing the editors to take on this book, and especially to Eric Stover of the Human Rights Center at the University of California, Berkeley for his suggestions.

The authors met for a conference in May 2004 to discuss drafts of their papers. We are deeply indebted to all the authors (every one of whom came through with a paper) as well as to several people who participated in the conference and made wise and helpful contributions: Priscilla Hayner of the International Center for Transitional Justice, and Professors Dinah Shelton and Garth Meintjes, both then of Notre Dame Law School. Many thanks as well to Darina Mackova, JSD Candidate at the Center, who transcribed the proceedings.

Javier Mariezcurrena also thanks Silvia Méndez and Laurel Cochrane, and dedicates this book to María Eugenia Roma.

Naomi Roht-Arriaza also thanks Faiz Ahmed and John Dermody for research assistance, and Hastings College of the Law for summer research support. For inspiration, she thanks Laura Arriaza for her enthusiasm and questions, Rafael Arriaza for his patience, and Gilberto Arriaza for his love and support (siempre!). She dedicates the book to Helen Geffen Roht, internationalist and early believer in a just world order, who started her down this road in the first place.

The new landscape of transitional justice

Naomi Roht-Arriaza

Darfur, Guantánamo, Iraq, Haiti. As this book goes to press, they are the headlines, today's sites of killing and mistreatment of civilians and torture of prisoners. Abuses during conflict are not new. Nor is the demand, in many parts of the world, that something be done in their aftermath, that there be justice. But there is a growing sense that something *can* and *must* be done, not only to stop the atrocities but also to bring those responsible to account, to make the facts known, and to succor the victims. The Security Council refers the situation in Darfur to the International Criminal Court. In 2005, Spanish courts sentence an Argentine naval officer to 640 years in a Spanish jail for throwing prisoners, alive but drugged, from airplanes into the sea a quarter-century before. Slowly, often after years have passed and sometimes in venues far from the scene of the crimes, demands for justice emerge. The past, unaccounted for, does not lie quiet.

The study of how societies emerging from periods of civil war or dictatorship deal with the legacies of the past became a full-fledged subject of academic inquiry and human rights activism during the 1990s. The term itself is a bit slippery: transitional justice can be defined as the "conception of justice associated with periods of political change, characterized by legal responses to confront the wrongdoings of repressive predecessor regimes."[1] That definition is somewhat problematic, in that it implies a defined period of flux after which a post-transitional state sets in, whereas in practice "transition" may cover many decades, and may last longer for some issues than for others. It also does not articulate what the state is "transitioning" *to*. Moreover, the same governments that carried out repression or war sometimes institute transitional measures: are those truly "transitional"? Finally, by privileging the *legal* aspects of coming to terms with the past, it overvalues the role of law and legislation, and may give short shrift to the roles of education and culture and of distributional justice.[2]

For these reasons, some people prefer to talk about "post-conflict" justice, but that label has its own problems, especially where what is at

1

issue was not primarily a conflict between two or more armed factions but massive repression by a government against its own unarmed people. In any case, for our purposes transitional justice includes that set of practices, mechanisms and concerns that arise following a period of conflict, civil strife or repression, and that are aimed directly at confronting and dealing with past violations of human rights and humanitarian law.

The universe of transitional justice can be broadly or narrowly defined. At its broadest, it involves anything that a society devises to deal with a legacy of conflict and/or widespread human rights violations, from changes in criminal codes to those in high school textbooks, from creation of memorials, museums and days of mourning, to police and court reform, to tackling the distributional inequities that underlie conflict. A narrow view can be criticized for ignoring root causes and privileging civil and political rights over economic, social and cultural rights,[3] and by so doing marginalizing the needs of women and the poor. On the other hand, broadening the scope of what we mean by transitional justice to encompass the building of a just as well as peaceful society may make the effort so broad as to become meaningless.

This book takes a narrower view, centered on the two central aspects of truth and justice. We focus on a few methods and techniques: prosecutions and criminal investigations, truth commissions, vetting or cleansing of security forces, and, to some extent, formal reparations programs.[4]

Post-conflict attempts at justice are not new: war crimes trials go back at least to the fourteenth century. In the wake of both World Wars there were trials, successful and not. Torturers were tried after the fall of the Greek dictatorship of the 1970s, while a consensus among elites postponed questions of justice and reparations in post-Franco Spain and in post-Salazar Portugal.[5] The decade that concluded with the fall of the Berlin Wall coincided with a wave of changes, negotiated or compelled, from military dictatorships to civilian governments in the Southern Cone of South America, the Philippines and in a number of African countries. The negotiated end of South Africa's apartheid regime, and ends to the civil wars of Central America, soon followed.

These events raised a lively debate regarding the proper strategy after a dictatorship falls or a civil conflict ends. Much of the debate was framed by the conditions of transition in Latin America and Eastern Europe. In the former, the prior dictators and their military and civilian supporters still wielded a good deal of power, and could credibly threaten mayhem if their interests were not respected. Moreover, these transitions were largely negotiated between elites, not compelled by the military defeat of one side in a civil conflict or by popular uprising. Under these circumstances, diplomats, political scientists and also some human rights activists argued that it was shortsighted to overwhelm newly installed, fragile civilian governments with demands for criminal prosecutions, Thus, amnesties were an inevitable concession, trading justice for the past in exchange for justice in the future.

In Argentina and later in Chile, incoming civilian governments commissioned broad-based commissions of notables to investigate and document the human rights violations of the prior regime. While both the Argentine Sábato Commission and Chile's Truth and Reconciliation Commission actually turned their findings over to the courts (and, in Argentina, members of the ruling juntas were prosecuted), the model of a "truth commission" gained force as a "second-best" option where trials were deemed too destabilizing. Truth commissions seemed less confrontational while still not ignoring the violations and doing something for victims. Such commissions focus on a defined period in the past, exist for a limited period, are official, and are tasked with, at a minimum, compiling a narrative of the past violations and recommending ways to repair the damage and prevent its repetition.[6]

The emphasis on "truth" required a theory of why the truth was so important. In Latin America, the rationale was tied to the nature of the repression. For the most part, the military governments did not openly kill their opponents. Rather, large numbers of people were disappeared, picked up by official or unofficial security forces that then refused to acknowledge the detention. Almost all were killed, often after extended torture, and in many cases the bodies were never found. Unofficial death squads wore civilian clothes and provided a measure of deniability. The families of those who disappeared were ostracized as a climate of generalized terror set in.

In Eastern Europe, the period of massive killings had usually passed long before, but there was a pervasive sense of constant surveillance and arbitrary punishment handed down by a state that hid its true face. Opening up of state archives and historical commissions, and efforts to remove the offenders from public office, were the principal Eastern European responses. Truth was needed to reverse the silence and denial of the dictatorship years, to establish the extent, origin and nature of the crimes, which were not well-known, and to know who had collaborated in an effort to limit their future influence. Even though the human rights violations in both places were usually common knowledge, there was a huge gap between knowledge and acknowledgment.[7] And the end of the Cold War meant that investigation of the past would not necessarily entail alignment with one superpower, or aid and comfort to the other.

Psychological research, especially with torture survivors, reinforced the notion that truth was important in itself. Survivors seemed to be helped by telling their story to a sympathetic listener and by setting it within a larger social context. It seemed reasonable that, just as individuals need "closure" to leave trauma behind, whole traumatized societies would benefit from a public airing leading to closure. Religious leaders chimed in, arguing that knowing the truth would allow the victims to forgive without forgetting and the perpetrators to confess and atone, thus setting the stage for former enemies to live together. Human rights lawyers began to argue for a "right to truth" independent of criminal prosecution.[8]

The South African experience became the best known of these experiments. An amnesty law was required in the country's interim constitution, but the Parliament decided to tie amnesty to full disclosure of the crimes by any individual seeking amnesty. They grafted this amnesty-for-truth process onto a Truth and Reconciliation Commission (TRC) aimed at hearing victims' stories, documenting the violations, and providing recommendations for change.

The backers of the South African TRC did not argue merely that a truth commission was a second-best alternative where trials were unavailable. Rather, they insisted, a well-run commission could accomplish things no trial could provide. It could focus on the overall pattern of violations, rather than zeroing in on just those cases that happened to be brought to trial. It could keep the focus of testimony and discussion on the victims rather than the perpetrators, and allow victims to testify in a supportive setting more conducive to healing than the sometimes brutal cross-examination of a criminal or civil trial. By offering amnesty in exchange for confession, it could elicit information from perpetrators that would be unlikely to emerge in a criminal trial where the burden of proof remained on the state. Moreover, non-judicial methods were better at dealing with the many shades of gray that characterize most conflicts. Trials divided the universe into a small group of guilty parties and an innocent majority, which was thereby cleansed of wrongdoing. In reality, however, large numbers of people supported those who committed the actual violations, and even larger numbers turned their faces away and were silent. Trials could not adequately engage with those nuances.[9] A restorative justice approach, focusing on the victims and on reintegration of offenders rather than the retributive justice ascribed to the criminal law, was preferable.

Truth commissions became a staple of the transitional justice menu. Over time, critiques arose. Such commissions assumed there was a single "truth" to be molded from the disparate strands of interests and experience. They could contribute to a compiling of "factual" truth, but not necessarily to the creation of a common narrative or common understanding. They frustrated and at times even retraumatized victims who, having unearthed their pain, were left wondering to what end. The model of short-term catharsis as a basis for healing was disputed by therapists, and the empirical evidence showed that testifying in public was beneficial for some victims, but not others. They did nothing to affect local power relationships.[10]

Moreover, the South African example, widely praised internationally, received a more critical reception at home. While it had many positive aspects, the TRC did not lead automatically to reconciliation either between blacks and whites or among blacks ("revealing is healing" turned out only to be true sometimes), almost no high-ranking officials of the apartheid government came forward to ask for amnesty, and the courts were largely unwilling to pursue cases, even well-founded ones, against those who disdained the offer of amnesty for truth. Although other countries emerging from conflict adapted parts of the South African scheme, none adopted it wholesale.

From country to country as well, a process of diffusion of experiences and ideas followed. Chileans advised the South Africans on their TRC; the South Africans inspired the idea of confession in exchange for amnesty or leniency in a number of places. Forensic scientists multiplied exhumation and forensics teams, using newly minted techniques around the world. The peace agreement drafters designed the Guatemalan Historical Clarification Commission to *not* mimic aspects of the earlier Salvadoran Truth Commission. But each place was also unique, influenced not only by international advisors and funders but by the strength of its own human rights movement, of opposing political forces and the nature and extent of the conflict.

While truth commissions became widely known, other elements of the transitional justice "toolbox" where used far less frequently. Vetting or cleansing of political leaders and security forces was a major component of efforts in the Czech Republic and elsewhere in Eastern and Central Europe, but was criticized for being overbroad and based on unreliable secret police records. Army officers were vetted in El Salvador; in Argentina, military promotions were contingent on human rights screening. Reparations programs were implemented in Argentina, Brazil, Chile, and (eventually, on a scaled-down basis) South Africa, and are just now being carried out in Guatemala and Peru. Beyond these, reparations programs are scarce, although they are a frequent TC recommendation.

By the time of the South African TRC in 1995, a further set of considerations had to be added to the mix. In the early 1990s, a bloody ethnic conflict in the former Yugoslavia left 200,000 dead. Western powers dithered, but eventually agreed to try to deter ongoing atrocities by setting up an international criminal tribunal. In addition to deterrence, the tribunal was supposed to contribute to reconciliation through justice, to create a historical record, and to remove some of the worst offenders from positions of power. It was set up via Security Council resolution, which in theory at least ensured the cooperation of all UN members. A year later, in 1994, the slaughter of over three quarters of a million people during three months in Rwanda, prompted the creation of a similar international criminal tribunal for Rwanda. Both tribunals were set up outside the situs of the conflicts, both because of security concerns and because it was felt that an outside court, staffed largely by outsiders, would have the advantages of impartiality, credibility and expertise that would be lacking in compromised or decimated national legal systems.

Criminal prosecution was seen as essential in these cases in part because the killings had been massive, open and notorious (indeed, broadcast on Rwandan radio) and so a "truth commission," by itself, was thought both inadequate and unnecessary.[11] Moreover, these were not cases where a rigid security force hierarchy under state control attacked perceived enemies of the state. Rather, they were much murkier, involving ethnic and resource-based conflict and looser chains of command. Often, ethnically based conflicts set community against community, neighbor against neighbor. Only trials could provide for the confrontation of evidence and witnesses that would create an unimpeachable factual record, Moreover, only trials could adequately individualize responsibility, holding the guilty parties liable without stigmatizing entire ethnic or religious groups. This was important to avoid continuing bouts of violence as well as the temptation of private revenge.

The Tribunals were praised for reaffirming the principle that accountability was an important international concern. Their statutes, rules of evidence and procedure, and rulings were milestones in the development of international criminal law, and they served as training grounds for a corps of international investigators, lawyers and judges. They developed important jurisprudence on genocide, crimes against humanity and war crimes, among other issues. They contributed to creating an authoritative record of the origins and nature of the violence, incapacitated a number of offenders, allowed some victims to tell their story, and limited the ability of some local authorities to do further mischief. They established that heads of state were not immune from trial before an international tribunal, and pioneered techniques like the use of sealed indictments and plea bargains in the international criminal context. As of February 2006, the Yugoslav Tribunal has indicted almost 100 individuals, including former president Slobodan Milosevic. The Rwandan Tribunal has tried or is currently trying 52 leaders of the Rwandan genocide, including the former army Chief-of-Staff, and another 17 detainees are awaiting trial.[12]

And yet, by the start of the new decade criticism mounted as well. The Tribunals were enormously expensive and time-consuming, and critics noted that the same resources might have been better spent on rebuilding the national legal systems. Their very distance, both literal and figurative, made them seem remote from the "target" societies, and it was doubtful whether the populations of the Balkans or Rwanda accepted the facts established in their rulings as authoritative or even knew of their work.[13] It was unclear what their long-term legacy would be, as domestic courts seemed woefully unprepared to take up the cases the Tribunals lacked resources to pursue even as the Tribunals faced deadlines to wrap up their activities.[14]

Two other events at the end of the 1990s raised the profile of international justice efforts: the creation of the International Criminal Court and the arrest of Augusto Pinochet. After a number of preparatory meetings, a conference convened in 1998 to create a permanent International Criminal Court. The ICC has jurisdiction over genocide, crimes against humanity, and war crimes taking place after July 1, 2002. (A fourth crime, aggression, will be added once defined.) Unlike the Yugoslav and Rwanda Tribunals, the ICC's jurisdiction is complementary to that of national courts: it can only prosecute when local courts prove unable or unwilling to do so. As of 2006, some 100 countries are parties to the ICC Statute. The prosecutor has announced his first investigations, but few indictments have been forthcoming as yet. In March 2005, the Security Council sent its first referral to the Office of the Prosecutor.

Scarcely three months after the signing of the Rome Statute, the former head of Chile's military government, Augusto Pinochet, was arrested in London under a provision of Spanish law providing jurisdiction in local courts for cases of genocide, terrorism and other international crimes under ratified treaties. The British House of Lords found that he had no immunity as a former head of state from charges of torture, and that torture constituted an "extradition crime." The highest Spanish criminal appeals court also upheld the prosecution under Spain's universal jurisdiction law. Eventually, Pinochet was found unfit for trial and sent home, but by that time the taboo on complaints against him had been broken. He was soon charged in a number of cases, his parliamentary immunity stripped, and as of this writing he is awaiting trial in both human rights and tax evasion cases; many of his closest associates are in prison. Transnational prosecutions seemed a viable option as a complement to national or international ones, or at least as a way to avoid creating safe-havens for traveling dictators. A rash of other transnational prosecutions followed.

These two major trends – the increasing use of investigative or "truth and reconciliation" commissions and the use of international and transnational trials – came together by the beginning of the new millennium. The debate about truth versus justice seemed to be resolving in favor of an approach that recognized them as complementary. Even those who had argued strenuously in favor of a non-prosecutorial, "truth-centered" approach recognized exceptions for crimes against humanity, while advocates of prosecution recognized that a truth-seeking and truth-telling exercise could serve as a valuable precursor or complement, even if not a substitute, for prosecutions. This mutual recognition combined with increasing attention at the international level to issues of reparations and structural reform. Practitioners and scholars began to speak of a "package" of measures, of an intertwined set of obligations arising in cases of massive or systematic violations, composed of truth, justice, reparation and guarantees of non-repetition.

Moreover, each element affected the shape and possibilities of the others, in an "ecological model"[15] of social reconstruction or reclamation. "Truth-telling" followed by neither reparations nor prosecutions seemed to make victims' accounts meaningless, while reparations without public acknowledgment of the facts looked to many victims like "blood money" paid for their silence. Prosecutions without a forum where a larger narrative could emerge created a partial, fortuitous view of history (dependent on evidence and the ability to apprehend defendants), while a truth commission without a tie to judicial actions against perpetrators begged the question of what the consequences of truth should be. Only by interweaving, sequencing and accommodating multiple pathways to justice could some kind of larger justice in fact emerge.

The next generation

As the new millennium began, there was an increasing consensus that in the wake of massive human rights and humanitarian law violations some kind of transitional justice measures were needed. The consensus was never absolute: Mozambique, for example, decided against officially confronting its past. However, by and large, for successor governments the no-action option was no longer either desirable or viable. For one thing, national and international human rights groups saw ending impunity as a key part of their agenda, and were quite capable of exerting pressure. Many of these governments, moreover, had international observers, missions, administrators or advisors present, and these people generally urged attention to transitional justice issues. Their concerns dovetailed with those of international banks and aid agencies, which had discovered that increased attention to the rule of law was a likely prerequisite to economic development.

One major strand of this new phenomenon is the simultaneous existence of a number of different mechanisms aimed at transitional justice. Truth commissions are now often seen as complements to criminal processes, and a number of them have coexisted with ongoing criminal investigations or have been explicitly designed to feed into such investigations. In other emerging proposals, prosecutions, amnesty, fact-finding and reparations to victims are all bound up together in a single multifaceted process. The creation of multiple institutions or multiple functions in a single institution results in both synergies and tensions, duplications and gaps. The relationships between these institutions necessarily become complicated, as they must navigate issues of evidence- and witness-sharing, division of labors, sequencing, and the similarities and differences in the narratives they produce.

Thus, Sierra Leone has had both a Truth Commission and a Special Court, and East Timor has had both a Commission for Truth, Reception and Reconciliation and Special Panels for Serious Crimes. The timing of these various efforts has varied: in some cases, the two mechanisms have operated simultaneously, while in others, including Argentina and Chad, a truth commission has preceded prosecutions, either deliberately or because conditions for prosecution have only opened up years after the commission finished its work. In a few cases, like the former Yugoslavia (and perhaps Mexico or Iraq), prosecutions came first, and only later did the value of a complementary truth commission become apparent.

Beyond the truth commission/court bifurcation a whole array of methods for combining truth-seeking and prosecutorial functions developed. Thus, for example, the Peruvian Truth and Reconciliation Commission contained a special unit whose job was to cumulate and organize evidence of crimes (and criminals) that could be presented to prosecutors. The Mexican Special Prosecutor, in contrast, has a citizen advisory committee that sees its job as compiling a historical record, and the current Colombian proposal envisions a Commission with the same job. Increasingly, the issue is simply one of carrying out multiple functions: compiling a factual record of the conflict, listening to and recording victims' stories, recommending changes to avoid repetition,

combining truth +
accountability.

imposing sanctions against at least the top perpetrators of serious crimes, and some method for both sanctioning and rehabilitating other perpetrators. The exact shape and timing of the mechanisms and institutions for carrying out these functions are more and more diverse, tailored to national conditions and constraints within a broad framework of international legal and political exigencies. As this flowering of approaches progresses, new questions arise, and some old ones are replayed.

Along another dimension, this new multilayered reality exhibits an increasingly complex set of relationships among the local, national and international planes. Early experiences with truth commissions and courts were almost completely national, as in South Africa or Chile (with some international funding), or completely international, like El Salvador. The ad hoc Criminal Tribunals were deliberately placed outside the country where the crimes took place. The Guatemalan Historical Clarification Commission and the Haitian Truth and Reconciliation Commission pioneered the use of a "hybrid" institution composed of both national and international commissioners and staff; a subsequent commission in Sierra Leone followed a variant of that model. "Hybrid" courts in East Timor, Sierra Leone, Kosovo, Cambodia and elsewhere also combine international and national authority and staffing in various ways.[16] In theory, these hybrid institutions can combine the independence, impartiality and resources of an international institution with the grounding in national law, realities and culture, the reduced costs, and the continuity and sustainability of a national effort. Or they can create orphan institutions fully owned by neither their international nor national progenitors.

Hybrid institutions are not the only possible intersection of the national and the international dimensions of transitional justice. International criminal tribunals – either ad hoc or, more recently, the permanent International Criminal Court – coexist with national courts. An emerging division of labor holds that international courts should focus on leaders and organizers of mass crimes, especially those where formal or informal immunities might bar national prosecutions, while national courts deal with the rest.[17] Indeed, the idea of *complementarity* is the cornerstone of the International Criminal Court, and variations on this idea are increasingly found in national legislation and jurisprudence as well. Exactly where those lines are, however, and whether such a two-track strategy responds to the needs of victims as well as to the realities of limited resources, are open questions. Prosecutions by international tribunals will always be limited, but often, as several cases in this book show, transnational investigations, extradition requests and prosecutions by national courts in countries other than those where the crimes took place may fill the gap. Such transnational procedures, like those involving Chile, Argentina or Chad, may under certain circumstances catalyze, jump-start or support domestic investigations or prosecutions. Human rights institutions, especially regional courts like the Inter-American Court of Human Rights, can play a similar role in developing legal standards and backstopping or opening up national efforts. Emerging national transitional justices strategies, like those of Colombia, must mold themselves around these new realities. Together, these developments create an increasingly porous legal fabric, where promises of amnesty or immunity made at the national level cannot be airtight and are subject to both international revision and domestic reevaluation.

However, international influence can also overwhelm and deform national processes. In places like Afghanistan and Iraq, the "transitional moment" is the result of violent external occupation. In those circumstances, the priorities of the occupying power may twist the available options and resources for transitional justice, raising questions of political legitimacy and civil engagement. The need for military stability may make transitional justice initiatives more difficult, and any action a government takes while the country is occupied may lack sufficient legitimacy to be successful. In a world where a single hegemonic power, the United States, is increasingly willing to use force to create political change in the name of democracy and human rights, an insistence on a modicum of both broad-based international cooperation and domestic support for specific initiatives may be imperative if such processes are to be successful and sustainable.

Two dimensions – national/international, or truth commission/trial – are no longer enough to map the universe of transitional justice efforts. Transitional justice now reaches down into the local village or neighborhood level, and makes use of a number of techniques drawn from or influenced by local customary law that combine elements of truth-telling, amnesty, justice, reparations, and apology. In East Timor, the Truth Commission organized Community Reconciliation Procedures where low-level perpetrators (none who had committed murder or crimes against humanity) were granted immunity from formal prosecution in exchange for appearing at a community-level hearing, recounting their crimes, and carrying out a sanction imposed by the community itself. In Rwanda, the government is carrying out a large-scale experiment in the use of village-level *gacaca* courts to judge alleged perpetrators of the 1994 genocide. Local-level justice processes can create a much tighter sense of community ownership than those that take place in far-off capital cities or, worse still, foreign lands. They can provide a more understandable process, one untainted by the perceived unfairness or remoteness of formal legal structures often inherited from a colonial power. They can also play a role, after "horizontal" conflicts involving ethnic- or territorially-based armed groups, in allowing neighbors who have been on different sides of a conflict to re-engage and to coexist. They can draw on indigenous and traditional ceremonies and authorities, tapping into profound spiritual and world-visioning symbols that are often non-Western, based on ideas of community harmony and well-being. Because of the culture-specific nature of these processes, it can be hoped that they will resist the tendency, so pronounced in the case of truth commissions, for politicians and negotiators to extrapolate a "formula" that can be applied, with few changes, to any and all situations.

These local-level initiatives also give a new, more fulsome meaning to the concept of reconciliation. During the early wave of experiences, reconciliation was conceived of as either a code word for impunity (the Latin American experience) or as an automatic by-product of other processes, especially of knowing the truth (the South African variant). However, a new understanding of reconciliation as a separate set of phenomena, with its own demands and time-frames, has slowly emerged. Definitions of reconciliation are still contested and murky, and the individual, community and polity aspects of such processes are still not well understood. Theorists talk about "thick" and "thin" processes, of "coexistence"[18] or "normalcy"[19] as the goals. We, like others,[20] have always preferred the term "social (and moral) reconstruction"; some chapters use reconciliation instead. As Weinstein and Stover write:

And so, at a group level, reconciliation involves the reconfiguring of identity, the revisiting of prior social roles, the search for common identifications, agreement about unifying memories if not myths, and the development of collaborative relationships that allow for difference. At the individual level, reconciliation may mean personal reconnection with friends and acquaintances from a former life – a reconnection that raises questions about trust, forgiveness, and attachments in a very intimate way. Societal development necessitates the construction of networks that promote collaboration across social groups.[21]

It is easier to visualize these multiple meanings once social reconstruction has been decoupled from other transitional justice processes, with which it is deeply interconnected, and once the community as mediating structure between the individual and the polity has become a key actor in at least some post-conflict settings. Finally, a more complex temporal dimension exists as well. While transitional justice efforts focus on the period shortly after a new government, committed to change, comes to power, it is now clear that ends to transitions cannot be decreed, and that certain aspects of the transitional justice agenda will endure for many years. Transitions may happen in bouts or waves, as new generations come of age and as the international context changes. A long-term perspective is therefore essential.

This book brings together case studies that explore one or more of these dimensions. Together, they illustrate the interplay of different functions, levels, mechanisms and goals in the current transitional justice agenda, and they point to some directions for the future. The cases are organized into two parts: Part I involves Truth and justice: Combinations and coordination. Part II centers on Levels of justice: Local, national and international. The overlap between the sections is substantial. The chapter on the East Timorese Community Reconciliation Procedure, for example, is about both combining truth and justice and combining local, national and international levels of justice, while the chapter on emerging efforts in Colombia reflects both the combination of functions and the strong influence of international factors, especially the Inter-American system and ICC, on domestic debates. Several of the case studies in Part II also involve multiple mechanisms or proposed mechanisms, while those in Part I reflect different (and in the East Timor and Sierra Leone cases, extensive) international shaping and participation. A concluding chapter draws out the lessons learned.

We chose the case studies because they illustrated one or more of the trends we were interested in: other places could have illustrated many of these same points, and raised others. We also looked for a balance of regions, how far along these processes were, and varying kinds of international influence. We looked for a mix of the relatively well-known, and of places much less-known and analyzed, at least in the English-speaking literature. We also looked for a mix of academics and practitioners, a combination of insiders describing the processes they helped establish and guide, and outsiders with intimate and long-standing knowledge of those processes. We brought the team of authors together (with a number of additional experts) at a workshop held at Notre Dame University's Center for Civil and Human Rights in 2004. Seeking a balance between specificity and comparability, after discussion of all the papers, we jointly came up with a rough template of questions for the chapters: questions about effectiveness, buy-in, constraints, continuity and sustainability, synergies and gaps. The chapters each reflect these concerns in their own way.

The study of how to come to terms with the past, to reconstruct the social and moral fiber of a society, is one of the most complex and daunting human endeavors. It is not just a rational intellectual exercise, but one that engages our deepest and most cherished notions of what it means to define ourselves and our memory, and to live in community and society. In all these stories, determined people, faced with a window of opportunity, looked to other places for ideas, borrowed from their successes and learned from their failures, taking outside constraints into account. And then, if they had the minimal security and leeway to do so, applied their own wisdom, ingenuity, imagination and traditions to create something unique to their particular time and place. We celebrate that creativity, determination, and drive, and we dedicate this book to those, in all the countries where we work, who act to make justice, in the largest sense of the word, a reality.

NOTES

1. Ruti Teitel, "Transitional Justice Genealogy" (2003) *Harvard Human Rights Journal*, 16, p. 69.
2. On the roles of education and culture, see Sarah Warshauer Freedman et. al., "Public Education and Social Reconstruction in Bosnia and Herzegovina and Croatia", in Eric Stover and Harvey Weinstein, eds., *My Neighbor, My Enemy* (Cambridge: Cambridge University Press, 2004). On distributional justice, see Rama Mani, *Beyond Retribution* (Cambridge: Polity Press, 2002).
3. See Jane Alexander, "A Scoping Study of Transitional Justice and Poverty Reduction" (January 2003), available at http://www.grc-exchange.org/docs/SSAJ56.pdf.
4. Reparations merits its own book, and in the initial design of this project the Notre Dame Center for Civil and Human Rights proposed two books, one on trials and truth commissions, and one on reparations. The International Center for Transitional Justice is also publishing a large study on reparations.
5. See M. Cherif Bassiouni, *Post-Conflict Justice* (Transnational Publishers, 2002) for early efforts; for the 1970s, see Alexandra Barahona de Brito et al., eds., *The Politics of Memory* (Oxford: Oxford University Press, 2001); for Spain's efforts, starting in the early 2000s, to finally confront the legacy of Francoism, see Equipo Nizkor's website, www.derechos.org/nizkor/spain.
6. Priscilla Hayner, *Unspeakable Truths* (Routledge, 2001), at p. 5.
7. Thomas Nagel made this point at an early conference on transitional justice sponsored by the Aspen Institute.
8. See, for instance, *Carmen Aguiar de Lapaco* v. *Argentina*, Inter-American Commission Case 12.059, Report 21/00, OEA/Ser.L/V/II.106 Doc. 3 rev. at 340 (1999).
9. See Laurel Fletcher and Harvey Weinstein, "Violence and Social Repair", (2002) *Human Rights Quarterly*, 24, pp. 573–639; Jaime Malamud, *War Without End* (Norman: University of Oklahoma Press, 1996).

10. See, e.g., Richard Wilson, *The Politics of Truth and Reconciliation in South Africa* (Cambridge: Cambridge University Press, 2001).
11. Aryeh Neier, *War Crimes: Brutality, Genocide, Terror, and the Struggle for Justice* (New York: Times Books/Random House, 1998).
12. Figures derived from indictments listed on the website of the ICTY, http://www.icty.org. ICTR data in letter dated 5 December, 2005, from the President of the ICTR to the President of the Security Council, available at http://65.18.216.88/ENGLISH/completionstrat/S-2005-782e.pdf.
13. Stover and Weinstein, *My Neighbor, My Enemy*, especially chs. 1,2, 9 and 10.
14. In the case of the ICTY, the Tribunal served a gatekeeper function in relation to national courts: for a local court to take up a war-crimes case, the Tribunal had to first find the case meritorious (the "rules of the road" agreement). In Rwanda, national courts proceeded to try several thousand defendants (and to arrest over 120,000) but the relationship with the ICTR was not one of close cooperation.
15. Fletcher and Weinstein, "Violence and Social Repair".
16. The UN is also pursuing a hybrid court process in Cambodia as well, where, under the proposal insisted upon by the Cambodian government, a majority of judges and senior officers of the Extraordinary Chambers will be Cambodian nationals. For further discussion of hybrid courts in these countries, see Suzannah Linton, "Cambodia, East Timor and Sierra Leone: Experiments in International Justice" *2001 Criminal Law Forum*, 12:185; relevant information is also available at http://www.cij.org. In 1999, the United Nations established a program of International Judges and Prosecutors in Kosovo. By the end of 2000, the Kosovo IJP program had evolved into a system of special international-majority trial and appellate panels, which could hear all war crimes cases, as well as all significant cases of organized crime and "power vacuum" and "payback" crimes, including terrorism, inter-ethnic violence, political assassinations, and corruption. See Michael E. Hartmann, *International Judges and Prosecutors in Kosovo: A New Model for Post-Conflict Peacekeeping* (USIP, 2003), available at http://www.usip.org/pubs/specialreports/sr112.html.
17. The Security Council has since at least 2000 supported the idea that the International Criminal Tribunals for the Former Yugoslavia and Rwanda should focus on civilian, military and paramilitary leaders and should, as part of their completion strategy, "concentrat[e] on the prosecution and trial of the most senior leaders suspected of being most responsible for crimes" while transferring cases involving lesser offenders to the national courts. Security Council Res. 1329, UN Doc. S/RES/1329, Nov. 30, 2000; Security Council Res. 1503, UN Doc. S/RES/1503, Aug. 28, 2003; also S/RES/1534 (2004). The Prosecutor for the International Criminal Court has similarly expressed his office's intention to focus on the leaders who bear most responsibility. "Paper on some policy issues before the Office of the Prosecutor" (Sept. 2003), available at http://icc-cpi.int/library/organs/otp/030905_policy_paper.pdf. National laws, e.g. in Argentina or Rwanda, sometimes make the same distinction, as does the Special Court for Sierra Leone.

18. See, e.g., Antonia Chayes and Martha Minow, eds., *Imagine Coexistence: Restoring Humanity After Violent Ethnic Conflict* (San Francisco: Jossey-Bass Publ., 2003).
19. Tina Rosenberg, "Latin America", in Alex Boraine, Janet Levy and Ronel Scheffer, eds., *Dealing with the Past: Truth and Reconciliation in South Africa* (Cape Town: Institute for Democracy in South Africa, 1994), p. 67.
20. See Stover and Weinstein, *My Neighbor, My Enemy*, pp. 13–20. See also Jose Zalaquett, "Balancing Ethical Imperatives and Political Constraints" (1992) *Hastings Law Journal* 43, no. 6.
21. Stover and Weinstein, *My Neighbor, My Enemy*, p. 18.

Part I

Truth, justice, and multiple institutions

Introduction to Part I

Naomi Roht-Arriaza

The authors in Part I look at the different ways in which the quest for truth and justice can be carried out at the same time. These experiences use a variety of institutional designs to create an authoritative and official record of past events, to criminally prosecute the worst offenders, to give victims a platform, and to recommend changes that will dignify victims, educate bystanders, and ensure that "never again" becomes a reality.

In Chapter 1, William Schabas discusses the Sierra Leone experience from his vantage point as a member of that country's Truth and Reconciliation Commission. Schabas concludes that, despite many fears and some real, and unexpected, problems, there is no inherent reason why a TRC cannot exist side by side with criminal trials, in this case the Special Court for Sierra Leone. Although the two institutions had different mandates and were created at different times, their goals were complementary, and by and large each pursued those goals unhindered. Schabas also raises questions about the advisability of retracting an already-granted amnesty, and about the degree of real change in political culture needed to support transitional justice endeavors.

In Chapter 2, Sigall Horovitz looks at Sierra Leone from the perspective of a former staff member of the Special Court. She describes the operation of the Court, and analyzes its strengths and weaknesses in light of prior experiences with international criminal tribunals, especially in terms of local ownership and long-term strengthening of local justice. She considers the relationship of the Court to the TRC, and concludes that, while it is possible for both mechanisms to operate simultaneously, from her perspective a better approach would be to sequence them, so that the conclusions of a TRC undergird and feed into subsequent prosecutions.

That is the approach taken by the Peruvian Truth and Reconciliation Commission as described by Eduardo González Cueva in Chapter 3. González Cueva takes up the challenges of using the information and testimony unearthed by a TC to catalyze domestic prosecutions, especially in a situation where the existing Public Prosecutor's office is not keen to do so. He describes the creation of a separate unit within the

19

TRC to prepare *dossiers* for the prosecutor, and the differences in approach of information-gathering for public hearings, for an overall report, and for specific crimes. He discusses the problems encountered, and some alternative strategies that might have facilitated optimal use of the resources and capabilities of both institutions.

While Peru embedded some prosecutor-type functions within its TC, Mexico created a new special prosecutors' office (SPO) instead of a TRC. In Chapter 4, Mariclaire Acosta, the former Assistant Secretary for Human Rights in the Fox administration, and Esa Ennelin trace the genesis and evolution of the SPO, charged with looking into notorious massacres, killings and disappearances from the 1970s and 1980s. They note the lack of clear civil society – or official – support for the SPO, its risky legal strategy, and the creation of a Citizens' Support Committee that, at least initially, was seen as a way to move beyond individual cases to look at overall causes, patterns and possible reforms.

Chapter 5 illustrates yet another variation on this theme: the emerging proposals for demobilization of paramilitary groups in Colombia. Colombian Helena Olea and Argentine María José Guembe, both human rights lawyers, look at the advances and limits of the legislation which, as it now stands, combines limited prosecution, "alternative punishment," reparations for victims and the compilation of a historical record into a single package. They point out some of the legal and practical challenges of tying these functions together. In addition, in a preview of the issues raised in Part II, they analyze the ways in which the Colombian government has had to respond to both the jurisprudence of the Inter-American system and the looming presence of the International Criminal Court as well as to US extradition requests in designing the demobilization legislation.

Chapters 6 and 7 concern East Timor, during the period when it was administered by the United Nations following a pro-independence referendum and the resulting Indonesian-instigated violence. In Chapter 6, Caitlin Reiger, former co-director of the East Timor Judicial System Monitoring Programme in Dili, looks at the combined national/international efforts to hold the perpetrators of the violence criminally responsible. Here as in Sierra Leone, a truth commission coexisted with specially created institutions for criminal investigation, in this case Special Panels for Serious Crimes and a Serious Crimes Investigation Unit. Reiger's chapter focuses on the constraints and difficulties of the criminal investigations, especially given Indonesian non-cooperation in extraditing or prosecuting the "big fish" and the ambivalence of both the United Nations and the Timorese government. Chapter 7 takes up the same time period from the perspective of the Commission for Reception, Truth and Reconciliation. It follows in Part II.

1   The Sierra Leone Truth and Reconciliation Commission

William A. Schabas

Truth and reconciliation commissions have become one of the standard options on the palette of transitional justice alternatives. They stand as something of a half-way house among approaches towards accountability for past atrocities and other human rights violations. The truth and reconciliation commission does not "forgive and forget," because it is predicated on public truth-telling, but nor does it encompass rigorous prosecution by criminal justice mechanisms. The South African model is probably the best-known, although it had some atypical features, such as the power to recommend amnesty to perpetrators who made full confession of their deeds.

The Sierra Leone Truth and Reconciliation Commission was established in July 2002. It presented its final report to the President of Sierra Leone on October 5, 2004. The actual operations of the Commission, consisting of both private and public encounters with victims and perpetrators, public hearings on thematic issues, and other research and investigation took only about eight months, however. The report provided Sierra Leone with a detailed narrative of the country's history, with a focus on the brutal civil war of the 1990s, analysis of various dimensions of political, economic and social life with a view to understanding the causes of the conflict, and a series of findings and recommendations.

Perhaps the most distinctive feature of post-conflict justice in Sierra Leone has been the parallel existence of an international criminal justice mechanism, the Special Court for Sierra Leone. In the past, truth and reconciliation commissions have often been viewed as an alternative to criminal justice that, sometimes only in an informal manner, obviates or at the very least suspends prosecutions. In Sierra Leone, the two institutions operated contemporaneously. This unprecedented experiment revealed some of the tensions that may exist between the two approaches. Yet it also demonstrated the feasibility of the simultaneous operation of an international court and a truth commission. The Sierra Leone experience may help us understand that post-conflict justice requires a complex mix of complementary therapies, rather than a unique choice of one approach from a list of essentially incompatible alternatives.

Creation and mandate of the Truth and Reconciliation Commission

Sierra Leone's civil war began on 23 March 1991, when forces styling themselves the Revolutionary United Front (RUF) raided a town near the border with Liberia. The declared objective of the RUF was to overthrow the corrupt and tyrannical government of Joseph Saidu Momoh and the All People's Congress (APC), which had ruled Sierra Leone since the late 1960s. The events that day were little more than a skirmish, but they heralded the beginning of a decade of violence that devastated the country. If the aims of the RUF might have been shared by many in Sierra Leone, who were frustrated by years of dictatorship, and by the descending spiral of poverty and underdevelopment that characterized the country since its independence from British colonialism in 1961, the war soon lost the veneer of any legitimate aspirations. Not only the RUF, but also both its allies and opponents, indulged in tactics of the utmost brutality.[1]

Like all wars, it had its phases, with a series of regime changes in the central government, transformations in the profile of the rebel groups, and unsuccessful attempts at compromise and peace negotiation. A promising attempt to resolve the conflict, reached at Abidjan, Côte d'Ivoire in late 1996, and brokered by various international actors including the United Nations,[2] soon broke down. The climactic conclusion was a devastating attack on the capital in January 1999, chillingly labeled "Operation No Living Thing." With Freetown in ruins, the government sued for peace. The formal beginning of the end of the conflict was the *Lomé Peace Agreement* of 7 July 1999, between the Government of Sierra Leone and the Revolutionary United Front of Sierra Leone.[3] The agreement provided a controversial amnesty, sometimes also referred to as a pardon or reprieve, for perpetrators of atrocities on all sides of the conflict.[4] The Special Representative of the Secretary-General of the United Nations, Francis Okelo, formulated a reservation to the amnesty provision, insisting that it could not apply to genocide, crimes against humanity, war crimes, and other serious violations of international law.[5]

The *Lomé Peace Agreement* pledged the establishment of a Truth and Reconciliation Commission (TRC), to be set up within ninety days. Although efforts were soon directed to this task,[6] legislation for the purpose was not adopted by Sierra Leone's Parliament until February 22,

2000.[7] Pursuant to section 6(1) of the *Truth and Reconciliation Commission Act 2000 (TRC Act)*, the Sierra Leone TRC was established "to create an impartial historical record of violations and abuses of human rights and international humanitarian law related to the armed conflict in Sierra Leone, from the beginning of the Conflict in 1991 to the signing of the *Lomé Peace Agreement*; to address impunity, to respond to the needs of the victims, to promote healing and reconciliation and to prevent a repetition of the violations and abuses suffered."

The Truth and Reconciliation Commission was a creation of the Parliament of Sierra Leone, in pursuance of an undertaking found in Article XXVI of the *Lomé Peace Agreement*. Although a national institution, the TRC had an international dimension because of the participation of the Special Representative of the Secretary-General for Sierra Leone and the High Commissioner for Human Rights in its establishment. These two senior United Nations officials were responsible for recommending the appointment of the three members of the Commission who were not citizens of Sierra Leone.[8] Virtually all of the financing for the Commission came from international donors, with the Office of the High Commissioner assuming the responsibility for fund-raising. Initially budgeted at $10 million,[9] poor donor response resulted in a reduction to less than $7 million. In the end, the TRC received approximately $4 million, a disappointing result that seems to indicate an indifference to its mission, despite grand statements to the contrary. In contrast, the Special Court for Sierra Leone, also funded by voluntary contributions from international donors, has a much larger budget, albeit one scaled down from an amount that originally exceeded $100 million to about $56 million over three years. The Office of the High Commissioner for Human Rights withheld 13 percent of the funds that it raised as an overhead or administrative fee.[10]

Although section 6 of the *TRC Act* might be taken to suggest a limit on the TRC's temporal jurisdiction from 1991, when the war began, until the *Lomé Peace Agreement* of July 7, 1999, in practice the Commission did not operate as if its investigations were confined by this period. The *TRC Act* also required the Commission to investigate and report on the "antecedents" of the "conflict," and this implied it could look well back from 1991.[11] Moreover, the TRC was also charged with addressing impunity, responding to the needs of victims, promoting healing and reconciliation and preventing a repetition of the violations and abuses suffered. This aspect of the mandate had no precise temporal framework. The TRC took it as authority to look at post-Lomé events. The final report of the Commission discussed the history of Sierra Leone in considerable detail, especially the colonial period. It addressed the long-standing dichotomy between the region surrounding the capital of Freetown, known as the Colony of Sierra Leone, and the enormous hinterland, designated as the Protectorate. The report also attempted to analyse the contribution of the various post-colonial regimes, which were marked by tyranny and corruption, to the origins of the conflict.

The *TRC Act* referred in several places to "victims and perpetrators," suggesting that these two groups made up the Commission's principal constituency. Special attention was focused on children, including child perpetrators, as well as victims of sexual abuse.[12] The Commission was also given a role in determining responsibilities, as well as in identifying the "causes"[13] and the "parties responsible,"[14] and here its attention was directed to "any government, group or individual".[15] The Commission listed the names of those holding positions of responsibility in the various parties to the conflict.

At the core of the Commission's mandate was the concept of "human rights violations and abuses." The *TRC Act* seemed to suggest that these could be committed by individuals as well as governments. Responsibilities could extend, for example, to transnational corporations or private security organisations.[16] Section 6 assigned the Commission to report on "violations and abuses of human rights and international humanitarian law," arguably a very broad concept. In contrast, the mandate of the South African TRC – a model familiar to the Parliament of Sierra Leone when it created the TRC – spoke only of "gross violations." According to Priscilla Hayner, the South African TRC was criticised for this narrow perspective, in that this presented a "compromised truth" that excluded a large number of victims from the Commission's scope.[17] The term "violations" is widely used within both human rights law and humanitarian law, but the term "abuses" is rather less familiar. Of some interest within the field of international human rights law is the frequent use of the term "abuse" in a very recent instrument, the *Protocol to the African Charter on Human and Peoples' Rights on the Rights of Women in Africa*, adopted in July 2003. It uses the term "abuse" in several provisions.[18] The context suggests that the term is used particularly with reference to acts committed by individuals against other individuals, rather than by states.[19] This construction of the term "abuses" is confirmed elsewhere in the *TRC Act*, which instructs the Commission to consider the acts of any "government, group or individual." Whether or not the drafters of the *Act* were aware of the debate in international human rights law about the liability of non-State actors, they certainly seemed to be of the view that it was not only governments that could breach fundamental rights.

The broad reference to "human rights and international humanitarian law" had another consequence. The Commission's work was not confined to the classic violations of bodily integrity, such as killings, rapes and other violent crimes, and to crimes of destruction of property or pillage. After some consideration, the Commission concluded that it should take its guidance from the comprehensive enumeration of human rights found in such instruments as the *Universal Declaration of Human Rights* and the *African Charter of Human and Peoples' Rights*. In other words, it was to consider not only civil and political rights but also economic, social and cultural rights. Instructions along these lines were given to statement takers as guidance for their interviews with victims.

The value of an approach stressing the indivisibility of human rights became abundantly clear when victims reported to the Commission. Although they would describe their initial victimization in terms of physical violence or destruction of property, by and large they told the Commission that they were not seeking compensation or restitution tied to these specific harms, but rather "schooling for my children", "medical care" and "decent housing." For the victims of terrible brutality, the future lay in the vindication of their economic and social rights, rather than some classic legal concept of *restitutio in integrum*.

The Commission's mandate had both fact-finding and therapeutic dimensions. As then-Attorney General Solomon Berewa (currently Vice-President) put it, "far from being fault-finding and punitive, it is to serve as the most legitimate and credible forum for victims to reclaim their human worth; and a channel for the perpetrators of atrocities to expiate their guilt, and chasten their consciences. The process was likened to a national catharsis, involving truth telling, respectful listening and above all, compensation for victims in deserving cases."[20] The "Memorandum of Objects and Reasons," which was attached to the *TRC Act*, noted that the Peace Agreement "envisaged the proceedings of the Commission as a catharsis for constructive interchange between the victims and perpetrators of human rights violations and abuses."

The work of the TRC consisted of two principal phases. The first, described as the "statement taking phase," began in December 2002. Approximately seventy "statement takers" were recruited throughout the country. Most were drawn from various sectors of civil society, such as NGOs and religious institutions. Attention was paid to ensuring that a significant percentage of the statement takers were women. Fluency in local languages was one of the main criteria in the hiring of statement takers. The statement taking proceeded until March 2003. Approximately 7,000 statements, mainly from victims but with a not unsubstantial number of perpetrators, were compiled. The statements were analysed in order to identify "window cases," that is, representative statements that served to illustrate important aspects of the conflict. All of the statements were also coded and entered into a computerized data base for the purpose of statistical analysis.

The second phase, known as the "hearings phase," began in April 2003 and continued until early August 2003. Many of the hearings brought together victims and perpetrators for what were sometimes quite dramatic exchanges, and the occasional public reconciliation. These hearings were held throughout the country, often in isolated towns that were only accessible by helicopter. Other hearings focused on thematic issues, such as the media, the legal profession, governance, and corruption.

Unfortunately, the hearings concluded with a rather unsatisfactory performance by President Tejan Kabbah. In contrast with all of the other leaders of various factions in the conflict, Kabbah refused to acknowledge any responsibility or to apologize to the people of Sierra Leone for his own role in the conflict.

H.E. Dr. Tejan Kabbah: Now, I think what you are asking me to do is this: to apologise to people for wrong doing . . . Of what use is that and I have mentioned this again in that record; I don't know, maybe it's a bit long you haven't read it all; but I said this, that I went round this country telling people, please I beg you, wrongs that have been done one way or the other, accept what it is, just forget about the past; let's live together; let's work together and rebuild our country . . . Now I just cannot understand what more I'm expected to do.

Leader of evidence: Your Excellency, the Leader of APC this morning, before the Commission, apologised for all the mistakes he had done. He had done that on the 14th, he did that again and he is using the platform of the Commission in fulfillment of all the efforts of your Excellency in this regard. Would your Excellency want to send a direct message to the people of Sierra Leone on reconciling the differences that did exist, and possibly do exist. That was my question Sir.

H.E. Dr. Tejan Kabbah: If you want to say . . . I will give you ok, I want peace, I want reconciliation, I would repeat it as many times as ever as you want. Please all Sierra Leoneans, all of us, let's work together, let's forget about the past; those that have to face the court, let them face the fact that they have to face the court and go on if they have justification, it depends, let them go ahead and do it. Now, those who have done something wrong to others, please go and apologise to them; and if they don't listen to you, go to the Vice President, come to me, we will go to your community get things organised.[21]

It was an unfortunate ending to the process, and a bad omen for the follow-up to the work of the Commission.

In parallel with these quite public activities, the Commission also undertook a more discreet program of research and investigation. Here it was terribly handicapped by poor resources. This part of the Commission's work is a story of missed opportunities, although the existing staff performed honourably and produced results of good quality.

The final phase of the Commission's work, the drafting of the report, took more than one year. Indeed, the Commission spent considerably more time writing up its results than it did in the operational phase of its mandate. The delays were partly the result of staffing shortages, and also the consequence of an overly ambitious vision of the report. It was decided that the report should be several volumes in length, perhaps so as to match that of the South African Commission. A shorter and more succinct report would have been far more accessible to Sierra Leoneans, and yet could have covered all of the essentials.

Findings and recommendations

Under the *TRC Act*, the Commission was charged with making findings and recommendations. According to section 17, "[t]he Government shall faithfully and timeously implement the recommendations of the report that are directed to state bodies and encourage or facilitate the implementation of any recommendations that may be directed to others." The findings and recommendations are, in effect, a summary of much of the report. Their implementation will be one of the tests of the effectiveness of the Commission.

It must be said at the outset that the causes of the conflict were not at all evident, and that there are many conflicting versions and accounts. In this respect, the Sierra Leone TRC differs fundamentally from the South African experience, where the root evil – *apartheid* – was never really in question. A condemnation of the racist regime and a dedication to political transition were the underpinnings of the South African TRC's work. There was nothing comparable in Sierra Leone. The *Lomé Peace Agreement* itself, which brought the civil war to a close and was at the origin of the call for a truth commission, was a cease-fire between warring factions, rather than a decisive victory by one side over the other, and a triumph for any particular vision or ideology. One of the most significant, but also potentially controversial, contributions of the Truth Commission is its analysis of the background of the conflict, and its attempt to identify causes.

Many accounts of the Sierra Leone conflict have laid most of the blame on external factors, for example charging Libyan leader Ghaddafi with fomenting the conflict and Liberian leader Charles Taylor with sustaining it. While it did not totally discount these factors,[22] the

Commission focused on internal factors, such as bad governance and corruption, and the betrayal of Sierra Leone by its political, financial and intellectual leaders. As the Report noted,

> . . . the civil war in Sierra Leone was largely the result of dysfunctional govern-ance and institutional processes in the country. Political actors failed to sustain the state's capacity to meet such critical challenges as the security, livelihood and participation in decision making of the overwhelming majority of Sierra Leoneans. The Commission shares the view that the failure of governance provided a context conducive for the interplay of poverty, marginalisation, greed and grievance that caused and sustained the civil war.[23]

The conclusion was a depressing one, because the Commission noted that many of these root causes remain unchanged in post-conflict Sierra Leone. Moreover, there is little or no commitment by those who govern the country to any meaningful attempt to address these factors. At the same time, it is a conclusion that is pregnant with optimism, for it provides Sierra Leoneans with a framework by which they can change their own destiny. An analysis focusing on external causes would have both exonerated Sierra Leoneans from responsibility and at the same time left them helpless to change things.

The atrocities committed by the RUF are well-known outside Sierra Leone, in contrast with those committed by the pro-government militias and similar forces. This is reflected within Sierra Leone in a tendency by some to overlook crimes committed by the anti-RUF forces, who, it is said, were fighting a just cause. The Commission rejected this "just war" approach to the conflict. Even if a right and wrong side in the conflict could be identified – something the Commission did not even consider – the TRC's mandate was to address violations and abuses, whatever the identity of the perpetrator. Anecdotal evidence and intuition that the RUF was responsible for the majority of the violations was confirmed in analysis of the Commission's data base. But the atrocities committed by the pro-government Civil Defense Forces (CDF), and notably by one sub-group of them known as the *kamajors*, were on a par with the worst the RUF had to offer.

A great deal of attention has also been paid to the role of mineral resources, and especially diamonds, which are found in abundance in Sierra Leone.[24] The Commission found that the rebels had not been focused on control of the diamondiferous regions of the country, at least in the early years of the conflict.[25] In other words, although low-technology diamond mining is one of the important features of Sierra Leone's economy, diamond smuggling cannot be viewed as a principal cause of the conflict. These findings in effect throw the ball back into the court of Sierra Leone's governing elite. Its historic greed and indifference to the lot of the ordinary people would appear to be the underlying theme in the conflict. This was certainly the source of the discontent that provoked the original rebel incursions, and generated much initial sympathy and support for the RUF. But in the end, the RUF had no greater vision of the future of the country than those it sought to overthrow.

In its findings, the Commission considered the amnesty provision that was included in the *Lomé Agreement*. Commissioners were well aware of the prevailing view in international law whereby such blanket amnesties are unacceptable.[26] Of course, the view was also reflected in the statement appended to the *Lomé Agreement* by the Special Representative of the Secretary-General. A judgment of the Special Court for Sierra Leone, issued in March 2004, declared the amnesty to be in breach of international law.[27] But the Commission felt it could not second-guess the negotiators at Lomé who had considered that amnesty and pardon were the only way the fighting could be brought to an end. The Commission's findings are set out in three paragraphs of the Report:

It is not clear why unconditional amnesty was accepted by the United Nations in November 1996, only to be condemned as unacceptable in July 1999. This inconsistency in United Nations practice seems to underscore the complexity of the problems at hand. The Truth and Reconciliation Commission is unable to condemn the resort to amnesty by those who negotiated the Lomé Peace Agreement. The explanations given by the Government negotiators, including in their testimonies before the Truth and Reconciliation Commission, are compelling in this respect. In all good faith, they believed that the RUF would not agree to end hostilities if the Agreement were not accompanied by a form of pardon or amnesty.

Accordingly, those who argue that peace cannot be bartered in exchange for justice, under any circumstances, must be prepared to justify the likely prolongation of an armed conflict. Amnesties may be undesirable in many cases. Indeed there are examples of abusive amnesties proclaimed by dictators in the dying days of tyrannical regimes. The Commission also recognises the principle that it is generally desirable to prosecute perpetrators of serious human rights abuses, particularly when they rise to the level of gravity of crimes against humanity. However amnesties should not be excluded entirely from the mechanisms available to those attempting to negotiate a cessation of hostilities after periods of brutal armed conflict. Disallowing amnesty in all cases is to deny the on-ground reality of violent conflict and the urgent need to bring such strife and suffering to an end.

The Commission is unable to declare that it considers amnesty too high a price to pay for the delivery of peace to Sierra Leone, under the circumstances that prevailed in July 1999. It is true that the Lomé Agreement did not immediately return the country to peacetime. Yet it provided the framework for a process that pacified the combatants and, five years later, has returned Sierra Leoneans to a context in which they need not fear daily violence and atrocity.[28]

The Commission's views on this subject may contribute to the ongoing debate on the appropriate attitude that transitional justice should take towards the issue of amnesty. The report also expressed concern about the decision by President Kabbah to withdraw the amnesty, at least partially, when he called for prosecutions by a United Nations-sponsored tribunal. This amounted to reneging on the agreement he had made with the RUF at Lomé. While Kabbah might himself argue that the RUF had also reneged on *Lomé*, and that this justified his decision, the whole business had the consequence of removing amnesty from the tool-box of future peace negotiators. Will it ever again be possible to convince armed insurgents to lay down their arms in return for amnesty, given what is now a genuine possibility that it will not be respected over time? For those who are uncompromising in their condemnation of amnesties, this is perhaps a welcome development. The Commission seemed to feel, however, that in certain circumstances an amnesty may well be an appropriate compromise to bring an end to conflict. However, its report did not attempt to unpack the relationship between amnesty, justice and reconciliation. In other words, the Commission did not take a position on how the amnesty might have contributed to reconciliation, and whether the alternative – an insistence upon criminal prosecution – would have hindered a healing process.

Many of the TRC's recommendations were without monetary implications. If the government is sincere in its commitment to implement the Commission's recommendations, in accordance with the *Act*, it cannot avoid these proposals. For example, in accordance with its finding that capital punishment was used essentially as a political tool by the various post-colonial regimes in order to suppress and terrorize their opponents,[29] the Commission called for the immediate abolition of the death penalty. It also called upon the president to commute all outstanding death sentences. The latter measure does not even require legislative approval, and can be accomplished immediately by presidential decree. In the same vein, the Commission called for all persons being illegally detained to be released without delay. A significant number – perhaps twenty or more – of RUF sympathisers have been in Freetown's Pademba Road prison since May 2000, and have been denied access both to legal counsel and their families. The Commission also demanded the repeal of legislation concerning sedition and defamatory libel. The laws are holdovers from the repressive colonial period, and have no place in a contemporary democratic society.

Although the TRC had no resources of its own to distribute to victims, it was authorised to make recommendations regarding the Special Fund for War Victims, whose establishment was provided for in Article XXIV of the *Lomé Peace Agreement*. More generally, the Commission was empowered to make recommendations with respect to the needs of victims. It has called for a robust program of compensation of victims, although question marks remain about the funding for this. Recommendations focused on services such as healthcare, education and access to microcredit rather than cash disbursements. Sierra Leone's economy remains in dismal straits, and any program with serious financial implications necessarily involves the support of the international donor community.

Women and the TRC

It was often said that the TRC was mandated to give special attention to issues concerning women in Sierra Leone, although there is actually nothing in the *TRC Act* to this effect. Section 17 of the *TRC Act* requires the Commission to give "special attention to the subject of sexual abuses." The TRC did in fact devote considerable attention to issues concerning women in the conflict and more generally within Sierra Leonean society.

Many women gave statements to the Commission and testified during its hearings. One day each week was reserved for testimony by women victims of sexual abuse. Their statements were taken in closed sessions, in the presence of women members and staff of the Commission. But frequently, women who had been victims of sexual abuse insisted upon testifying publicly. Their dramatic testimony was often punctuated by terrible pauses, by tears and sobs, but despite the emotional strain they courageously continued. It is often said that African women do not like to speak openly about sexual assaults; but it is unlikely that women anywhere like to speak openly about sexual assaults. Certainly the public hearings of the Sierra Leone TRC showed that any suggestion that African women are particularly demure about such things is an unfounded stereotype. The willingness to speak in public must show an outrage and intolerance of such practices that is translated into the need for public denunciation.

Issues concerning women inevitably were confronted with traditional practices that discriminate against women. For example, one of the features of the conflict was the widespread capture and enslavement of women, who were then described euphemistically as "bush wives." In fact, they were domestic and sexual slaves. The Commission rejected any suggestions that the circumstances of their abduction were cured once women had spent a significant period of time with their captors. One of the features of Sierra Leonean culture that reflects the subjugation of women is the very widespread practice of female genital mutilation. It was not strictly speaking a human rights violation with a significant *nexus* to the conflict. But if the Commission were to view corruption and bad governance as causes of the conflict, could it not also treat female genital mutilation on the same plane? The issue was too controversial, even among the commissioners, for a clear view to emerge. In the end, the Commission made no findings or recommendations on this point, except to urge Sierra Leone to ratify the recently adopted *Protocol to the African Charter on Human and Peoples' Rights on the Rights of Women in Africa*, which requires the prohibition "through legislative measures backed by sanctions, of all forms of female genital mutilation, scarification, medicalization and para-medicalization of female genital mutilation and all other practices in order to eradicate them."[30]

Children and the TRC

Children were very much at the heart of the TRC's mandate. They seemed to be the incarnation of the contradictions that gripped the entire country, in that one and the same child might be both a victim and a perpetrator. In one case, a young teenager reported on how he had been forced to watch while his parents were slaughtered, and then forcibly recruited into the RUF where he became a killer. When he testified before the Commission, he had returned home to live with relatives and was back in school. But many others were much less fortunate, and still live as street children in the alleyways of Freetown, or are condemned to lives of inactivity in amputee camps.

The Commission worked closely with various international and local child protection organizations. Special counselling was available when child witnesses were heard. Witnesses under eighteen were not even allowed the option of testifying in public; they too would be heard with victims of sexual assault in closed hearings. Many children were, of course, also victims of sexual crimes.[31]

 A "child-friendly version" of the TRC report was also prepared. While the intentions were honorable, it is difficult to determine how effective such a measure can really be. The assumption is that a single version, written in a highly simplified and somewhat paternalistic tone, is appropriate for "children." This must surely be an oversimplification of the situation. Nobody would go to a bookstore and ask to purchase a book "appropriate for a child under eighteen." A copy of *The Cat in the Hat*

would not suit a child of seventeen any more than an unabridged version of *Anna Karenina* would be right for one of six. Children vary enormously, depending upon age and other factors that influence levels of maturity. What is surely required are several "child-friendly versions" rather than a single "one size fits all" volume.

A variety of recommendations dealt with the special concerns of children. In one proposal , reflecting the priorities of the *Convention on the Rights of the Child*, the Commission calls for a prohibition on corporal punishment. Children were also the backbone of the combatant forces. Their immaturity made them particularly vulnerable to manipulation by the adult leaders of different groups. The use of narcotic drugs may have contributed to the process, although their role in the conflict has probably been exaggerated. Evidence before the Commission indicated that the military leaders of both the RUF and the pro-government militias had begun their careers as child-soldiers themselves. They had been recruited to British colonial forces in the 1950s, when they were in their early teens. Apparently it was the British who coined the term "Small Boys Units," used in the 1990s as a label for combat units of children as young as ten. This is not to excuse their conduct – recruitment of child-soldiers is now recognised as a war crime – but it certainly helps account for the origins of the practice.

The TRC and the Special Court

Perhaps the most distinctive aspect of the Sierra Leone transitional justice programme was the parallel existence of a truth and reconciliation commission and an international criminal tribunal.[32] This was not part of a master plan, but rather the result of circumstances subsequent to the decision to establish the TRC. A renewal of fighting in May 2000 stalled the creation of the TRC, but also revived debate about the legitimacy of the amnesty. The Government of Sierra Leone "reassessed"[33] its position with respect to the amnesty, and requested that the United Nations establish a special tribunal. On August 14, 2000, the Security Council supported the creation of a court to try "persons who bear the greatest responsibility" for serious violations of international humanitarian law and the laws of Sierra Leone, and mandated the Secretary-General to negotiate an agreement with the government of Sierra Leone to this effect.[34] Like the TRC, this too took some time to materialize, and it was only in January 2002 that the United Nations and the Government of Sierra Leone reached formal agreement on the project.[35] In April 2002, the *Special Court Agreement (Ratification) Act 2002* was adopted to enable the effective operation of the Court and to implement Sierra Leone's commitments under the agreement with the United Nations.

In March 2003, the Special Court issued eight indictments against several obvious and well-known suspects. The first trials began in June 2004, at about the same time that the TRC wound up its work. The date at which the temporal jurisdiction of the Special Court begins, November 30, 1996, coincides with the signature of the *Abidjan Peace Agreement*, reached between the Government of Sierra Leone and the rebel Revolutionary United Front (RUF).[36] The Secretary-General had recommended this be chosen so as not to impose a "heavy burden" on the Court, although the conflict is generally agreed to have begun in 1991. In mid-2001, the Government of Sierra Leone unsuccessfully requested the United Nations to extend the temporal jurisdiction to the beginning of the conflict in 1991. The explanation given by the United Nations for limiting the jurisdiction is not very convincing. Perhaps the United Nations was itself uncomfortable with involvement in pre-Abidjan prosecutions because it had not objected to the amnesty provisions at the time, in contrast with the position it took three years later at Lomé.

In a letter to the Security Council in 2001, as the Court's legal framework was still being negotiated, Kofi Annan said that "care must be taken to ensure that the Special Court for Sierra Leone and the Truth and Reconciliation Commission will operate in a complementary and mutually supportive manner, fully respectful of their distinct but related functions."[37] Once it became clear that the two institutions would operate in parallel, there was intense speculation about how they might interact. Those who were suspicious of truth commissions and oriented towards criminal prosecution, saw the opportunity to marginalise the TRC, subordinating it to the Court as a kind of investigative arm or grand jury. For example, Amnesty International wrote that the TRC's "contribution to ending impunity is likely to be extremely weak or non-existent." Furthermore, it recommended that "the government of Sierra Leone and the international community should acknowledge that, while the TRC may be able to make an important contribution to establishing the truth about human rights abuses and understanding the nature of the conflict in Sierra Leone, it should not be a substitute for prosecuting those responsible for serious crimes under international law."[38]

Those who favoured restorative justice approaches responded by insisting upon the relevance of a strong and dynamic TRC as a complement to prosecution. In this spirit, as early as October 2001 the United States Institute of Peace, the International Human Rights Law Group, and the International Center for Transitional Justice held an expert round-table on how the two bodies would relate to each other.[39]

In December 2001, as part of its activities to prepare for the establishment of the TRC, the Office of the UN's High Commissioner for Human Rights (OHCHR) and the UN's Office of Legal Affairs convened an expert meeting in New York City. The meeting was described as follows in the report of the High Commissioner:

The expert meeting on the relationship between the TRC and the Special Court was organised by OHCHR and the Office for Legal Affairs (OLA) of the United Nations in New York on 20 and 21 December 2001. The participants discussed the important issue of an amicable relationship between the two institutions that would reflect their roles, and the difficult issue of whether information could and should be shared between them. The pros and cons of a wide range of possibilities regarding cooperation between the Commission and the Court were examined. Based on those discussions, the participants agreed on a number of basic principles that should guide the TRC and the Special Court in determining modalities of cooperation. These principles include the following:

> (i) The TRC and the Special Court were established at different times, under different legal bases and with different mandates. Yet they perform complementary roles in ensuring accountability, deterrence, a story-telling mechanism for both victims and perpetrators, national reconciliation, reparation and restorative justice for the people of Sierra Leone.
> I. While the Special Court has primacy over the national courts of Sierra Leone, the TRC does not fall within this mould. In any event, the relationship between the two bodies should not be discussed on the basis of primacy or lack of it. The ultimate operational goal of the TRC and the Court should be guided by the request of the Security Council and the Secretary-General to "operate in a complementary and mutually supportive manner fully respectful of their distinct but related functions" (S/2001/40, paragraph 9; see also S/2000/1234).
> II. The modalities of cooperation should be institutionalised in an agreement between the TRC and the Special Court and, where appropriate, also in their respective rules of procedure. They should respect fully the independence of the two institutions and their respective mandates.[40]

In addition to the UN-sponsored meetings, some international NGOs developed some rather elaborate proposals on the type of provisions that might be governed by a relationship agreement. Although there was consideration of the possibility of joint or common efforts at witness protection, translation and public awareness, most of the reflection on how the two bodies might cooperate tended to dwell on what was called "information sharing," something the December expert meeting had agreed was a "difficult issue."

The various proposals mainly attempted to govern the modalities of "information sharing" between TRC and Special Court. In practice everyone understood this would be a one-way street. It was quite unthinkable that the Prosecutor of the Special Court – not to mention the defense – would share its files with the Commission. From the TRC standpoint, the concern was that access by the Court to its materials would have a chilling effect on perpetrators who might otherwise have been tempted to cooperate with the Commission. For example, the Secretary-General indicated that the RUF was "receptive" to the TRC, but that it had expressed "concern over the independence of the Commission and the relationship between it and the Special Court."[41] According to Human Rights Watch, doubts about the ability of the TRC to obtain information in confidence "could potentially undermine the willingness of persons to come before the TRC to provide testimony."[42]

In the result, there was never any formal agreement between the two bodies, nor was there any information sharing. Neither institution showed any interest in cooperation. Both seemed to value polite, neighbourly relations, and nothing more. The Prosecutor of the Special Court, David Crane, very helpfully declared that he was not interested in seeking information from the TRC, a move that may have reassured some perpetrators who were concerned that any information they might provide to the Commission would be used to build a case against them at the Special Court.

After the TRC had concluded its public hearings, in August 2003, some detainees of the Special Court asked to give public testimony to the TRC. Even more surprisingly, the Prosecutor then opposed the initiatives taken by the TRC with a view to facilitating such public hearings. A ruling by the Court's President, Geoffrey Robertson, allowed defendants to appear before the Commission, but did not authorise a public hearing.[43] Judge Robertson explained:

30. What is actually proposed by this application may be described in different ways: it may appear as a spectacle. A man in custody awaiting trial on very serious charges is to be paraded, in the very court where that trial will shortly be held, before a Bishop rather than a presiding judge and permitted to broadcast live to the nation for a day or so uninterrupted. Thereafter for the following day or days, he will be examined by a barrister and then questioned from the bench by the Bishop and some five or six fellow Commissioners. In the immediate vicinity will be press, prosecutors and "victims." His counsel will be present and permitted to interject but there are no fixed procedures and no Rules of Evidence. The event will have the appearance of a trial, at least the appearance of a sort of trial familiar from centuries past, although the first day of uninterrupted testimony may resemble more a very long party political broadcast. It is not necessary to speculate on the consequences of this spectacle: there may be none.

There may be those the Prosecution fears which could lead to intimidation of witnesses and the rally of dormant forces. There may be those that doubtless informed the original advice of his lawyers against testifying – namely fodder for the Prosecution, an adverse effect on public perceptions of his innocence and a consequent disheartening of potential defence witnesses. There will probably, I fear, be this consequence, namely intense anxiety amongst other indictees, especially from rival factions, and concerns over whether they should testify to the TRC as well, or in rebuttal. The spectacle of the TRC sitting in court may set up a public expectation that it will indeed pass judgement on indictees thus confronted and questioned, whose guilt or innocence it is the special duty of the Special Court to determine.

31. I cannot believe that the Nuremberg Tribunal would have allowed its prisoners to participate in such a spectacle, had there been a TRC in Germany after the war, or that the International Criminal Tribunals for the Former Yugoslavia or Rwanda would readily permit indictees awaiting trial to broadcast in this way to the people of Serbia or Rwanda. If it is the case that local TRCs and international courts are to work together in efforts to produce post-conflict justice in other theatres of war in the future, I do not believe that granting this application for public testimony would be a helpful precedent.[44]

Deprived of the platform they had been seeking, the defendants ultimately refused to cooperate with the TRC. Unfortunately, the tensions generated by this litigation left a sour taste in relations between the TRC and the Special Court. In reality, it was little more than an incident in what had been an essentially serene relationship.

The issue of testimony by Special Court detainees might have been addressed from the standpoint of a division of labour between the two institutions. There had been suggestions that the TRC would, in effect, concern itself with the "small fish" while the Court focused on the "big fish." There was certainly no doubt that the Court's mandate was confined to "those who bear the greatest responsibility," something spelled out explicitly in Article 1 of its Statute. During establishment of the Court, the Security Council had stressed that it would be preferable for juvenile offenders to be dealt with by the TRC, perhaps suggesting that the Council understood the relationship between the two bodies as involving some sort of identification of distinct spheres of interest.[45] But in pursuing the testimony of alleged offenders being held in custody by the Special Court, the Commission demonstrated that it considered even the "big fish" to fall within its own terms of reference. Indeed, it could not be otherwise, given that the TRC was tasked with preparing an historical record of the conflict, something that necessarily involved a consideration of the role of the principal participants.

Observers in the field continue to report that people in Sierra Leone are confused about the distinctions between the two bodies. This is presented as a problem, for which the solution proposed is further campaigns of sensitization. Yet confusion about the mandates and functions of these two bodies would seem to be not only inevitable but quite natural and understandable. After all, most European law students have trouble explaining the distinctions between the European Court of Human Rights and the European Court of Justice. The average citizen of the United States would be challenged to distinguish between the Chief Justice of the Supreme Court and the Attorney-General. Who can really expect uneducated, illiterate peasants in the countryside of Sierra Leone to do better? Perhaps the "confusion" about the two bodies is proof of success, not failure. To the extent that the people of Sierra Leone understand that the two bodies exist, and that they have some shared objectives, such as accountability for human rights violations, then the message has been delivered and "sensitization" achieved.

The TRC accomplished its mandate, although it suffered terribly from poor funding and administrative weaknesses. In particular, it was able to prompt the cooperation of many perpetrators, who testified in public or private to their deeds. In this respect, it was probably no better or worse than the many other truth commissions have been. To be sure, there is nothing simple about convincing those who have committed atrocities to admit to their crimes. Moreover, the Sierra Leone TRC did not have the carrot of amnesty that the South African TRC had used as an incentive for perpetrator admissions.

The willingness or reluctance of perpetrators to participate in accountability processes – be they truth commissions or courts – may have far less to do with promises of amnesty or threats of prosecution than many may think. Just as criminals often confess, despite "Miranda" warnings about the right to silence, not to mention stern admonition from their lawyers, some perpetrators of serious human rights violations may feel the need to unburden themselves, to "tock dee troot" as they say in Krio, Sierra Leone's lingua franca. At the other extreme, there are those who are incapable of admitting to what they have done, even when promised immunity from prosecution. And this suggests that truth-telling may or may not work, regardless of the threat of criminal trial.

Conclusion

Sierra Leone has provided the evolving discipline of transitional justice with a laboratory in which to examine how the two bodies, special "internationalized" courts and truth commissions, relate to each other. As experience has now shown, much of the speculation about potential problems and relationships has proven to have been somewhat wide of the mark. The relevance of this work to other post-conflict justice situations cannot be underestimated. Virtually everywhere, the two concepts have their promoters, although they are often presented in the alternative. Sierra Leone has demonstrated that the relationship of the two mechanisms is rather more synergistic than many might have thought. The complexities of the matter are well-illustrated in the saga of attempts to establish a truth commission for Bosnia and Herzegovina, and the evolving view of the International Criminal Tribunal for the former Yugoslavia from one of virtual opposition[46] to one that might be characterized as benign tolerance.[47] These issues are likely to be at the top of the agenda of the Prosecutor of the new International Criminal Court as he wrestles with the adequacy of domestic responses to atrocity in assessing the potential admissibility of cases under Article 17 of the Rome Statute.[48] Perhaps the unfolding practice in Sierra Leone will convince him of the usefulness of a genuinely complementary approach, by which international prosecution coexists with alternative accountability mechanisms, rather than the context of antagonism and confrontation that many observers expect.

Although there had been some discussion within Sierra Leone about the importance of a truth commission prior to its establishment, the idea was obviously borrowed from elsewhere. It seems open to question whether Sierra Leone would have organised a truth commission had this not been promoted and encouraged by the "international community." If the United Nations had insisted that Sierra Leone contribute a reasonable proportion of the costs of the venture, it would probably never have seen the light of day. Sierra Leone is an extremely poor country, and it could never have been expected to shoulder a large part of the expense of a truth commission. Still, the insignificant participation in the TRC's funding by Sierra Leone and by Sierra Leoneans can only have affected negatively the sense of ownership. Sierra Leone is a graveyard to wonderful international initiatives, established by generous funders, which are left abandoned and decaying when the foreign support concludes. Why should the TRC be any different?

With the presentation of its report, the Commission formally went out of existence. The *Truth and Reconciliation Act 2000* provided for follow-up mechanisms, to ensure that the recommendations are implemented. It seems likely that the real successor of the Commission may be the new Human Rights Commission, which will be a permanent institution. The Truth and Reconciliation Commission has fulfilled its general objectives, and it seems likely that the Special Court will do the same. The problem is not with the viability of the transitional justice institutions, but with the limited nature of the overall transition within Sierra Leone.

A useful comparison can be made with South Africa, where the transitional justice institutions were part of a much broader social transformation, driven by an extremely dynamic civil society. Sierra Leone lags far behind South Africa in this respect. And this sad conclusion inevitably limits the potential of the Sierra Leone Truth and Reconciliation Commission to influence the future of this troubled country.

NOTES

1. See, for background: Paul Richards, *Fighting for the Rain Forest: War, Youth and Resources in Sierra Leone* (Portsmouth, NH: Heinemann, 1996; Oxford: James Currey, 1998).
2. Peace Agreement between the Government of the Republic of Sierra Leone and the Revolutionary United Front of Sierra Leone (RUF), November 30, 1996.
3. For discussion of the legal status of the agreement, see: *Prosecutor* v. *Kallon et al.* (Case Nos. SCSL-2004-15 and 16-AR72(E)), Decision on Challenge to Jurisdiction (Lomé Accord Amnesty), March 13, 2004.
4. *Peace Agreement between the Government of Sierra Leone and the Revolutionary United Front of Sierra Leone*, Lomé, July 7, 1999, Art. IX. See, e.g.: Daniel Macaluso, "Absolute and Free Pardon: The Effect of the Amnesty Provision in the Lome Peace Agreement on the Jurisdiction of the Special Court for Sierra Leone", (2001) *Brooklyn Journal of International Law* 27, p. 347.
5. UN Doc. S/1999/836.
6. Richard Bennett, "The Evolution of the Sierra Leone Truth and Reconciliation Commission", in *Truth and Reconciliation in Sierra Leone* (Freetown: UNAMSIL, 2001), pp. 37–51.
7. *Truth and Reconciliation Commission Act 2000*, Supplement to the Sierra Leone Gazette Vol. CXXXI, No. 9.
8. *Truth and Reconciliation Commission Act 2000*, s. 3. The Commission's three international members were the author, Satang Jow, a former Minister of Education of the Gambia, and Yasmin Sooka, a South African human rights lawyer and member of that country's TRC. The national members were Bishop Joseph Humper, the chair, Laura Marcus-Jones, an ex-judge, Professor John Kamara, a college principal and veterinary surgeon, and Sylvanus Torto, a professor of public administration.
9. "Fourteenth report of the Secretary-General on the United Nations Mission in Sierra Leone", S/2002/679, para. 27.
10. Volume I of the TRC's Report, at pp. 130–66 presents the financial issues in detail. There is also a fairly detailed account of the Commission's financing, including the donor-related matters, in the 2003 Annual Report of the High Commissioner for Human Rights.
11. *Truth and Reconciliation Commission Act 2000*, s. 6(2)(a).
12. *Truth and Reconciliation Commission Act 2000*, s. 7(4).
13. *Ibid.*, s. 6(2)(a).
14. *Ibid.*, s. 7(1)(a).
15. *Ibid.*, s. 6.

16. L. Sanders, "Rich and Rare are the Gems they War: Holding De Beers Accountable for Trading Conflict Diamonds", (2001) *Fordham International Law Journal* 24, p. 1402; William A. Schabas, "Enforcing International Humanitarian Law: Catching the Accomplices", (2001) *International Review of the Red Cross* 83, p. 439.

17. Priscilla B. Hayner, *Unspeakable Truths, Facing the Challenge of Truth Commissions* (New York/London: Routledge, 2002) pp. 74–75.

18. Articles 5(d), 12(1)(c), 12(1)(d), 13(m), 22(b), 23(b).

19. The same expression appears in an earlier instrument, the *Declaration on the Elimination of Violence against Women*, GA Res. 48/104, Art. 2(a) and (b), and in the Vienna Declaration and Programme of Action of 1993.

20. Solomon Berewa, "Addressing Impunity using Divergent Approaches: The Truth and Reconciliation Commission and the Special Court", in *Truth and Reconciliation in Sierra Leone*, note 6 above, p. 59.

21. Testimony of Ahmed Tejan Kabbah, President of Sierra Leone, August 5, 2003.

22. Volume 3B of the Report contains a chapter entitled "External Actors in the Conflict". See *Witness to Truth: Report of the Sierra Leone Truth and Reconciliation Commission*, Vol. 3B (Freetown, 2004), Chapter II.

23. *Witness to Truth*, Vol. 2, p. 6.

24. Ian Smillie, Lansana Gberie and Ralph Hazelton, *The Heart of the Matter: Sierra Leone, Diamonds and Human Security* (Toronto: Partnership Africa/Canada, 2000).

25. *Witness to Truth*, Vol. 3B, Chapter I.

26. See, for example, "The Rule of Law and Transitional Justice in Conflict and Post-Conflict Societies, Report of the Secretary-General", UN Doc. S/2004/614, para. 64(c).

27. *Prosecutor* v. *Kallon* (Case No. SCSL-2004-15-AR72(E)), Decision on Challenge to Jurisdiction: Lomé Accord Amnesty, March 13, 2004, *Prosecutor* v. *Kamara* (Case No. SCSL-2004-16-AR72(E)), Decision on Challenge to Jurisdiction: Lomé Accord Amnesty, March 13, 2004.

28. *Witness to Truth*, Vol. 3B, Chapter VI, paras. 10–12.

29. A series of executions carried out by the Kabbah government in 1998 was recently declared by the United Nations Human Rights Committee to be a violation of Article 6 of the International Covenant on Civil and Political Rights: *Mansaraj et al.* v. *Sierra Leone* (Nos. 839, 840 and 841/1998), UN Doc. CCPR/C/64/D/839, 840 and 841/1998.

30. Art. 5(b).

31. *Witness to Truth*, Vol. 3B, Chapter IV.

32. See chapter 2 (on the Court) in this volume. See also William A. Schabas, "The Relationship Between Truth Commissions and International Courts: The Case of Sierra Leone", (2003) *Human Rights Quarterly* 25, p. 1035.

33. Solomon Berewa, note 23 above, pp. 55–60, at p. 56.

34. UN Doc. S/RES/2000/1315. On the Court, there is now a considerable literature, too extensive to cite here.

35. The establishment of the Court is discussed in some detail in *Prosecutor* v. *Kallon et al.* (Case Nos. SCSL–2004–15, 16 and 17–AR72-E), Decision on Constitutionality and Lack of Jurisdiction, March 13, 2004.

36. *Peace Agreement between the Government of the Republic of Sierra Leone and the Revolutionary United Front of Sierra Leone*, Abidjan, November 30, 1996.

37. "Letter dated 12 January 2001 from the Secretary-General addressed to the President of the Security Council", UN Doc. S/2001/40, para. 9.

38. "Sierra Leone: Renewed Commitment to End Impunity," AI index: AFR 51/007/2001, September 24, 2001.

39. Richard Bennett, note 6 above, at p. 43.

40. UN Doc. E/CN.4/2002/3, para. 70.

41. "Eleventh report of the Secretary-General on the United Nations Mission in Sierra Leone", S/2001/857, para. 44.

42. "Human Rights Watch Policy Paper on the Interrelationship Between the Sierra Leone Special Court and the Truth and Reconciliation Commission", April 18, 2002, p. 2. Letter from PRIDE to ICTJ, cited in International Centre for Transitional Justice paper: "Exploring the Relationship Between the Special Court and the Truth and Reconciliation Commission of Sierra Leone", June 24, 2002, p. 8.

43. *Prosecutor* v. *Norman* (Case No. SCSL–2003–08–PT), Decision on Appeal by the Truth and Reconciliation Commission for Sierra Leone and Chief Samuel Hinga Norman JP Against the Decision of His Lordship, Mr Justice Bankole Thompson Delivered on 30 October 2003 to Deny the TRC's Request to Hold a Public Hearing With Chief Samuel Hinga Norman JP, 28 November 2003.

44. *Ibid.*

45. "Letter dated 22 December 2000 from the President of the Security Council to the Secretary-General", UN Doc. S/2000/1234, p. 1.

46. "Fifth annual report of the International Tribunal for the Prosecution of Persons Responsible for Serious Violations of International Humanitarian Law Committed in the Territory of the Former Yugoslavia since 1991," July 27, 1998, UN Doc. A/53/219–S/1998/737, annex, para. 225.

47. See, for example, the speech of then-President Claude Jorda of May 12, 2001 delivered in Sarajevo, of which the full text is contained in the Press release of May 17, 2001, JL/P.I.S./591–e, available at www.un.org/icty, under "Latest developments", in the folder "Archived Press Releases".

48. *Rome Statute of the International Criminal Court*, UN Doc. A/CONF.183/9. The parameters of prosecutorial discretion in this area are set out in Article 53 of the *Statute*. For an overview of the *Statute*, see William A. Schabas, *Introduction to the International Criminal Court*, 2nd edn, (Cambridge: Cambridge University Press, 2003).

2 Transitional criminal justice in Sierra Leone

Sigall Horovitz

> I believe that crimes of the magnitude committed in this country are of
> concern to all persons in the world, as they greatly diminish respect for
> international law and for the most basic human rights. It is my hope
> that the United Nations and the international community can assist
> the people of Sierra Leone in bringing to justice those responsible for
> those grave crimes.
>
> *Letter sent by the President of Sierra Leone, Ahmad Tejan Kabbah,*
> *to the UN Secretary-General, dated June 12, 2000.*

Receptive to Sierra Leone's cry for help, the United Nations concluded an
agreement with the Government of Sierra Leone establishing the Special
Court for Sierra Leone (Special Court), mandated to try persons bearing
the greatest responsibility for international crimes and certain domestic
crimes committed within the country since November 30, 1996. The
Special Court is the first modern international criminal tribunal located
within the country where the prosecuted crimes were committed. It is
also the first such tribunal that was created by a bilateral treaty, coexisted
with a truth and reconciliation commission, has a far-reaching outreach
program, and relies mostly on national staff.

The Court's geographical location and the national institutional support it receives facilitate the collection of physical evidence and the
preparation of witnesses, increasing the efficiency of its process. These
factors also provide the Court with an excellent opportunity to engage in
local capacity-building initiatives aimed at enhancing its ability to leave
behind a legacy. The Court's reliance on national staff ensures that once it
completes its work, Sierra Leone will be left with professionals capable of
supporting a rule of law society.

The Special Court became operational in August 2002. Its two first
trials commenced in mid-2004, and a third trial started at the beginning
of 2005. Although its mandate will result in only a few individuals being
charged, the Court was created to "contribute to the process of national
reconciliation and to the restoration and maintenance of peace."[1] At first
glance, it seems the Court is well positioned to promote these national

transitional justice goals: by bringing perpetrators to justice it could deter further violence and allow the population to break from a violent past and build a future based on respect for human rights and equality before the law. Its process, moreover, could promote a sustainable peace by helping restore the rule of law and eradicate the culture of impunity in Sierra Leone. Nonetheless, the Court's ability to promote such goals could be curtailed by an array of elements including its own limited funding and jurisdiction, the volatile state of security in the country, and varying levels of local opposition. To help restore the rule of law, the Court must be seen as a role model for the administration of justice, and to promote deterrence it must be deemed credible. In light of these unique realities, this chapter examines the potential success of the Special Court as a cornerstone of transitional justice in Sierra Leone.

Background: The conflict

Sierra Leone gained independence from British rule on April 27, 1961. In March 1991, forces of the organized armed group known as the Revolutionary United Front (RUF) led by Foday Kankoh, with help from Liberian forces, entered Sierra Leone from Liberia, declaring their aim was to overthrow the government. International and local pressure led to democratic elections on February 26, 1996, in which Ahmad Tejan Kabbah of the Sierra Leone People's Party (SLPP) was elected President. On election day, the RUF attacked central towns in Sierra Leone. In response, various civil militia forces, including organized groups of traditional hunters, united into a centralized force which became known as the Civil Defense Forces (CDF). The CDF fought against the RUF, alongside the Sierra Leone Army (SLA). The national coordinator of the CDF forces was Sam Hinga Norman, who subsequently became Deputy Defense Minister in Kabbah's government. On November 30, 1996, President Kabbah and RUF leader Foday Sankoh signed a peace agreement in Abidjan (Abidjan Accord).[2] Shortly after, army elements calling themselves the Armed Forces Revolutionary Council (AFRC) overthrew the government. The AFRC was led by Johnny Paul Koroma, who immediately after the coup invited the RUF to join the government. Combined AFRC/RUF forces began attacking the CDF as well as civilians deemed to be collaborating or sympathetic to the CDF, while the CDF did the same with perceived AFRC/RUF collaborators. International efforts produced a cease-fire agreement on May 18, 1999 between President Kabbah, acting on behalf of the government, and Sankoh, acting on behalf of the AFRC/RUF.[3] Subsequently, a peace agreement was signed on July 7, 1999 in Lomé, Togo (Lomé

Agreement).[4] In October 1999, the UN established the United Nations Mission to Sierra Leone (UNAMSIL).[5] The AFRC/RUF forces neither disarmed nor released abducted civilians, and despite the Lomé Agreement resumed attacks on the CDF and on the civilian population.[6] In May 2000 AFRC/RUF forces took hostage and abused about 500 UN peacekeepers. Sankoh was arrested on May 17, 2000.[7] British troops were immediately deployed in Sierra Leone to deter violence and train the local army and police forces. A cease-fire agreement was signed in November 2000 and AFRC/RUF forces began surrendering their arms to UN peacekeepers.[8] Another cease-fire agreement was signed in May 2001.[9] On January 18, 2002, Sierra Leone's civil war was officially declared over.[10]

The war killed between 50,000 and 75,000 people. It rendered almost half of the country's population of 5 million either internally displaced persons or refugees.[11] The prevalence of rape and other sexual assaults during the war resulted in the widespread increase of sexually transmitted diseases, especially HIV/AIDS. The notorious amputation campaigns carried out by the rebels against the civilian population left many disabled. The impact on infrastructure and property was enormous – many hospitals, schools, community facilities and private houses were demolished; telephone and electric infrastructure was destroyed; roads and bridges were severely damaged. Around 45,000 ex-combatants, including 5,600 child-soldiers, were disarmed and demobilized. Efforts are presently being made to reintegrate refugees, internally displaced persons, ex-combatants and victims into their communities. Despite instability in neighboring countries, Sierra Leone today seems internally stable for the first time in over a decade.

The establishment of transitional justice mechanisms

The Lomé Agreement, like previous unsuccessful peace agreements in Sierra Leone, granted a sweeping amnesty to all combatants for all crimes committed during the conflict.[12] It also accorded powerful political positions to AFRC/RUF leaders.[13] In lieu of prosecutions for the crimes committed during the war, the Lomé Agreement called for the creation of the Truth and Reconciliation Commission (TRC).[14] The UN representative to the peace negotiations appended a reservation to the Lomé Agreement, stating that the amnesty cannot apply to international crimes.[15] The UN High Commissioner for Human Rights insisted that peace was incompatible with impunity.[16] International NGOs also opposed the "blanket" amnesty and demanded prosecutions.[17]

Following the abduction of about 500 UN peacekeepers by rebels and Sankoh's arrest in May 2000, the UN Secretary-General stated that

Sankoh should be held responsible for the recent crisis in Sierra Leone.[18] On May 26, 2000, touting the importance of establishing accountability for the attainment of a sustainable peace, Sierra Leone's president declared that Sankoh would face trial; the Finance Minister stated that the government would prefer to see Sankoh tried by an international tribunal, as a local court could not guarantee his safety.[19] Civil society requested the creation of an international tribunal.[20] US and UK officials demanded that those responsible for the atrocities be held accountable.[21]

On June 12, 2000, almost a year after signing the Lomé Agreement, President Kabbah wrote a letter to the UN Secretary-General requesting the UN's assistance in bringing to justice RUF members responsible for the atrocities committed in Sierra Leone's war. In the letter, the president acknowledged that "Sierra Leone does not have the resources or expertise to conduct trials for such crimes" and that "there are gaps in Sierra Leonean criminal law as it does not encompass such heinous crimes."[22] On August 14, 2000, the Security Council requested the UN Secretary-General to negotiate the establishment of the Special Court with the Government of Sierra Leone.[23]

International pressure demanding prosecutions for Sierra Leone's atrocities increased following the August 25, 2000 abduction of eleven British soldiers by the AFRC splinter group, the "West Side Boys". However, it was not until January 16, 2002 that an agreement was concluded between the UN and the Government of Sierra Leone on the establishment of the Special Court (Special Court Agreement).[24] Thus, the Court is a treaty-based, international institution. In March 2002, in accordance with constitutional requirements, the Sierra Leone parliament enacted domestic legislation implementing the Special Court Agreement.[25] In concluding the Special Court Agreement and in enacting the implementing legislation, although allegations to the contrary exist, neither the UN nor the government reneged on the Lomé Agreement's amnesty: the UN never considered it applicable to international crimes,[26] and the government considered it applicable only in national courts.[27]

In August 2002 the Special Court became operational, and its work will extend at least into 2007. A trial against three former CDF leaders, including Sam Hinga Norman, commenced on June 3, 2004.[28] Another trial, against three former RUF leaders, commenced on July 5, 2004.[29] A third trial, against three former AFRC leaders, commenced on March 7, 2005.[30] Additional trials may take place if or when the Special Court obtains custody over two further indictees,[31] former AFRC leader Johnny Paul Koroma, and former Liberian president Charles Taylor, who allegedly assisted the AFRC/RUF. Theoretically, new indictments could be issued, although it is unlikely at this stage due to the limited funding and duration of the Court.

The jurisdiction of the Special Court

Article 1 of the *Statute of the Special Court for Sierra Leone* (*Statute*) limits the Court's temporal jurisdiction to violations that occurred after November 30, 1996, the date the Abidjan Accord was signed. The temporal jurisdiction is open-ended. The signature date of the failed Abidjan Accord was chosen as it was considered a non-politically biased date, which provided a time-frame that ensures the Court would not be overburdened while it still addresses the most serious atrocities committed during the war, in all geographical areas and by all parties involved.[32]

The Special Court's subject matter jurisdiction is limited to crimes against humanity and war crimes,[33] as well as to the domestic crimes of sexually assaulting young girls and setting fire to property.[34] Despite the Court's mandate to try domestic crimes, the indictments to date charge accused persons only with international crimes, consistent with the Court's view that the Lomé Agreement's amnesty does not cover such crimes, at least insofar as they are prosecuted by a foreign or international tribunal.[35] The Special Court has primacy over national courts;[36] while the national courts exercise concurrent jurisdiction over post-Lomé crimes, they have not yet chosen to exercise it.[37]

Former RUF and AFRC members are charged with extermination, murder, rape, sexual slavery and other forms of sexual violence, enslavement, and inhumane acts as crimes against humanity; with acts of terrorism, collective punishment, murder, outrages upon personal dignity, mutilation, and pillage as violations of Common Article 3 to the Geneva Conventions and of Additional Protocol II; and with the use of child-soldiers and attacks against peacekeepers as "other serious violations of international humanitarian law."[38] The former CDF members are charged with murder and inhumane acts as crimes against humanity; with murder, cruel treatment, pillage, acts of terrorism, and collective punishment as violations of Common Article 3 and of Additional Protocol II; and with the use of child-soldiers as "other serious violations of international humanitarian law".[39] The accused persons are charged with these crimes by virtue of having commanded the perpetrators, pursuant to the doctrine of command responsibility, as well as for having directly perpetrated the crimes. Direct perpetration under international law includes having planned, ordered, instigated, aided and abetted the crimes, or having participated in a joint criminal enterprise which produced them.[40]

Article 1 of the Statute limits the Court's personal jurisdiction to those bearing "the greatest responsibility" for the atrocities.[41] This restriction is not only the result of resource limitations and urgency of legal action but also of the infeasibility of bringing to justice over 40,000 combatants. Furthermore, in Sierra Leone, many of the combatants were children who were abducted and manipulated by the commanders to commit atrocities; bringing them to justice does not reflect their limited volition and may adversely impact their rehabilitation and reintegration into society. Children between fifteen and eighteen years old are not excluded from the jurisdiction of the Court, but the Special Court's Prosecutor from the outset made clear that juvenile offenders would not be indicted or prosecuted.

It is widely accepted that the "selective prosecution" approach could, if adopted wisely, advance transitional justice goals. The challenges lie in establishing the selection criteria. This task is left to the Special Court's Prosecutor,[42] who must decide on a strategy which on the one hand will satisfy international expectations of "cost effective" justice by efficiently establishing accountability, and on the other hand will advance national goals such as the promotion of a sustainable peace and the restoration of the rule of law. This is not a new strategy: the Argentine trial of the Juntas in the early 1980s followed a similar approach, as discussed in Chapter 12. Despite starting with the trial of a "small fry", Dusko Tadic,[43] the International Criminal Tribunal for the former Yugoslavia (ICTY) eventually adopted a similar selective approach in order to successfully complete its mission.[44] Similarly, on trial before the Special Court are not only top echelon leaders but also mid-level commanders whose position of authority, combined with the seriousness of the crimes they allegedly committed, encouraged the perpetration of grave atrocities by others. Nevertheless, there are victims throughout the country who feel that they are denied justice because the "small fry," especially those involved in attacks against their area or their relatives, are not brought before the Court.[45]

Even some Sierra Leoneans who accept the need to follow the "selective prosecution" approach criticize the Prosecutor's exercise of discretion, believing that some of the mid-level commanders who are testifying before the Court, themselves bear the "greatest responsibility" for some of the war's atrocities and should be prosecuted. This skepticism is exacerbated because important leaders and commanders are currently not facing trial before the Special Court as they are either dead or at large. Former RUF leader Foday Sankoh was indicted by the Special

Court but died while in its custody; his deputy, Sam Bockarie, was indicted by the Special Court but was murdered in Liberia; former AFRC leader, Johnny Paul Koroma, was indicted but is either dead or at large; and, former Liberian president, Charles Taylor, who allegedly supported and assisted the AFRC/RUF forces in carrying out their mission, was indicted by the Special Court but nonetheless long enjoyed the protection of political asylum in Nigeria. This diminishes the Court's relevance and credibility in the view of some Sierra Leoneans.[46] Recent indications, nonetheless, show that the Special Court is becoming accepted locally as part of the Sierra Leonean reality.[47]

The Special Court's treaty-based nature removes it from subordination to the Sierra Leonean court system and thus renders it an international tribunal.[48] Nonetheless, it is often referred to as a "hybrid" tribunal since its jurisdiction extends over both domestic and international crimes; since its staff comprises about 60 percent nationals;[49] since it was built on government-owned land;[50] and since it relies on national authorities to enforce many of its orders, including arrest warrants.[51] In addition, the *Statute* authorizes the Special Court's judges to be guided by Sierra Leone's 1965 *Criminal Procedure Act* when amending the Special Court's Rules of Procedure and Evidence (Special Court Rules).[52] Furthermore, the Sierra Leonean government participates in the Court's Management Committee and is involved in the selection of the Court's judges, prosecutor and deputy prosecutor.[53]

A hybrid, in-country court raises delicate issues about the relationship between the government and the court. For some, there is no genuine partnership between the government and the international community, but rather an outside imposition. Such skeptics base their claim on the limited scope of government participation in the Special Court's process and on the lack of consultation with the Sierra Leonean public prior to the Court's establishment. However, this view misconstrues the nature and purpose of this joint venture. Deeper institutional involvement of the Sierra Leonean authorities could have resulted in an overburdened domestic court system, a depleted national treasury and a government deprived of experienced personnel; factors which inevitably interfere with other transitional justice goals such as institutional development and judicial reform. Furthermore, had the government been more involved in the Special Court's process, the Court's appearance of impartiality would have been compromised, especially with respect to the already problematic proceedings against the CDF leaders.

On the other hand, strong international involvement attracts greater funding resources and experienced international lawyers. Interestingly, the Court's staff includes numerous Sierra Leonean professionals who have spent the last years living and working in western countries, who now provide an important cultural bridge between the Court's national and international personnel. In fact, the Court's hybrid staff represents a successful synthesis of diverse approaches that promotes the common causes shared by all its members. While allegations of prejudice exist, they seem to be marginal. Indeed, claims of bias attributed to one of the Court's international judges entailed his being percluded from sitting in one of the cases, but such claims could have equally been aimed at any Sierra Leonean judge.[54]

The enforcement capacity of the Special Court

The Special Court, in contrast to the International Criminal Tribunal for Rwanda (ICTR) and the ICTY (collectively: ad hoc tribunals), was not established by the Security Council under Chapter VII of the UN Charter (Chapter VII). It therefore does not benefit from certain international enforcement measures that such a legal basis confers.[55] Nonetheless, the Special Court is a product of a bilateral treaty under which the Sierra Leonean authorities are legally obligated to comply with its orders.[56] Hence the Court's treaty-based nature, to a certain extent, facilitates a greater enforcement capacity than that of the ad hoc tribunals; a point clearly demonstrated by the effective arrests made during 2003 by the local police force pursuant to orders of the Special Court. Furthermore, certain provisions in UN Security Council Resolutions 1470 and 1478 urge third states to cooperate with the Special Court.[57] However, these provisions lack Chapter VII enforcement powers.[58] Nonetheless, Liberia cooperated with the Special Court when a Liberian district court issued search warrants for Taylor's homes in Monrovia to Special Court officials in March 2004.[59] The lack of Chapter VII powers explains in part the Court's long failure to obtain custody over Charles Taylor, who at the time of writing this chapter resided in Nigeria where he was granted asylum.

There were other forms of pressure encouraging the surrender of Taylor to the Court. UN Security Council Resolution 1532, issued pursuant to Chapter VII, calls on all states to freeze funds and assets owned or controlled by Taylor.[60] Interpol, pursuant to the Court's request, issued a Red Notice against Charles Taylor on December 4, 2003.[61] The Special Court's Prosecutor frequently met with US, European and West African government officials in an effort to encourage, through diplomatic means, international pressure on Nigeria to surrender Taylor to the Court.[62] In the meetings it was stressed that since Nigeria is party to the Convention against Torture and the Geneva

Conventions, it must pursuant to those treaties either extradite or prosecute suspects of war crimes and torture.

The structure of the Special Court

In accordance with Article 11 of the *Statute*, the Court's structure resembles the tripartite organization of the ad hoc tribunals and the International Criminal Court (ICC), consisting of the Chambers, Registry and Office of the Prosecutor. However, in accordance with Rule 45 of the Special Court Rules, the Court also uniquely incorporates a Defense Office, which despite having been set up by the Registry, functions independently from the latter.[63] Examination of the experience of defense counsel at the ICTR, who complained about the lack of resources and the poor quality of assistance received from the Tribunal, brought about the creation of the Special Court's Defense Office.[64] The Defense Office is headed by the Principal Defender and its functions include giving initial advice and assistance to suspects and accused persons, providing administrative and substantive support to defense counsel, and assigning defense counsel to suspects and accused persons who lack the financial means to secure legal representation.

The Court's Chambers comprise two Trial Chambers and an Appeals Chamber, the former consisting each of three judges (one nominated by the Government of Sierra Leone and two by the UN Secretary-General), and the latter consisting of five judges (two nominated by the Government and three by the UN Secretary-General). Almost half of the judges are African (five out of eleven), a characteristic that could mitigate public opposition based on a view that the Court is a "Western imposition."[65]

Jurisprudential contribution

The Special Court's jurisprudence contributes to the development of international criminal law. In establishing, for example, that a "forced marriage" constitutes a crime against humanity,[66] and that the recruitment of children under fifteen to an armed force constitutes a serious violation of international humanitarian law,[67] the universal prohibition of these acts is strengthened. This development, in turn, could have ramifications within Sierra Leone, since awareness of the Court's decisions regarding the international prohibition of such acts may help prevent their reoccurrence in Sierra Leone.

Two landmark decisions by the Special Court's Appeals Chamber which not only enrich the jurisprudence of international criminal law but also bear the potential to promote deterrence in Sierra Leone, are those asserting that neither the position of an accused as a head of state nor the granting of a national amnesty to perpetrators, preclude prosecution for international crimes by international tribunals.[68] These two decisions may operate to restrict "traditional methods" for averting penal consequences of international crimes; "traditional methods" which perpetuate impunity.

The Appeals Chamber's decision establishing that heads of states are not immune from prosecution by international tribunals was given in the case against Charles Taylor, who was indicted for his alleged involvement in Sierra Leone's war, while still in office as Liberia's president.[69] Taylor's defense counsel argued before the Special Court's Appeals Chamber that under customary international law, heads of states enjoy immunity from criminal prosecution in foreign or international courts. The Appeals Chamber rejected this argument, finding that under customary international law, "the principle seems now established that the sovereign equality of states does not prevent a Head of State from being prosecuted before an international criminal tribunal or court."[70] This decision sends an important message to African and other leaders. Taylor's surrender to the Special Court strengthens this message. Unfortunately, until the rule of law is reinforced throughout West Africa tyrants may continue evading justice, even after having been indicted by international criminal tribunals.

In its decision concerning the national amnesty, the Special Court's Appeals Chamber ruled that "[w]hatever effect the amnesty granted in the Lomé Agreement may have on a prosecution for such crimes as are contained in Articles 2 to 4 [of the *Statute*] in the national courts of Sierra Leone, it is ineffective in removing the universal jurisdiction to prosecute persons accused of such crimes that other states have by reason of the nature of the crimes. It is also ineffective in depriving an international court such as the Special Court of jurisdiction."[71] This view is consistent with the reservation appended to the Lomé Agreement by the UN representative, as well as with the growing body of opinion which maintains that under international law such blanket amnesties cannot apply to international crimes. Referring to this trend, the Special Court acknowledged "that such a norm is developing under international law."[72]

Indeed, the Special Court's Appeals Chamber affirmed that "[e]ven if the opinion is held that Sierra Leone may not have breached customary law in granting an amnesty, this court is entitled in the exercise of its discretionary power, to attribute little or no weight to the grant of such amnesty which is contrary to the direction in which customary international law is developing."[73] Finally, it is worthwhile stressing that the Special Court's decision does not abolish the institution of post-conflict amnesties, but rather renders such amnesties inapplicable in international or third-state proceedings to certain persons with respect to particular crimes.

Witness protection

In contrast to the Nuremberg Trials, most evidence before the Special Court is testimonial. Hence the success of trials before the Special Court depends on the ability and willingness of witnesses to testify. Since the security situation in Sierra Leone has still not completely stabilized, many witnesses feel that testifying before the Court will entail retaliation. The fact that RUF supporters and CDF supporters live in mixed communities increases this apprehension.[74] Fears of retraumatization and stigmatization may also prevent certain witnesses, especially victims of sexual violence, from testifying before the Court.

The war left Sierra Leone with a seriously damaged justice system, hardly capable of enforcing protection measures, and with army and police forces which are still identified with various parties to the conflict and considered unreliable.[75] The Special Court must therefore afford protection to its witnesses. Psychological and psycho-social support must also be accorded to witnesses who, by testifying and reliving painful experiences may become retraumatized. Moreover, if victims testify in a safe and protective environment, their testimony can be a positive and rehabilitating experience.[76] The Court's Witnesses and Victims Section provides security arrangements as well as psychological and medical assistance to witnesses.[77] The judges issue orders aimed at protecting witnesses by concealing their identities from the public;[78] delaying the disclosure of their identities to the defense;[79] and minimizing their confrontation with the accused.[80] The Special Court Rules on victim participation are not nearly as extensive as those of the *Rome Statute* of the ICC,[81] but Rule 75(C) of the Special Court Rules does provide that "[a] Judge or a Chamber shall control the manner of questioning to avoid any harassment or intimidation." Still, there have been instances where cross-examinations caused victim-witnesses to feel as though they were accused themselves, or where extensive legal arguments were advanced by the parties "over the heads" of victim-witnesses, making them feel dispensable and at times interrupting their testimony in a disrespectful manner. Finally, it is important to ensure that protective measures are available to witnesses after they testify, even after the Court completes its work. Resource limitations render this difficult. The Special Court intends to leave the responsibility of protecting the physical well-being of witnesses after they testify to the national police, despite the fact that it is unclear whether the police force has the capacity to carry out this assignment. Arrangements are being made to ensure that certain NGOs will afford psychological support to those who have already testified.[82] With regard to the installment of witness relocation programs after testimony, especially for potential witnesses who are currently in foreign countries as a result of protective measures undertaken by the Court to secure their testimony, it is hoped that the state where they reside will fund their stay, or that they will be able to support themselves in those countries without financial assistance.

Special Court, TRC and transitional justice in context

Especially where an amnesty regime exists, the operation of a truth commission or another truth-seeking mechanism is crucial in order to promote acknowledgment of past violations. However, other mechanisms must also be established to ensure the restoration of justice. In Sierra Leone, the circumstances eventually brought about the nullification of the amnesty for certain leading perpetrators with respect to particular crimes, and the establishment of a distinctive prosecutorial process alongside the TRC and the amnesty regime that still applies to most ex-combatants.

The roles of the TRC and Special Court in part overlap, as they both promote accountability and the preservation of a historical record. The TRC's process complements the Court's prosecutions by establishing, albeit in a non-prosecutorial manner, the accountability of many of the "small fry" perpetrators, while the Court plays a necessary punitive role with respect to the accountability of the "big fish." The TRC, moreover, was in a better position than the Court to address the accountability of the child-soldiers involved in the war.[83] In addition, while the Special Court is mandated only to prosecute the atrocities which occurred after November 30, 1996, the TRC investigated and recorded atrocities which took place throughout the entire duration of the armed conflict, thereby facilitating a complete historical account of the war. On the other hand, the Court is better equipped to ascertain the truth in relation to certain events, given its greater capacity to obtain evidence, its larger financial resources, and the high standard of "proof beyond a reasonable doubt" required by the Court to allow the inclusion of evidence in the historical account it establishes.[84] For example, given the reluctance of many Sierra Leoneans to voluntarily express opinions against the CDF, the Court, by trying top-echelon CDF members, may be in a better position than the TRC to discover the truth about the CDF's involvement in the atrocities.

The coexistence of the Special Court and the TRC could in theory enhance the attainment of their respective, non-shared goals, provided the means to achieve their ends are undertaken wisely. For example, the TRC's report could be introduced as evidence before the Special Court, thus facilitating the latter's judicial process. In a decision rendered by the Special Court's Appeals Chamber, Judge Geoffrey Robertson stated that "[j]udicial notice might be taken of [the TRC report], and it might provide considerable assistance to the Court and to all parties as an authoritative account of the background to the war."[85] Unfortunately the report was not available when the trials commenced, but it may be useful as trials continue.

Furthermore, information held by the TRC which exculpates individuals who are accused before the Special Court could perhaps be shared with their defense counsel to promote a fair trial. Such a course of action must, however, be considered in light of witness protection issues and the desirability of using information which was provided to the TRC in confidence. In addition, each of these institutions' statement-taking process could prepare the society for the other's, since "training" the people to testify before a formal body may reduce their apprehension and encourage their involvement in transitional justice processes. Finally, it is worthwhile mentioning that while the TRC's report aims to identify the root causes of the war, the Special Court's process addresses some of these root causes by promoting accountability and respect for human rights.

If conducted unwisely, however, each entity's work towards different goals may undermine that of the other. The coexistence of the TRC and the Special Court in Sierra Leone was not planned in advance but was rather a result of circumstance. The TRC initially resisted the idea of establishing the Special Court. Such resistance was partially based on the TRC's above discussed opposition to the notion that the Lomé Agreement's amnesty provision is inapplicable to international crimes. The TRC's attitude also emanated from the perception that the Court's existence would threaten its own process, a theory based on the assumption that perpetrators would refuse to cooperate with the TRC for fear of being subject to prosecution based on the information they provided.[86] Nonetheless, the Special Court's Prosecutor, upon his arrival in Sierra Leone, publicly announced that he would refrain from using evidence obtained by the TRC for the Special Court's purposes. This relaxed the TRC's initial resistance to the Court, and in December 2002, the Special Court's Prosecutor and the Chairman of the TRC publicly announced mutual support between the institutions.[87] Had these personalities adopted a different approach, the work of both institutions would have been jeopardized, as a hostile relationship between them would have generated negative public opinion and deterred the population from participating in their respective processes.

As a result of the lack of advance planning in the contemporaneous establishment of the Special Court and the TRC, there was initially much confusion within the population with regards to their respective roles. In addition, some sectors felt the need to support one mechanism rather than the other.[88] However, once mutual respect was publicly declared, such sentiments lessened considerably, although even after this public announcement there were incidents where mutual respect appeared to be lacking.[89]

To ensure the synergies between a truth and reconciliation commission and a transitional prosecution institution, both mechanisms must convey a strong message of mutual respect. Otherwise, they risk undermining each other's process. The success of their coexistence should not depend on the personalities leading their respective processes but rather on advance planning and consultation. Such advance planning should include a comprehensive sensitization program prior to the creation of the mechanisms to educate the public on their respective roles, demonstrate their mutual respect and promote a perception that the mechanisms are complementary rather than competing.

Perhaps a better way to promote the efficiency of truth commissions and prosecutorial processes is to prevent their contemporaneous existence, especially when their coexistence was not planned in advance. Concluding prosecutions before setting up a truth and reconciliation commission makes little sense because prosecutions are extremely time-consuming, and reconciliation efforts must be initiated as soon as relative stability is achieved. The reverse order must therefore be considered.

In Sierra Leone, certain problems would have been eliminated, or at least mitigated, had the TRC concluded its operations prior to the commencement of the Special Court's process. Such sequencing would have eliminated public fragmentation, mitigated public confusion with regards to the respective roles of the two institutions, precluded hostile "press fights" between the entities, and perhaps enhanced public co-operation with the TRC.[90] This sequencing could have also enabled the Special Court to benefit from the TRC's report by admitting it into evidence early on. Moreover, identification by the TRC of the main perpetrators prior to the establishment of the Special Court could have reduced negative public perception of the Court. Finally, with the passage of time, the security and political realities in Sierra Leone could have been more favorable to the Court's work.

On the other hand, had the Special Court been set up at a later stage, getting hold of suspects and evidence would have been much more difficult. The passage of time would have also increased witness fatigue and reluctance of victims to recount their distant painful past. In addition, the trials would have been less relevant to the local population and therefore less effective in terms of achieving transitional justice goals such as reconciliation and judicial reform. Furthermore, a delay of even a year or two could have eroded the political will to set up such a court. Hence, under the circumstances, the simultaneous establishment of both transitional justice mechanisms, albeit not envisaged, was not a poor choice.

National relevance and legacy

As an institution which sits at the locus of the crimes and encourages national involvement in its process, the Special Court has great potential to promote national judicial reform and restoration of the rule of law. The employment of nationals by the Special Court facilitates the permeation of international standards into the domestic sphere,[91] and ensures that once the Court completes its work Sierra Leone will be left with legal and law-enforcement professionals. Currently, out of a total of 255 staff members, 149 are nationals.[92] Furthermore, there is a legacy that the Court will leave behind: jurisprudence which could provide guidance to national courts, Special Court Rules which could stimulate the reform of Sierra Leone's 1965 *Criminal Procedure Act*, a video record of its process which could be used as a future reference in judicial reform activities,[93] and a double-chambered courthouse which will be left to the government. This could provide the "building blocks" for a sustainable reformed national justice system. However, for these "building blocks" to be used by Sierra Leoneans, the Special Court must be considered locally as a role model for the administration of justice. To this end, Sierra Leoneans must deem the Court credible and relevant to their lives.

To allow the public to assess their relevance, the trials must be transparent. This means that the proceedings must be public, accessible, and easily understood. The majority of the population is too poor to travel to Freetown to observe trials. Even Freetown residents are hesitant to attend trials, not only due to financial constraints but also in light of the intimidating number of armed security guards and barbed wire surrounding the Court's site, which from the outside resembles a high security prison. Daily radio broadcasts of the trials would have best promoted transparency, as most Sierra Leoneans listen regularly to the radio. Such broadcasts could have also advanced deterrence goals. However, undertaking this measure could enhance the security risk to certain witnesses as their testimonies often reveal identifying information. Redacting recorded testimonies prior to broadcasting them was considered but deemed too costly.[94] Currently, 10–15 minute-long summaries of the proceeding are broadcasted on a weekly basis,[95] but the extent to which this promotes transparency is debatable.

Nonetheless, the Court's national relevance is enhanced through participation of Sierra Leoneans in its process – as witnesses, staff and receptive audiences. An emerging civil society engaged in a "bottom up" process of NGO formation and coalition-building ensures future attention to criminal justice and human rights issues.[96] In addition, the judges as well as the Defense Office engage in workshops, university seminars and other initiatives aimed at educating the next generation of Sierra Leonean lawyers on due process and rights of the accused.[97] This process is further reinforced through various activities undertaken by the Court's Outreach Section (OS).

The outreach program started in the Office of the Prosecutor, but was moved to the Registry to maintain an appearance of neutrality. The OS became fully operational in early 2003, and initially pursued its aims through conducting workshops for special groups – such as ex-combatants, victims, military representatives, policemen, and youth groups – with the intention of preparing them for the trials while taking into account their peculiar needs and roles in society.[98] In mid-2003, the OS began employing District Officers who are based in the provinces, to conduct community meetings updating the public on the Court's proceedings. These educative activities, conducted nationwide and in local languages, enhance the national relevance of the trials by rendering clear and understandable an otherwise incomprehensible process. The OS organizes public meetings where the Prosecutor and Principal Defender discuss their respective functions; conducts educational programs for school children; funds victims' journeys to the Court; promotes a book it has published about the Special Court in basic English; and encourages radio programs discussing the Court's process.[99] Such initiatives could have been undertaken by other organizations which are less costly than an international criminal tribunal. However, it was felt that the Court was well-positioned to educate on its mission, as it is able to explain its process while demonstrating it at the same time.[100]

Outreach activities go beyond informing the population of the Court's mandate, to ensure that the principles promoted by the Court remain in the country. To meet this objective the OS, after consultation with the government's "customary law" expert, began training "lay magistrates" on issues such as the presumption of innocence and due process of law.[101] These "lay magistrates" are traditional chiefs who engage in adjudication, and although too marginalized by the national legal institutions to receive formal training they still have a stronghold throughout the nation.[102] To promote a sustainable respect for the law and human rights, the OS established the "Accountability Now Club" (ANC), which comprises representatives of thirteen higher education facilities throughout Sierra Leone. While the ANC's short-term goal is to promote the participation of students in the Court's process, its long-term goal is to ensure student involvement beyond the Court's tenure in advocating broader legal and social transformations.[103] The Court does not intend to substitute for other judicial reform programs;[104] nonetheless, Court officials felt that the institution was ideally placed to contribute to judicial reform goals, and that it would be dishonorable not to do so.[105]

Outreach initiatives are also in place to listen to public concerns and address them accordingly, not just to win the public's hearts and minds but also to improve the Court's processes. The OS established the "Special Court Interactive Forum" (SCIF) to provide a link between the public and the Court. SCIF members currently include representatives of 28 local organizations, who on the one hand inform people in remote areas of the Court's progress, and on the other hand direct public concerns to the Registrar's attention.[106] Having learned that among other concerns, the public is anxious to be compensated for the past injustices, the OS initiated a consultation process concerning a victim commemoration scheme, which also addressed the issue of reparations.[107] An interesting suggestion made once by the Registrar, was that the diamond industry be approached and asked to assist in creating a trust fund for compensating victims, not as an admission of guilt but rather as an expression of the industry's concern for the victims of atrocities in a diamond producing country.[108]

Despite extensive outreach efforts, unfavorable public perceptions of the Court remain. A significant sector thinks the indictments of CDF leaders, in particular, are unfair because of the CDF's role in resisting the RUF. In addition, with respect to the CDF trial, some believe that it is unfair that Norman is on trial while President Kabbah, who was Norman's official superior when Norman allegedly committed the crimes, was not even indicted.[109] Others regard the trials as inconsistent with the amnesty provided by the Lomé Agreement. There are also those who believe the trials frustrate the attainment of peace as they will destabilize the nation by bringing back into the spotlight former rebel leaders,[110] and by increasing existing tensions between RUF supporters and CDF supporters who often live in the same communities. In addition, some critics regard the Court as an imposition of the West, complaining that despite presidential and parliamentary approval, Sierra Leoneans were not involved in a South Africa-like broad-based consultation process prior to its establishment. Others may be influenced by declarations made by those opposing the Court, that the US$80 million spent so far to support the Court could have been used to compensate the victims, or to rebuild their houses and villages.[111] And still others feel the discrepancies between local and international standards in terms of maximum punishment and detention conditions undermine the Court's credibility as an institution of justice.[112] Even Sierra Leoneans who currently approve of the Special Court may change their position if the Court fails to successfully try Charles Taylor, or if not enough convictions take place to justify its process.

The public's resistance to the Special Court seems to lessen, however, as the trials proceed.[113] This may be a result of the revelations made in the trial against CDF members, which drew attention to the egregious practices of the CDF, or simply due to a form of "critic's fatigue." Recently conducted regional conferences relating to transitional justice issues, revealed that the Court is generally considered as legitimate by the public.[114] They also revealed that those who still oppose certain aspects of the Court's process now tend to consider that the issues they challenge will be resolved within the framework of the Court.[115] Opposition based on the funds supporting the Court's operation has also lessened. It is worthwhile mentioning in this context that despite what seems like an enormous budget compared to the national budget of Sierra Leone, or even to the amounts raised by the TRC, the Court has been hampered by budgetary shortfalls. The Court's budget pales in comparison to that of the ICTY or ICTR, where the yearly budget exceeds the amount available to the Court for three years of operation.[116] The perceived waste of resources by the ad hoc tribunals accounted for the decision to fund the Special Court through voluntary contributions, resulting in the Court's restricted financial resources.[117] The Court's limited funds may ultimately pose a greater hurdle to its success than negative public opinion.

Conclusion

Despite antagonistic views and financial constraints, even the Court's critics agree that it will send a message of accountability to those who commit mass atrocities. Hopefully, this will remove the threat of further violence and enable Sierra Leone to rehabilitate itself and undergo a transition towards a more egalitarian rule of law society. Nonetheless, without additional measures employed by the government and the international community to promote sustainable transformation and to put an end to endemic corruption and mismanagement, as effective as the Court may be in conducting the trials, it will be unsuccessful in promoting sustainable peace and reliable justice. The Court's achievements can only constitute preliminary steps towards an improved society where human rights and rule of law prevail. Only a long-term commitment by the local authorities, coupled with international assistance, can ensure transition from the evils of war and the harms of violence towards an environment in which the development of the individual is encouraged and a high standard of living is attainable.

The international community cannot overlook the fact that for transitional justice mechanisms to have a sustainable effect, attention must be given to fighting poverty and encouraging development. Perhaps international entities (including those in the justice sector) whose presence in the country over the past few years contributed to the local economy should reconsider their approaching mass exodus, which may seriously destabilize the economy, risking further impoverishment and an increase in the already high unemployment level.[118] Alleviating poverty will enable the population to engage in social and political reform; it will also mitigate public bitterness which may easily serve to promote the political agendas of opportunistic and corrupt elements within the society.

Justice is about fairness and equality. If the Court can promote a public belief that there is a willingness within the society to treat people fairly and equally, it can assist in advancing transitional justice goals. If its judicial process is transparent, it can demonstrate to the Sierra Leonean society how to operate an impartial judicial system that enshrines due process of law and fairness of proceedings, while also promoting a break from a violent past. If it succeeds in ensuring that Sierra Leoneans feel parties to its process, as opposed to bystanders, it is headed in the right direction towards advancing transitional justice in Sierra Leone.

The Special Court's judicial process will condemn the dreadful practices Sierra Leoneans have witnessed in the past decade and hopefully deter their reoccurrence and restore respect for the law. The historical narrative established by the Court and the TRC will advance the public's awareness of the gravity of the atrocities committed, which in turn may help facilitate social and political reform consistent with human rights protection and rule of law. The war's root causes have been identified by the TRC. It is now up to the government to ensure that the "justice" in "transitional justice" does not remain "transitional".

NOTES

1. UN Doc. S/RES/1315, August 14, 2000, para. 7. For a critical view see P. Penfold, "Will Justice Help Peace in Sierra Leone?", *The Observer*, October 20, 2002.
2. Peace Agreement between the Government of Sierra Leone and the Revolutionary United Front of Sierra Leone, Abidjan, November 30, 1996, UN Doc. S/1996/1034 (Abidjan Accord).
3. Agreement on Ceasefire in Sierra Leone, May 18, 1999. Available at www. sierra-leone.org/ceasefire051899.html.
4. Peace Agreement between the Government of Sierra Leone and the Revolutionary United Front of Sierra Leone, Lomé, July 7, 1999 (Lomé Agreement). Available at www.sierra-leone.org/lomeaccord.html.
5. UN Doc. S/RES/1270, October 22, 1999. UNAMSIL replaced the UN Observer Mission to Sierra Leone (UNOMSIL), which was established under UN Doc. S/RES/1181, July 13, 1998.
6. M.P. Scharf, *The Special Court for Sierra Leone*, ASIL Insight, Oct. 2000 (Scharf, *The Special Court*), para. 3; Human Rights Watch, *Sierra Leone Rebels Violating Peace Accord*, August 30, 1999 (available at www.hrw.org).
7. "Sierra Leone News and Information Archives", available at www.sierra-leone.org (SL News Archives), news of May 8–17, 2000.
8. The Abuja Ceasefire Agreement of November 10, 2000.
9. The Ceasefire Agreement of November 10, 2000 was renewed in Abuja on May 4, 2001.
10. NPWJ Executive Summary, p. 33.
11. Government of Sierra Leone, *Sierra Leone Vision 2025 "Sweet Salone" – Strategies for National Transformation*, August 2003 (Sweet Salone, August 2003), p. 32, a pamphlet published with support from United Nations Development Programme (UNDP). This is the source of the details in the rest of this paragraph.
12. Lomé Agreement, Article IX.
13. Lomé Agreement, Article V, granted Foday Sankoh the chairmanship of the Commission for the Management of Strategic Resources, National Reconstruction and Development, and the status of Vice-President. It also granted four additional cabinet posts and four Deputy Minister posts to RUF members. Johnny Paul Koroma received chairmanship of the government's Commission for the Consolidation of Peace.
14. Lomé Agreement, Article XXVI(1).
15. Reference to this reservation is found in the Seventh Report of the Secretary-General on the United Nations Military Observer Mission in Sierra Leone, UN Doc. S/1999/836, July 30, 1999, paras. 7 and 54.
16. SL News Archives, news of July 9, 1999.
17. Press releases available at www.hrw.org and www.amnesty.org.
18. SL News Archives, news of May 22, 2000.
19. SL News Archives, news of May 26, 2000.
20. The Director of the local NGO "Campaign for Good Governance" called for the establishment of an international tribunal to prosecute Sierra Leone's atrocities. SL News Archives, news of May 26, 2000.

21. The British Foreign Secretary supported Sankoh's prosecution, emphasizing that the Lomé Agreement's amnesty provision only applies to acts committed before its signature. US Senator Gregg stated that the United States will "demand that brutal thugs are held accountable for their atrocities." SL News Archives, news of June 6, 2000.

22. Letter dated June 12, 2000 from President of Sierra Leone to the Secretary-General, UN Doc. S/2000/786, Annex.

23. UN Doc. S/RES/1315, August 14, 2000.

24. Agreement between the United Nations and the Government of Sierra Leone on the Establishment of a Special Court for Sierra Leone dated January 16, 2002 (Special Court Agreement), available at www.sierra-leone.org/specialcourtagreement.html. The delay in concluding the Special Court Agreement was due to the instability in Sierra Leone and difficulties in finding funds for the Special Court.

25. *The Special Court Agreement (Ratification) Act 2002.* In accordance with section 40(4) of the Constitution of Sierra Leone (1991) treaties must be approved by parliament.

26. Consistent with the reservation appended to the Lomé Agreement by the UN representative.

27. Kabbah's August 5, 2003 Statement to TRC, para. 35.

28. *Prosecutor* v. *Sam Hinga Norman, Moinina Fofana, Allieu Kondewa*, Case No. SCSL–2004–14.

29. *Prosecutor* v. *Issa Hassan Sesay, Morris Kallon, Augustine Gbao*, Case No. SCSL–2004–15.

30. *Prosecutor* v. *Alex Tamba Brima, Brima Bazzy Kamara, Santigie Borbor Kanu*, Case No. SCSL–2004–16.

31. They cannot be tried in absentia, in accordance with Article 17 of the *Statute of the Special Court for Sierra Leone (Statute). Statute* available at www.sierra-leone.org/documents-specialcourt.html. Taylor was detained in Nigeria and turned over to the Court in March 2006. Subsequent proceedings are beyond the scope of this chapter.

32. Report of the Secretary-General on the Establishment of a Special Court for Sierra Leone, UN Doc. S/2000/915, October 4, 2000 (SG Report on Court's Establishment, UN Doc. S/2000/915), paras. 25–28. Schabas, in chapter 1, questions whether this date was not selected because the United Nations had failed to attach a reservation to the amnesty provision in the Abidjan Accord, similar to that attached to the Lomé Agreement. In Penfold, *Will Justice?* para. 16, the author theorizes that the date was chosen because violence in Freetown broke out in 1997 (criticizing the international community's greater concern with Freetown than with the rest of the country).

33. The Court's jurisdiction extends to violations of Common Article 3 to the Geneva Conventions and of Additional Protocol II, and "other serious violations of international humanitarian law." The Court lacks jurisdiction over genocide.

34. The international crimes are punishable under Articles 2–4 of the *Statute*; the domestic crimes under Article 5.

35. *Prosecutor* v. *Morris Kallon, Brima Bazzy Kamara*, SCSL–2004–15–AR72 (E), SCSL–2004–16–AR72(E), Decision on Challenge to Jurisdiction:

Lomé Accord Amnesty, March 13, 2004 (Lomé Amnesty Decision, March 13, 2004). See related discussion below.

36. Article 8(2) of the *Statute*.

37. Article 8(1) of the *Statute* establishes the concurrent jurisdiction of the Special Court and the national courts; since the Lomé Agreement's amnesty provision is considered applicable domestically, such concurrent jurisdiction applies in practice to post-Lomé crimes.

38. *Prosecutor* v. *Issa Hassan Sesay, Morris Kallon, Augustine Gbao*, SCSL–2004–15–PT, Indictment, February 5, 2004; *Prosecutor* v. *Alex Tamba Brima, Brima Bazzy Kamara, Santigie Borbor Kanu*, SCSL–2004–16–PT, Indictment, February 5, 2004. The former RUF and AFRC members are charged with the same crimes, as they are alleged to have participated in a joint criminal enterprise which produced these crimes, even if they did not physically perpetrate or order them. On criminal responsibility resulting from participation in a joint criminal enterprise, see S. Powles, "Joint Criminal Enterprise – Criminal Liability by Prosecutorial Ingenuity and Judicial Creativity?" (2004) *Journal of International Criminal Justice*, 2, p. 606. Also see ICTY case: *Prosecutor* v. *Milutinovic et al.*, IT–99–37–AR72, Decision on Dragoljub Ojdanic's Motion Challenging Jurisdiction – Joint Criminal Enterprise, May 21, 2003, para. 20.

39. *Prosecutor* v. *Sam Hinga Norman, Moinina Fofana, Allieu Kondewa*, SCSL–2004–14–PT, Indictment, February 5, 2004.

40. See A. Cassese, *International Criminal Law* (New York: Oxford University Press, 2003), pp. 181 and 191.

41. Art. 1 of the *Statute* also adds that such persons may include "those leaders who . . . have threatened the establishment of and implementation of the peace process in Sierra Leone." According to the Secretary-General, these words "do not describe an element of the crime but rather provide guidance to the prosecutor in determining his or her prosecutorial strategy." Letter dated January 12, 2001 from the Secretary-General addressed to the President of the Security Council, UN Doc. S/2001/40, para. 3.

42. Report of the Planning Mission on the Establishment of the Special Court for Sierra Leone, UN Doc. S/2002/246, Annex, March 8, 2002, para. 29: "the selection for prosecution of those 'who bear the greatest responsibility' necessarily entails a measure of discretion on the part of the Prosecutor."

43. *Prosecutor* v. *Dusko Tadic*, Case No. IT–94–1–T, available at www.un.org/icty.

44. This approach was endorsed in UN Doc. S/RES/1503, August 28, 2003, defining the ICTY's "completion strategy".

45. There will not be domestic prosecutions of these lesser offenders with respect to crimes committed prior to the signing date of the Lomé Agreement, July 7, 1999, due to the amnesty provision therein, but it is not completely inconceivable that "small fry" will be tried by national courts for crimes committed after July 7, 1999.

46. See "Sierra Leone: Rebels 'Criminally Gutted an Entire Nation' Says International Prosecutor", Freetown, July 5, 2004. Article available at www.allafrica.com/stories/200407060022.html.

47. Interview with Nikolaus Toufar (Completion Strategy Coordinator at Special Court's Registry), Freetown (by phone), March 10, 2005. See relevant discussion on the "National Victims Commemoration Conference of Truth, Justice and Reconciliation" which took place in Freetown on March 1–2, 2005, and on the regional preparatory conferences.

48. Report of the Secretary-General, S/2000/915, paras. 9 and 39; *Prosecutor v. Morris Kallon, Sam Hinga Norman, Brima Bazzy Kamara*, SCSL–2004–15–AR72(E), SCSL–2004–14–AR72(E), SCSL–2004–16–AR72(E), Decision on Constitutionality and Lack of Jurisdiction, March 13, 2004.

49. See First Annual Report of the President of the Special Court for Sierra Leone, for the period December 2, 2002–December 1, 2003, (Special Court's First Annual Report), p. 20, available at www.sc-sl.org.

50. Article 5 of the Special Court Agreement.

51. Article 17 of the Special Court Agreement.

52. Article 14 of the *Statute*.

53. The Management Committee for the Special Court is an oversight committee which supervises funding and administrative arrangements related to the Court's operation. See Special Court's First Annual Report, page 30. See Articles 2, 3 and 7 of the Special Court Agreement.

54. *Prosecutor v. Issan Hassan Sesay*, Case No. SCSL–2004–15–AR15, Decision on Defense Motion Seeking the Disqualification of Justice Robertson from the Appeals Chamber, March 13, 2004. The defense argued that Judge Geoffrey Robertson's expressions about the RUF which were included in a book he wrote (G. Robertson, *Crimes Against Humanity – The Struggle for Global Justice* (2002)) demonstrated clear bias, and alternatively that they objectively gave rise to the appearance of bias. Accordingly, the defense requested that the judge withdraw from the Appeals Chamber or that the other members of the Appeals Chamber disqualify him from the Chamber. Consequently, the Court's Appeals Chamber held that the views expressed in the book objectively gave rise to the appearance of bias and precluded Judge Robertson from participating in the case against the former RUF members.

55. Security Council resolutions under Chapter VII constitute actions against states that are threatening international peace and security and are considered binding on all UN Member States.

56. Article 16 of the Special Court Agreement; section 21 of the *Special Court Agreement (Ratification) Act 2002*.

57. UN Doc. S/RES/1470, March 28, 2003, para. 11: "[The Security Council] . . . urges all states to cooperate fully with the [Special] Court." UN Doc. S/RES/1478, May 6, 2003, preamble: "[The Security Council] . . . Calling on all States . . . to cooperate fully with the Special Court".

58. Resolution 1470 was not issued under Chapter VII. With regard to Resolution 1478, while its operative part was issued under Chapter VII, its preamble is not governed by Chapter VII.

59. Interview with Alberto Fabbri (Legal Advisor to Special Court's Prosecutor), Freetown, August 5, 2004.

60. UN Doc. S/RES/1532, March 12, 2004, para. 1.

61. See Interpol website www.interpol.int/public/ICPO/PressReleases/PR2003/
    PR200334.asp.
62. Interview with Alberto Fabbri (Legal Advisor to Special Court's Prosecu-
    tor), Freetown, August 5, 2004.
63. Interview with Simone Monasebian (Principal Defender of the Special
    Court), Freetown, August 19, 2004. Also see Special Court's First Annual
    Report, page 18.
64. Interview with Robin Vincent (Registrar of the Special Court), Freetown,
    August 4, 2004.
65. The Appeals Chamber judges are: Judge Ayoola from Nigeria, Judge King
    from Sierra Leone, Judge Fernando from Sri Lanka, Judge Winter from
    Austria, and Judge Robertson from the United Kingdom. The First Trial
    Chamber judges are: Judge Itoe from Cameroon, Judge Thompson from
    Sierra Leone, and Judge Boutet from Canada. The Second Trial Chamber
    judges are Judge Doherty from Northern Ireland, Judge Sebutinde from
    Uganda, and Judge Lussick from Samoa. Hence in total there are five
    African judges out of eleven judges.
66. *Prosecutor v. Alex Tamba Brima, Brima Bazzy Kamara, Santigie Borbor Kanu*,
    SCSL–2004–16–PT, Decision on Prosecution Request for Leave to Amend
    the Indictment, May 6, 2004.
67. *Prosecutor v. Sam Hinga Norman*, SCSL–2004–14–AR72(E), Decision on
    Preliminary Motion based on Lack of Jurisdiction (Child Recruitment),
    May 31, 2004.
68. *Prosecutor v. Charles Ghankay Taylor*, SCSL–2003–01–AR72(E), Decision
    on Immunity from Jurisdiction, May 31, 2004 (Taylor Immunity Decision,
    May 31, 2004); Lomé Amnesty Decision, March 13, 2004.
69. Taylor was charged with seventeen counts, including extermination,
    murder, enslavement, inhumane acts, rape, sexual slavery and any other
    form of sexual violence as crimes against humanity; with acts of terrorism,
    collective punishment, murder, cruel treatment, and pillage as violations
    of Common Article 3 to the Geneva Conventions and of Additional Pro-
    tocol II; and with the use of child-soldiers and attacks against peacekeepers
    as "other serious violations of international humanitarian law." See *Prosecu-
    tor v. Charles Ghankay Taylor*, SCSL–2003–01–I, Indictment, March 7,
    2003.
70. Taylor Immunity Decision, May 31, 2004, para. 52. Considering that at the
    time of the hearing Taylor was no longer head of state, the Court held that
    "[t]he immunity *ratione personae* which he claimed had ceased to attach to
    him. Even if he had succeeded in his application the consequence would
    have been to compel the Prosecutor to issue a fresh warrant." See Taylor
    Immunity Decision, May 31, 2004, para. 59.
71. Lomé Amnesty Decision, March 13, 2004, para. 88. The Chamber also
    noted that the President of Sierra Leone acknowledged that "the intention of
    the amnesty granted was to put prosecution of such offences outside the
    jurisdiction of national courts." See Lomé Amnesty Decision, March 13,
    2004, para. 74.
72. Lomé Amnesty Decision, March 13, 2004, para. 82.

73. Lomé Amnesty Decision, March 13, 2004, para. 84. See the view of the TRC as expressed by Schabas in chapter 1. In fact, this is the fundamental issue which caused tension between the TRC and the Special Court.

74. Stressing that witnesses face threats from within their own communities, see *Prosecutor* v. *Allieu Kondewa*, SCSL–2003–12–PT, Ruling on the Prosecution Motion for Immediate Protective Measures for Witnesses and Victims and for Non-Public Disclosure and urgent Request for Interim Measures until Appropriate Protective Measures are in Place, October 10, 2003, para. 24. See also *Prosecutor* v. *Sam Hinga Norman, Moinina Fofana, Allieu Kondewa*, SCSL–2004–14–T, Decision on Prosecution Motion for Modification of Protective Measures for Witnesses, June 8, 2004, para. 34.

75. Referring to the fragile security situation in Sierra Leone, see e.g. *Prosecutor* v. *Issa Hassan Sesay, Morris Kallon, Augustine Gbao*, SCSL–2004–15–T, Decision on Prosecution Motion for Modification of Protective Measures for Witnesses, July 5, 2004, para. 23.

76. Interview with An Michels (clinical psychologist at Special Court's Witnesses and Victims Section (WVS)), Freetown, August 2, 2004.

77. Article 16.4 of the *Statute* requires the WVS personnel to "include experts in trauma, including trauma related to crimes of sexual violence and violence against children."

78. Rules 75 and 79 of the Special Court Rules authorize the judges to order measures to this effect.

79. Disclosure of the identity of a witness to the accused is usually delayed until 21 or 42 days before the witness' appearance in trial, pursuant to Rule 69(A) of the Special Court Rules, thus protecting the witness from intimidation and retaliation while providing sufficient time for the accused to prepare his or her defense.

80. Many child-soldiers developed a sense of loyalty towards their leaders as they were often separated from their biological family at an early age and had since lived with their abductors. To protect them from the trauma involved in testifying in the presence of an accused, as well as to preserve the quality of their testimony, the Court orders measures to minimize their direct confrontation with the accused, for example, by allowing them to testify through a closed circuit television, pursuant to Rule 75(B)(iii) of the Special Court Rules.

81. See *Rome Statute*, Article 19.3, 15.3, 68.3.

82. Interview with An Michels, Freetown, August 2, 2004.

83. On the handling of children by the TRC, see discussion in chapter 1, pp. 32–33.

84. Some who observed the public statements given before the TRC by those who testified as perpetrators, expressed skepticism about their truthfulness.

85. *Prosecutor* v. *Sam Hinga Norman*, SCSL–2003–08–PT, Decision on Appeal by the Truth and Reconciliation Commission for Sierra Leone and Chief Samuel Hinga Norman JP Against the Decision of His Lordship, Mr. Justice Bankole Thompson delivered on 30 October 2003 to Deny the TRC's Request to hold a Public Hearing with Chief Samuel Hinga Norman JP, November 28, 2003, para 7.

86. Interview with David Crane (Prosecutor of the Special Court), Freetown, July 29, 2004.

87. *Ibid.*

88. Penfold, *Will Justice?* para. 8.

89. E.g. the malevolent exchange of press releases on behalf of the two institutions regarding the incident surrounding the TRC's request to conduct a public hearing with Norman. See discussion in chapter 1, pp. 36–37.

90. See related discussion on the theory that the Special Court's process had a "chilling effect" which prevented perpetrators from testifying before the TRC, in chapter 1, p. 36.

91. See J. R. W. D. Jones, C. Carlton-Hanciles, H. Kah-Jallow, S. Scratch and I. Yillah, "The Special Court for Sierra Leone – A Defence Perspective", (2004) *Journal of International Criminal Justice*, 2, 211, pp. 229–30.

92. See First Annual Report, p. 20, available at www.sc-sl.org.

93. Such video record is currently produced by the Court's Public Affairs Office. It will include footage of the trials, interviews with staff and deliberations between trial attorneys and other main actors. Interview with Sativa January (Special Court's Video Producer), Freetown, July 13, 2004.

94. Interview with Robin Vincent (Registrar of the Special Court), Freetown, August 4, 2004.

95. Interview with Peter Andersen (Special Court's Public Affairs Officer), Freetown (by phone), February 16, 2005.

96. The proliferation of local human rights organizations in Sierra Leone also facilitated the operation of numerous international NGOs. Some of the international NGOs themselves contributed to the Court's national relevance by sensitizing the population to the Special Court's mandate and mission during the months before it became operative.

97. Interview with Rupert Skilbeck (Defense Advisor at the Special Court's Defense Office), Freetown, July 30, 2004.

98. Approximately 2,000 people participated nationwide in these workshops, which were conducted by Outreach representatives in cooperation with the NGO "No Peace Without Justice".

99. Interview with Mohamed Suma (representative of Outreach Section), Freetown, June 18, 2004.

100. Interview with Robin Vincent (Registrar of the Special Court), Freetown, August 4, 2004.

101. Interview with Binta Mansaray (Special Court's Outreach Coordinator), Freetown, August 5, 2004.

102. *Ibid.*

103. Interview with Mohamed Suma (representative of Outreach Section), Freetown, June 18, 2004.

104. For example, the British Department for International Development is currently leading a US$50 million justice program in Sierra Leone.

105. Interview with Robin Vincent, Freetown, August 4, 2004.

106. *Ibid.*

107. This process culminated with the "National Victims Commemoration Conference of Truth, Justice and Reconciliation", a conference organized by local NGOs and facilitated by the Special Court's Outreach Section.

This conference took place in Freetown (not in a Special Court facility) on March 1–2, 2005. It involved the participation of 250–300 civil society representatives, and in its course expert opinions were expressed by representatives of UNAMSIL, the international NGO "International Center for Transitional Justice" (ICTJ), and local NGOs. Interview with Nikolaus Toufar (Completion Strategy Coordinator at Special Court's Registry), Freetown (by phone), March 10, 2005.

108. Interview with Robin Vincent, Freetown, August 4, 2004.
109. On this matter see also brief discussion in chapter 1, p. 37.
110. Penfold, *Will Justice?* para.12.
111. Penfold, *Will Justice?* para. 23–24. Nonetheless, had the Court not been established, it is an open question whether these funds would have been disbursed to Sierra Leone.
112. E.g., while the death sentence constitutes a legal and acceptable punishment under Sierra Leonean law for domestic offences which are less grave than the offences prosecuted by the Special Court, such punishment cannot be imposed by the Special Court. See Penfold, *Will Justice?*, para. 22.
113. Interview with Peter Andersen (Special Court's Public Affairs Officer), Freetown (by phone), February 16, 2005.
114. Interview with Nikolaus Toufar, Freetown (by phone), 10 March 2005.
115. For example, those who believe Norman is innocent, try to find and provide the defense with exculpatory evidence. Interview with Nikolaus Toufar, Freetown (by phone), March 10, 2005.
116. The annual budget of the ICTY is US$120 million and that of the ICTR is US$110 million.
117. R. Zacklin, "The Failings of Ad Hoc International Tribunals", (2004) *Journal of International Criminal Justice*, 2, pp. 541–45. Recent efforts have resulted in the UN's approval to finance the third year of the Court operation through assessed compulsory contributions of UN member states. However, the Court will operate for more than three years, so without a UN commitment to fund the Court's fourth year, the threat of Treasury draining remains imminent.
118. Sierra Leone was ranked last in the 2004 UNDP *Human Development Report 2004*. Available at www.undp.org/hdro.

3 The Peruvian Truth and Reconciliation Commission and the challenge of impunity

Eduardo González Cueva

Introduction

The Peruvian Truth and Reconciliation Commission (*Comisión de la Verdad y Reconciliación* – CVR), which released its Final Report in August 2003, has laid a strong claim to be remembered as one of the most notable among similar experiences of accountability and historical clarification. The CVR produced a large final report as complex and ambitious as those issued by previous commissions, including those of South Africa and Guatemala. With a budget above 13 million dollars,[1] and a staff of over 500 professionals who processed the testimonies of almost 17,000 victims,[2] the magnitude of the CVR operations was second only to the South African Truth and Reconciliation Commission (TRC).

Like the South African TRC, the CVR steered an eminently public process. Not only did it organize public hearings[3] where the victims of violence had an opportunity to share their experiences with the population, but it also conducted a highly visible set of activities aimed at winning public support for the prosecution of those persons who allegedly perpetrated the worst crimes under the Commission's mandate.

The CVR raised expectations on a wide range of issues, including: the clarification of the whereabouts of the disappeared, whose number was established at over 8,500;[4] the exhumation of clandestine burial sites, of which over 4,600 were identified;[5] comprehensive reparations to individual victims;[6] and the prosecution of perpetrators, many of whom were named in the Final Report. However, in line with the experience of other commissions, the distance between those social expectations raised high by the truth, and what the state authorities were ready to grant, has left frustration in its wake, especially in the field of criminal justice.

Unlike other commissions, the CVR saw part of its job as helping to advance criminal prosecutions. At the end of its work, the CVR handed over the dossiers of 43 cases[7] to the Office of the Prosecutor General (*Ministerio Público* – MP), in addition to the dossiers of four cases it had previously delivered. The CVR made several specific recommendations on subjects including indictments, exhumations, measures to ensure the appearance of the defendants (*medidas cautelares*), witness protection and the request of further information from the security forces. However, progress has been slow in the MP and most of the cases have been remanded to local prosecutors for further investigation.

The MP – and more generally, the Peruvian judicial system – has the undistinguished record of being too pliable in the face of political pressure. Its lack of diligence follows an historical pattern of unresponsiveness and inefficiency. However, even recognizing that systemic limitation, common to most transitional countries, the options chosen by the commission need to be carefully examined to ascertain whether they were the best possible. This chapter posits that the relationship between the CVR and the MP suffered from the lack of a commonly agreed-upon prosecutorial strategy that would address the complexities of massive, systematic crimes. The CVR did not have a prosecution strategy at the beginning of its work, but a vague set of criteria built upon the anxiety not to let some cases be forgotten. Only by the end of its work did the CVR build a strategy focused on larger patterns of violations and going beyond isolated cases, but by then it had limited time to build support around it and faced a series of tensions with the MP that have made a sustainable prosecution strategy more difficult.

This chapter situates the choices made by the CVR in the political context in which the Commission was created. It reviews the legal developments in the struggle against impunity and the changes in the political climate as the Commission neared the end of its mandate. It also examines the work of the legal teams within the CVR before and after the presentation of its Final Report and it summarizes the advantages and disadvantages of the CVR strategy and highlights possible lessons to be learned.

The Peruvian transition and the creation of the CVR

Two violent evils, fanatical insurgence and authoritarianism, painfully branded the last two decades of the Peruvian twentieth century. A fragile democracy was challenged in the cradle by the armed insurgence led by two groups: the Maoist "Shining Path" (*Partido Comunista del Perú – "Sendero Luminoso"*), that began its actions in 1980, and the smaller Tupac Amaru Revolutionary Movement (*Movimiento Revolucionario Túpac Amaru* – MRTA), launched in 1984.

Insurgent actions caught by surprise the civilian elites that, in 1983, gave carte blanche to the armed forces for a massive military response that escalated the conflict and eventually put most of the country under a prolonged state of emergency. The combined action of guerrilla organizations, military units and local self-defense groups acting under the command, or with the acquiescence of the state, between 1983 and 1993 caused the bulk of the 69,000 deaths that the CVR would estimate for the whole twenty-year period.

The government of Alberto Fujimori, elected in 1990, decided to meet the challenge of armed insurgency with a strategy predicated upon the suppression of civil liberties and a fundamental erosion of political accountability. Faced with the resistance of the civilian opposition in congress, Fujimori opted for a coup d'etat. In April 1992, in alliance with the military and with the assent of most of the population, Fujimori illegally dissolved the National Congress and declared the judiciary in reorganization. He quickly assuaged international concerns by organizing new elections that established a new parliament with constitutional drafting powers. A new, strongly presidential constitution was approved in a referendum in 1993, but international acceptance and political normalization did not translate into respect for the rule of law. Peru's political life experienced a steady decline towards a corrupt autocracy, whose legitimacy was maintained by economic stability and the success of the security forces.

Fujimori benefited from the effects of a new counter-insurgency strategy that the armed forces had implemented since the late eighties: it combined draconian counter-insurgency laws that transformed the judicial system into a machine to produce convictions, leniency toward insurgent deserters and – most critically – renewed alliances with peasant and indigenous communities. Abimael Guzmán, leader of the "Shining Path", was captured in September of 1992 and capitulated later, declaring the armed insurgency over and calling for peace negotiations.[8] The survival of maverick insurgent units or the general threat of a terrorist revival was constantly used to justify the continuity of emergency measures and the growing powers of the intelligence services (*Servicio Nacional de Inteligencia* – SNI), during most of the period of government.

In time, growing corruption and a lack of accountability eroded the government's legitimacy. In addition, human rights organizations worked to engage international institutions to protect the rights of victims. The government had invested serious efforts to reassure international partners and local public opinion that counter-insurgent war was being waged without the brutal tactics employed by the security forces under the administrations of both President Fernando Belaúnde (1980–85) and Alan García (1985–90). However, in 1995, in response to judicial investigations of atrocities committed by death squads operating under army control, the government passed legislation enacting a blanket amnesty to security forces personnel involved in violations of human rights.[9] Human rights organizations exposed the systematic character of state abuse in Peru and cited notorious cases that led to rulings against the Peruvian state in the Inter-American Court of Human Rights (IACHR),[10] which severely damaged the government's image. Even state institutions established by governmental initiative would prove to be fiercely independent, such as a human rights ombudsman's office[11] and an independent office that reviewed the trials of those sentenced for terrorism, and recommended that hundreds receive presidential pardons.[12]

Public outrage against human rights abuses was not mobilized around a general sense of widespread abuse, but around specific cases that became *causes célèbres*: the execution by a death squad of nineteen people at a party held a few blocks from the National Congress, in the working-class neighborhood of Barrios Altos; the disappearance of nine students and a professor from La Cantuta, the campus of a state university, during a military-enforced curfew; the torture and execution of SIN agents, suspected of having leaked information of abuses to the press.

In contrast to what had happened during the worst moments of the conflict during the eighties, when observers lacked access to areas of conflict, the cases of *Barrios Altos* and *La Cantuta* had massive visibility: they took place in Lima, in areas or institutions completely under the control of the security forces. A sustained stream of leaks to the press, presumably from alienated members of the military, exposed the work of a shadowy death squad, the "*Grupo Colina*" under the direct control of the government.

The government's 1999 decision to unilaterally withdraw from the jurisdiction of the IACHR after an adverse decision condemned Peru's anti-insurgent criminal framework[13] became one of the main issues of concern for the national opposition and for international observers.[14] Peru's return to the jurisdiction of the IACHR would be one of the key pressure points against the Fujimori government, providing a rallying point for a political opposition that had been deeply divided during the initial years after the coup.

In the end, Peru's transition would not be the result of a negotiated arrangement, like the Spanish or the Chilean transitions that were the paradigm for many Peruvian democratic politicians.[15] The scandal created by the release, in September of 2000, of videos with evidence of high-level corruption led to the announcement that Fujimori would cut his mandate short and that new elections would be organized in a year's time. After a few weeks of uncertainty, not even that appearance of an orderly retreat could be maintained. Fujimori left the country in November, under the pretense of attending to international commitments, and resigned from the presidency after arriving in Japan. There, he would eventually claim Japanese citizenship, in an attempt to shield himself from the possibility of extradition.

Fujimori's escape, that of his intelligence advisor Vladimiro Montesinos and many other leaders of the government, combined with a wave of arrests against generals, businessmen and politicians involved in the corruption network unveiled by the videos, left the democratic opposition in an apparently unbeatable situation from the standpoint of comparable transitions. The authoritarian regime had entirely collapsed without any capacity to leave in place institutional safeguards against the prosecution of its members: the military was too weakened and divided by extensive corruption to protect the fallen leaders; no real political movement sustained the disgraced *caudillo*; a challenge to the amnesty laws left by Fujimori was due to be considered at the IACHR.

In addition, the Peruvian transition did not have to deal with any serious armed challenge against the state. No peace process was part of the agenda and the international community did not pressure Peru for talks with the rebels. The conflict was largely over; the "Shining Path" had imploded since the capture of its leader and the MRTA's last active cell had been destroyed in a failed attempt to take high-level hostages in 1997.

Demoralized members of Fujimori's party in Congress abandoned their posts or defected to the opposition. The collapse of *fujimorismo* permitted the creation of a new pro-democracy majority and the appointment of an opposition leader as the new President of Congress and also of Peru until new elections were held, in accordance with constitutional procedure.

In these extraordinarily favorable circumstances, the new President, Valentín Paniagua announced that his government would not be just a low-profile caretaker administration. He called a non-partisan cabinet of notables presided over by former United Nations Secretary-General Javier Pérez de Cuéllar and joined by respected experts. One of the cabinet's first actions was to announce that Peru would radically change Fujimori's human rights policies, recognize again the jurisdiction of the IACHR, and join newly created international institutions like the International Criminal Court. The new Ministry of Justice, led by prominent jurist and human rights advocate Diego García Sayán, created a Working Group, with the participation of ministries, members of the security forces and civil society, to study the creation of a truth commission and recommend a mandate.[16]

The Working Group was insulated from pressures, since the cabinet was non-partisan and parties in congress were actually discussing a parallel truth commission project that would not go too far. This factor, in addition to the political irrelevance of the supporters of the fallen regime or the old insurgency, enabled the commission's mandate to be supportive of prosecutions and resulted in a commission composed without representatives of party lines. Moreover, the composition of the commission was not the object of comprehensive negotiations to include members of all shades of the political spectrum and, as a result, the commission did not have to carry the burden of political compromises.

The mandate of the CVR and its interpretation

The mandate, as approved by the Working Group and ratified, with some changes, by President Paniagua in the decree that created the Commission,[17] was simple in form yet comprehensive and ambitious. The truth commission was charged with "clarifying the process, facts and responsibilities of the terrorist violence and human rights violations produced from May 1980 to November 2000, whether imputable to terrorist organizations or State agents, as well as proposing initiatives destined to affirm peace and harmony among Peruvians".[18]

The aim of clarification required the Commission to produce both an interpretation of the historical period and case-specific fact-finding. The Presidential decree specified that the "societal conditions and institutional behaviors" that constituted the breeding ground for violence had to be analyzed, and established that the Commission should also identify responsibilities for the crimes listed in the mandate.[19]

Responsibilities would be identified "when appropriate" and "to the extent possible" and would feed into the legal functions that, according to the Constitution, are reserved to the MP and the courts. The decision as to the "appropriateness" of identifying criminal responsibilities was left to the Commission, with the proviso that, if such decisions were taken, any responsibilities so established would be only presumptive.

The subject-matter jurisdiction of the Commission was defined as a list[20] of those crimes generally considered to violate non-derogable rights, such as the rights to life, personal integrity and legal protection: murder, kidnappings, enforced disappearance of persons, and torture. The list, however, was not a *numerus clausus*: it left two possibilities open for the inclusion of crimes considered analogous in nature to those explicitly mentioned. After "torture" were the words "and other serious injuries." These would be used by the Commission to include sexual crimes under the mandate; the Commission used another clause, at the end of the list, to examine crimes committed against children, forced displacement of persons, and violations of due process and to analyze whether the agents of violence may have committed the crime of genocide.

The subject-matter jurisdiction of the commission inevitably raised the question of the applicable law. At the time of the formation of the Working Group, the Ministry of Justice had explicitly mentioned international human rights law and international humanitarian law as forming the basis for the definition of the crimes committed by both sides of the conflict.[21] The Working Group, however, found it impossible to reach consensus on the inclusion of international humanitarian law. The representatives of the security forces resisted the inclusion of the laws of war, since, in their view, that would implicitly recognize that the confrontation with the "Shining Path" and the MRTA had amounted to an internal armed conflict, and that groups that they considered "terrorists" would be endowed with belligerent status.

The Working Group dropped the reference to the laws of war, but resisted the characterization of anti-state agents as "terrorists". Both the Ministry of Justice's terms of reference for the group, and the proposal issued by the Working Group defined those organizations as "subversive," a term that, although widely used in the media with a pejorative connotation, only described the position of the "Shining Path" and the MRTA regarding the existing political order. President Paniagua, however, dropped the term "subversive" and replaced it with "terrorist",[22] therefore leaving in the mandate an ambiguous and inevitably politicized definition. In the end, the Commission agreed on a common definition of "terrorism" on the basis of a survey of international law and used it mainly to refer to the strategy of the Shining Path.

The decree specified that the Commission would examine conduct attributable to state agents, members of "terrorist organizations" and members of paramilitary organizations.[23] Later in the life of the Commission, the interpretation of the mandate included the investigation of the self-defense groups that, in some areas, acted directly under the orders of the armed forces.

The question of what to do about the validity of the amnesty laws passed by Fujimori's Congress in 1995 in favor of the security forces was answered in April 2001, two months before the creation of the CVR, when the IACHR ruled in the *Barrios Altos* case that amnesty laws that impeded the investigation and punishment of serious human rights violations were void and contrary to the obligations accepted by states under the American Convention of Human Rights.[24] The Court later clarified that the ruling applied in all other cases, not just in this massacre.[25] After this ruling, the Supreme Court of Peru declared the decision of the IACHR to be binding on the Peruvian judicial system, making it unnecessary for Congress to vote on the issue and automatically reopening cases that had been closed in 1995.

The inclusion of insurgents raised another issue: the situation of those persons belonging to insurgent groups and sentenced for the crimes of terrorism and treason (*traición a la patria*), under draconian laws passed by Fujimori's government shortly after the 1992 coup. The laws, in the view of the IACHR in the *Castillo Petruzzi* case,[26] violated elementary rights to due process. Would the Commission pronounce itself on those violations of due process? And if so, would it recommend new trials? The expectation about this possibility resulted in specific policies by the members of the "Shining Path" and the MRTA in prison. Initially, they attempted a mixed policy of pressure and rapprochement before the Commission, giving testimony while demanding a general amnesty for former members of the insurgent organizations, who considered themselves "war prisoners" or "political prisoners". However, when the Constitutional Court of Peru (*Tribunal Constitucional*), on the basis of the IACHR's *Castillo Petruzzi* ruling, opened the way for new trials for persons accused of terrorism .and treason, their attitude changed.[27] Members of the insurgent organizations now kept their testimonies in safe terrain, avoiding self-incrimination and justifying the crimes as regrettable errors, for which few would accept responsibility.

Finally, the temporal jurisdiction of the Commission, encompassing events from the beginning of the Maoist insurgency in May 1980 to Fujimori's escape in November 2000, raised its own challenges. It was not always evident that the Commission would include the eighties. Although it was generally perceived that the conflict had raged under the administrations of Fernando Belaúnde (1980–85) and Alan García (1985–90), some public opinion leaders believed that the Commission should not examine what had occurred under democratically elected governments, and should limit itself to the period after the 1992 coup d'etat, whose atrocities were fresh in the public's memory . Ultimately, the CVR would be tasked with the examination of the whole period; this meant that it had to work on two distinct phases of the violence: a growing internal conflict fought under democratically elected governments until the late eighties, and the establishment of a victorious authoritarian regime, focused on suppressing the political opposition, after the capture or killing of armed opponents. The test of political independence for the Commission would not be its attitude to investigating the universally condemned actions of the fallen regime, but those crimes committed under democratic governments whose leaders were back as members of the political mainstream.

These and other unresolved issues would plague the investigation of the Commission, especially when dealing with cases where it had to be decided whether the mandate applied. An interpretation of the mandate to limit it to the context of insurgency and counter-insurgency was needed, but it would never be fully and explicitly asserted. The Commission was criticized for excluding cases of violations without relation to the conflict but under its temporal mandate, such as the apparent cooperation of the Peruvian military with the continent-wide "Operación Cóndor" in June 1980 to kidnap Argentinian guerrillas present in Lima; the torture and execution of intelligence agents under the government of Fujimori; or the forced sterilization of women in the Andean highlands during population control campaigns in the late nineties. As a general policy was lacking, not every part of the Commission would interpret the mandate in a uniform way.

An additional complexity was the fact that after the end of the transitional government, new President Alejandro Toledo ratified the Commission but added the mandate of contributing to national reconciliation, without much clarity as to the meaning or the sense of this additional function. This would be a permanent source of political tensions between the Commission and different constituencies, since some feared that reconciliation would be the excuse for state impunity, while others suspected that the concept would be used to support an amnesty for insurgent leaders.

The investigative powers of the Commission

The mandate of the CVR provided it modest powers in relation to the wide task assigned. The foundational Presidential Decree allowed the Commission to interview public officials, request information, carry out inspections, hold public and private hearings, and request measures of protection for witnesses.[28] The commission did not receive powers of subpoena or search and seizure. It had to rely on its own capacity of friendly persuasion to obtain the materials and testimonies it needed.

These weaknesses were attributed to the fact that the Commission was a special body created by decree rather than by legislation: this was probably the price to pay for a course of action that prioritized the prompt establishment of a commission in a process largely insulated from the kind of political horse-trading that would have probably taken place in Congress in the fluid situation of the transition.

The Commission interpreted its powers in a bold and comprehensive way, allowing it to conduct proceedings that carried some political and institutional risk. For example, the Commission took the initiative to propose to the Prosecutor General the carrying out of exhumations, to which the Commission brought independent experts. Similarly, the Commission obtained the permission of the Ministry of Justice to visit all the prisons that held persons sentenced for terrorism or treason and to conduct interviews and hearings, including lengthy interviews with the main leaders of the subversive groups.

Boldness of initiative contrasted with the diplomatic composure transmitted by the Commission's leadership. The Commission showed a deferential treatment toward state institutions and leaders and rarely used public pressure to achieve its objectives. Its notoriety and high levels of public support made it politically costly to oppose it or to appear to be obstructing its tasks. Upper-echelon military leaders, including former chiefs of the "emergency zones" in charge of counter-insurgent action appeared before the Commission; all the former presidents of the Republic gave testimony; substantial documentation was made available from the security forces and all the major imprisoned leaders of the insurgent organizations met the commission for long interviews.

Research at the CVR and investigative strategy

The initial discussions in the CVR about the interpretation of its mandate revolved around the kind of truth that needed to be unveiled. Different commissioners and teams presented competing positions regarding the pre-eminence of either an interpretive, "historical" focus, or a fact-finding, "juridical" focus. The tension between explaining what happened and finding legal evidence of what happened was never adequately solved, and ended up with the creation of parallel investigative units in charge of studying the situations under the mandate from diverging perspectives based in law or the social sciences. Also, early in the life of the Commission, as it was decided to study specific cases an additional rift emerged within the legal researchers, between those lawyers that worked on the establishment of general "patterns" of human rights violations that should be investigated and those working on cases that would eventually be sent to the MP.

In practice, each investigative unit worked independently from the others and reported to a responsible commissioner, who would provide the only link to other investigations. The investigative units initially established at the CVR were the Legal Team (*Equipo Jurídico*), focused on establishing whether the human rights violations in the mandate had attained the character of a generalized or systematic pattern; the National Processes Team (*Proceso Nacional de la Violencia*) was in charge of historical reconstruction of the conflict and the strategies of its actors;

the In-Depth Studies Area (*Area de Estudios a Profundidad*) examined specific scenarios, trying to reconstruct the social and cultural context prevalent during the conflict with a sociological and anthropological focus; the Regional Histories Area (*Historias Regionales*) reconstructed the history of the conflict as perceived by the regional actors; and the Reparations and Reconciliation Team (*Equipo de Secuelas, Reparaciones y Reconciliación*) investigated the consequences of the conflict in local communities, preparing a policy of reparations and reconciliation.

The absence of a central Research Directorship meant that there was significant overlap in several areas of the investigation that would be remedied partially through internal reorganizations at the last stage of the Commission's life, during the preparation of the Final Report. At that point, a newly created Editorial Committee was tasked with identifying internal inconsistencies in the work of the different investigative teams, catalyzing cooperation among them and commissioning additional research.

There was not, at the beginning, a specific group working on cases with the aim of submitting them for criminal prosecution, and the Legal Team sought to establish general patterns not cases. The CVR created a Legal Team charged with the investigation of specific cases only after the first public hearings, held in April 2002, seven months into the life of the CVR, which had made obvious that criminal justice was one of the top priorities of the victims. But how would any team deal with the mass of possible cases that the Commission would receive in thousands of public and private testimonies?

Well before a team of researchers was assembled, the Commission sketched the guidelines of an investigative strategy. It was impossible to prosecute all cases; in most situations, the available information would be scant. In that situation, the cases would be dealt with in a statistical manner, constituting the bulk of the "patterns" being researched by the existing Legal Team. In the minority of situations where information was abundant, the Commission could exercise its discretion to identify cases that appeared to be particularly suitable for prosecution due to the availability of evidence and testimony.

The next important issue was the selection criteria among the available cases. In general, the CVR decided that the cases to be investigated would be those "explanatory" of the patterns of violations observable in the conflict.[29] In practice, however, the CVR would often confuse "explanatory," that is, an exemplary case that sheds light on a larger situation, with "representative," that is, a case that, taken together with others, constituted a mini-universe of the situations examined by the Commission in a catalog-like fashion. This would have consequences later, as the commission presented "a list" of cases for prosecution to the MP and Peruvian public opinion was left with a collection of seemingly disparate cases but no clarity about the consistent nature of the brutal strategies implemented by the state and the insurgents.

A true "explanatory" approach would have required the selection of cases capable of showing how the specific crime being unveiled constituted part of a well-thought-out strategy applied with knowledge and intent. Given the fact that the CVR dealt with systemic crimes, the approach would have required, for example, the joint preparation of cases that took place in a given period and place, consistent with a statistically demonstrable pattern to show how a veritable criminal organization was in place deciding from above. This would have allowed a focus on leaders and organizations more than on seemingly isolated events.

Instead, the approach was to assemble a number of cases that represented different types of violations, committed at different moments of the conflict, in different places and by different actors, trying to be as inclusive and comprehensive as possible. As cases were selected not for their capacity to unveil a larger strategy but for their own intrinsic merits, it soon became evident that the impact that the cases had had in the national life would emerge as an additional criterion for inclusion.

A Special Investigations Unit (*Unidad de Investigaciones Especiales*) was created in mid-2002 to investigate a list of potential cases forwarded by the Commissioners. As the Unit would have to gather sensitive information and deal with witnesses, it was designed to work separately from the rest of the Commission. That decision would make the Special Investigations Unit run parallel to the rest of the Commission and deepen the gap between different approaches. The Unit would have no substantive contact with the existing Legal Team or with the social science teams.

The isolation of the Special Unit facilitated its investigative work in some ways: it obtained access to key witnesses and valuable evidence and identified the whereabouts of alleged perpetrators without the risk of leakage, and it enjoyed considerable leeway to build its cases in the way it considered fit. However, the Unit's isolation also created problems: the most complex one would be the apparent inconsistency with the work of the pre-existing Legal Team. When the work on the Final Report started the editorial committee identified the apparent inconsistency between the chapters produced by the Legal Team – focused on examining whether the number and extension of the violations reached the threshold of international crimes – and the cases prepared by the Special Unit, built solely on the basis of national law.

An implicit challenge for the Commission was to select cases providing leads to the role of higher-ups in the organizations participating in the armed conflict. It was intuitive, although not explicitly affirmed, that justice would not be served by forwarding to the MP cases leading to the prosecution of low-level perpetrators. It was not clear, however, how to establish the responsibility of chiefs and commanders. Without substantive contact with the Legal Team to select cases that would fit into patterns, the Special Unit had to work alone to craft theories on how to identify responsibilities that went beyond the direct perpetrators. In practice, the Unit found itself grouping the individual cases it had received from the commissioners into small patterns and making connections in order to identify a chain of command. In this way it put together, for example, the main cases attributed to the first military commander of the emergency zone, General Clemente Noel in 1983, or to the "Grupo Colina" in the early 1990s. Had the Special Unit and the Legal Team identified synergies, their task would have been easier; at the very least, the Unit would not have been forced to repeat the work of identification of patterns already undertaken by the Legal Team.

The Unit used the theory of "indirect authorship through an organized power apparatus" disseminated in continental criminal law by the German jurist Claus Roxin.[30] According to the argument, crimes executed through organizations are distinguishable from others because the objective elements of the crime take place as a result of the commands of a hierarchical leader, with the power to use different and in essence interchangeable subordinates to implement the orders. The structure in question must be a criminal organization, have a rigid hierarchy, the direct author has to be interchangeable and operate under the automatic control of a superior.[31] Proving this set of facts placed stringent requirements on the shoulders of the Special Unit and led to a very complex and protracted process of case approval by the Commission.

An additional complication emerged when deciding how to apply this theory to situations that took place in different moments of the conflict. While it was useful to deal with the cases of the insurgent organizations and the clandestine death squads organized under the authoritarian regime led by President Fujimori, there were doubts about its applicability to the actions of the state security forces under democratic regimes in the 1980s. In order to use its theory, the Commission had to interpret the situation of the eighties as one in which entire sections of the legally constituted security forces slipped into illegality, therefore constituting criminal apparatuses of power. However, while that characterization could apply to the security forces "at some places and moments of the conflict,"[32] it would not affect the whole of the State. The Commission, therefore, while being able to investigate the responsibility of military commanders, found it extremely difficult to point to the personal responsibility of political superiors, such as elected authorities, and in particular the presidents of the Republic during the 1980s.

Even though the challenges were many, the Special Unit experienced an accelerated learning process during its existence. While the first cases under analysis focused on specific incidents where it was possible to identify the immediate author, subsequent endeavors included more complex situations. For example, one of the first cases fully documented by the Special Unit was the January 2002 identification of the Army captain responsible for the massacre of eight peasants in Chuschi. The case, forwarded to the MP as soon as it was finished, was a relatively simple one. Soon enough, the Special Unit dealt with the more complex case of hundreds of disappearances in the Huanta Stadium, a sports complex transformed by the Navy into a detention center run by an especially vicious commander. The case, also transferred to the MP before the end of the Commission's mandate, pointed to the responsibility of the Army general in charge of the Emergency Zone during the year when most of the disappearances took place.

The relationship between the CVR and the Prosecutor General's Office

The Commission had achieved early in its mandate a written agreement with the MP in order to establish general forms of cooperation: information sharing, exhumations and witness protection. At the time of the establishment of this agreement, however, little attention was given to the issue of when to share information, or the criteria for sharing it, particularly in those investigations considered confidential by the CVR.

The CVR understood that it would develop its investigation and gather evidence to the point where a robust case was built, so that it could be forwarded to the MP ready for prosecutorial action. This arrangement in effect gave the initiative to the Commission, and it could have worked assuming that both institutions shared a common purpose and previously agreed strategy; however, no real process of consultation existed to establish principles and priorities, distribute tasks or allocate resources within state and civil society stakeholders.

It was only realistic to expect that there would be friction between the CVR and the MP. Some investigations overlapped since the 1995 amnesty laws had been voided and cases were being investigated by local prosecutors at the time when the Commission was pursuing its own work. As the media found out that high profile cases were under investigation, prosecutors would demand access to the evidence, creating confusion and no little confrontation, since the Commission preferred to control its investigative process and not to share information in the middle of a still unfinished case.

Conflicts over access to information characterized the investigation of the massacre of over one hundred persons accused or sentenced for terrorism in the prison island of El Frontón in 1986. Former members of the Navy who had participated in the massacre approached the CVR in the hope of exchanging information for protection in the form of material benefits or foreign travel. The prosecutor in charge of the case discovered this and issued a subpoena against the Commission. However, a judge ruled that the CVR, as an Executive branch agency, had confidentiality privileges and it should finish its work before sharing information with the MP. So, in this case, the Commission prevailed in the short term but at the cost of an inopportune affirmation of the principle of executive privilege against prosecutorial interests.

An additional factor in the poisoning of the relations between prosecutors and commissioners was the imbalance of capacities and resources. Since it was a unique institution benefiting from the extraordinary circumstances of its creation, the CVR had been able to obtain significant resources and secure expertise for specialized investigative tasks, such as exhumations. This would result, in some cases, in institutional jealousy from typically understaffed and under-budgeted local prosecutors who would perceive the Commission as competition. For example, the first exhumation conducted by the MP under initiative of the CVR and the Ombudsman's office took place in the community of Chuschi, in the department of Ayacucho. The CVR's experts, members of the Peruvian Forensic Anthropology Team (*Equipo Peruano de Antropología Forense – EPAF*), would in fact conduct most of the work, while the experts of the MP would find themselves confined to the backseat, due to the technical complexity of a task for which they had received no training. Although the exhumation concluded in the successful identification of all the remains found, serious confrontations emerged between the MP and the EPAF and by extension the CVR. Eventually the tensions derived from this hostility led to a costly rupture between the EPAF and the Commission.

After the exhumation at Chuschi, the Commission proposed a mechanism to reach specific agreements on which exhumations to conduct. The CVR, the MP, the Ombudsman's office and the *Coordinadora* created an ad hoc group, the Exhumations Platform (*Plataforma de Exhumaciones*), to put together views and make suggestions to the MP. However, although the group would manage to organize two additional exhumations, those continued to be hindered by confrontation and hostility. More substantively, as important as they may be, agreements on technical proceedings like exhumations did not substitute for the lack of a general prosecutorial strategy. In the absence of a common will and strategy, the agreement signed by the CVR and the MP was simply too generic to address the problems raised by the existence of the Commission and – although the primacy and constitutional authority of the MP was never challenged – in practice the Commission was successful in imposing its criteria on access to information and witnesses.

Another source of estrangement between the CVR and the MP was the question of the validity of the testimonies and evidence gathered by the Commission for further prosecutorial work. The Commission, although conscious of its mandate to contribute to prosecutions, did not apply standards that matched the stringent demands of judicial evidence. So, for example, even in cases where no direct corroboration of a testimony was possible, the Commission would examine it against the mass of similar testimonies existing in the database or surrounding circumstances and conclude, on a balance of probabilities, about its truthfulness.[33] The MP would, after the demise of the CVR, argue against the validity of the Commission's evidence, although it did so in a probably unhelpful way, pointing to the fact that the testimony had not been obtained in the presence of a prosecutor.

The CVR tactics to encourage prosecution

Confronted with growing signs of hostility from the MP, the Commission was left with the task of devising tactics to prod the MP into action. It turned to conducting a public strategy that would mobilize the support of different segments of civil society in favor of prosecution.

The public hearings held by the CVR starting in April 2002 successfully focused public attention on the work of the Commission. The enormity of the crimes that were aired, and the opportunity to hear for the first time victims of violence speaking in their own terms about the experience they had suffered, built support for prosecution. By September, after nine highly publicized hearings in the main cities of the country and the exhumation conducted in Chuschi, a public opinion poll in Lima discovered that 60.1 percent of those interviewed thought that "punishing the criminals" was the policy that would most contribute to national reconciliation.[34]

The Commission must have understood that public support for prosecutions was one of the most valuable assets it had to persuade the MP to act. As early as June, during an institutional retreat, some Commissioners were comparing the public hearings with "advance releases" of the Final Report that were successfully gaining public support for truth-seeking, and wondered whether other "advance releases" could obtain similar support for reparations and justice. "Advance announcements" or any kind of rapprochement to the Ministry of Economy on reparations were considered premature. Advance work on prosecution, however, was considered possible: the Commission could work on one of its cases and develop a full-fledged investigation that it would later publicly hand over to the MP with such an array of supporting material that it would not be possible for the MP to excuse itself from investigation.

In December 2002, the CVR handed over the case of the Chuschi executions to the MP and issued a press release to let the public know the details of the case, including the pseudonym of the Army captain allegedly responsible for the massacre. The CVR chose to present the MP with a report (*informe*) and not with an accusation (*denuncia*), since it was unclear in the mandate whether the CVR could act as an accusing party in a criminal complaint. The Chuschi Report reconstructed the case, based on evidence gathered at the exhumation and the testimony of eyewitnesses. The report identified the name and whereabouts of the alleged perpetrators, and recommended that the MP issue indictments and provide protection to witnesses.

The Chuschi Report was an attempt to test the system and measure the reaction of the MP in what appeared to be a relatively simple case, entirely manageable within the limits of domestic law, involving crimes characterized as aggravated kidnapping (*secuestro agravado*) and murder with cruelty (*asesinato con crueldad*). Some international human rights experts[35] suggested alternative tactics, such as prioritizing larger, more complex cases, showing the functioning of a criminal chain of command and pointing at high-level perpetrators. The Commission, however, maintained course, hoping that a successful case against mid-level perpetrators could be the beginning of a thread leading to the higher-ups. However, the Chuschi case proved that the MP would not be easily prodded into action. The MP cast doubt on the information submitted by the Commission and announced that it would conduct its own investigations. No warrants for the arrest of the alleged perpetrators were issued immediately, in spite of journalistic investigations that uncovered the identity of the killers. The MP only issued a formal indictment in the last months of the life of the CVR.

The Huanta case, a more complex one, was similarly forwarded to the MP as the Report of a completed investigation. It detailed the operations of the detention center run by the Navy in the Sports Stadium of the city, the apparent responsibility of General (retired) Clemente Noel as former commander of the emergency zone, and three especially gruesome cases committed by forces based in the Stadium: the execution of a group of members of a local church, the disappearance of a local journalist, and the discovery of a mass grave with remnants of people last seen alive in detention. Sections of the report were read in public in March 2003 by the President of the Commission, Dr. Salomon Lerner, after a visit to the Huanta Stadium.[36] In his speech, he gave details of the three cases and recommended the indictment of some Navy officers and General Noel. As with the Chuschi case, the MP did not act immediately and the case remains to date under investigation. The Chuschi and Huanta cases showed that publicity did not necessarily provide an impetus for pro-active prosecutorial action. If the MP was not prepared to expeditiously issue an arrest warrant for a mid-level perpetrator, it was even less prepared to do so against former generals. After the Huanta case, the Commission concentrated on completion of the Final Report.

The Final Report would be the ultimate test for the CVR. The MP was presented with 43 cases demanding immediate action. However, some issues dented the ability of this tool to prompt the MP to act. In the first place, the Commissioners decided that the Special Investigations Unit would have to prepare, in addition to the cases under its responsibility, additional cases "only for purposes of the Report," that is, not the kind of casework leading to a Report to the MP but short summaries of cases to provide symbolic acknowledgment to the victims. The Commissioners may have felt that the public would react adversely to the Final Report if it presented only cases technically ready for prosecution, since these usually involved the security forces, while ignoring other high-profile cases provoked by the subversive groups that proved to be notoriously more difficult to clarify.[37]

However, this decision would prove to be a diversion of energies at a crucial time, since cases had to be identified, prepared and approved. Although 43 cases were on the original list of the Special Unit,[38] 73 were finally included in volume VII of the Final Report and a smaller number appeared as specific illustrations of crimes after chapters contained in other sections. Confusion resulted, since the press assumed that the Commission had given 73 cases to the MP, ready for immediate action. Speakers for the MP were eager to declare disingenuously that a good number of the cases presented by the CVR were not at all material for serious investigation. This was certainly true for the cases as published in the Final Report, since the report featured either summaries of the dossiers prepared by the Special Unit, or short narratives compiled from secondary sources.

A serious additional problem was that the Commission had mostly overlooked the central problem of whether to name perpetrators in the Final Report. In general, the commissioners had assumed that they were under an obligation to name names if they obtained them, since the foundational mandate made clear that the CVR would identify "as far as possible, presumptive responsibilities."[39] No policy on this issue had been prepared, however. Due process emerged as a concern during the public hearings, since in some cases the victims decided to accuse perpetrators by name. The hearings' rules of procedure clearly provided a mechanism for those persons accused to respond if they wanted to challenge the testimony of the victims, and the CVR held special *in camera* hearings to receive those responses. In preparing the Final Report, the CVR understood that it would suffice to notify those about to be accused of serious crimes that the CVR had been convinced of their alleged culpability, and it would provide them an opportunity to respond to the charges.[40]

The commissioners, however, after receiving specific pleas from the Armed Forces, decided to further consider the issue. The argument that they had to consider was that naming somebody in the Final Report – even as an "alleged" perpetrator – would amount to a sentence in the court of public opinion. In addition, if a mistake were made, the work of the Commission would be discredited. The Commission had to balance the right of the victims to know the truth to the utmost extent possible and the propriety of disclosing all the truth even above the alleged perpetrators' rights to their personal reputation.

Although a decision was reached, it had elements of ambiguity and formalism that made it moot. The CVR decided that it would present the cases to the best of its knowledge and conviction, but it would not publish an accusation of specific crimes. Therefore, the cases published in volume VII included the names of the doers and provided all the details of the crimes committed, but they avoided language that would sound like an indictment. In reality, the new guidelines were only partially incorporated in the Final Report and several sometimes inconsistent formulations appear in the final text. As far as the CVR was concerned, it had not given the names of doers *as perpetrators*, so that remained a pending task that the MP would have to discharge in formal indictments. Consequently, the CVR included a proviso in volume VII of the Final Report stating that the Commission expected diligent action by the MP but that, if after a prudential lapse of thirty days no evidence of action existed, it would ask the Ombudsman's office to make use of its constitutional right to formulate an accusation against the perpetrators of the cases investigated for prosecution.[41]

The result of this decision was ambiguous: the press immediately seized the opportunity to read the cases and draw obvious conclusions, making lists of perpetrators on the basis of what was already said in the Report.

The objective of protecting the reputation of the alleged perpetrators from the court of public opinion was thus soundly defeated, but this was only some kind of societal, symbolic justice. The main objective, to obtain the indictment of perpetrators, was not achieved: the MP sternly reminded the press that no deadlines existed for prosecutorial action and that, therefore, the CVR's proviso was ineffective. The Ombudsman's office, in turn, did not act on the Commission's recommendation.

Two years after the Final Report of the CVR was issued, at the time this chapter is written, progress has been mixed. On the positive side, all branches of the state have taken significant strides to implement the CVR recommendations: Congress passed a policy of collective reparations; the Constitutional Court has consistently upheld the right to truth in a number of cases and struck down as unconstitutional aspects of a 2004 bill on military justice; the Executive has accepted responsiblity in a number of cases before the Inter-American system of human rights and pursued friendly settlements; a path-breaking National Human Rights Plan was approved in 2005, and 22 of the 47 cases forwarded by the CVR to the MP are already in the trial phase. Significantly, the MP established a specific prosecutor for human rights cases and the judiciary established a court for human rights cases by widening the mandate of a pre-existing Anti-Terrorism Court.[42]

However, much remains to be done, while political tensions and institutional sclerosis continue to bedevil accountability efforts. Strenuous opposition by the armed forces to the report and to the prospect of having members of the military on trial has weakened the resolve of the institutions in charge of prosecutions. Of 252 arrest warrants for indicted persons, 209 were never complied with due to the permanent presence of procedural errors that provided the excuse not to go ahead with the orders. Of over 1500 victims included in the cases sent by the CVR to the MP less than 25 percent have legal representation, mostly by human rights NGOs, while all defendants in the security forces have lawyers paid by the government. Witness protection remains weak and inefficient and there have been numerous cases of intimidation. The most worrisome development, however, remains the continuous attempts by the military to assert the jurisdiction of the military justice system over human rights cases through legislative proposals that have garnered the support of significant sectors of the political elite.

Conclusions

Not every truth commission is mandated to cooperate with criminal justice. When they are, the situation raises complex challenges that include the question of the appropriateness of conducting specific case investigations, the question of primacy of jurisdiction, the timing, conditions and forms of information-sharing, and the like.

A truth commission, however, is an ad hoc body with a limited life span and resources operating after a prolonged period of judicial weakness. It would be unreasonable to expect a commission to fully tackle multiple needs, such as the building of technical capacities in prosecutorial authorities or the building of a comprehensive consensus to act against impunity.

However, a commission has the advantage of initiative and visibility. Even in the absence of special investigative powers (normally in the hands of prosecutorial authorities) a commission can make a difference by setting priorities and establishing criteria to develop prosecutions in close consultations with stakeholders.

The Peruvian Truth and Reconciliation Commission had several strategic advantages, such as favorable public opinion, the mobilization of groups of victims, the support of civil society organizations and the availability of resources. It decided to work in an exemplary manner, to set the standards for subsequent action by the *Ministerio Público* once its mandate was over. The Commission utilized public hearings, exhumations and criminal investigations to mobilize public support and prod the MP into action.

The major weakness of the Commission, however, was its inability to design in time a comprehensive prosecutorial strategy that could be the object of consensus among the different stakeholders. During the life of the Commission, only the outlines of such a strategy were built, by trial and error and successive approximations. The master guidelines remained the same: the identification of paradigmatic cases that would be acted upon by the MP and would eventually encourage the judicial authorities to continue on their own the struggle against impunity. Significant resources were assigned to this task, but the Commission could have used better coordination of its investigative teams in order to shorten the learning curve and identify potentially productive strategies.

The assumption that the Commission would hand over only finished cases to the MP was not completely shared by all the relevant stakeholders, which resulted in unsolved overlapping and lack of coordination. The relations between the Commission and the MP could not avoid misunderstandings and tension. When the Final Report was issued, the MP was unreceptive. Confusion regarding the issue of naming perpetrators added to the estrangement between both institutions, with the regrettable result of a slow and half-willed investigation into the cases left by the Commission.

In spite of its shortcomings it cannot be doubted that the Peruvian Truth and Reconciliation Commission acted with zeal for justice and that the protection of victims' rights was its paramount interest. Its best efforts had to deal with the formidable unwillingness and inability of the MP and the structural weaknesses of the Peruvian state. In this regard, the CVR went through the same experiences of human rights organizations struggling against impunity. Its boldness and good faith continue to deserve better results.

NOTES

1. Including the work of a handover commission, the total budget came to 13.2 million US dollars of which the CVR directly raised 6.3 million among international donors.
2. The CVR received 16,986 testimonies.
3. The CVR conducted 27 public hearings: 8 case hearings, 7 thematic hearings, 5 institutional hearings and 7 local hearings.
4. On April 1, 2004, the Ombudsman's office presented the report "Missing Peruvians: Preliminary List of Persons Disappeared between 1980 and 2000", an initiative launched during the existence of the CVR. The list identified 8,558 disappeared.
5. Comisión de la Verdad y Reconciliación, *Informe Final*, Vol. IX, p. 211. The CVR registered 4,644 burial sites and conducted preliminary assessments in 2,200 of them. Additionally, it compiled 1,884 *Ante Mortem* files with information usable for the identification of the remains of missing persons.
6. The CVR proposed a comprehensive program of reparations: symbolic, services and financial. *Informe Final*, Vol. IX, pp. 117–208.
7. A summary version of the cases appears in the Final Report of the CVR (*Informe Final*, Vol. VII), published August 28, 2003. Detailed files for the 43 cases, including confidential information regarding evidence were handed over to the Prosecutor General's Office by memo 04–2003–CE on September 3, 2003.
8. Fujimori made public in October 1993 a series of letters written by Guzmán asking for peace negotiations between the Peruvian state and the "Shining Path". Although serious discussions were never undertaken, the position of their leader demoralized and divided the rank and file of the "Shining Path".
9. Law 26479 of June 14, 1995; Law 26492 (compulsory interpretation of Law 26479) of June 28, 1995.
10. In 2000, the final year of Fujimori's government, over 300 cases against Peru had accumulated in the Inter-American System of Human Rights.
11. The *Defensoría del Pueblo* was created by Law 26520, signed by the President on August 8, 1995.
12. The "Commission Charged to Recommend to the President of the Republic the Concession of Pardons to Persons Sentenced for Terrorism and Treason" was created by Law 26655 on August 17, 1996.

13. *Castillo Petruzzi et al* v. *Peru,* Judgment of May 30, 1999, Inter-American Court of Human Rights, Series C No. 52. In the sentence, the Court unanimously finds that "the proceedings . . . are invalid, as they were incompatible with the American Convention on Human Rights, and so orders that the persons in question be guaranteed a new trial in which the guarantees of due process of law are ensured" (No. 13 of the Judgment).

14. The unilateral withdrawal was one of the main issues raised by the Inter-American Commission of Human Rights in its "Second Report on the Situation of Human Rights in Peru" OEA/Ser.L/V/II.106 Doc. 59 rev. 2 June 2000.

15. The 30th Ordinary Session of the OAS General Assembly approved on June 5, 2000, the creation of a special mission to Peru led by the Foreign Affairs Minister of Canada, Lloyd Axworthy, and by the Secretary-General of the OAS, César Gaviria. (AG/RES. 1753). Upon its recommendation, the OAS appointed in July 11, 2000, a special mission to encourage dialogue between the government of Peru and the opposition.

16. Supreme Resolution 304–2000–JUS, Dec 9, 2000.

17. Supreme Decree 065–2001–PCM, June 2, 2001.

18. Supreme Decree 065–2001–PCM, Art 1.

19. Supreme Decree 065–2001–PCM, Art 2. lit a, b.

20. Supreme Decree 065–2001–PCM, Art. 3. "The Truth Commission shall focus its work on . . .

  (a) Murders and kidnappings;
  (b) Forced disappearances;
  (c) Torture and other serious injuries;
  (d) Violations of the collective rights of the country's Andean and native communities;
  (e) Other crimes and serious violations of the rights of individuals."

21. Supreme Resolution 304–2000–JUS. Preamble: "in the development of the process of violence that shook the country since 1980, serious violations of Human Rights and International Humanitarian Law took place."

22. Supreme Decree 065–2001–PCM. Preamble: "in May 1980 terrorist organizations unleashed violence against humanity and thousands of Peruvians ended up as victims of the violation of their most elemental rights both as the work of said terrorist organizations and that of some agents of the State."

23. Supreme Decree 065–2001–PCM, Arts. 1, 3.

24. IACHR, Sentence (*Chumbipuma Aguirre et al* v. *Peru*), March 14, 2001.

25. IACHR, Interpretive Sentence (*Chumbipuma Aguirre et al* v. *Peru*), September 3, 2001.

26. *Castillo Petruzzi et al.* case, Judgment of May 30, 1999. This sentence sparked the unilateral and illegal withdrawal of Fujimori's Peru from the jurisdiction of the Court.

27. Judgment of the Constitutional Court Voiding Certain Aspects of the Anti-terrorist Laws of the Fujimorista Regime. EXP. No. 010–2002–AI/TCLIMA, action presented by Marcelino Tineo Silva and over 5,000 citizens.

28. Supreme Decree 065–2001–PCM, Art. 6.

29. Comisión de la Verdad y Reconciliación, *Informe Final*, Vol. I, cap. 4, pp. 228–29.
30. Comisión de la Verdad y Reconciliación, *Informe Final*, Vol. I, cap. 4, pp. 233–40. Claus Roxin, *Autoría y dominio del hecho en Derecho penal* (Mexico: Pons Librero, 2000).
31. Comisión de la Verdad y Reconciliación, *Informe Final*, Vol. I, cap. 4, p. 235.
32. Comisión de la Verdad y Reconciliación, *Informe Final*, Vol. VIII, General Conclusions, p. 362.
33. See the Magdalena Monteza case on sexual violence. Comisión de la Verdad y Reconciliación, *Informe Final*, Vol. VI, cap. 1. 5, pp. 384–90.
34. Grupo de Opinión Pública de la Universidad de Lima, *Estudio* 165, *Barómetro* (Lima Metropolitana y Callao, September 2002).
35. *Reunión Técnica Internacional sobre Judicialización*. Held by the TRC in Lima, December 6–7, 2002, with sponsorship by the UN Office of the High Commissioner of Human Rights and the International Center for Transitional Justice. Minutes taken by the rapporteur, Alejandro Valencia Villa.
36. *Informe a la Fiscalía de la Nación sobre el caso Huanta*, March 10, 2003.
37. Comisión de la Verdad y Reconciliación, *Informe Final*, Vol. I, cap. 4, p. 229.
38. Not counting the already presented cases of Chuschi and Huanta.
39. D.S. 65–2001–PCM, Art. 2, lit. b.
40. "The CVR has undertaken all reasonable efforts to ensure that any person whose name is mentioned as an alleged perpetrator had the opportunity to present her or his version of the facts. In particular, it was provided that the person was heard or, at least, called upon." CVR *Informe Final*, Vol. I, p. 227.
41. *Informe Final*, Vol. VII, p. 21.
42. Administrative Resolution 170–2004–CE–PJ.

4   The "Mexican solution" to transitional justice

Mariclaire Acosta and Esa Ennelin *

The political context for human rights and the Mexican transition to democracy

The legacy of a repressive regime

The current government of Mexico, led by Vicente Fox, came to power thanks to the first truly democratic and competitive national election held in the past 90 years. The vote that resulted in his victory in the year 2000 ended the 71-year-old monopoly of state power held by the Institutional Revolutionary Party (*Partido Revolucionario Institucional* – PRI) since 1929, when it was founded by a coalition of *caudillos* and revolutionary generals after two decades of revolution and civil war.

The very fact that the Mexican electorate was able to produce such a result was the product of generations of struggle. It was also the first time in the history of the country that political change did not result from the use of violence and bloodshed, but was carried out by the peaceful exercise of political rights. This in itself is no small matter, but a fact which tends to be overlooked, given the stable nature of Mexico's protracted authoritarian regime. The election that brought Vicente Fox, a candidate of the center-right opposition party, National Action Party (*Partido Acción Nacional* – PAN) to power, was the result of the consistent and peaceful mobilization of thousands of people for the effective exercise of civil and political rights, and especially for the basic right to participate in free, fair and authentic elections. This fact makes it an historic turning point of great significance.

The gradual and prolonged transition to democratic rule has not automatically delivered respect for all human rights. However, it has produced some significant changes which have had an impact on the way that these rights are perceived by large sectors of society and in the government, especially at the federal level. Respect for human rights has become a legitimate political claim and is now widely perceived as an obligation of the government. This is certainly a far cry from the prevailing situation of just a few years ago, when political violence and systematic repression accounted for numerous cases of disappearances and extra-judicial executions, as well as the generalized use of torture and arbitrary detention of real or perceived political opponents.

In this context, it is imperative to ensure accountability for the state-sponsored crimes of the past four decades. These range from massacres by security forces of peaceful protesters which took place in Tlatelolco (1968), in Jueves de Corpus in Mexico City (1971), in Aguas Blancas, Guerrero (1995) and in Acteal, Chiapas (1997), to name but a few. The disappearances, torture and extra-judicial executions of countless victims which were implemented on a large scale in the period of the so-called "dirty war" against the armed opposition groups during the 1970s and part of the 1980s and have continued sporadically up to the present, also need to be investigated and punished.[1]

These crimes are systemic in nature. They were originally planned and executed by security forces operating under the direct command of the President of the Republic and the highest-ranking officials in the successive PRI governments. This was the case of the notorious *Dirección Federal de Seguridad*, disbanded in 1984 after pressure from the United States government for its involvement in drug corruption scandals.[2] Under the PRI regime, when serious social and political dissent appeared in regions marked by inequality and oppression of its indigenous *campesino* population, such as Chiapas, Oaxaca and Guerrero, governors and local power bosses or *caciques*, would take over law enforcement activities, and reproduce the original pattern of state repression, always with the knowledge and complicity of the federal government.[3] Unfortunately, in some of these areas the situation seems to have changed little.

Thus, if Mexico wants to consolidate the gains made by its incipient electoral democracy, it must move forward decisively to clarify a murky past of state-sponsored violence and implement a second set of reforms for the construction of new institutions and practices in order to ensure real democratic governance. Foremost among these reforms is the need to overhaul law enforcement agencies and the justice system in order to provide a minimum of public and judicial security to the population. Given the nature of the previous political system, more akin in many ways to that of the ex-Soviet Union than to the authoritarian dictatorships of the rest of Latin America, police organizations, prosecutors, judges and other legal actors have operated in a context where the monopoly of power and machine-style politics encouraged corruption, impunity and lawlessness.

The emergence of civil society and a movement for human rights

In comparison with other countries in the region, Mexico only fairly recently developed an organized and articulated movement demanding explicit respect for human rights. The 1968 student movement was really about civil liberties, although its rhetoric was couched in the revolutionary Marxist terms of the era. A few years later in the 1970s, after repression had turned peaceful protest into armed revolt, the quest for members of the guerrilla groups abducted and disappeared by security forces spawned the first mobilizations of relatives, which were similar to other movements in the region. These groups banded with leftist political parties to create a short-lived national front against repression.

The López Portillo government, inaugurated in 1976, realized that the repressive policy of its predecessors had led to more revolt and bloodshed than to pacification. But the issue of the *desaparecidos* remained unresolved. After several high profile mobilizations by organizations such as *Comité Eureka* and the Committee of the Mothers of the Disappeared for Political Reasons (*Comité de Madres de Desaparecidos Políticos*), the Attorney General of the Republic presented a public report in 1979 which stated that the majority of the alleged *desaparecidos* had died in armed confrontations or were still fugitive.[4]

It was not really until the mid-1980s – well after the PRI had reached an agreement with the previously outlawed left-wing parties that led to their participation in the national elections of 1982 – that the first independent human rights organizations emerged.[5] These two social movements, the "anti-repression" movement of the radical left, on the one hand, and the nascent human rights movement, on the other, never completely understood one another, thus weakening their respective causes. As we shall see further on, these differences were to become very apparent in the first years of the Fox government over the issue of how to confront the legacy of repression and human rights abuse.

The use of international human rights protection mechanisms in Mexico was initially introduced in 1989 by the opposition party *Partido Acción Nacional* (PAN), as part of its strategy for contesting rigged government elections. At present, there are approximately 100 individual petitions from Mexican nationals in the Inter-American Human Rights system. Approximately 800 more are lodged in the various human rights protection mechanisms of the UN Human Rights Commission. Most of these cases deal with violations of the right to life, physical integrity, freedom and due process committed during the decade of the nineties.[6]

The government of Carlos Salinas (1990–94), tainted by the questionable election that brought him to power as well as by notorious human rights abuse, surprised the country by decreeing the creation of a national ombudsman – tied to the government – charged with the protection of human rights. Thus the National Human Rights Commission (*Comisión Nacional de Derechos Humanos* – CNDH), which succeeded a modest office for human rights in the Ministry of the Interior, came into being. In time, similar state commissions emerged and a national system for the protection of human rights was formed. Nine years later, the CNDH became fully independent of the government. This state-managed human rights system has had a relatively modest impact. It is led primarily by political appointees and is staffed mostly by bureaucrats from the different law enforcement agencies. The CNDH inherited an incipient program for the investigation of the fate of hundreds of disappearances during the "dirty war" initiated by its predecessor as part of a promise made by President Salinas on his inauguration day to Rosario Ibarra de Piedra, mother of a disappeared activist and founder of *Comité Eureka*.

Transitional justice and the strategy of the Fox administration

First steps

In his inaugural address, President Fox started out by stating that human rights would be a central concern of his government and that he would put together a very forceful policy in this area. He repeated his campaign promise to establish a truth commission that would explore human rights abuses of the past[7] and subsequently reinforced the seriousness of his commitment to human rights by signing an ambitious cooperation agreement with the UN High Commissioner for Human Rights. Unfortunately, as with almost everything else in the Fox government, these promises were largely unfulfilled. Undoubtedly his government has done more for human rights than the preceding ones. But, as with many of his campaign promises and attempts at reform, his administration proceeded to protect human rights in a haphazard fashion, without a consistent and coordinated set of efforts to tackle the deeply ingrained structural problems of the country that impede their enjoyment.

During the five-month transition period following the elections, Fox had sent several signals indicating that his campaign promises for human rights were serious. He met with several ex-guerrillas in a highly publicized event and reiterated his promise for a truth commission. He also set up a team charged with reforming the justice system. A well-respected human rights lawyer was a prominent member of this team, which came up with a blueprint for a complete overhaul of the system. It was leaked to the press that the team leader was to be appointed Attorney General of the new government. However, a few days before his inauguration, President-elect Fox suddenly switched course and designated a general on active duty who had been the military prosecutor in the previous government, Rafael Macedo de la Concha. This surprise designation sent an extremely negative signal to the human rights community. Macedo de la Concha's human rights record was tainted and he was accused of many notorious abuses that had received ample international attention.

With these mixed signals, during the first months of his tenure, President Fox relegated human rights almost entirely to the sphere of foreign policy, perhaps on the assumption that the rest of his government, by virtue of its having come to power in a peaceful, democratic election, would be automatically committed to human rights. For the time being, he ignored the promise to create a truth commission.

An important benchmark of Foreign Minister Jorge Castañeda's new human rights policy was the treatment of the case of Ricardo Miguel Cavallo, a former Argentine military officer living in Mexico who was involved in a fraudulent operation related to the mandatory registration of vehicles with a private institution called RENAVE. The case is interesting because it was the first time that Mexican institutions showed an attitude of openness around the treatment of gross human rights violations.

In 1996, a group of victims of the Argentine military dictatorship, some of whom lived in Spain, asked a Spanish judge to initiate a criminal prosecution against the Argentine military. Based on the principle of universal jurisdiction, Judge Baltazar Garzón started an investigation for the crimes of terrorism, genocide and torture.

A few weeks after the election of Vicente Fox, the Mexican newspaper *Reforma* revealed that Ricardo Miguel Cavallo, president of RENAVE, was a former member of the Argentine navy, accused of participating in gross human rights violations in the *Escuela Mecánica de la Armada* (ESMA), the largest clandestine detention center used by the military during the dictatorship in that country. The International Police (Interpol) detained Cavallo at the Cancun airport while he was attempting to flee to Argentina where his impunity would be guaranteed. The following day, Madrid's Central Criminal Investigation Court No.5 of the *Audiencia Nacional* asked the Mexican government to detain Cavallo while an extradition request was processed.

The case confronted Mexican authorities with an interesting challenge. On the one hand, since the crimes had not been committed in Mexico and the victims were not Mexican, any decision in this case would not constitute a precedent. However, the public's reaction to this decision would be a good indicator of popular response to the opening of criminal investigations for the so-called Mexican "dirty war". On the other hand, since this was a universal jurisdiction case, which attracted significant attention outside of Mexico's borders, a favorable decision would allow the newly-elected government to demonstrate to the international community that an important change had taken place regarding human rights.

On October 5, 2000, the Ministry of Foreign Affairs forwarded a formal extradition request from the Spanish authorities to the judicial branch in order to obtain an opinion. In January 2001, Judge Jesús Guadalupe Luna Altamirano[8] ruled that Cavallo should be extradited to Spain in order to face trial for his probable responsibility for the commission of the crimes of terrorism and genocide. The Supreme Court confirmed the Judge's decision and authorized Cavallo's extradition.[9] The Supreme Court did not apply international law in its decision, and it neither acknowledged nor denied the principle of universal jurisdiction. Cavallo was extradited in June, 2003, and as of February 2006 still awaits trial in Spain.

Following the Cavallo case, the Legal Advisor of the Foreign Ministry made an extraordinary effort to bring Mexico up-to-date in relation to its pending ratifications and accessions to international conventions in the field of human rights. The effort was only partly successful because the Senate blocked the ratification of the Rome Statute, which established the jurisdiction of the International Criminal Court, and Protocol II of the Geneva Conventions. It also added an interpretation to the Inter-American Convention on Forced Disappearance, stating that the Convention will not apply to those events of forced disappearance which took place before the Convention's entry into force.[10]

Human rights had a high profile in the new government's rhetoric but the initial efforts to consolidate a consistent policy for their advancement were eventually undermined by the joint action of the Ministry of Defense, the Attorney General's Office and the Ministry of the Interior, often in an alliance with the National Human Rights Commission. Despite the high visibility of the issue, little was achieved in the struggle against impunity and in the everyday behavior of the security forces, especially at the local level. The creation of a truth commission was not mentioned again in public by the government, despite its announcement and the fact that it had been a reiterated campaign promise.

The debate on how to deal with the past

Nonetheless, the issue of how to deal with the legacy of the past was debated in the press and inside the government, where the discussion over whether or not to establish a truth commission was intense. In June 2001, the President finally approved the creation of a body charged with the public investigation of human rights abuses and corruption. This project of a truth commission, initially announced at Fox's inauguration, was designed by a group of independent experts under the direction of Adolfo Aguilar Zinser. The human rights community was not consulted, and the project was never implemented.

Santiago Creel, Minister of the Interior and PAN Senator Diego Fernández de Cevallos, led the offensive against the project. They argued that a truth commission would have disastrous effects on the nascent Mexican democracy by spurring an indiscriminate witch-hunt against the perpetrators of past crimes. Many of these people were still powerful and held important positions in the Congress. To expose them would mean losing any support for important reforms like the badly needed reform of the tax system. These two politicians were backed by a less visible but very effective coalition of former officials, intellectuals, and prominent figures such as Felipe González, former Prime Minister and head of the Socialist Party of Spain.[11]

The violent death, in suspicious circumstances, of Digna Ochoa, a widely known and respected human rights defender in October of 2001 created a huge national and international uproar. This forced President Fox to take his responsibilities in the field of human rights more seriously. Some of his boldest initiatives correspond to the immediate aftermath of this event, such as the liberation of victims of abuse like Montiel and Cabrera, two environmentalist peasants, and General Gallardo, all of them prisoners of conscience adopted by Amnesty International. He also took decisive steps for the implementation of some form of response to the demand for accountability for past abuses.

The National Human Rights Commission, miffed at the thought that the Ministry of Foreign Relations' proactive human rights policy was leaving them behind, entered the scene at the bidding of Santiago Creel. The investigation of the abduction and disappearance of 532 victims of the "dirty war," initiated by the Salinas government in 1988, was taken out of the freezer and speedily completed.

On November 27, 2001, in a highly charged formal ceremony held at Lecumberri, a former prison turned into the seat of the National Archives, José Luis Soberanes, President of the CNDH, read excerpts from a 3,000-page report which disclosed the findings of the institution on the fate of these 532 persons. Of these cases, 275 were of people who had "disappeared" following detention by state authorities. Evidence, albeit inconclusive, existed of the involvement of the authorities in another 97 cases. The CNDH had been unable to reach a conclusion on a further 160 cases, but the possibility of their "disappearance" should not be discounted in any future investigation.[12]

The National Human Rights Commission stated that the *modus operandi* of the security forces during the "dirty war" was clearly illegal. It went on to describe the integration of the special task forces set up to carry out the task of persecuting the guerrillas (who had also committed illicit activities), namely the *Brigada Especial* or *Brigada Blanca*, composed of members of the former *Dirección Federal de Seguridad* and aided by officials from other federal and state government agencies. Finally, it documented the impunity of these actions, by making clear that despite the fact that these "disappearances" had been duly reported to the authorities by the victims' relatives, the Commission found no evidence that they had ever been investigated by the relevant authorities, thus violating the right to justice of the victims.[13] The report recommended that the President instruct the Attorney General to designate a special prosecutor for the investigation and punishment of these crimes, in order to ensure full respect for human rights in the future.[14]

The ceremony was attended by the President, who received the report and the recommendations, the Minister of the Interior, the Minister of Defense, the Attorney General and other prominent members of his cabinet. In a highly unusual move, Soberanes also handed Fox a closed envelope with the names of the alleged perpetrators of the crimes he had just described in detail, on the grounds that they were only suspects and he could not reveal their names in order to protect their good name and reputation. This was contrary to the usual procedure followed by the ombudsman, who always makes the names of alleged perpetrators of human rights abuse public and is mandated to do so by the law, without this giving rise to any liability.[15] Santiago Creel then proceeded to announce the creation of a special prosecutor's office to investigate these crimes.

The report received mixed responses on the part of civil society. The non-governmental organizations that attended the presentation, agreed that the fact that the government had finally acknowledged state responsibility in the practice of forced disappearances, after decades of official secrecy and denial, was of paramount importance. According to them, the report should be regarded only as a first step towards the truth, because the "truth" represented in the report was not enough. They stated that the full depth of the problem was still unknown, including the details of where many of the *desaparecidos* are located. They also demanded that the revelation of the truth be followed by justice and reconciliation.[16]

The leaders of the organizations representing the victims' families were the ones with the most reservations and doubts towards the report. The most critical were Rosario Ibarra, president of the *Comité Eureka*[17] and the vice-president of the *Asociación de Familiares de Desaparecidos de México* (AFADEM), Julio Mata Montiel. Rosario Ibarra claimed that the only thing that the CNDH had done was to revisit the cases that *Eureka* had presented eleven years before and claim them as its own.[18] Julio Mata Montiel indicated the existence of more than 800 cases registered by AFADEM in the state of Guerrero alone and observed that the CNDH had presented less than 600 cases for the whole country.[19]

In contrast, the report was accepted quite well by the political elites. All the parties represented in the Congress, from right, left and center, had positive opinions about this particular modality for dealing with the need to know the truth about the forced disappearances and finding justice for the victims, without seeking revenge. According to press reports, they all agreed that this was fundamental for political, institutional and ethical reasons.[20]

Officially, the Armed Forces remained silent after the release of the report, but unofficially, military sources claimed that the Mexican Army as an institution had acted legally during the "dirty war" in the combat against the guerilla groups. The Army had protected the constitutional order of the country. The claim by the CNDH that some military bases, such as the *Campo Militar Número Uno*, had been used as detention and torture facilities for more than one and a half years, was absurd. There may have been some detentions, but the detainees were turned over to the corresponding authorities. They made it clear that in the event that there were concrete accusations against some members of the Army, and if the relevant authority verified their guilt, they would agree to the judicial consequences, but to judge an institution as a whole was unacceptable.[21]

The Army kept its word. As we shall see later on, it accepted the legal consequences of the actions of some high-ranking military officers during the "dirty war." But it pre-empted civilian justice by deciding to prosecute them under military law.

Mechanisms for transitional justice

Finding a "Mexican solution"

The Special Prosecutors' Office for the Attention of Matters Allegedly Related to Federal Crimes Committed Directly or Indirectly by Public

Servants Against Persons Linked to Social or Political Movements of the Past (*Fiscalía Especial para la Atención de Hechos Probablemente Constitutivos de Delitos Federales Cometidos Directa o Indirectamente por Servidores Públicos en Contra de Personas Vinculadas con Movimientos Sociales y Políticos del Pasado, FEMOSPP*) was the result of a Presidential Decree. It had full power to name and gather evidence against the perpetrators of human rights violations, including the Tlatelolco massacre of 1968, the murder of student protesters by paramilitary gangs in 1971, and the cases related to the state sponsored "dirty war," up to the recent past.[22]

The Presidential Decree contained the framework of a transitional justice policy in Mexico. First, the President requested the Attorney General, General Rafael Marcial Macedo de la Concha to create a Special Prosecutor's Office (SPO). Second, the President requested that the Attorney General create a Citizens' Support Committee to aid and offer advice to the Prosecutor. Third, the President ordered the Minister of Defense to ask the Military Prosecutor to provide the Attorney General with any information required to fulfill the functions mentioned in the Decree. Fourth, the Interior Minister was instructed to form an interdisciplinary committee to study, analyze and present proposals to determine the form of just compensation and reparation to the victims who were affected by the violence. Fifth, the President ordered the opening of tens of thousands of previously classified documents and records held by former secret service institutions, to be sent to the National Archive.[23]

In the opinion of Paul Seils of the International Center for Transitional Justice, the request for the creation of the SPO was based on a number of relatively narrow factors. First, it relied on the exercise of federal jurisdiction regarding crimes allegedly committed by public servants. This means that in general the SPO will not deal with matters committed by public servants at the state level, ruling out of the investigation, for example, acts committed by the local state police. In addition, the investigations exclude the members of the guerrilla groups who were convicted and later granted an amnesty in 1978.[24] The SPO must also demonstrate a link between the victim and social or political movements, a task which may prove difficult and is dependent on the SPO's and the Court's interpretations, since the Decree offers no definition of these and no guidance on the criteria to be applied. In addition, the Presidential Decree did not state any exact time limit for the prosecution and investigation and did not explicitly mention the nature of the crimes to be investigated.[25]

Prior to the release of the Presidential Decree, it had been agreed in the cabinet that Alberto Székely, a prominent environmental and human rights lawyer, and former Legal Advisor to the Ministry of Foreign Affairs, was to be designated Special Prosecutor under the authority

of the President himself. The Citizen's Support Committee was to
be staffed by respected members of the human rights community. In
fact, some of them had already been invited and had agreed to participate. Upon learning that the Decree had been changed at the last
minute, giving the nomination of the Special Prosecutor to the Attorney
General, Székely declined the invitation and the candidates for the
Citizen's Support Committee followed suit.[26] This problem, which
was not made public until much later, delayed the process of setting
up the SPO. However, on January 4, 2002, almost two months after the
Presidential Decree was issued, the Attorney General nominated an
academic and former public servant, Dr. Ignacio Carrillo Prieto.

After his nomination, Ignacio Carrillo began work on what he called
the "Mexican solution" to deal with the human rights crimes of the past.
In an interview with Kate Doyle, Head of the Mexico Project of the
National Security Archives, he spelled out the terms of this enterprise by
pointing out that truth, justice and reparations all go together. "We
cannot trade truth for justice. We cannot trade money for justice. The
Mexican Solution is a very appropriate response to impunity, a new
model," he is quoted as saying.[27] In fact, the task that Carrillo Prieto
was assigned was not easy, and the Presidential Decree did not make it
any easier, because it did not lay out clearly how the work of the SPO was
to be carried out.

Although this "Mexican solution" in the form of a Special Prosecutors
Office was the first of its kind in Latin America, it is not unique. There
have been other experiments of a similar kind.[28] However, only limited
efforts were made to consult about the possible structure of the SPO,
and because of that, it missed an opportunity to learn from past mistakes
at an earlier stage.[29]

In March 2002, the newly chosen Special Prosecutor introduced
the five members of his Citizens' Support Committee to the public.
These were drawn mostly from academia, survivors of the Tlatelolco
massacre of 1968 and former guerrillas. He also presented his Action
Plan for the new office.

The Special Prosecutor's Office

The Action Plan for the Office of the Special Prosecutor contains five
programs with 64 activities. It is divided into three main areas (*ejes*):

1. Legal investigation
2. Information and analysis
3. Cooperation, citizen participation and institutional relationships

The objective of the legal investigation area is to consolidate investigations, centralize the cases under federal jurisdiction and support bringing criminal cases before the corresponding courts. It comprises three different programs and one sub-program, dealing with forced disappearances, 1968–71 massacres, 1990s massacres, and legal problems. Altogether these programs have more than 1,000 cases under investigation.

The area of information and analysis gathers and analyzes historical evidence in order to clarify how the crimes of the past were linked to social and political movements. Finally, the area of cooperation, citizen participation, and institutional relationships is intended to take care of the needs of victims affected by the violence and repression. It also cooperates with human rights organizations, academic institutions and professional groups. This program also has a sub-program, dedicated to the dissemination of information on the activities of the SPO.

The Citizens' Support Committee mentioned in the Presidential Decree does not have a clear mandate. It is made up of experts in the fields of law, history and social sciences, and offers advice and support to the SPO. The Committee started its work with five people and in 2003 was enlarged to sixteen after the Prosecutor complained of lack of support. The objective of the Committee is to monitor the work of the SPO and denounce it if it does not complete its mission. Its main function is to give a voice to the victims, the citizens, and to society at large.[30] The Interdisciplinary Committee or working group mentioned in the Presidential Decree, charged with presenting proposals for the reparation of the abuses investigated by the SPO, has not been established to date.

The SPO began work with 40 to 50 individuals. However, in late 2003, in the wake of the publication of a critical report by Human Rights Watch on the performance of the SPO[31] and of the scandal created by the closure of the Deputy Ministry for Human Rights and Development,[32] the Special Prosecutor obtained more support and the number of personnel was increased to more than 100 individuals. The SPO presently has over 170 officials and most of them (at least 50 investigators) are working in the Legal Investigations Programs.[33]

When one reads the reports published every 100 days by the Special Prosecutor's Office with all the details of the work they have accomplished during nearly three years, it is difficult not to be impressed with the sheer size of the office's workload. According to their latest statistics, the SPO's investigators have, for example, started almost 500 new inquiries and conducted hundreds of interviews with the families of victims. They have also organized thousands of pages of unclassified documents and studied them. Most of the investigation resources are

concentrated in high profile cases of the 1960s and 70s, with the rest
investigating the alleged 662 homicides of *PRD* supporters in the early
1990s, which are almost half of the cases in the SPO.

After Carrillo Prieto accepted his post as the head of the Special
Prosecutor's Office, he stated that he would bring to justice all of those
responsible, despite the positions they had held in government during
the "dirty war."[34] He certainly proved to have the will to do it, but he
seemed to have underestimated the huge obstacles that he and his office
were going to face in the months and years to come. Unfortunately,
convictions of alleged perpetrators, in other words, the concrete results
that people are waiting for, are still lacking. Only eight arrest warrants
have been issued as a result of the hundreds of cases investigated, and
only Miguel Nazar Haro, former head of the infamous *Dirección Federal
de Seguridad*, is in detention awaiting trial.

There are many reasons for the slow progress. which does not seem to
depend on the political will of the Prosecutor, but rather on the structural obstacles and financial difficulties that his office is facing. First,
building court cases is a time-consuming process. Despite having expressed a new attitude and new commitment to human rights, the army
is not yet fully cooperative. It still hides or withholds information and
refuses to give crucial names or data. It still loses archives or it does not
have time to look for them.[35] The *Archivo General de la Nación* (AGN),
or Mexican National Archives, holds an astonishing collection of millions of documents and files useful for these criminal investigations.
Almost half of the documentation was obtained from the *Dirección
General de Investigaciones Sociales y Políticas* (General Directorate for
Social and Political Investigations), a twin of the infamous *Dirección
Federal de Seguridad*, and moved to the AGN in 1994.

Unfortunately though, the AGN failed to create any kind of index or
system to help the investigators in their search for documents. It took
over 18 months for the SPO investigators to organize the documents
they needed.[36] Researchers are forced to submit a written list of documents of interest held in the AGN, and then trust that the archive
staff will identify and locate them, all of which causes delays.[37] Many
investigators complain of arbitrariness, and fear that the Ministry of the
Interior may be monitoring the use of the records.

Second, since its creation there have been severe internal conflicts
inside the SPO that have affected its performance and working conditions. In the short lifetime of the institution, there have been constant,
and at times turbulent, personnel changes. Third, the slow process of
convictions is obviously still very much dependent on the political will of
the members of the justice system, and of the President, who has

declined to give enough political support and resources for this process. As criticism of the SPO's achievements has mounted, the Prosecutor himself has revealed that President Fox did not, for example, provide the promised funding for the exhumation of suspected mass graves in the southern state of Guerrero.[38] According to officials, there is not enough funding to hire a new Director of Psychological Support for the Victims, which is of great concern since aid for the victims and the reparation of damage is one of the most important tasks that the SPO was ordered to accomplish. Moreover, the SPO depends financially on the Attorney General's office or *Procuraduría General de la República*, raising serious doubts about its autonomy despite protestations of support from the former Attorney General.[39]

Fourth, there is a powerful political opposition to the SPO. For example, two arrest warrants issued by the SPO have not been carried out, a fact denounced by Carrillo Prieto himself. Last but not least, the SPO has had to fight against the Mexican justice system, notorious for its long history of corruption and incompetence.[40] Despite this, prosecutions are slowly moving forward and the SPO has managed to win and lose a few significant court cases. In March 2003, the Special Prosecutor's Office first attempted to indict former officials of the *Dirección Federal de Seguridad* on charges of forced disappearance, illegal detention and kidnapping in the case of Jesús Piedra Ibarra, a guerrilla allegedly kidnapped by police and intelligence agents in Monterrey in 1975. He has never been found. The federal judge refused to issue arrest warrants, arguing that the statute of limitations had expired. The SPO appealed to the Supreme Court, and in November 2003 the Supreme Court unanimously rejected the ruling of the federal judge. It ruled that the statute of limitations did not apply to kidnapping as long as the victim was missing, giving federal prosecutors the ability to charge former government officials responsible for "dirty war" disappearances with that crime.[41]

After the Supreme Court ruling, in December 2003 a judge issued an arrest warrant against three former officials accused of participation in the enforced disappearance of Jesús Piedra Ibarra. In February 2004, the federal authorities finally managed to arrest Miguel Nazar Haro in Mexico City. He was held for several months in the Topo Chico prison of Monterrey awaiting trial, and has recently enjoyed the benefit of house arrest given his advanced age and deteriorated state of health. The two other suspects in the case, Luis de la Barreda Moreno and Juventino Romero Cisneros, remain fugitives. In the spring of 2004, the Mexican authorities issued five arrest warrants for suspected perpetrators of the enforced disappearance in 1975 of Ignacio Salas Obregón, founder of the *Liga Comunista 23 de Septiembre*, but to date only Nazar Haro has been captured.[42]

In June 2004, Ignacio Carrillo Prieto won another significant case. In a ruling similar to its decision on kidnapping of December 2003, the Supreme Court stated that cases of forced disappearance by state authorities could be prosecuted if the victims were still missing,[43] even if the disappearance occurred before this crime became a part of Mexico's criminal code in 2001. Prior to this ruling, charges of enforced disappearance could not be applied to the hundreds of cases of victims who vanished three decades ago. Instead, those cases could only be tried as kidnappings, a lesser charge which carries a sentence of six months to three years, rather than 15 to 40 years for forced disappearance.[44]

A month later, the Special Prosecutor put the nation's judicial system to the test once more. In a bold and surprising move, he charged former President Luis Echeverria, two of his former aides, three army generals, and a few other officials with genocide for the intent to destroy a national group in the massacre of at least 25 student protesters on Corpus Christi day in June 10, 1971.

The Special Prosecutor pressed the charges of genocide because, under existing laws, there was apparently no other way around the statute of limitations in massacre cases. The case presented against Echeverria and his associates was enormous: 9,382 pages of evidence and testimony. The following day, a federal judge threw out the request for an arrest warrant without reading all of the evidence presented to him, simply deciding that the 30-year statute of limitations had passed. After this ruling, Carrillo Prieto appealed once more to the Supreme Court, arguing that the genocide charges should stand because the PGR had investigated the case in the year 1982, interrupting the running of the statute of limitations. In June 2005, the Supreme Court ruled that in Echeverria's case the statute had been tolled by official immunities, although for a number of other defendants the charges were dismissed on grounds that no immunity ever applied and that Mexico only ratified the treaty making genocide imprescriptable in 2002, years after the events at issue. The case now returns to the lower courts, where it faces an uncertain future. The Special Prosecutor has indicated several times that if he fails with the courts he will take this case to the Inter-American system.[45]

In the interim, criticism of Ignacio Carrillo Prieto and of the SPO has grown stronger and more strident. The PRI leadership issued a press release announcing the creation of a panel of distinguished jurists and members of the party to contest the case. Among those jurists was Sergio

García Ramírez, former Prosecutor of Mexico City in 1971 when the massacre occurred, and at the time President of the Inter-American Human Rights Court. After much prodding from the press, García Ramírez denied his intention to form part of such a panel. The Secretary of Defense, General Ricardo Clemente Vega, stood up in a graduation ceremony of the Defense Academy and made a strong speech asking for forgiveness and "pardon" of the military. He subsequently attempted to tone down this statement, which caused a strong impact coming as it did from a four-star general and Secretary of Defense.

Even President Vicente Fox seems to have distanced himself from the Special Prosecutor. He recently stated in an interview that if Carrillo Prieto suffers a defeat in the Supreme Court, the President would then consider, once more, the possibility of creating a truth commission.[46] The Special Prosecutor immediately opposed the idea of a truth commission and said that: "With a truth commission, governments make a pact with the Devil. Our office looks for ways to send the Devil to jail."[47] A few days later, a more subdued Carrillo Prieto said that if it comes to the creation of a truth commission, it will operate inside the SPO and it will handle only those cases which cannot be judged in the Mexican justice system.[48]

Military justice

The Office of the Special Prosecutor is not the only institution investigating past abuses. In fact, under an ad hoc mechanism agreed to between the Ministry of Foreign Affairs and the Inter-American Human Rights Commission in 2001, several state prosecutors' offices are also investigating crimes of the past under the supervision of this body. Among these are some cases in the military prosecutor's office.

In September 2003, the Army made its first move to acknowledge its responsibility for the human rights violations committed during the dirty war, when it announced an arrest warrant for Generals Mario Arturo Acosta Chaparro and Francisco Quirós Hermosillo and Major Francisco Javier Barquín, accused of the homicide of 143 people who disappeared during the 1970s. The three of them are presently in prison on charges related to drug trafficking. Apparently, in the course of the inquiry, a protected witness and former military pilot, gave evidence that they had detained more than a hundred peasants and held them in the military barracks of Pie de la Cuesta, close to Acapulco, from where they were thrown into the ocean in helicopters belonging to the Air Force.[49]

The military prosecutor immediately began proceedings, although in fact, according to the constitution, the case should have been dealt with by civilian authorities.[50] Sadly, this first move of acknowledgment proved to be a failure. The Supreme Military Tribunal ruled that because of lack of evidence the three officers could only be tried for the deaths of 22 persons. In July 2004, a military judge exonerated Acosta Chaparro because of "loss of documents." The other two perpetrators were to be released with the same excuse.[51]

Synergies and conflicts between the mechanisms for transitional justice

Although Carrillo Prieto and the military prosecutor appear to be fighting the same battle to bring perpetrators of crimes against humanity to justice, there are fears that the simultaneous use of the two parallel systems is leading to impunity. Serious cases of human rights violations against civilians involving members of the Mexican armed forces such as the one described above should be under the jurisdiction of the SPO instead of the military.

Military tribunals are separate from civilian courts in Mexico. Ordinary practice has been that cases concerning members of the Armed Forces are immediately turned over to the military prosecutor's office. According to a novel constitutional interpretation by former federal Attorney General Rafael Macedo de la Concha, military personnel cannot be tried in civilian courts for human rights abuses committed against civilians.[52] This position was reinforced by the reservation prompted by the military, PRI and conservative members of PAN to the ratification of the Inter-American Convention on Forced Disappearance of Persons in 2002 by the Senate.[53]

It is well-known that the Mexican military have a tradition of protecting their own and have allowed abuses to go uninvestigated and unpunished. Furthermore, the military justice system lacks the necessary independence to carry out reliable investigations, and its operations are not transparent.[54] For example, the Code of Military Justice states: "In the cases where its importance requires it, the prosecutor should request instructions from the Secretary of the Military and Navy."[55] Amnesty International has observed that in investigations in the military justice system, access to the case file is virtually impossible.[56] Some NGOs have demanded that the SPO take a more active role in confronting its difficulties with the military prosecutor's office.[57]

Attempts at local ownership of the process

Almost three years have passed since the creation of the SPO and criticism of its meager results has grown stronger. The media and civil society, especially several international human rights organizations and institutions are keeping close watch on the ongoing process to bring past human rights crimes to justice. Although the Citizen's Support Committee has failed to live up to most of its expectations, it is planning a report called "The White Book" in an attempt to tell the truth about the repressive policy that involved the various agencies and institutions of the State during the "dirty war". The intention of this report is to give Mexican society and new generations an objective vision of the past, and in this way play something of the role of a "truth commission", focusing on overall patterns and responsibilities. So far, however, there is no clear indication that this "White Book" is seriously under way.[58]

Perhaps the media, both Mexican and international, have been the most active actors in publicizing and keeping the public in touch with the "dirty war" and the prosecuting process. The Mexican newspapers carry abundant reports and statements about the "dirty war", the SPO and the role of the military. Although a democratic opening in the Mexican press started in the 1970s, it took three decades for *El Universal*, one of the main Mexican newspapers, to publish for the first time twelve shocking pictures of the 1968 Tlatelolco massacre. The newspaper timed the publication of the photographs with the opening of the Special Prosecutor's Office in February 2002.[59] Undoubtedly *Proceso*, a widely respected weekly news magazine founded in 1976 by a group of former journalists after they were ousted by President Echeverría from the newspaper *Excélsior*, is the most faithful follower of the SPO. Julio Scherer, its founder, has even written a book, co-authored with Carlos Monsiváis, one of the country's leading commentators, with some of the material gathered by the SPO.[60]

Mexican civil society organizations, especially human rights activists and members of the victims' organizations were, and still are, very suspicious of the SPO. The motives and arguments vary according to their composition. Human rights NGOs claim to have preferred a truth commission and have voiced their doubts about the creation of a special prosecutor, alleging the incompetence and failure of many of the special prosecutors nominated to investigate diverse crimes in the past decade.[61] They do not seem to think that the process of democratization has made much of a difference in this matter. Instead, human rights groups have turned to the Inter-American system as their strategy of choice for dealing with the past. Cases now pending include several within the mandate of the SPO.

The victims' groups are more divided. Some have cooperated with the office and are awaiting results.[62] Others, like *Comité Eureka*, headed by Rosario Ibarra de Piedra, mother of Jesús Piedra, claim that the relatives of the disappeared do not believe in truth commissions or in special prosecutors.[63] AFADEM *(Asociación de Familiares de Desaparecidos de México)*, made up mostly of rural victims of the "dirty war" and its sequelae in Guerrero cooperated at first with the SPO. They approved of the establishment of a subsidiary office of the SPO in the town of Atoyac and supported the victim's families who brought denunciations to the SPO, but they were reluctant to fully endorse Carrillo Prieto's office. After three years they are extremely critical.

In February 2003, one year after the nomination of Carrillo Prieto, sixteen human rights NGOs signed and released a document that strongly criticized the creation, goals and methods of the SPO.[64] In October 2003, a second report was released and presented to the Inter-American Commission of Human Rights at its 118th session. Its criticisms can be summed up as follows: the SPO is not an independent entity since it is an organ of the PGR; it is working with limited resources and insufficient personnel; the SPO is reporting poorly on its activities and results; it has not persisted in its effort to reclaim the cases that are in the hands of the military courts; and finally, the SPO was created without a process of political dialogue, which would have created social support for the organization.[65]

International organizations and institutions, both governmental and non-governmental, have been more nuanced in their critiques. Amnesty International and Human Rights Watch have released reports criticizing the SPO and the military justice system for their lack of results in the prosecution of perpetrators of crimes during the "dirty war". In 2003, Human Rights Watch especially criticized the Fox administration and the military for not providing the SPO with the support it needed to carry out its mandate.[66] The International Center for Transitional Justice (ITCJ) has participated in the work of the SPO since the beginning. In April 2003, ICTJ staff members visited Mexico and discussed an agreement with the Special Prosecutor and his staff, which resulted in a technical assessment of the SPO, and released a report which is cited extensively in this chapter.

No justice without truth?

Is the glass half empty or half full? It is obvious that the consolidation of democratic rule in Mexico is a slow and halting process. It is also clear that the Fox government misread the election results and has lacked the strength and political will to rally the forces that would have helped it to overcome the enormous and active resistance to change posed by the

PRI establishment and its allies, who continue to have a considerable hold on power and on the institutions of the justice system.

Early on, the human rights policies laid out by the most progressive elements in the newly formed democratic government, led by Jorge Castañeda and Adolfo Aguilar Zinser, were supported by the President but never really protected from the powerful interests which they directly threatened. When Aguilar Zinser was nominated to another post and Castañeda stepped down, these policies floundered and lost their intention and thrust.

The original strategy for transitional justice was reduced to the creation of a Special Prosecutor's Office lacking the necessary autonomy and resources to perform its task. Organized civil society – with the exception of a few groups of survivors, political activists and demobilized guerrillas of the 1960s and 70s – has never really been consulted and has not become part of the process of designing and producing the mechanisms for transitional justice that the country needs. On the other hand, the current members of most of the human rights organizations belong to a generation who did not suffer the repression of the "dirty war", so they have no way to gauge the importance of the SPO, however meager its results. The victims' groups, with the notorious exceptions already mentioned, have tried to cooperate. They found themselves without the necessary support from either the Prosecutor's Office or the human rights community. The fact that it took two years for Carrillo Prieto to make his first arrest has frustrated them. So they have decided to keep their distance and criticize the process from afar.

The end result has been that at every stage of the process, the strategy for transitional justice seems to have been systematically diverted from its original intent by the powers that be. The project for a truth commission was shelved as a response to pressures from the PRI and the more conservative elements of Fox's own party. Hence the role of the National Human Rights Commission – discredited from the start by its previous lack of interest in the matter – which was called into action and asked to report on the crimes of the "dirty war". The report was a good one, but the Commission kept the names of the alleged perpetrators secret, adding to the mistrust of the victims. The former Attorney General maneuvered at the last moment to keep the Special Prosecutor's Office under his control with the consequences that we have seen. The military paid lip service to the project, but have dragged their feet since then, especially when asked to cooperate. Besides, they continue to hold on to their unconstitutional privilege to prosecute and judge their own when they have committed crimes against civilians. The majority of the members of the Senate have also contributed to this chain of events by ratifying international instruments designed for dealing with crimes against humanity with reservations which weaken their thrust, almost without a murmur.

Despite everything, one cannot claim that there have been no advances. The Special Prosecutor is daring, he works hard, and he is imaginative and brave. The media inform the public regularly on the performance of the SPO. The international community, especially the NGOs, continue to monitor and lend their critical support to the effort. And last but certainly not least, the Supreme Court has, so far, largely produced enlightened decisions, which have allowed the Special Prosecutor to navigate the difficulties and pitfalls of the domestic legal system. Slowly, slowly, the process has taken hold of the country's consciousness, and even recalcitrant objectors, like Rosario Ibarra, have grudgingly conceded some positive results.

Obviously, the continuing legal fight on the culpability of former President Echeverria in the commission of genocide will determine the future of the Special Prosecutor and his Office. It is difficult to envisage him continuing to work as if nothing has happened if the courts do not rule in his favor. The political backlash would be enormous. It is probable that his Office would continue to exist, but under the direction of a lesser figure, one who would let it wither away and die, in the manner of previous special prosecutor's offices. The choice to focus on genocide, rather than, say, the 500-plus disappearance cases, was therefore a risky one.

But even if Carrillo Prieto were to succeed in convicting a powerful ex-President, with unforeseen consequences, the problem of the path taken by the Fox government for dealing with the crimes of the past lies in the difficulties faced by the SPO for delivering the rest of the elements that are required in a strategy of transitional justice. It is one thing to arrive at the legal truth of the crimes that the SPO is prosecuting, and quite another to reconstruct the historical truth of the systemic nature of these crimes. That truth is to be discovered still, and the Citizen's Support Committee of the Special Prosecutor, which some of us mistakenly took for a viable alternative to a truth commission,[67] has so far proven its total inability to undertake such a task. In the present political context, it is difficult to envisage that this will be accomplished in the near future, given the strength of resistance to initiatives of this nature and the lack of a strong demand from organized civil society.

The use of penal law for systemic crimes obviously has many advantages, but only if punishment is really delivered. Putting aside considerations as to the real capacity of the Mexican justice system to effectively punish these types of crimes, the use of penal law as an exclusive strategy might hinder the development of an overall understanding of the patterns of repression and those responsible for it, thus making it difficult for Mexican society to undergo a real process of transitional justice.

The Mexican people will not obtain an official historical account of these events at least for a long time coming. This would have been the result of a truth commission, but that mechanism was strongly opposed by the PRI – which still controls the Congress and the majority of state governments – as well as by the governing party. Instead, the government attempted to merge the functions of punishment with those of truth-telling in the same mechanism. The fact that the "Mexican solution" has not really addressed comprehensive truth-seeking initiatives – involving the stories of the victims and ability to reveal the identity of the perpetrators of the past crimes and their position in the chain of command – does not bode well for the other objectives of reparation, reconciliation and guarantees of non-repetition, allegedly part of the Fox government's strategy for transitional justice.

Serious judicial reform is a necessity if Mexico is to become a modern, law-abiding country with an improved human rights record. This means many things aside from reforming the institutions that deal with public security and the administration of justice. It also requires the incorporation of international human rights law into domestic law, and the teaching and training of lawyers, judges and law enforcement officials how to use it. It also means upgrading the official human rights commissions and helping civil society organizations build and enhance their capacities. None of this can be achieved if the complex web of complicities and cover-ups of past state crimes, especially the systematic use of torture and enforced disappearance of political opponents, is not revealed and the perpetrators of these crimes are not brought to justice.

The situation of the rule of law in Mexico is still very precarious. The current administration's meek attempts at reforms in the justice system have so far failed. The legacy of the authoritarian past is very present and the current political context – a weak presidency and an independent legislature – is highly favorable to special, powerful and privileged interests which do not need to comply with legal restrictions. This does not bode well for the possible outcome of the "Mexican solution" to transitional justice. In fact, for the moment, it looks like the Mexican people might be left, once again, with very little justice, scant truth and no reconciliation.

NOTES

*The authors wish to express their gratitude to Sofia Ramos and Maria José Guembe for their support in the legal interpretation of many aspects of this paper.

1. See Julio Scherer and Carlos Monisváis, *Los patriotas. De Tlatelolco a la Guerra sucia* (México: Nuevo Siglo Aguilar, 2004), p. 199; Sergio Aguayo, *1968, Los archivos de la violencia* (México D.F: Grijalbo, Reforma, 1998), p. 331.

2. Coletta Youngers and Eileen Rosin, *Drugs and Democracy in Latin America, The Impact of US Policy* (Boulder: Lynne Rienner Publishers, 2004), p. 274.

3. For example, in the massacres of Aguas Blancas and Acteal there is evidence that these operations were planned at the highest level of the respective state governments of Guerrero and Chiapas. There is also evidence that the federal authorities were at least aware of these preparations.

4. Alicia de los Rios, "Testimonio" in Comisión de Derechos Humanos del Distrito Federal, et al., *Memoria, Seminario internacional. Tortura, reparación y prevención. Comisiones de la verdad, Foro Público. Perspectivas y Alcances. El caso de México, Ciudad de México, 20 de julio de 2002* (México, 2003), pp. 520, 434.

5. The first two human rights organizations to emerge in this period were the Centro de Derechos Humanos Fray Francisco de Vitoria O.P. (1984) and the Academia Mexicana de Derechos Humanos (1984).

6. This information was obtained by the author when she was acting as Deputy Minister for Human Rights and Democracy in the Ministry for Foreign Relations, in July 2003.

7. Alan Zamembo, "Mexico's History Test", *Newsweek International,* July 2, 2002, in Louis Bickford, "Transitional Justice in Mexico", Dec. 2005 *Journal of Human Rights* 4, pp. 537–57.

8. Case 5/2000, Juzgado Sexto de Distritos de Procesos Penales en el Distrito Federal, January 11, 2001.

9. Writ of "Amparo" under revision 140/2002, June 10, 2003. Extradition for torture was denied on statute of limitations grounds.

10. Inter-American Commission on Human Rights, www.cidh.oas.org/basicos. The Convention already had a reservation that permitted military jurisdiction over any crime committed by a member of the Armed Forces.

11. Sergio Aguayo, "El derecho a la información: hacia una comisión de la verdad", CDHDF, note 4 above, p. 460.

12. Mexico, "Disappearances: an ongoing crime", Amnesty International, AI index: AMR 41/020/2002, 2002. http://web.amnesty.org/library/Index/engAMR410202002?OpenDocument&of=COUNTRIES%5CMEXICO

13. Comisión Nacional de Derechos Humanos, *Recomendación 26/2001, Informe especial sobre las quejas en materia de desapariciones forzadas ocurridas en la década de los 70 y principio de los 80.*

14. *Ibid.*

15. Ley de la Comisión Nacional de los Derechos Humanos publicada en el Diario Oficial de la Federación el 29 de junio 1992 (Ultima reforma aplicada 26/11/2001).

16. Juan Manuel Venegas and Victor Ballinas, "Castigo a funcionarios de alto nivel por su responsabilidad en la *guerra sucia*, piden ONGs", *La Jornada*, November 28, 2001.

17. The Committee for the Defense of Prisoners, the Persecuted, the Disappeared and Political Exiles founded in 1978 is also called Comité Eureka.

18. Georgina Saldierna, "Cuestiona Ibarra objetivos de la fiscalía especial", *La Jornada*, November 28, 2001.

19. "Desconfían ONGs de Macedo y la fiscalía", *El Universal*, November 28, 2001.

20. Jesús Aranda, Ciro Pérez and Victor Ballinas, "Hablar de *desaparición* impedirá que prescriban hechos de la *guerra sucia*", *La Jornada*, November 28, 2001.

21. Jesús Aranda, "Rechazan militares que instalaciones del Ejército se hayan usado en la *guerra sucia*", *La Jornada*, November 28, 2001.

22. Poder Ejecutivo de la República, *Acuerdo por el que se disponen diversas medidas para la procuración de justicia por delitos cometidos contra personas vinculadas con movimientos sociales y políticos del pasado*, November 27, 2001; See Kate Doyle, "Forgetting is not Justice, Mexico Bares its Secret Past", Reportage, *World Policy Journal*, Summer 2003, pp. 61–72.

23. Poder Ejecutivo de la República, Articles 1 to 8.

24. Many members of the other side of the conflict have already been killed or punished with long prison sentences, torture and other inhumane practices.

25. Paul Seils, "A Promise Unfulfilled? The Special Prosecutor's Office in Mexico", International Center for Transnational Justice (2004), p. 11.

26. Sergio Aguayo offers an interesting account of this process in Ricardo Ravelo, "Ahora falta la verdad", *Proceso*, July 25, 2004.

27. Kate Doyle, "Forgetting is not Justice", p. 69.

28. The Ethiopian Transitional Government established a similar kind of office in September 1992.

29. Paul Seils, *A Promise Unfulfilled?* p. 37.

30. David Vicenteño, "Reclaman al Presidente Fox su promesa de castigar los crímenes del pasado", *Reforma*, June 10, 2004.

31. Daniel Wilkinson, "Justice in Jeopardy: Why Mexico's First Real Effort to Address Past Abuses Risks Becoming Its Latest Failure", *Human Rights Watch* (2003) Vol. 15, No. 4 (B).

32. *La Fiscalía Futil, entrevista al Fiscal Especial*, October 2003.

33. *FEMOSPP.* "Informe", (January 2002 – March 2004), 509–21.

34. Denise Dresser, "Cuentas por saldar", *Nexos*, August 20, 2004.

35. Wilkinson, "Justice in Jeopardy".

36. *Ibid.*, p. 25.

37. Interviews with the workers of the SPO on September 24, 2004.

38. Kevin Sullivan, "New Genocide Charges Planned in Mexico", *Washington Post*, September 2, 2004.
39. See, for example, David Viceteño Ortiz, "Da Mecedo total libertad a Fiscalía", *Reforma*, June 12, 2004.
40. Dato Param Coomaraswamy, presented in accordance with resolution 2001/ 39 of the UN Human Rights Commission, Economic and Social Council, E/ CN.4/2002 Add.1, January 24, 2002, p. 11. The special rapporteur on the independence of judges and lawyers visited Mexico in 2001.
41. Resolución del asunto 1/2003 de la sala SCJN.
42. Silvia Otero, "Ordenan más capturas por 'guerra sucia'", *El Universal*, February 27, 2004.
43. SCJN June 29, 2004, 49/2004.
44. Reuters, "Mexico High Court Boosts 'Dirty War' Trial Arsenal", June 30, 2004.
45. Interview with Ignacio Carrillo Prieto, August 11, 2004.
46. Ginger Thompson, "Mexico's leader to Pursue Genocide case", *New York Times*, September 1, 2004.
47. Ginger Thomson and Tim Weiner, "When Promises to Bring Justice in Mexico Come to Naught", *New York Times*, July 26, 2004.
48. Fuerza Informativa Azteca, "Comisión de la Verdad ya estaba prevista: FEMOSPP", September 2, 2004, http://www.todito.com/paginas/noticias/ 160103.html.
49. Jorge Alejandro Medellín, "Consignarán más involucrados en guerra sucia", *El Universal*, April 26, 2004.
50. Artículo 13, *Constitución Política de los Estados Unidos Mexicanos*, 5ª ed., Texto Vigente, México, Comisión Nacional de los Derechos Humanos, 2002.
51. Jesús Aranda, "Exculpan de vuelos de la muerte a Acosta Chaparro", *La Jornada*, July 9, 2004.
52. http://www.mexicosolidarity.org/news_july5_04.ht.
53. The reservation was to Article 9: "persons alleged to be responsible for the acts constituting the offence of forced disappearance of persons may be tried only in the competent jurisdictions of ordinary law in each state, to the exclusion of all other special jurisdictions, particularly military jurisdictions."
54. See Human Rights Watch, World Report 2003, p. 154–55.
55. See Código de Justicia Militar, Art. 81–IV.
56. AI, Mexico: *Unfair Trials, Unsafe Convictions*, AMR41/007/2003.
57. *La impunidad en México*, Report of Mexican organizations to the Inter-American Human Rights Comisssion, 117th Session, Washington DC, February 2003.
58. Comité Ciudadano de Apoyo al Fiscal Especial para Movimientos Sociales y Políticos del Pasado, Oficio No. FEMOSPP/CCAFE/0094/2004.
59. Kate Doyle, "Forgetting is not Justice".
60. Scherer and Monisváis, *Los patriotas*.
61. Centro de Derechos Humanos Miguel Agustín Pro, "Reseña del contexto mexicano", CDHDF, note 4 above, pp. 419–30.
62. See Alicia de los Rios, "Testimonio".

63. Rosario Ibarra de Piedra, "La lucha por la verdad y la justicia", CDHDF, note 12 above, pp. 447–51.
64. The title and the authors of the document are the same as in the document presented at the 117th Session of the Inter-American Human Rights Commission in Washington DC.
65. *Ibid.*
66. See Human Rights Watch, note 32 above.
67. See Mariclaire Acosta, "Ajuste de cuentas con el pasado: la experiencia mexicana", CDHDF, note 4 above, pp. 17–19.

5 No justice, no peace: Discussion of a legal framework regarding the demobilization of non-state armed groups in Colombia

*Maria José Guembe and Helena Olea**

Introduction

After more than 50 years of political violence, Colombia confronts the possibility of negotiating the disarmament, demobilization, and reintegration of at least one of its armed actors. Colombians and the international community welcome the possibility of putting an end to the increasingly bloody internal armed conflict and consequently reducing the number of executions, disappearances, kidnappings, and wounded and displaced persons. However, the fact that there are two types of non-state armed actors, guerrillas and paramilitaries, who have committed grave crimes, including human rights violations and crimes of war, and that most of these groups are involved in drug trafficking complicates any resolution to the conflict. The new interplay between domestic and international legal systems and standards also presents interesting challenges.

For two years the Colombian Congress considered different versions of governmental initiatives on differentiated criminal treatment for members of armed groups willing to disarm and demobilize. The first draft introduced by the Uribe administration in October 2003 included elements of punishment, conditional parole, and reparations, but also had a number of shortcomings. Domestic and international actors pressured the government to modify the draft legislation. Congress became dissatisfied with the executive's amended draft and no effort was made to move forward. The executive submitted another draft to Congress in February 2005 after earlier efforts to submit a joint initiative with a group of Congress members failed. By March 2005 eight congressional initiatives, in addition to the executive's draft bill, had been submitted to Congress. The government soon succeeded in obtaining support for its initiative, which was approved with minor changes by Congress in June 2005.

The Colombian government and the armed actors are slowly beginning to realize that developments in international law limit the possible solutions to the conflict. Negotiating the termination of an armed conflict today is not as simple as it was ten or even five years ago. Blanket amnesties and general pardons are not an option, not only because of the political pressure that victims groups may exert, but also because these practices do not stand the test of international standards and institutions. Trying to ignore or defy these standards will simply trigger one or more of the mechanisms that protect victims' rights to truth, justice and reparation.

The approved bill will have to stand the test of international standards set forth by the Inter-American Court of Human Rights, the UN Human Rights Committee, and the Colombian Constitutional Court. It will also have to take into account that Colombia ratified the Statute of the International Criminal Court (ICC) and is subject to the ICC's jurisdiction, which any peace settlement should avoid triggering.[1] Additionally, the criminal justice interests of other states may pose a constraint on possible peace settlements. Other states have initiated criminal investigations and prosecutions, and have requested the extradition of members of the armed groups for crimes committed in Colombia because of the victim's nationality, or because part of the crime was committed in another state, as in the case of drug trafficking. These extradition requests, actual and potential, play a role in each side's maneuvering around peace negotiations, and hang over any attempts at settlement.

Colombia's solutions should take into account the experiences of other countries in terms of strengthening democracy and the rule of law by supporting accountability for war crimes and crimes against humanity. They should also be pragmatic, taking into account the capabilities, strengths and shortcomings of the justice system that will have the burden of implementing the mechanism created by the new law. As some have described it, a balance needs to be found where there is as much justice as possible, and as much impunity as is necessary. However, it appears that the outcome fails to find such a balance.

This chapter describes the tensions and opportunities created by the interplay between domestic and international constraints on the negotiation process. We begin with a brief overview of the armed conflict and the peace negotiations. Next, we describe the main elements of the recently approved legislation. We then proceed to analyze it in light of the international legal framework and present our conclusions.

Complexities that explain the conflict

Colombia is in the midst of an internal armed conflict in which most of the victims are civilians. The origins of this conflagration can be traced back to the period known as *La Violencia* (The Violence).[2] The period began with the slaying of Jorge Eliécer Gaitán, an independent presidential candidate for the Liberal Party, in 1948. And it continued with a massive violent outbreak that resulted in the assassination of thousands of persons by members of the opposing political party. *La Violencia* was mainly a rural phenomenon and its victims were mostly candidates for public office and community leaders. In 1953, against the backdrop of chaos and violence, Augusto Rojas Pinilla, General in Chief of the Colombian Army, led a coup and seized power. Rojas Pinilla's rule lasted until 1958, when after mounting pressure he was ousted by an alliance of conservative and liberal leaders who drafted and promoted the *Frente Nacional* (National Front) accord. Under the accord, the agreement of the major parties to alternate governmental control succeeded in decreasing the number of political assassinations but also eliminated political alternatives outside of the Liberal and Conservative parties. As an unintended consequence of the agreement, both parties lost their ideological and electoral base because their rotation into power was assured. In spite of the termination of the *Frente Nacional* in 1970, the Conservative and Liberal parties failed to build a clear political agenda, turning into purely electoral machineries at the local, departmental, and national level.[3]

Guerrilla groups emerged in Colombia in the 1960s influenced by social revolutionary ideas, and in response to military repression, political violence and the lack of political options for the left. Small-scale communist organizational efforts in rural areas were violently repressed, leading to the creation of *Fuerzas Armadas Revolucionarias de Colombia* – FARC (Revolutionary Armed Forces of Colombia).[4] Almost simultaneously, another guerrilla group emerged, *Ejército de Liberación Nacional* – ELN (National Liberation Army), formed by urban middle class intellectuals influenced by the Cuban revolution.[5] Subsequently, myriad smaller guerrilla groups surfaced, including *Ejército Popular de Liberación* – EPL (Popular Liberation Army), *Manuel Quintín Lame*, *Partido Revolucionario de los Trabajadores* – PRT (Revolutionary Workers Party), and *Movimiento 19 de Abril* – M-19 (the 19th of April Movement). Since their formation, Colombian guerilla groups have claimed allegiance to leftist ideologies and justified their use of force as a response to the impossibility of winning public office in a corrupt and closed political party system.

Due partially to the Armed Forces' frustration with its incapacity to defeat the guerrillas militarily and also to the rising influence of drug lords who created private armies to protect themselves and their property, paramilitary or self-defense groups emerged in the 1980s. These groups of armed men were able to fight the guerrillas unbounded by the rule of law, unlike the military, which was feeling increasingly constrained by human rights monitoring. The Armed Forces envisioned that the creation of these groups would allow them to gain the upper hand in their struggle against guerrillas. Other sectors of society, particularly landowners and corporations, politically and financially supported the creation of paramilitary groups as part of their defense strategy against guerrilla groups, which were targeting them through kidnappings and extortion schemes. Numerous incidents of connivance, cooperation, or lack of effective will to curb the unlawful actions of paramilitary groups unequivocally illustrate the ties between Armed Forces units, commanders and officers, and the paramilitaries.[6] By the 1990s most paramilitary groups were organized under an umbrella organization, *Autodefensas Unidas de Colombia* – AUC (United Self-Defense Forces of Colombia), but a few small groups remained independent.[7]

In order to fill the vacuum left by the disintegration of large drug cartels in Colombia (e.g., the Cali and Medellín Cartels) and as a way to augment significantly their incomes, both guerrillas and paramilitaries moved into the drug business. Their incursion into drug trafficking also reflected changes in the production of coca and heroin. Drug cultivation, production and commercialization are today essential to the economic sustainability of illegal armed actors in Colombia.[8] Their strength has multiplied, as measured by the number of active soldiers and weaponry. Today, guerrillas and paramilitaries control distinct areas of the country where they extort from landowners and corporations in proportion to the income earned, in an illegal taxation scheme. Their enforcement mechanisms include killings, torture, and kidnappings.

The intervention of the United States exacerbated the cycle of violence. The US government provides significant military assistance to Colombia claiming that it is part of their counter-narcotic strategy.[9] Since the 1980s, the US government has requested Colombia's cooperation in the extradition of drug traffickers. As the link is established between drug trafficking and guerrillas and paramilitaries, the United States is now requesting the extradition of high-ranked members of these unlawful groups mostly on drug trafficking charges. US assistance has augmented the military capacity of all armed actors, and thus an increase in military confrontations and casualties, while the extradition policy has fueled the increasing belief by leaders that there are few alternatives to waging war.[10]

In the last ten years, the increased military power of both guerrillas and paramilitaries has resulted in their effective control of portions of territory.[11] As the military strength of non-state parties has grown, so has their propensity to infringe the laws of armed conflict. Indeed, they now commit serious crimes on a scale not seen before. This is in part explained by the fact that the armed parties' military strength has come as a result of targeting civilians, rather than actually combating each other and the state's armed forces.

Negotiations with guerrillas and paramilitaries

Presidents Belisario Betancur (1982–86), Virgilio Barco (1986–90), César Gaviria (1990–94) all attempted peace negotiations. During the Samper administration (1994–98), the government attempted to negotiate once more with the remaining active guerrilla groups, FARC and ELN. Those efforts proved futile, however. President Andrés Pastrana (1998–2002) was elected on a peace negotiation platform. Negotiations with FARC failed, even though, as requested, FARC was granted full control of a demilitarized zone the size of Switzerland. The Pastrana administration also engaged in unsuccessful negotiations with ELN. The possibility of negotiations with AUC or any paramilitary forces was never considered.[12]

In May 2002, Alvaro Uribe was elected on a strong military platform that promised the defeat of the guerrillas and urged the Armed Forces to combat paramilitary groups. A few months after taking office, government officials began discreet and confidential talks with AUC. In contrast to negotiations with paramilitaries, the Uribe administration has achieved very little with guerrilla groups. While Uribe demands a cease fire as a prerequisite to negotiations, FARC and ELN request a demilitarized zone where they can concentrate their combatants. Discussions with FARC have not progressed satisfactorily, despite national and international efforts.[13] Similarly, negotiations attempts with the ELN have encountered numerous obstacles.

Until 2002, the possibility of negotiating the disarmament of paramilitary forces was not considered viable, as the legal framework and political environment did not support it. Unlike the guerrilla groups, AUC lacks even a stated political agenda, which creates a legal and political constraint in negotiations with them. On December 1, 2002 AUC announced a unilateral and unlimited cease-fire as a demonstration of their willingness to move forward with peace negotiations. The

AUC gesture was a calculated one, as Congress had just passed draft legislation that opened the possibility of these negotiations.

On December 23, 2002, President Uribe approved Law 782 of 2002, which modified Law 418 of 1997, the statute that set forth mechanisms for peace negotiations, including demobilizations. These earlier laws provide amnesties for certain crimes and economic benefits to all members of illegal armed groups who voluntarily desert or demobilize, so long as they have not been charged with the commission of a serious violation of international human rights or humanitarian law. The modification removed the requirement for unlawful armed organizations to be of a political nature in order for the government to negotiate with them. Law 782 of 2002 thus opened the way for negotiations and demobilization of paramilitary groups, an opportunity that both the Uribe administration and AUC were eager to exploit. A few days later, a commission was created to explore alternatives for negotiations with the paramilitaries.[14]

Formal negotiations between the parties began in January 2003. Simultaneously, members of the Uribe administration – including the President – began to speak of possible alternatives to detention and prison terms for guerrillas and paramilitaries who committed heinous crimes yet agreed to participate in a peace process. On July 15, 2003, the Uribe administration and AUC signed a formal agreement, the *Acuerdo de Santa Fe de Ralito* (Santa Fe de Ralito Accord) and announced that by December 2005, around 13,000 men would demobilize.[15] Two dissident paramilitary groups announced their willingness to join the peace negotiations, which would mean the demobilization of another 6,000 armed men. On November 24, 2003, the President suspended arrest orders for the leaders of *Bloque Cacique Nutibara* (BCN),[16] an AUC group comprised of around 850 men. BCN members subsequently handed over their weapons and returned to their homes.[17] A second smaller group comprised of 155 men from *Autodefensas Campesinas de Ortega* demobilized on December 7, 2003. In short, for all practical purposes the demobilization process had effectively begun.

On April 16, 2004 Carlos Castaño, the political commander of AUC, disappeared. The negotiation process stumbled for a few weeks, but continued under the leadership of Salvatore Mancuso. In 2005, Ramón Isaza Arango assumed the role upon Mancuso's demobilization. On May 12 and 13, 2004, the Uribe administration and AUC adopted an agreement establishing an area in Tierralta, Córdoba for AUC representatives to settle while negotiations take place.[18] On July 1, 2004, negotiations formally began. Even though a cease-fire, a stated requirement of the whole process, has not been completely observed, negotiations continue.[19] By February 2006, 22,842 AUC combatants have put down their weapons in 30 demobilizations. They have also returned land comprising 6,500 hectares, buildings, vehicles, 14,141 weapons and ammunition.

Demobilizations take place in three phases under the responsibility of the Ministry of Justice and Interior. In the first phase, AUC presents the government with a list of men, weapons, vehicles, and communication equipment that will be demobilized. In the second phase, AUC members gather in a public act before government officials; they provide some basic information about themselves, attend workshops, and receive subsistence aid. The Prosecutor's Office determines whether there are any pending criminal proceedings against them. The third phase depends on the Prosecutor's findings. If a criminal investigation, charge or conviction is pending for conspiracy or lesser crimes, they are pardoned and the criminal charges or investigations are terminated.[20] Subsequently, they are allowed to return to their places of origin where local authorities are responsible for providing them with basic services and assistance. If the Prosecutor's Office finds that they have criminal charges or convictions for serious crimes, they have to remain in a "concentration zone" awaiting a special process under the criminal justice system to be specifically established for demobilized combatants.

The definition of a special, more lenient framework for individuals responsible for grave crimes that cannot be granted amnesties or pardons under the existing legal framework is the object of the justice and peace legislation discussed in this chapter. Among the demobilized, an undisclosed number of men stand accused or convicted of serious crimes and await a definition of their legal situation in Santa Fe de Ralito.[21] The rest of the demobilized men who are charged or convicted of lesser crimes will benefit from Law 782 of 2002 and either their criminal investigations will be closed, charges will be dropped or they will be pardoned.

The legislation: "Justice and Peace Law"

In October 2003, President Uribe submitted to Congress a legislative initiative that established alternatives to imprisonment for members of armed groups. The Uribe administration claimed that this initiative, known as the Alternative Criminal Law, solved the prohibition on granting amnesties and pardons for atrocities set forth in criminal legislation and in Law 782 of 2002.[22] The government claimed to have based the initiative on the example of Northern Ireland. The two cases differ substantially, however. While in Northern Ireland the issue at stake was finding a legal framework for the release of the Irish Republican Army members in prison, in Colombia very few combatants are in prison and a very small number of criminal investigations result in prosecutions against or convictions of perpetrators of serious or lesser crimes.

In 2004 and 2005, several attempts to reach a consensus on modifications of the bill among Congress members and cabinet members failed as opposing views on accountability for grave crimes became more apparent. Finally, and under the leadership of President Uribe, a new version titled "Modified Draft Bill to the Justice and Peace Law" (JPL) was submitted to Congress, which borrowed elements from prior drafts. The JPL was approved by Congress on June 21, 2005 and was signed by President Uribe on July 25, 2005.[23]

The JPL claims that its purpose is to facilitate peace processes and the integration into civilian life of groups or individuals who are members of illegal armed groups, guaranteeing the victims rights to truth, justice and reparations. It aims to achieve those objectives by creating a legal framework for the investigation, judgment, punishment, and granting of benefits to members of illegal armed groups who demobilize and who may not be granted amnesties, pardons or any other benefit established in Law 782 of 2002. The bill establishes an alternative system of criminal justice, which entails the suspension of a criminal sentence and its replacement with an alternative punishment. Benefits are granted commensurate with the individual's contribution to attaining peace, justice, and reparations to the victims, as well as her or his resocialization.

The JPL defines an "illegal armed group" as a guerrilla or self-defense group, or a significant or integral part thereof, such as a *bloque* or *frente*, capable of launching sustained military actions, under a responsible command. It defines victims as persons who individually or collectively suffered direct damage as a result of crimes committed by illegal armed groups. Damage includes physical or mental injuries, emotional distress, economic loss, or violation of fundamental rights. The spouse, parent or child of a victim who was assassinated or disappeared is also a victim. The JPL also includes definitions of the rights to justice, truth, and reparations.

The JPL sets different conditions for individual and collective demobilizations. In the case of collective demobilizations, benefits may be granted to members of an illegal armed group who are investigated, accused or convicted for crimes committed in relation to their participation and membership in this group, and who may not benefit from Law 782 of 2002. As established in that law, their names must appear on the lists of demobilized individuals that the President sends to the

Prosecutor's Office. Other requirements established in the JPL include that: the group must have agreed with the executive branch to its demobilization and dismantling; property obtained as a result of illegal activities must be handed over; minors recruited to the group must be handed over to the state's child welfare agency; groups must put an end to all illegal activities and cease all obstruction of the free exercise of political rights; and that groups must not have been created for drug trafficking or illegal profit-making purposes. Members of illegal armed groups who are detained at the moment of the demobilization may benefit from the JPL.

Beneficiaries of individual demobilizations must fulfill similar requirements, including a need to show that the purpose of their activities could not have been drug trafficking or making illegal profits. In addition, individuals must provide information and collaborate in dismantling the organization to which they belonged.

The JPL provides for an oral hearing. Issues raised during the hearing must be resolved there, and notice of decisions is given during the hearing, pursuant to the newly implemented criminal procedure code. Beneficiaries may appoint defense counsel, and if they do not desire to do so, one will be appointed by the Public Defender's Office. The JPL creates a Special Unit for Peace and Justice within the Prosecutor's Office responsible for investigating the crimes to which this legislation applies and prosecuting them.[24] *Tribunales Superiores de Distrito Judicial* (Appellate Tribunals) are the competent courts for this special procedure. Additionally, the JPL creates a Judicial Counsel (*Procurador*) for Justice and Peace in order to assist victims.

In practice, the special procedure would work as follows. The Prosecutor's Office receives the names of those individuals who are demobilizing, and may open, or continue pending, criminal investigations against them. Individuals demobilizing may choose to submit their version of the facts to the Prosecutor, describing the crimes they committed, with the aid of an attorney. This is also the procedural opportunity to surrender any property for reparations to victims. If the individual enters a guilty plea, the Tribunal holds a hearing to confirm that he is doing so voluntarily. Once that is confirmed, a sentencing hearing is held in the next five days. If from other evidence or testimonies, the Prosecutor determines that one of the individuals demobilizing committed other crimes and omitted to mention them in his oral statement, he will ask the Tribunal to hear the charges.

All crimes committed by an individual while he was a member of the illegal armed group are integrated into one procedure, resulting in one conviction and one sentencing. Additionally, any prior convictions and sentences will be cumulated to this one. However, if the individual enters a guilty plea to some but not all the charges against him, the crimes for which he is not admitting his responsibility will continue to be dealt with under the regular criminal procedure. The punishment for the crimes for which he entered a guilty plea and/or collaborates as a witness or informant is cumulated to the alternative punishment. Furthermore, if after a ruling under the JPL or Law 782 of 2002 there is reason to believe that the individual committed other crimes related to his participation in the illegal armed group prior to his demobilization, those crimes will be investigated, prosecuted and judged under the ordinary criminal law. However, that individual may receive an alternative punishment if he enters a guilty plea or collaborates with the investigation of the crime. In that case, the alternative punishment would be cumulated to the punishment already imposed, abiding by the maximums set forth in the JPL. Finally, the decisions of the Tribunal may be appealed.

Reparations are considered in the same hearing, pending a prior request from the victim, the Prosecutor or the *Procurador*'s delegate. The Tribunal holds a hearing in the next five days in which evidence and arguments on reparations are presented. Parties are encouraged to reach a settlement. If that is not possible, the Tribunal rules on the reparations motion during sentencing.

During the sentencing phase, the Tribunal rules on the regular punishments the individual would otherwise face, as well as on alternative punishment. In the sentence, the Tribunal describes the actions the individual must undertake, the economic and moral reparations he must pay to the victims and any loss of property to be used for reparations. Alternative punishments consist of a prison term of between five and eight years, depending upon the nature of the crimes and the degree of collaboration offered. Beneficiaries must contribute to their resocialization through work, study or teaching during their imprisonment term, and promote the demobilization of the illegal armed group to which they belonged. Additional prison term reductions are not applicable. However, the principle of lenity applies and accordingly, if an individual is sentenced to a prison term of less than five years, he will serve that term instead of an alternative sentence. Additionally, once the alternative prison term is served, the individual is released on probation for one half of the prison term served. The alternative punishment may be revoked if the individual fails to comply with the probation terms, which entail obligations such as appearing periodically before the Tribunal, informing of any change of address; refraining from committing any crimes; and observing good behavior.

The JPL grants the government the power to determine where alternative prison terms should be served. It provides that those places should be similar to the rest of the prisons in terms of "safety and austerity", but contemplates the possibility of serving prison terms abroad. Additionally, up to 18 months of the time individuals spent in the concentration zones during the negotiation process, should be counted as time served.

The JPL establishes that the state has the obligation to protect the rights of the victims: to privacy; to their safety, and that of their relatives and witnesses; to reparations, provided by the perpetrator of the crime; to be heard and be permitted to present evidence; to receive adequate information for the protection of their rights; to know the truth about the crimes committed against them; to be informed of the decision to prosecute and to challenge it; to be represented by an attorney or the Procurator's Office; to receive assistance for their physical or mental recovery; and to a translator or interpreter if necessary; and to receive humane and dignified treatment.

In those cases in which it is not possible to identify the perpetrators, but the link between the harm caused and the illegal armed group benefiting from this law is established, the Tribunal should order the Reparations Fund to pay reparations to the victims. The JPL defines reparations as the duties to restitution, compensation, rehabilitation and satisfaction. Accordingly, for a beneficiary of the JPL to be released on probation, he must have handed property for reparations over to the Victims Reparations Fund (VRF), carried out the reparation actions he was ordered to do, and collaborated with the National Commission on Reparations and Reconciliation (NCRR), or signed an agreement with the Tribunal promising to comply with such obligations. The JPL lists the following as reparation actions: handing over to the state illegally obtained property; public statements that re-establish the victims' dignity; public acknowledgment of the harm caused to the victims, expressing remorse, asking for forgiveness and promising not to commit those crimes again; and providing effective collaboration in finding and identifying kidnapped or disappeared persons and the human remains of victims.

The JPL creates the NCRR. Its members are the Vice-President, the *Procurador* General, the Minister of Interior and Justice, the Minister of Finance, the Director of the Social Solidarity Network, the Ombudsman, and two representatives of victims' organizations. The JPL also creates Regional Commissions for the Restitution of Property, responsible for promoting actions to reclaim property rights, and a Victims

Reparations Fund administered by the Social Solidarity Network. The assets of the Fund will be the property handed over by the beneficiaries of this law, public resources and donations.

The NCRR is created for an eight-year term. Its functions include: to guarantee the participation of victims in judicial proceedings and in the protection of their rights; to submit a public report on the reasons for the emergence and evolution of illegal armed groups; to follow up and verify demobilization processes (including the possibility of inviting international organizations or foreigners to participate in this activity); to follow up and periodically evaluate reparations – as established in this law – and make recommendations; to submit a report to the government on reparations to victims; to recommend reparations criteria to the VRF; to supervise the administration of the VRF; to coordinate the Regional Commissions for Restitution of Property; and to carry out reconciliation actions aimed at preventing new violent acts.

The JPL establishes the obligation of the state to preserve historic memory, which in this case includes the causes, developments, and consequences of the actions of illegal armed groups. It also indicates that the right to truth entails the preservation of archives and that access to them should be permitted to victims and their relatives, as well as to researchers, ensuring the right to privacy of victims of sexual violence, and avoiding causing unnecessary harm to the victims.

The JPL considered under international standards

The JPL represents a leap forward in contrast to the blanket amnesties passed in other countries of the region on the 1970s and 1980s. It contemplates a procedure to investigate the facts, pass judgment on the crimes, punish the perpetrators, and provide redress to the victims, while demobilizing combatants. As such, it reflects both a perceived need to meet the demands of international and regional law and to "talk the talk" of transitional justice. However, some important aspects of the legislation need to be improved in order to render it consistent with international standards. Next, we examine issues in the JPL that are cause for concern.

First, the JPL assumes that there is an effective, functioning justice system, with ongoing criminal investigations on cases relating to the armed conflict. That is not the case, however. There are significant gaps and failures in the collection of evidence, cases do not result in convictions, and worse still, many cases do not reach the indictment stage. It is important that the government considers the conditions under which the JPL will be implemented, in order to create a realistic and sensible mechanism. The government has not followed previous recommendations of international bodies concerning the justice system. The inefficient justice system is probably one of the most important factors in the human rights crisis in Colombia. Thus, there is no reason to think that, without sustained attention, the new institutions will fare any differently, yet the entire scheme rests on the fragile base of existing criminal investigations and proceedings.

Second, from a practical perspective, it is necessary to consider the implications of the procedure set forth in the JPL. The Prosecutor's Office has only 60 days to carry out the criminal investigation resulting in charges against an individual. Allowing ample time for the investigation is fundamental in light of the complexity of the crimes, the armed groups' organization and command responsibility structure, and the difficulties in gathering evidence. However, once the individual is charged with an indictment, the procedure is swift, particularly if the individual decides to enter a guilty plea. Special consideration should be given to the rule that orders the cumulation of all criminal procedures against an individual into one single procedure as it presents practical difficulties, given that investigations will not advance simultaneously. It may force the Prosecutor to close pending investigations in order to comply, thus leaving crimes unsolved.

Third, the JPL favors the interests of demobilized individuals over those of the victims and society at large. A demobilized individual may obtain an alternative punishment for crimes for which he was convicted prior to the demobilization, during the demobilization, and even after he was sentenced to an alternative punishment. In all of these cases, it is sufficient that he collaborates with the criminal investigations or that he enters a guilty plea. The victim, on the other hand, has only one procedural opportunity to request a reparations motion. Additionally, for convictions that do not take place during the demobilization, the victim must initiate reparation motions according to the regular, more cumbersome, procedure.

Fourth, the allocation of resources is essential for the success of the JPL. Therefore, concerns have been raised regarding whether the Prosecutor's Unit specially created by the JPL will have sufficient staff and resources to carry out all the pending criminal investigations and prosecutions. This is a crucial element to ensure that the process does not result in impunity. Accordingly, efforts should focus on strengthening the capacity and resources of this Unit.

Fifth, victim status granted under the JPL should abide by international standards. A remarkable feature is that its definition of victims applies the standards set forth by the Inter-American Court, that is, it considers the victims' relatives as victims themselves. However, it also includes in its definition of victims members of the Armed Forces and the Police who suffered direct harm as a result of the action of non-state armed groups, and their relatives. Granting victim status to members of state armed groups flies in the face of basic norms of international humanitarian law, as it blurs the fundamental principle of a distinction between combatants and non-combatants.

Sixth, the JPL should be consistent with its main objective of demobilizing combatants, rather than attempting to achieve contradictory goals. Following the procedure set forth in Law 782 of 2002, which contemplates individual and collective demobilizations, the JPL sets forth the possibility of granting alternative punishments in both situations. While supporters of individual demobilizations consider them necessary to encourage desertions from non-state armed groups, opponents criticize them for deflecting efforts to bring pressure for collective demobilizations. The JPL establishes that demobilizing individuals must collaborate in dismantling the organization to which they belonged. The underlying purpose is to co-opt combatants. Rather than focusing on offering conditions that ensure that combatants effectively and safely demobilize, and that allow them to find a livelihood unrelated to the conflict, the JPL promotes betrayal and demands that combatants continue to be involved in the conflict.

Seventh, the confession of demobilized individuals should be a requirement of the JPL. There have been ample discussions concerning whether confession should be mandatory or voluntary. The JPL has opted for the latter, arguing that individuals cannot be forced to incriminate themselves, much less when the result of a confession is a conviction.[25] Demanding confessions and admissions of their participation in an armed group could have provided invaluable information to ensure and protect the victims' right to truth as well as the general truth-seeking process. This seems particularly relevant for a society in which the links between illegal armed groups, state agents, and private actors merits disclosure and debate in order to facilitate dismantling these organizations and resolving the conflict. Such a requirement would also assist the reparations process set forth in the JPL. Additionally, individuals would not be forced to incriminate themselves, but would do so willingly in exchange for an alternative punishment, similar to other plea bargains.

Eighth, alternative punishments fail to consider the crimes committed, focusing only on the threat of future violence. The punishments established in the JPL are more lenient than regular ones in several ways. These include their duration; the possibility that up to 18 months of the time spent in a concentration zone during the negotiation and investigation of the crime be counted as time served; the possibility that they may be served in another country; and the special facilities in which they will be served. Bases for granting alternative punishments include the individual's contribution to achieving peace, his collaboration with the justice system, the payment of reparations to the victims, and his resocialization.[26] The lack of focus on the severity, scope and role in the crimes committed, privileging the status of the perpetrators and their possible contribution to a peace process undermines the victims' rights to justice, truth, and reparations, and rewards perpetrators. Furthermore, it creates incentives for recidivism and impunity.

Ninth, victims have no voice during the process: they are only heard during the reparations motion and if the Prosecution calls them as witnesses during the trial. On the other hand, because it is not in the victims' power to initiate a criminal investigation, if the Prosecutor decides to ask the Judge to close an investigation or a case, they will not have an opportunity to find out what happened. From another perspective, the swiftness of the procedure can also damage the right to know the truth. These failures could have been partially resolved by the NCRR. However, the NCRR's mandate is to explore the causes of the armed conflict and the evolution of armed groups, but not account for the victims and human rights violations in general. The draft does, however, establish the obligation to preserve the archives, which may in the future result in complementary mechanisms that guarantee and protect the victims' rights.

Tenth, the JPL does not establish the state's responsibility to pay reparations to the victims in cases in which state agents participated in the crimes or when the state failed to ensure and protect the victims' rights. Even though the JPL contemplates the victims' right to reparations, it is contingent on the demobilization of the armed group or the individual perpetrator. According to some international human rights bodies, the state is obliged to pay reparations for violations committed by paramilitary groups acting in connivance with state agents. The Inter-American Court established the responsibility of the Colombian state in the creation and support of self-defense groups, which later became paramilitary organizations dedicated to unlawful activities.[27] In the case of *19 Merchants* v. *Colombia*, the Court ordered the state to pay reparations for material and immaterial damages, offer medical and psychological assistance to the victims, and undertake other actions in the form of non-monetary reparations, including a public apology, investigation and disclosure of all that can reasonably be known about the fate of the victims, access to archives, and effective measures to prevent violations from recurring.[28]

Eleventh, the JPL has limited application and victims of most crimes committed during the armed conflict will not have procedural opportunities to seek reparations. The JPL only applies to the gravest crimes, for which amnesty cannot be granted, when the authors of such crimes are demobilizing. Hence, most crimes committed during the armed conflict will not be investigated or punished and their victims will have to seek reparations through a civil action when perpetrators demobilize, in application of Law 782 of 2002, or through a reparations motion in a regular criminal proceeding if the crimes are investigated and prosecuted and the perpetrators have not effectively demobilized. Victims of state agents' actions will have to claim their right to reparations through a regular procedure, provided that they can demonstrate state responsibility. This creates unnecessary divisions among victims.

Twelfth, the JPL should allocate sufficient funds for reparations. As established in the JPL, individuals demobilizing will pay reparations with property unlawfully obtained. It is problematic, to say the least, that their obligation to pay reparations is limited to unlawful property and that the rest of their patrimony is exempted. If property unlawfully obtained is insufficient, reparations should be covered through the Victims Reparations Fund. On the other hand, the JPL establishes that the VRF will be ordered to pay reparations in cases where the perpetrator could not be identified, but the harm and its link with the activities of the illegal group was demonstrated. This is a positive addition aiming at protecting the victims from impunity. However, it may still result in a serious obstacle for victims because, in many cases, they may lack evidence and adequate representation to demonstrate the armed group's responsibility.

As described above, there are three sources of funding for the VRF: unlawfully obtained property handed over by individuals and groups demobilizing, public resources, and donations. The VRF will most likely face a shortage of funds as the JPL does not specify the proportion of state contributions. On the other hand, experiences from other countries show that reparations are not particularly attractive to donors. Victims' rights cannot be subject to the uncertain expectation of receiving donations.

Thirteenth, in terms of non-economic reparations, the actions demobilized individuals must carry out seem to follow the criteria established by international law. However, some of them are more likely the responsibility of the state. For example, the JPL establishes the obligation of demobilized individuals to perform certain actions in order to reestablish the victims' dignity. It is difficult to imagine that victims' dignity depends on the perpetrators' actions; the state has a paramount role to play. Satisfaction measures and the assurance that events will not happen again would also contribute to this objective.

Fourteenth, definitions of related crimes and political crimes in the JPL should be carefully considered as they will have a significant impact in a post-conflict society. Illustrative of the importance of drug trafficking in Colombia, the issue that has generated the most heated debates has been whether drug related crimes should be treated as related crimes and thus cumulated and included in the alternative punishment scheme. Drug trafficking crimes committed by armed groups to fund their activities, and also the possibility that drug traffickers could pose as members of armed groups and benefit from alternative punishment, constitute major concerns. While granting alternative punishments for crimes against humanity and war crimes generates little hesitation among government officials, this is not the case with drug trafficking. Drug crimes capture more attention and concern in Colombia than crimes against humanity and war crimes. Furthermore, there is more awareness of the issue of extradition to the United States on drug trafficking charges, than for crimes committed against foreigners on the basis of passive personality or universal jurisdiction. This also reflects the tension between those who reject and those who accept the penetration of drug trafficking within Colombian society.

The extradition issue lurks in the background of the talks. It surfaces, for example, in the debate over the reformulation of the crime of sedition to include self-defense groups. The paramilitaries are interested in attaining the status of political offenders, in an attempt to shield themselves from extradition.[29] The Uribe administration has explained its support of a wider definition of sedition, in an effort to equate paramilitaries with guerrillas, acknowledging the political nature of their organization and their crimes. In practical terms, reformulating the crime of sedition would have no impact on paramilitaries' cases, since this crime would be covered under Law 782 of 2002 and amnesty would be granted for it. Again, concerns regarding the possibility of extradition – particularly for drug related crimes – rather than principled opposition to granting political status to paramilitaries have weighed on this debate.

Fifteenth, the International Criminal Court (ICC) constitutes a new international factor conditioning the resolution of the conflict.

The Rome Statute came into effect for Colombia on November 1, 2002.[30] A few days after its ratification, the government revealed that it had invoked Article 124, which allows states to limit the jurisdiction of the Court over war crimes for a seven-year period. However, to the extent that the crimes involved constituted widespread or systematic attacks on civilians, the ICC will have jurisdiction under Article 7 regarding crimes against humanity.

The ICC has jurisdiction only if the state "is unwilling or unable genuinely to carry out the investigation or prosecution." Among the circumstances under which the Court would find unwillingness on the part of the state, the Rome Statute mentions domestic prosecutions for the purpose of shielding. There might be some discussion regarding Colombia's willingness to prosecute and whether the JPL is a form of shielding.

The JPL appears to have been conceived in an effort to try to avoid triggering the ICC's jurisdiction. First, it is framed not as an amnesty law, but as a criminal proceeding that results in an alternative sentence. If there were no prosecution efforts at all, but rather a refusal to investigate or prosecute, Articles 17 and 20 of the Rome Statute would not be applicable and thus the ICC would have jurisdiction over the crimes. The existence of a proceeding, however flawed, raises Articles 17 and 20 barriers, shifting the burden to the Prosecutor who has to show that the proceedings are being carried out without adequate independence, or that there is an undue delay.

An indicator of shielding could be a disproportionately lenient sentence in light of the gravity of the crime. According to the Rome Statute, when imposing a sentence, the Court should take into account such factors as the gravity of the crime and the individual circumstances of the convicted person. The Court itself is to issue sentences of up to thirty years or life imprisonment, and may reduce them in exchange for cooperation. However, any sentence reduction must be the result of an individualized hearing, and may only take place after the person has served two-thirds of the sentence (or 25 years).[31] While this would suggest that the Court may regard across-the-board probation or even five- to eight-year sentences as too lenient, Article 80 seems to give states some leeway in imposing sentences, as it establishes the principle of non-prejudice to the application of domestic penalties and laws. It is not clear whether a post-conviction suspension of sentence or probation, even in exchange for information or reparations, would be considered within this margin of leeway, or whether, as we believe, it would be so disproportionate, given the heinous nature of the crimes at issue, as to inevitably constitute evidence of shielding.

Conclusions

A peace process that brings a resolution to Colombia's long lasting and bloody internal armed conflict may become a foundational moment that would help to cement a society respectful of human rights. In this scenario, the interplay of domestic and international legal factors exerts pressure towards a political process where certain ethical and legal imperatives must be respected. In this process international standards and institutions will play a pivotal role.

As the discussion on the legality and wisdom of the JPL proceeds, the main underlying issue is whether it takes all necessary and possible steps towards dismantling illegal armed groups. This issue is linked to truth related efforts. Many claim that in the case of paramilitary groups, there are strong interests opposing truth-seeking and truth-telling mechanisms as they would result in uncovering the identities of prominent figures who funded and supported such groups. Another key element is the relationship between drug trafficking and armed actors. Finding a way to differentiate drug trafficking as a funding source for paramilitaries or guerrillas and drug traffickers trying to become paramilitaries or guerrillas in an effort to benefit from the political status granted to armed actors has become crucial. In spite of international and domestic pressures to separate these actions, they appear to be intertwined. Thus, the resolution of this issue will be fundamental for the success or failure of the paramilitary demobilization process and its legal framework.

A number of issues emerged as the JPL was approved by Congress. First, the Uribe administration lacks a clear plan for carrying out the demobilization process and seems oblivious to the appropriate legal framework that should inform that process. Second, the Uribe administration's position of denying the existence of an armed conflict has had a negative impact on the legislative process creating confusion and contradiction among legislators. This denial results in the lack of an open public debate about what Colombian society is willing to accept in exchange for the demobilization of an armed actor. Third, the lack of information and understanding of international legal standards and of the conditions that would trigger the action of international criminal justice and human rights bodies is evident. Further educational and promotional efforts are necessary in order to create the conditions for informed decisions. Fourth, a greater commitment on the part of armed actors to a peace process and unilateral gestures such as respect for declared cease-fires, release of kidnapped persons, or information on the disappeared would contribute to the process as indicators of the good will of all parties. Fifth, the voices of the victims have not been adequately represented in this debate and thus have not been duly considered.

The success of the negotiation process will depend on the creation of a democratic procedure aimed at dismantling non-state armed actors by legal means. Hence, it is important to convoke broad segments of society, particularly victims. The JPL does very little to allow victims, as opposed to perpetrators, a voice. In order to complement the action of justice, initiatives that enable the narrative integration of the past need to be considered. Victims should be granted an opportunity to give their own fullest account of events. Testimonies are crucial to overcome impunity and demand that memory be exercised as a social practice. Additionally, these projects further contribute to create a narrative that will give meaning to past events, and thus help to buttress a broad social agreement demanding that grave acts of violence should not be repeated. These initiatives also create the opportunity for an integral revision of the past and of the conditions that made such violence possible.

The state has ample room to maneuver to ensure and protect the victims' rights. There are no pre-set formulas: it is possible to turn to available tools, adapt mechanisms used in other countries, or create new ones that respond to emerging needs. In this process the participation of judges is crucial because they are the only ones who can guarantee the right to justice, embracing the rights of the accused to due process and the legal acknowledgment of the victims.

The legality of the JPL has already been challenged in the Colombian Constitutional Court, and debates around it continue. Internal and international influences will impact the process and influence its outcome. Domestic and international legal frameworks create opportunities and also establish limits to state actions. If the Colombian state fails to abide by those standards, international bodies will have the opportunity to act. The pressures of the armed actors to receive the most favorable treatment will confront an international legal regime that establishes the right to truth, justice, and reparations.

The challenge is for the JPL to stand both the test of the Colombian legal system and international legal standards. The experience of other Latin American countries cannot be disregarded. After more than two decades, the attempts to unilaterally close efforts to obtain justice have been unsuccessful. The argument that impunity strengthens democracy has been proven wrong: impunity undermines democracy. Recent history shows that democracy will grow strong if it is capable of ensuring that those who break the law and undermine democracy pay a heavy price. That is the lesson that any pacification process should leave engraved on Colombian hearts and minds.

NOTES

*The authors wish to express their gratitude to Naomi Roht-Arriaza, Juan E. Méndez, Andreas Feldmann and Steve Kostas for their comments and suggestions. Authors appear in alphabetical order.

1. Approved by Congress through Law 742 of 2002, reviewed by the Constitutional Court of Colombia, Judgment C-578, July 30, 2002.
2. There are no reliable statistics, but it is estimated that between 100,000 and 300,000 persons were killed between 1948 and 1957. Marco Palacios, *Entre la Legitimidad y la Violencia, Colombia 1875–1994* (Santafé de Bogotá: Editorial Norma, 1995), pp. 221–35; and Gonzalo Sánchez, "La Violencia y sus Efectos en el Sistema Político Colombiano", in Rafael Pardo, ed., *El Siglo Pasado, Colombia: Economía, Política y Sociedad*, (Bogotá: Centro de Estudios de la Realidad Colombiana and Red Multibanca Colpatria, 2001) p. 325.
3. See, Robert H. Dix, *The Politics of Colombia*, (New York: Praeger Publishers, 1987), pp. 31–156; and Gabriel Silva, "El Origen del Frente Nacional y el Gobierno de la Junta Militar", in Rafael Pardo, ed., *El Siglo Pasado*, pp. 351–88.
4. Alfredo Rangel, "Las Farc-Ep: una Mirada Actual", in *Reconocer la Guerra para Construir la Paz*, ed. Malcolm Deas and Maria Victoria Llorente (Santafé de Bogotá: Cerec, Ediciones Uniandes, Grupo Editorial Norma, 1999), pp. 21–51.
5. Andrés Peñate, "El Sendero Estratégico del ELN: del Idealismo Guevarista al Clientelismo Armado", in *Reconocer la Guerra para Construir la Paz*, ed. Malcolm Deas and Maria Victoria Llorente (Santafé de Bogotá: Cerec, Ediciones Uniandes, Grupo Editorial Norma, 1999), pp. 53–98.
6. Human Rights Watch, *Colombia: the Ties that Bind: Colombia and Military-Paramilitary Links* (Washington DC: Human Rights Watch, 2000).
7. Mauricio Romero, *Paramilitares y Autodefensas 1982–2003* (Bogotá: IEPRI and Editorial Planeta Colombiana, 2003).
8. See Camilo Echandía, "Expansión Territorial de las Guerrillas Colombianas: Geografía, Economía y Violencia", in *Reconocer la Guerra para Construir la Paz*, eds. Malcolm Deas and Maria Victoria Llorente, pp. 99–149; and Bushnell, *The Making of Modern Colombia*, pp. 259–68.
9. Military and Police assistance programs to Colombia have fluctuated between: 88.6 in 1997; 112.5 in 1998; 308.8 in 1999; 765.3 in 2000; 242.6 in 2001; 401.9 in 2002; 621 in 2003; 549.7 in 2004; and it is estimated to reach 629.5 in 2005 (figures in millions of dollars). See Center for International Policy, Colombia Program http://www.ciponline.org/colombia/aidtable.htm.
10. Bruce Michael Bagley, "Colombia y la Guerra contra las Drogas", in Rafael Pardo, ed., *El Siglo Pasado*, pp. 389–423.
11. Vicepresidencia de la República, Programa Presidencial de los Derechos Humanos y Derecho Internacional Humanitario, Observatorio de los Derechos Humanos en Colombia, cited in United Nations Development Program, *El Conflicto, Callejón con Salida. Informe Nacional de Desarrollo Humano, Colombia – 2003* (Bogotá: United Nations Development Program, 2003), http://www.pnud.org.co/indh2003, 53.

12. For the success and failures of these efforts see, e.g. José Noé Ríos, "El Conflicto Armado Interno en Perspectiva," in Hernando Roa Suárez, Vicente Torrijos R. eds., *¿Es Posible la Paz en Colombia?* (Bogotá, Escuela de Altos Gobiernos, ESAP, 1998), pp. 61–74.

13. International Crisis Group, *Hostages for Prisoners: A Way to Peace in Colombia?* Latin America Briefing International Crisis Group (Bogotá/Brussels: March 8, 2004).

14. Resolution 185, December 23, 2002.

15. Santa Fé de Ralito Agreement to Contribute to Peace in Colombia between the Government and Autodefensas Unidas de Colombia, July 15, 2003, available at http://www.altocomisionadoparalapaz.gov.co/acuerdos/acuerdos_t/jul_15_03.htm (March 28, 2004).

16. The AUC is divided into *Bloques* (Blocks), which exercise military control over a geographical area.

17. One year later, most of those men were studying primary, secondary, or college education, and/or receiving job training. Of the 850 demobilized BCN members, 660 were hired by the Medellín Mayor's Office. On the other hand, 15 demobilized BCN members were assassinated, and 34 were detained for crimes committed after their demobilization.

18. Arrest warrants will be suspended as long as the men remain inside the location zone. The agreement came into force on June 15, by Resolutions 091 and 092 of 2004, and is renewable every six months. Agreement between the National Government and the AUC for the Location Zone in Tierralta, Córdoba, available at http://www.altocomisionadoparalapaz.gov.co/c_conjuntos/comunicado.htm

19. See, Asociación de Familiares de Detenidos Desaparecidos, Asfaddes and others, letter to Sergio Caramagna, Head of the OAS Mission to Support the Peace Process in Colombia (MAPP/OAS), June 30, 2004.

20. According to Law 782 of 2002, serious crimes include terrorism, kidnappings, genocide, and homicide against a person who is hors de combat or against a defenseless victim. All others are lesser crimes.

21. They are investigated or charged with crimes of kidnappings, forced disappearances and homicides.

22. República de Colombia, Proyecto de Ley Estatutaria 085 de 2003 Senado, *Por la cual se dictan disposiciones en procura de la reincorporación de miembros de grupos armados que contribuyan de manera efectiva a la consecución de la paz nacional* (October 6, 2003).

23. República de Colombia, Ley 975 dc 2005 (July 25, 2005).

24. The Special Unit for Peace and Justice would consist of: 20 Prosecutors, 20 Assistant Prosecutors, 150 crime investigators, 15 secretaries, 15 judicial assistants, 20 drivers, 40 bodyguards, and 15 assistant crime investigators.

25. The example of the South African Truth and Reconciliation Commission has been invoked to claim that a confession can only be demanded in exchange for amnesty.

26. Alternative punishments consist of a prison term of between five and eight years and an additional probation term of one half of the prison term served. Regular punishments established in the Penal Code for crimes for which the

JPL apply range from 8–15 years for torture, to up to 40 years for genocide or aggravated homicide.

27. Case of *19 Merchants* v. *Colombia*, Judgment of July 5, 2004, Inter-Am. Ct. H.R. (Ser. C) No. 109, par 116, 118, 124.
28. Case of *19 Merchants* v. *Colombia*, para. 229.
29. As described previously, the Colombian legal framework does not allow extradition for political crimes. However, it should be noted that members of FARC have been extradited to the United States for drug-trafficking crimes, regardless of other indictments pending against them in Colombia for other crimes, including political crimes.
30. Rome Statute of the International Criminal Court, July 17, 1998, 2187 U.N.T.S. 90.
31. Rome Statute, Articles 77 and 110.

6   Hybrid attempts at accountability for serious crimes in Timor Leste

Caitlin Reiger

Introduction

We are all here to build a high quality of justice - this Special Panel takes part in the building of international justice and hereby the international community to stop impunity.[1]

[T]he objective of prosecuting and punishing the perpetrators of the serious crimes committed in East Timor in 1999 is to avoid impunity and thereby to promote national reconciliation and the restoration of peace.[2]

After twenty-four years of illegal military occupation by Indonesia, in late 1999 East Timor emerged into a transition period of United Nations administration for two and a half years. Recovery from the violence and devastation wrought by the departing Indonesian forces was not yet complete when the new nation of the Democratic Republic of Timor Leste was declared on May 20, 2002.[3] During the intervening period, the first trial for crimes against humanity committed by pro-Indonesia militia members took place before Timor Leste's Special Panels for Serious Crimes in the capital Dili, opening and closing with the grand aspirations described in the above quotations. Like Sierra Leone and other states described in this volume, Timor Leste adopted a twin track to the question of accountability and reconciliation with the country's difficult past, combining retributive and restorative justice through criminal trials as well as a Commission for Reception, Truth and Reconciliation (CAVR). Simultaneously, neighboring Indonesia has now conducted its own trials for crimes committed in 1999 in Timor Leste, through its Ad Hoc Human Rights Court. As the CAVR is analyzed in greater detail in Chapter 7 below, it will be examined here only to the extent of its overlap and interaction with the formal prosecution of serious crimes.

One of the defining features of Timor Leste's experience with transitional justice has been the coexistence of these multiple and hybrid efforts to provide accountability for the human rights violations that

143

had occurred in the territory. A congruence of political and historical factors has seen the various efforts sometimes overlapping, sometimes competing, sometimes complementing one another. It is in this context that this chapter examines the development and implementation of formal justice initiatives for serious crimes within Timor Leste.[4] The Special Panels for Serious Crimes are often described as a hybrid tribunal due to the blend of national and international features, although a strikingly different hybrid model to the Special Court for Sierra Leone, the hybrid courts in Kosovo or the proposed Extraordinary Chambers in Cambodia.[5] They exemplify some of the dangers and limitations, as well as the potential, of these hybrid efforts.

This chapter will only briefly consider the history and nature of the human rights violations, leaving most of the historical information to Chapter 7. It will outline the national and international imperatives for transitional justice in Timor Leste, and the sequencing and establishment of the Special Panels for Serious Crimes and the Serious Crimes Unit to investigate and prosecute those violations. The next sections will consider the complementary and conflicting relationships of these institutions with both the CAVR and the Jakarta trials. Finally, the achievements of the Special Panels are evaluated in the light of the assumptions that are increasingly made about hybrid tribunals: that they can provide an international standard of justice at reduced cost and at a faster pace than the ad hoc international criminal tribunals for the former Yugoslavia and Rwanda; that they have the potential for a legacy of a justice process that is relevant to the local community, especially the victims; and finally, that they can help rebuild a sustainable justice system based on the rule of law.

As recounted elsewhere, Indonesia invaded the Portuguese colony of Timor Leste on December 7, 1975. Over the next 24 years, it carried out military offensives against pro-independence guerilla forces, during which hundreds of thousands of Timorese died as a result of massive military assaults against civilians, starvation and disease resulting from forced displacement. Torture, disappearances, land confiscation, forced sterilizations and general intimidation followed. In January 1999, new Indonesian President Habibie agreed to hold a UN-supervised referendum, leaving security in the hands of Indonesian military and police. These security forces attempted to control the outcome of the referendum through the creation of East Timorese militias. When, on August 30, 1999, the population overwhelmingly voted for independence, the security forces and militias exacted vengeance through massive forcible displacement and violence that left at least 1,300 people dead and near total devastation of the territory's property and infrastructure.[6] Thus, while the post-ballot violence was extreme because of its intensity and the scale of the physical destruction, it occurred against a backdrop of almost 25 years of protracted abuses and followed familiar patterns.

Transitional justice imperatives

After a multinational peacekeeping force had re-established security, the UN Security Council placed the half-island under the full executive and legislative control of the UN Transitional Administration for East Timor (UNTAET) with the objective of preparing the territory for independence.[7] Although the Security Council mandate included specific responsibility for "the administration of justice", it made only general mention of the need for justice for past abuses and the importance of reconciliation, neither of which received any coordinated early attention by UNTAET due to the overwhelming humanitarian crisis.[8] UNTAET's task included managing the initial post-conflict humanitarian emergency of a largely homeless population, establishing the ground-work for developing basic state infrastructure, including governance institutions and a public administration. It was also tasked with disarming FALINTIL, the resistance guerilla force, managing relations with Indonesia and facilitating the return of the large numbers of displaced people still in camps in West Timor under the control of militias.[9] At the very least, however, there was a clear "moral imperative" for the UN to make some arrangements towards justice.[10] The Secretary-General told the General Assembly in late 1999 that:

[a]ccounting for the violations of human rights which occurred in the aftermath of the consultation process is vital to ensure a lasting resolution of the conflict and the establishment of the rule of law in East Timor.[11]

East Timorese demands for justice focused on the establishment of an ad hoc international criminal tribunal, such as those created for the former Yugoslavia and Rwanda. These calls were echoed by UN-commissioned reports into the causes of the atrocities,[12] which concluded that accountability was a matter of international collective responsibility:

the United Nations, as an organization, has a vested interest in participating in the entire process of investigation, establishing responsibility and punishing those responsible and in promoting reconciliation. Effectively dealing with this issue will be important for ensuring that future Security Council decisions are respected.[13]

Nevertheless, the international community preferred a double-track of *national* mechanisms for accountability: within Indonesia, as well as within Timor Leste.[14] Indonesia's fragile democratic development after the fall of the Suharto regime was still dependent on the support of the powerful military, whose actions would have been directly challenged by the establishment of an international tribunal, a risk that the Security Council was not prepared to take. Whether or not the East Timorese people were prepared to take such a risk is difficult to assess, as the Indonesian withdrawal had left a power vacuum and the resistance leadership was largely consumed with the humanitarian crisis.

Yet it was not simply the case that purely *national* processes were to achieve this *international* aim. Leaving aside the Indonesian process for a moment, action within Timor Leste could never be merely a national effort, not least because of the hybrid nature of the situation. National sovereignty was temporarily being exercised by the international community on behalf of the East Timorese. The UN's highest human rights official, Mary Robinson, stated that the international community had a duty under international law and practice to do its utmost to hold perpetrators accountable and provide justice to victims.[15] Whether or not UNTAET was under a duty to prosecute those responsible for the international crimes, either in its national or international capacity it at least had the right to do so.

The establishment of a parallel Commission of Inquiry by the Indonesian Human Rights Commission was seen as an encouraging sign. However, human rights observers (both internationally and within Timor Leste) never believed that relying on Indonesia to provide accountability was a feasible solution, particularly due to the power still exercised by the Indonesian military. Three UN Special Rapporteurs recommended in December 1999:

Unless, in a matter of months, the steps taken by the Government of Indonesia to investigate TNI [Indonesian Armed Forces] involvement in the past year's atrocities bear fruit, both in the way of credible clarification of the facts and the bringing to justice of the perpetrators – both directly and by virtue of command responsibility, however high the level of responsibility – the Security Council should consider the establishment of an international criminal tribunal for the purpose.[16]

It was no coincidence that the reluctance within the Security Council to pursue this recommendation occurred at a time of well-publicized donor fatigue and sustained criticism of the International Criminal Tribunals for Rwanda and the former Yugoslavia over the lengthy duration of trials and the lack of recognisable results in those tribunals.[17] While the transitional justice goals of an independent Timor Leste were not elaborated much further by the international community than the extracts noted above, it is clear that newer – and what were hoped to be faster and cheaper – hybrid models of international/national justice were gaining favour, as the parallel developments in Cambodia and Kosovo demonstrate.

At the same time, however, UNTAET's primary task in terms of justice was the creation from scratch of a judicial system and re-establishment of the rule of law. At a physical level, all infrastructure such as court and prison buildings, books and records had been comprehensively destroyed during the "scorched earth" method employed during the withdrawal of the TNI and militias. A far greater problem was the lack of human resources. All previously serving judges and prosecutors, and the majority of lawyers and court staff, had been Indonesians who had fled the territory.[18] Widespread and ongoing lawlessness was a serious problem, which meant that the issue of justice for past atrocities became caught up in the realities of providing present and future justice through the creation of a temporary court system staffed by inexperienced, newly appointed East Timorese judges and lawyers. International judges were initially rejected on the basis that they would undermine local ownership of the justice system, but it soon became apparent that the newly appointed judiciary needed considerable help.[19] While the newly appointed East Timorese judges certainly saw themselves as appointed to deal with past crimes,[20] the key UNTAET judicial policy maker at the time has since noted that the East Timorese lawyers were "so inexperienced as to be unequal to the task of serving in a new East Timorese justice system"[21] and in particular, that the "prosecution and trial of legally and factually complex criminal offences such as crimes against humanity . . . should not be left solely to largely inexperienced lawyers, however committed they may be."[22]

A belated realization of the enormity of the task seems to be the primary explanation for the reversal of the initial policy decision that subsequently saw the focus shift from national empowerment to reliance on international judges to cover the national skills gap. Given the lack of political and financial support for a separate international tribunal, the task therefore fell on UNTAET to combine the retributive and reconciliation goals already mentioned with the additional demand to build the capacity of the fledgling East Timorese judiciary. Yet the shift was not accompanied by a considered assessment of how to ensure a sustainable process.

Initial investigations

Prior to the creation of the Special Panels, investigations into the recent atrocities were being undertaken by the UNTAET Human Rights Unit (HRU) during late 1999, as the pressing tasks of preserving evidence demanded attention.[23] In early 2000 a separate Serious Crimes Investigation Unit (SCIU) was established to take over the task, with the UN Civilian Police to conduct the criminal investigations. This marginalized many of those involved at the early stage and resulted in the loss of critical continuity in the process. Several months later, responsibility shifted again. When the Special Panels were established in mid-2000, UNTAET also created a Public Prosecution Service, which included a specialized unit to prosecute serious crimes.[24] At this point, the SCIU was transferred from the HRU to the responsibility of the international General Prosecutor. In contrast to the HRU, the initial personnel brought in to staff the SCIU have been widely criticized for their failure to involve East Timorese in their work, in particular some of the key national human rights organizations who had extensive documentation and information about the violations. Unlike the new SCIU staff, many HRU officers were recruited by the UN Office of the High Commissioner for Human Rights from international human rights organizations and had both local language skills and long-standing connections with local NGOs, which were lost once the responsibility for the investigations was transferred. The new investigators were either unaware of the level of expertise available within the community, or from an intended impartiality were suspicious of offers of assistance.

At a local level this lack of early consultation and respect led to a refusal to cooperate by these national organizations when later approached, a situation which severely hampered both community relations and the progress of investigations.[25] In particular, early SCIU investigations were criticized for failing to focus on the systematic nature of the violations that had occurred during 1999 and the role played by the Indonesian military apparatus, instead treating them as individual criminal cases, which was reflected in the fact that initial indictments included only ordinary domestic charges of murder, rather than crimes against humanity.[26]

The establishment of the Special Panels for Serious Crimes

In mid-2000 UNTAET established Special Panels of the Dili District Court to try cases of "serious criminal offences".[27] It was intended that they could "reconcile the need for expeditious prosecution and trial of serious crimes with the requirement of ensuring experience and expertise in the process", given "the potential impact on the reconciliation process both within East Timorese society and between East Timor and Indonesia."[28] The idea was drawn from the only other UN peacekeeping mission that was also acting as a temporary governing authority, the UN transitional administration in Kosovo, which was planning to establish a specialized mixed War and Ethnic Crimes Court, although that proposal never in fact proceeded.[29] In Timor Leste as in Kosovo, there was no possibility of creating a hybrid court by treaty as was subsequently done in Sierra Leone and Cambodia, as there was no independent national government with whom to contract; it was simply a matter of national legislative action, albeit exercised by the United Nations. The mixed jurisdictional basis for the creation of the Special Panels arose both from UNTAET's power as territorial ruler after the withdrawal of the de facto occupying power, as well as from universal jurisdiction over crimes against humanity on behalf of the international community.[30]

The UNTAET regulation stated that each Special Panel was to be composed of two international judges and one East Timorese judge, with similarly constituted panels of the Court of Appeal.[31] Two panels were constituted, along with the Appeals panel. These judges were selected by a Transitional Judicial Services Commission, but its home within a UN peacekeeping mission saw the recruitment process bound by bureaucratic requirements. None of the judges chosen had any background in international criminal law, or in some cases even criminal law. While one of the first judges appointed was from Portuguese-speaking Brazil, as the primary language of East Timorese lawyers was Indonesian and it was difficult to find appropriate interpreters, this judge found it easier to work in English. As was the case throughout the new judicial system, the Special Panels had no administrative or research support, and were funded from the meagre trust fund established for the reconstruction of the nation by voluntary contributions from international donors, leading to frequent staff turnover and consequent disruption and delays. Conceptually, the Special Panels were clearly part of the *national* court system, albeit a transitional one. Furthermore, they were established as part of what can also be seen as a little used and much maligned formal justice system, which for many East Timorese remained quite separate from their daily experiences with traditional village-level justice mechanisms.

The reliance on international involvement that characterized the recruitment of judges, prosecutors and investigators, however, was not matched in the other aspects of the Special Panel system. A small Public Defenders' Office was initially staffed only by several young East Timorese lawyers with minimal resources, who were also handling all basic legal assistance in matters before the ordinary courts. While some additional defense lawyers were seconded by international NGOs, it was not until late 2002 that a separate Serious Crimes Defense Unit was established by UNMISET (UN Mission for Support for East Timor), UNTAET's successor mission. International staff members within the unit soon reported no interaction with the East Timorese defense lawyers working on ordinary crimes, who seem to have lost what limited interest they may have had in defending those accused of serious crimes.[32] Similarly, only minimal attention was ever paid to court administration and chambers support for the Special Panels.[33] After sustained criticism of the functioning of the Special Panels, in late 2002 UNMISET finally created a small support unit for the judges, including researchers and translators, composed almost entirely of international staff.

The law applied by the Special Panels was also a hybrid, as the Indonesian laws previously in force continue to apply, subject to any inconsistency with international human rights law and any laws subsequently made by UNTAET.[34] The jurisdictional scope of the Special Panels included the international offences of war crimes, crimes against humanity, genocide and torture (whenever and wherever they occurred), and the national crimes of murder and sexual offenses that occurred within the territory of East Timor between January 1, 1999 and October 25, 1999. The definitions of the international crimes, as well as the modes of criminal liability and defenses, were adopted largely verbatim from the ICC Statute.[35] The definitions of the national crimes came from the Indonesian Penal Code. An UNTAET transitional criminal procedure code applied to both serious and ordinary criminal proceedings, that itself was a combination of civil and common law as well as elements from the ICC Statute and Rules of Procedure. In addition to the legal confusion, hearings were frequently conducted in all the four official languages of the Special Panels (Portuguese, English, Tetun and Indonesian).

In summary, it is important to note that the creation of the Special Panels and what became the Serious Crimes Unit (SCU) was not an integrated process based on any prior planning; it was a series of ad hoc responses to a crisis situation. The two organs developed quite separately, and never really functioned as a single institution. Nor is there evidence of any meaningful consultation between UNTAET and the East Timorese authorities at the time, and the subsequent lukewarm support for the Special Panels from key Timorese decision makers suggests a lack of any clear policy towards national prosecutions both at the time and since. The pressures to develop a functioning national court system at the same time as demonstrating that serious crimes were being dealt with contributed to poorly planned integration of the investigative and judicial organs of what ultimately became the Special

Panels. While it is not surprising that investigations commenced first, there was no structure within which they were supposed to fit for many months. Similarly, the continuation of the disparity between the attention and resources paid to the development of the SCU on the one hand, and the court system and provision of defense services on the other hand (even once a structure had been created), has led to critical credibility problems of the process as a whole. Furthermore, whereas in Sierra Leone the Truth and Reconciliation Commission was part of the political settlement of the conflict and predated the plans to create the Special Court, in Timor Leste the process was reversed. This has meant that the Special Panels and the criminal investigations of serious crimes have enjoyed at best an ambiguous relationship with political settlement efforts. The attempts to induce senior militia leaders to return from West Timor, along with the East Timorese refugees in camps under their control, have often seemed to contradict and undermine the SCU's commitment to accountability.[36]

Achievements of the Serious Crimes Process

Slightly over four years after it was established, the SCU came to an end in May 2005 after the Security Council mandate for UNMISET finally concluded. Investigations were stopped in November 2004 and the final trials completed before the Special Panels in April 2005. However, this was a completion date necessitated by the lack of support to continue, and many investigations were simply unable to be completed before the Security Council imposed deadlines. A total of 95 indictments were issued against 391 individuals. Of the 101 defendants that came before the Special Panels, 87 received final verdicts, with the remaining cases either withdrawn or dismissed.[37] In comparison with other international criminal tribunals this seems like a remarkable achievement in many respects. While initially most of the indictments contained isolated charges of murder only against seemingly unconnected individuals, this was primarily due to the need to process detainees who had been in custody for long periods while the major investigations were still continuing. The vast majority of those early indictees were low-level militia members, often illiterate peasants whose circumstances meant that poverty or lack of other options made them vulnerable to recruitment – forced or otherwise – into the plans of the Indonesian armed forces. The long-term nature of the occupation and the popular resistance to it also meant that many of these young men or old farmers who appeared in court, testified as to their concurrent role in the clandestine resistance movement and emphasized their lack of choice. Only one former member of the resistance guerilla force, FALINTIL, has been indicted and was one of the first to be tried and convicted. Since those early months, however, the majority of the indictments ultimately issued included charges of crimes against humanity, on counts such as murder, persecution, inhumane treatment, torture and several major rape cases. The progress of the investigations higher up the chain of command also led to many of the later indictees being members of the Indonesian armed forces or senior militia leaders, culminating in the indictment of General Wiranto, the former head of the Indonesian military.

Despite the inclusion in the subject-matter jurisdiction of the Special Panels, no indictments included charges of genocide or war crimes. Characterizing the atrocities during this period as war crimes was legally more difficult given that one of the parties (FALINTIL) to the conflict had remained cantoned during 1999.[38] While references to genocide had been made during the Indonesian occupation, none of the reports or investigations found evidence of genocidal acts during 1999.[39]

Of the 75 people convicted, several were convicted of lesser offences than those charged in the indictment and three were acquitted on all charges.[40] All persons tried were East Timorese. Observers expressed concern about adherence to human rights and fair trial standards, noting that many accused persons spent long periods in pre-trial detention and that the rate of progress may in part have been due to the poor quality of the defense.[41]

The funding and personnel support to the Special Panels and SCU remained heavily dependent on UNMISET, which inherited the serious crimes project from UNTAET. UNMISET's mandate was initially due to expire in May 2004, and there were protracted discussions over the future of both the SCU and the Special Panels and the completion strategy for the caseload. Both an internal review conducted by UNMISET in September 2003 and an independent report in January 2004 recommended the extension of the SCU mandate and significant ongoing support for the Special Panels.[42] They warned that otherwise, the Serious Crimes Project as a whole in Timor Leste would effectively collapse, as the domestic capacity had not yet reached a stage – nor were the domestic financial resources sufficient – to complete even the existing cases, let alone continue investigations.[43] The downsizing of the SCU began in August 2003, when offices in outlying areas were closed. The Security Council granted a reprieve of a further year, after the Secretary-General emphasised the weak state of the justice sector in general as well as it being "essential to make progress towards completing the serious crimes process."[44]

With the closure of the SCU, it remains unclear whether the government of Timor Leste will also close the Special Panels.

Relationship with the CAVR

The Commission, known by its Portuguese acronym "CAVR", was established in July 2001. In stark contrast to the establishment of either the Special Panels or the SCU, the CAVR was the result of careful planning and consultation, which revealed a clear community demand for reconciliation that did not involve forgetting about justice.[45] Its seven national commissioners were selected by a Panel composed of a broad range of civil society groups, including victims' organizations, and it also had regional offices and staff. It was an independent statutory authority established to inquire into and report on human rights violations committed in the context of political conflicts in the territory between April 1974 and October 1999. Its initial two-year mandate was extended until 2005, and its final national public hearing was completed in late March 2004. The Commission submitted its final report to the President on October 31, 2005.

The Commission was consciously designed as a complementary mechanism to the Serious Crimes process, as well as in recognition of the low capacity of the ordinary justice system. For this reason, its functions went beyond truth-seeking and making recommendations to government. As discussed in Chapter 7, a key function was to facilitate community-level reconciliation by overseeing local panels, known as Community Reconciliation Procedures (CRPs), to mediate between victims and low-level perpetrators of lesser crimes with the aim of reaching agreements that involve non-penal forms of accountability (such as public apologies or community work). These agreements were then registered with the local court and operate as a bar to future prosecution. The CAVR did not have the power to grant amnesties and, most significantly, was never intended to deal with serious criminal offences that fell within the jurisdiction of the Special Panels.

Nevertheless, in both theory and practice there were areas of potential overlap and ambiguity. Many of the crimes that became the subject of CRPs included serious beatings and intimidation, arson and killing of livestock. Yet many of these same acts, if knowingly committed as part of a widespread or systematic campaign against the civilian population, could well have been classified as persecution or inhuman treatment amounting to crimes against humanity. The regulations that defined the relationship between the SCU and CAVR were drafted so that the reference point in distinguishing between their respective mandates focused on the *crimes* committed rather than the *role* played by the individual. The nature of widespread international crimes depends on the involvement of large numbers of perpetrators, and so focusing on the crimes may mean that lower level perpetrators of serious crimes are caught between the various processes. Over time, the SCU, in line with the tendency in other international tribunals and after legitimate early criticism, moved towards focusing its resources on investigating and prosecuting those who bear greater levels of responsibility despite the lack of any statutory guidance on this aspect of personal jurisdiction of the Special Panels.

In order to ensure that cases involving serious crimes were not inadvertently taken up by the Commission, all statements received from offenders were to be vetted by the General Prosecutor within fourteen days. This added a significant burden to the existing work of the SCU, which in turn caused frustrating delays for the Commission. A Memorandum of Understanding between the CAVR and SCU was entered into to formalize the relationship between the institutions but was not entirely successful. The Commission noticed a lack of consistency in the decisions taken within the SCU that was attributed to insufficient clarity of prosecutorial strategy on issues that could be covered by the mandates of both institutions. Within the SCU the lack of consistency was explained as depending on which particular prosecutor was tasked to deal with the statement. Mostly, the name of the CAVR deponent wishing to participate in a CRP was simply fed into an SCU database to see if it matched that of a suspect under investigation, rather than handled through a considered legal analysis of the evidence and the possible criminal characterization. Given the range of extremely common name combinations in Timor Leste, this was not a particularly reliable method.[46] Finally, the registration of CRPs was often not possible due to the relevant local district court not being fully operational.

However, the CAVR, both as an independent body and as a non-prosecutorial mechanism, was able to remedy several of the obstacles facing the Special Panels and SCU. Reconciliation and justice are not just required between those who supported independence and those who did not. Old political differences, united by resistance to the Indonesian occupation, have begun to re-emerge within a democratic framework, and remain a subject of considerable sensitivity. Although an attempt in 2002 immediately after independence by President Gusmão to introduce an amnesty law for all past crimes was widely criticized and immediately thwarted within Parliament, the issue has not disappeared entirely from the agenda. While there are still loud calls for justice to be done for the crimes of 1999, there is clearly far more political ambivalence in relation to the pre-1999 period, particularly those allegations of crimes committed by the resistance movement.[47] The fact that the General Prosecutor is East Timorese and formally part of the government has made it more difficult for him to proceed with investigations against FALINTIL leaders.[48] The SCU was not able to progress with investigations, much less prosecutions, of atrocities that occurred prior to 1999 even where political ambivalence may not have existed, whereas the CAVR conducted several major public hearings into various aspects of the 1974–98 period. Besides the initial violence immediately following the Indonesian invasion, East Timorese often cite such notorious incidents as the 1983 Kraras massacre in Viqueque and the 1991 attack on mourners at the Santa Cruz cemetery in Dili as more deserving of justice than "lesser incidents" during 1999 that have been the subject of trials before the Special Panels.

The complementary nature of the CAVR's design was a creative response to the particularities of the situation and community expectations in Timor Leste. However, it was founded on several presumptions about the operation of both the SCU and the court system as a whole. These included a presumption, which did not become reality until quite late in its life, that the SCU was directed by clear prosecutorial strategy about the prosecution of lower-level perpetrators of serious crimes and agreed policy between the two institutions about how to resolve the areas of jurisdictional overlap, and furthermore, overly optimistic expectations that the ordinary formal court system would be able to fulfill its part of the process by becoming fully operational by the time CRPs were being registered.

Relations with Indonesia

Throughout the life of both the Special Panels and the CAVR, relations with Indonesia have been ever present. The security situation in general is now relatively stable, with the exception of ongoing occasional border incursions from West Timor. There has not been outright public opposition to the Special Panels' decisions (as opposed to frustration), although that is no doubt due to the fact that many of the supporters of those accused and convicted are not in the territory or are in the minority. Considerable numbers of pro-Indonesian East Timorese militia leaders and members have remained in Indonesia since they withdrew together with the departing forces. If they were to return, the situation could well change. Yet encouraging them – and with them the thousands of East Timorese living in poor conditions in camps under their control – to return continues to be a political priority for President Xanana Gusmão, and to some extent for the United Nations, which maintains an ongoing although dwindling military and civilian presence.[49] Furthermore, a sentiment often expressed in Timor Leste is that reconciliation will remain limited unless all who are responsible for the atrocities of the past are present.

Indonesia did eventually proceed with trials of its own as it had promised the Security Council in late 1999. In November 2000 a Law on Human Rights Courts was adopted, granting jurisdiction over crimes against humanity and genocide.[50] An ad hoc court was established under this law to hear cases relating to Timor Leste, although its jurisdiction was constrained further by temporal and geographic restrictions imposed by Presidential Decrees. Only eighteen individuals were tried as part of this process.

A full consideration of the Jakarta trials is beyond the scope of this chapter, but they have been the subject of extensive criticism by observers.[51] Despite the strong recommendations for prosecution contained in the original Indonesian Human Rights Commission's Inquiry, only a handful of senior military officers were prosecuted; most trials resulted in either acquittals or incredibly lenient sentences. The charges in the indictments were weak, and crucial evidence in support was not offered to the Court despite cooperation from the SCU in Dili that extended to facilitating the transfer of two witnesses. While there was never any formal relationship between the Special Panels and the Ad Hoc Human Rights Court, the mutual implications of each process may be examined further in future. Fifteen of the eighteen Jakarta defendants were also indicted by the SCU, and four of these were convicted of crimes against humanity and sentenced to several years' imprisonment. Any application of the prohibition on double jeopardy or being tried twice (*ne bis in idem*) contained in the Timor Leste Transitional Rules of Criminal Procedure would require judicial consideration of whether the Jakarta trials were conducted in accordance with international due process standards and an intention to bring the person to justice.[52]

Furthermore, the significance of the Jakarta trials becomes apparent when contrasted against the lack of enforcement mechanisms available to the Special Panels. Unlike the ICTY or ICTR, there was no direct Security Council authorization under Chapter VII of the UN Charter compelling states to cooperate with the Special Panels or SCU. Of the 440 people ultimately indicted, an estimated 339 remain in Indonesia and effectively beyond the reach of the Special Panels, including the vast majority of those indicted as part of the ten priority cases and all of the highest level accused. Efforts to gain custody of these indictees (and other suspects), many of whom are just across the land border with Indonesian West Timor, focused on overwhelmingly unsuccessful negotiations with Indonesia. A Memorandum of Understanding (MOU) was signed by the former Attorney-General of Indonesia and UNTAET during 2000, under which each party agreed to cooperate in matters of criminal investigations and witnesses.[53] The SCU made numerous requests to Indonesia, which were all refused or ignored, including on the basis that the MOU was never validly incorporated into Indonesian law. Perhaps most significant was the lack of international pressure brought to bear on Indonesia in this regard.[54] Although there is still no extradition treaty between Indonesia and Timor Leste, the SCU registered 263 arrest warrants for indictees with INTERPOL, including against a number of Indonesians.[55] These Indonesians include several high-ranking members of the Indonesian military who were indicted by the SCU for a broad range of crimes against humanity, including murder, forced deportation and persecution. The accused included the former Indonesian Minister of Defense and Commander of the Armed Forces, General Wiranto. In May 2005, none of these warrants had been executed.

The lack of cross-border enforcement powers was probably one of the single greatest design flaws in the entire serious crimes process, and it became the main obstacle to its success in the eyes of many national and international observers. This prompted the need to find alternate legal strategies. Although there was some limited internal consideration of a "Rule 61 procedure" as exists at the ICTY, whereby a public hearing is conducted after the non-execution of an arrest warrant, this was never taken up by either UNTAET or the East Timorese government. Perhaps even more creative was the filing of a motion by the Deputy General Prosecutor for Serious Crimes, seeking a public hearing before the Special Panels on the *issuing* of an arrest warrant against General Wiranto in late January 2004 to address concerns about political inter-ference in the judicial process and provide an opportunity for a public airing of witness testimony.[56] The inability to proceed with many of these major cases has arguably resulted in the CAVR public hearings, rather than the trials, presenting the main opportunity for the establish-ment of an historical record. While this may be convenient and a more appropriate role for a non-prosecutorial mechanism, the lack of coordination between the institutions suggests that this may be more serendipitous than the result of any planned strategy.

Although President Gusmao explicitly stated his opposition to pro-ceeding against Indonesian senior figures, within the Timorese political leadership the messages were initially more confused, fluctuating be-tween renewed calls for an international tribunal to an increasing con-sensus to focus on building better security, political and economic relations across the border.[57] This culminated in the establishment in March 2005 of a bilateral Commission for Truth and Friendship established by the governments of Timor Leste and Indonesia, to deal with issues related to the violence of 1999. While the Commission is empowered to recommend amnesties for those responsible for human rights violations and to rehabilitate those who have been "wrongly accused", it has no mandate to recommend reparations and, according to its terms of reference, its process "will not lead to prosecutions." As a result, it has been widely criticized by both East Timorese and international human rights groups.[58]

Providing an international standard of justice

Although the notion that international justice is of a "better" quality than national efforts is problematic, adherence to international fair trial standards is a useful benchmark. Arguably the area of greatest concern was to bring an international standard of justice to the internationalized process to ensure respect for the rights of the accused. The disparity between the defense and prosecution before the Special Panels described earlier was self-evident: in the first fourteen trials not a single defence witness appeared. The lack of expertise among both national and international judges, and financial and administrative hurdles to adequate staffing, resulted in confusing judgments where only minimal and contradictory reference was made to international jurisprudence.[59] The hybrid composition of the Special Panels and the restrictions imposed by both the UN's recruitment practices and domestic political preferences for Portuguese-speakers cumulatively resulted in frequent turnover of international judicial staff on short-term contracts, which led to disruptions and long delays between hearings.

Hybrid justice may be possible at a lower cost than international justice, but it still needs sufficient resources to complete its task. The Special Panels were established by UNTAET without the benefit of prior planning or assessment of the potential financial, personnel and other resource needs. In Dili, UNTAET's attention was stretched in many directions due to its role as temporary governor of the territory; although judges were appointed, some law declared and a courthouse refurbished, the practicalities of running a justice system received little priority. The Special Panels were not initially given any separate budget, but expected to function out of the same small pool of funds established for the entire transitional justice sector.[60] Although the Special Panels enjoyed some better facilities than the other national courts, they continued to suffer from inadequate resources. While the SCU accessed general UN funds ("assessed contributions"), the Special Panels were funded out of voluntary contributions.

Should internationalized tribunals be treated with more flexibility and understanding than international criminal courts on the issue of compliance with fair trial standards? There is a risk that international involvement will just confer "unwarranted legitimacy" on sub-standard processes.[61] It would seem that such an approach simultaneously undermines the original justification for such a hybrid process yet also reflects the realities of post-conflict situations, leading one observer to warn that "the UN must not, as it has in East Timor, use the hybrid status of [a] tribunal to justify its failure to meet international standards of judicial fairness and integrity."[62] Interestingly, these problems were foreseen to an extent by the UN Special Rapporteurs who visited Timor Leste in late 1999. In their report to the UN General Assembly they acknowledged the enormity of the task of fully investigating and documenting responsibility for the crimes that had occurred, stating: "[t]he East Timorese judicial system, which still needs to be created and tested, could not hope to cope with a project of this scale."[63]

National relevance

The Special Panels were created not by a national government, but by foreigners acting in its place. Rather than being the result of careful consideration and consultation with the East Timorese community, the process was developed within the UN mission in response to the exigencies of the situation at hand, by reference to a model that had been planned for Kosovo.[64] This affected the levels of East Timorese participation in the Special Panels, the accessibility and local understanding of the process, and the extent to which it interacted with other restorative justice and national political initiatives. However, there seems to be a sense that while prosecutions were international initiatives, they were generally welcomed as consistent with community demands for justice. The problem, initially at least, lay in the practical implementation.

The physical presence in Timor Leste of the Special Panels should have provided a visible sign of commitment to punishing those responsible and restoring dignity to victims. Yet a largely illiterate population, scattered throughout inaccessible mountains with poor communications needed more than a court sitting in the capital. Despite the combined international attention and interest within the East Timorese community, no official public outreach program exists for publicizing or explaining the court's work.[65] Whereas all the indictments before the Special Court for Sierra Leone to date have relied exclusively on international offences, in Timor Leste an early lack of clear prosecutorial strategy led to an initial tendency to "undercharge" some accused on domestic individual murder charges, which created misunderstandings of the court's jurisdiction and gave the impression that these cases were either unconnected or not as serious as others.[66] While initially there was great frustration among victim communities and East Timorese NGOs that the Court was too slow and focusing on the "small fry" rather than targeting the leaders behind the human rights violations, several stakeholders noted that this perception shifted significantly after the indictment of General Wiranto.[67]

At a general level, however, there was no real contact between victims' organizations and the Special Panels. The management and strategic direction problems within the SCU in its first two years led to a lack of continuity and communication as part of the investigation and evidence gathering process, which caused unnecessary grief for victims and families when this resulted in repeated interviews and even multiple exhumations of relatives' graves.

Particularly telling on the limits of national ownership of these processes was the controversy which arose after the issuance in early 2003 of the long awaited indictments that contained allegations which provided the macro picture of how the campaign to comprehensively destroy Timor Leste was conceived of, planned, prepared for, executed and covered up by high-ranking individuals. Yet while community groups and human rights NGOs in Timor Leste and internationally welcomed the indictments, there was a conspicuous silence by both UN officials in Timor Leste and the national government. The silence was broken by President Xanana Gusmão, one of the strongest advocates of reconciliation and forgiveness in the name of forging a stable peace, who announced that he believed the indictments were not in Timor Leste's national interest, which depended on good relations with Indonesia. He went on to reiterate that because the SCU was a UN creation, "then the international community must hold the responsibility for administering that justice and organising the structures and mechanisms to that effect."[68]

Even more curiously, UN officials in Dili were simultaneously publicly denying responsibility for the indictments, while quietly ordering the then-Deputy General Prosecutor (herself a UN employee) to reissue the indictments on the letterhead of the Public Prosecution Service of Timor Leste, rather than the UN letterhead upon which all other serious crimes indictments had been issued previously. The UN Mission of Support in East Timor issued a separate press release to that of the Serious Crimes Unit, "clarifying" that:

[w]hile indictments are prepared by international staff, they are issued under the legal authority of the Timorese Prosecutor-General. The United Nations does not have any legal authority to issue indictments.[69]

While UNMISET was in the process of winding down its role in Timor Leste, an internal report stated that:

[the Serious Crimes Program (SCP)], which has been largely internationally operated is clearly perceived by the Government as the responsibility of the international community. It is also reasonably clear that it is politically and financially convenient to the Government of Timor-Leste for the responsibility for the SCP to rest with the international community, particularly in the context of Timor-Leste's continued reliance upon the international community for financial support, and in the face of the emerging realities of the politics of the Indonesian-Timor-Leste bilateral relationship.[70]

Within the upper echelons of East Timorese politics, the Special Panels were simultaneously regarded as not enough like a proper international tribunal, or indeed all too close to one. The hybrid tribunal lurched from a joint national/international enterprise to one in which both the national and international authorities publicly disowned it. The conceptual confusion led to the abdication of responsibility by both parties. Research suggests that broader popular expectations may not accept this denial of national responsibility.

As the international community withdrew further from the control of the Special Panels and SCU, national elite politics seemed to be privileging a particular narrative that not only obscures responsibility for past crimes committed by the pro-independence resistance, but also protects present and future relations with a large and formerly aggressive neighboring state. Despite their shortcomings, if the Special Panels had been created in a way that ensured greater levels of national political ownership of the process, these considerations might well have dictated developments from the outset. The detailed allegations contained in the indictments that were issued, even if they are never tested at trial, at least provide a formal – although partial – legacy through a record which seeks to contradict the popular revisionism that still prevails within Indonesia that the atrocities were the result of disgruntled East Timorese who opposed independence and a few rogue soldiers who helped them.

Contributing to the reconstruction of a justice system

Besides the legacy that may emerge through the establishment of an historical record, a more tangible legacy that should rightfully be expected of a hybrid tribunal would include the creation or furthering of a process that is sustainable beyond the inevitably temporary involvement of the international community. As described above, when the first East Timorese judges were provisionally appointed in early 2000, many were of the impression that they would be judging the serious crimes cases from 1999.[71] The fact that the Special Panels were created *within* the national court system raised a presumption that they would be part of a long-term transfer of skills and an ensuring that the process would be sustainable by national actors once the internationals withdrew. Yet besides the on-the-job training and mentoring that the two East Timorese Special Panel judges received, no attempt was made to rotate other East Timorese judges into the Special Panels or to conduct training that crossed over between the jurisdictions. Unless the international involvement is spread throughout the judicial system, as has been the case in Kosovo, the involvement of international colleagues should not be assumed to automatically result in a transfer of skills to the national level. Furthermore, the specialized and high-profile nature of the Special Panels with their international backing, while co-located within a struggling national justice system, led to the alienation of those national judicial officials who were excluded from participation. In Timor Leste, the differences in remuneration and appointment processes between national and international judges led to strikes and resentment within the East Timorese judiciary.[72]

These difficulties reflect a fundamental confusion about where justice for past atrocities fit into the puzzle of a UN peacekeeping operation that was also charged with preparing the country for independence. The tasks of developing the local judiciary and prosecuting serious crimes were all being undertaken by the UN, so the ambiguity was not at first apparent. Yet as the complexity of the longer-term needs of Timor Leste's justice system became clearer, the international community (through the UN budgetary committee) made it clear that while it was prepared to continue supporting the SCU as part of fulfilling its collective obligations to provide justice for gross violations of human rights, its provision of direct support to a domestic justice system was far more limited.[73] By the time UNTAET was handing over to the smaller follow-on mission UNMISET, the Secretary-General admitted to the Security Council that Timor Leste's judicial system was not yet fully functioning and still suffered from inadequate resources and not yet competent personnel, demanding ongoing international assistance for the foreseeable future.[74] By the time of UNMISET's conclusion, the situation was not significantly different. The process of building a justice system from scratch is necessarily a long and slow process, which in many ways seems antithetical to the primary goal of speedy, high quality justice.

The Special Panels were neither an independent international tribunal which may have been able to produce more efficient and just results, nor a fully integrated process dedicated to building local capacity throughout the system. Rather than being a hybrid model that strategically combined the best features of national and international tribunals, they have often seemed like a misfit that inherited the worst of both.

The implications of this have been far-reaching for both Timor Leste's search for justice and the development of international models of accountability. These are discussed further in the final section of this chapter.

Conclusion

Any evaluation of the Special Panels as a transitional justice mechanism must be seen in the light of the particular contextual factors facing Timor Leste, many of which are unlike other societies in transition. There was a total departure of the occupying forces (and the majority of perpetrators), the lack of a skilled national legal profession, special constraints imposed by the nature of emergency peacekeeping operations, the novelty of a UN transitional administration, and the post-colonial politics of an emerging nation.

Timor Leste's Special Panels were created entirely under an international umbrella, in the form of a UN transitional administration, but acting in the role of a national government. Structurally, they were localized within the national court system, but they were also just one of several institutions addressing the question of accountability for the past. This fluidity about the status of the Special Panels was both beneficial and constraining. Although the Special Panels and the SCU enjoyed some important "successes" in identifying and punishing a small handful of those East Timorese perpetrators responsible for the atrocities during 1999, the "fragmented accountability" that sees the high-level organizers and planners of the destruction remain out of the court's reach in Indonesia was an ongoing frustration for all involved.[75] Although a benefit of internationalization of such a process should have been to bring the weight of international pressure to bear, the repeated refusal by Indonesia to cooperate with the Timor Leste process, both in terms of access to evidence and transfer of suspects, left the SCU in the invidious position where its most important indictments against senior members of the Indonesian military were unlikely ever to proceed to trial. In the post-September 11 international environment, where the stability and goodwill of the world's largest secular Muslim nation assumes particular importance, it remains doubtful whether Indonesia will ever be held to account internationally. In February 2005, the UN Secretary-General established a three-member independent Commission of Experts to assess the progress made in bringing to justice those responsible for the serious violations of international humanitarian law and human rights in Timor Leste in 1999, both in terms of the Jakarta trials and the Special Panels.[76] On May 26, 2005, the Commission presented its report. It urged the Security Council either to continue supporting the SCU and Special Panels or to create some equivalent mechanism; to specifically investigate the high-level cases of Indonesian officers in Indonesian courts and, if credible investigations were not forthcoming, to reopen the question of an international ad hoc tribunal. In September 2005, the Security Council asked the Secretary-General to study the issue again.[77]

The international aspects of the Special Panels seemed to attract no discernible advantage over a fully integrated national process. Likewise, they did not produce the benefits of local relevance; instead, the aspects of the system that had barely been touched by the benefits of internationalization – namely the defence and judiciary –only belatedly received long overdue resources, and then at the cost of making the whole project more international, not more hybrid, as it did not lead to greater integrated involvement by East Timorese staff.

The Special Panels for Serious Crimes in Timor Leste therefore blur the lines between international and national efforts to prosecute serious human rights violations. They offer both hope and disappointment to those who desire to locate the new model of mixed tribunals still within the context of the teleological drive towards increased "internationalization" of accountability for human rights violations. They bore the weight of international expectations, but were faced with national realities; yet those same national realities are no longer acceptable excuses. Depending on the degree of political constraints and imperatives, hybrid courts can both represent international progress and conversely a retraction from international justice. It is exactly these contradictions that provide the adaptability and appeal of hybrid approaches to justice for international crimes, yet they also carry their own set of dangers.

The fact that Timor Leste's Special Panels were grafted onto the new national court system, rather than being created as a separate institution was due more to the coincidence of circumstances than any deliberate design as to whether they should have been primarily national or international in character. UNTAET was already in the process of building a new national judicial system from scratch, so it did not make any sense to create an entirely separate institution requiring duplication of scarce personnel and resources. However, the Panels' position within the ordinary court structure meant that they suffered many of the same teething problems and lack of support that affected the entire judicial system. The only way to remedy this was to increasingly treat the Special Panels as a separate institution, which contradicts much of the rationale behind their establishment. By way of contrast, Sierra Leone's Special Court arose from a national request, yet the UN had the relative luxury of being able to consider the concept and design an institution with greater clarity than in Timor Leste, as it was not bound by the same national imperatives. Within Timor Leste, the CAVR's independence from other institutions, and the time taken to consult and plan for its establishment, set it on a far stronger base.

Furthermore, the demands of providing speedy, efficient and fair prosecutions in a post-conflict environment are often quite different from the demands of rebuilding a justice system. Building capacity takes significant time and patience, and necessarily involves some mistakes as well as slows down the substantive work. Surely both need to occur together, and both are necessarily resource-intensive projects. On the one hand, there has been an increased focus on the importance of giving priority to national rule of law development after conflicts, and while this attention seems to be occurring mostly within policy and donor organizations, it is slowly spreading to planners of UN peace operations. On the other hand, the international criminal justice and human rights movements have been successful in making accountability for atrocities an imperative after conflicts. A hybrid tribunal of some sort does have the potential to become a bridge between national and international responses, but this may not always be possible, and requires careful forethought about the national and international contexts, and their compatibility with the specific national and international objectives. The tensions between the need to go fast and slow, to look to the past and the future, to rebuild while still trying to understand why it fell apart, must all be grappled with in all transitional justice projects. While Timor Leste's attempts at justice have only seen limited success, their coexistence with the CAVR at least means that the trials – be they national, international or something in between – are not expected to bear this burden alone.

NOTES

1. Opening statement of the Deputy General Prosecutor for Serious Crimes, Jean-Luis Gillisen of Belgium, at the commencement of the trial in the *Joni Marques* case on July 9, 2001 (transcript on file with author).
2. *Prosecutor* v. *Joni Marques and Others* Case no. 9/2000, Special Panel of the Dili District Court, judgment, December 11, 2001, paras. 979–80.
3. As East Timor changed its name to Timor Leste on independence, the new name will be used for consistency as much as possible.
4. Although informal justice initiatives through customary forms of dispute resolution have also occurred, they are beyond the scope of this paper.

5. For detailed discussion of Sierra Leone, see Chapters 1 and 2. Generally, see Suzannah Linton, "Cambodia, East Timor and Sierra Leone: Experiments in International Justice", (2001) *Criminal Law Forum*, 12, pp. 185–246.

6. A Security Council Mission was shocked by the level of destruction on their visit to the territory soon afterwards: *Report of the Security Council Mission to Jakarta and Dili 8 to 12 September 1999*, UN Document S/1999/976, September 14, 1999.

7. UNTAET was created by Security Council Resolution 1272, UN Document S/RES/1272, October 25, 1999.

8. Sidney Jones, *Human Rights and Peacekeeping in East Timor* (April 2001), Draft Paper prepared for the Aspen Institute (copy on file with author).

9. For further discussion of the breadth of UNTAET's mandate, see Joel Beauvais, "Benevolent Despotism: A Critique of UN State-Building in East Timor", (2001) *New York University Journal of International Law and Politics*, 33, 1101.

10. See Hansjorg Strohmeyer, "Making Multi-Lateral Interventions Work: The UN and the Creation of Transitional Justice Systems in Kosovo and East Timor", (2001) *Fletcher Forum of World Affairs*, 25, 107; also, Security Council Resolution 1264, UN Document S/RES/1264, September 15, 1999.

11. *Progress Report of the Secretary-General on the Question of East Timor*, UN Document A/54/654, December 13, 1999, para. 42.

12. *Special Rapporteurs' Report*, UN Document A/54/660, "Situation of Human Rights in East Timor", December 10, 1999, at para. 73; UN Document A/54/726, S/2000/59, "Report of the International Commission of Inquiry on East Timor to the Secretary-General", January 31, 2000.

13. *Ibid.*, para. 47. See also Security Council Resolution 1338, UN Document S/RES/1338, January 31, 2001 para. 8.

14. See, for example, the compromise resolution of the UN Commission for Human Rights in which it affirmed that "the international community will exert every effort to ensure that those responsible are brought to justice, while affirming that the primary responsibility for bringing perpetrators to justice rests with national judicial systems." Resolution adopted by the Special Session on East Timor, UN Doc. E/CN.4/S-4/L.1/Rev.1 at para. 4.

15. *Report of the High Commissioner for Human Rights on the Human Rights Situation in East Timor*, UN Document E/CN.4/S-4/CRP.1, September 17, 1999, para. 4.

16. *Ibid.*, para. 74.6.

17. For a detailed analysis of this issue, see *Report of the Group of Experts on the Effective Operation and Functioning of the International Criminal Tribunal for the Former Yugoslavia and of the International Criminal Tribunal for Rwanda*, UN Document A/54/634, November 22, 1999.

18. Hansjorg Strohmeyer, "Policing the Peace: Post-Conflict Judicial System Reconstruction in East Timor", (2001) *The University of New South Wales Law Journal*, 24, pp. 171–82 at p. 175.

19. For detailed criticism of the decision to place inexperienced East Timorese jurists in such positions without further prior intensive training, see Frederick Egonde-Ntende, "Building a New Judiciary in East Timor", (2001) *Commonwealth Judicial Journal*, 14(1), 22. Egonde-Ntende is a

Ugandan High Court Judge who was initially appointed as a judicial mentor and became one of the first international judges to serve on the Court of Appeal.

20. Jones, *Human Rights and Peacekeeping in East Timor*, note 8 above.

21. Strohmeyer, "Collapse and Reconstruction of a Judicial System: The United Nations Missions in Kosovo and East Timor", (2001) *American Journal of International Law*, 95, 46.

22. Strohmeyer "Making Multi-Lateral Interventions Work" above note 10.

23. For a detailed discussion of this early period, see Jones, *Human Rights and Peacekeeping in East Timor*, note 8 above.

24. *Regulation on the Establishment of a Public Prosecution Service* (June 6, 2000), UNTAET/REG/2000/16.

25. Interviews with Human Rights Unit staff and members of the NGO Yayasan Hak, Dili, September 2003.

26. See the discussion in Linton, "Cambodia, East Timor and Sierra Leone: Experiments in International Justice", note 5 above at p. 206, quoting the East Timor Action Network.

27. *Regulation on the Establishment of Panels with Exclusive Jurisdiction over Serious Criminal Offences* (June 6, 2000), UNTAET/REG/2000/15 (UNTAET Regulation 2000/15).

28. Strohmeyer, "Policing the Peace", note 18 above at p. 176; Strohmeyer, "Making Multi-Lateral Interventions Work", note 10 above at p. 118. Strohmeyer was the Acting Principal Legal Advisor in UNTAET during the time the Special Panels were created, having worked immediately prior to that in UNMIK in Kosovo.

29. See Suzannah Linton, "New Approaches to International Justice in Cambodia and East Timor", (2002) *International Review of the Red Cross*, 84, p. 93; Strohmeyer, "Making Multi-Lateral Interventions Work", note 10 above at 118–20.

30. Universal jurisdiction is explicitly asserted in the Regulation that created the Special Panels: section 2.

31. UNTAET Regulation 2000/15.

32. Interview with international public defenders and UNMISET staff, Dili, September 2003.

33. For further detail see "Judicial System Monitoring", *Justice in Practice: Human Rights in Court Administration* (November 2001), Thematic Report No. 1, Judicial System Monitoring Program http://www.jsmp.minihub.org/Reports/JSMP1.pdf.

34. Regulation on the Establishment of the United Nations Transitional Administration in East Timor (November 27, 1999) UNTAET/REG/1999/1.

35. A notable exception is the ICC defence of superior orders: section 21, UNTAET Regulation 2000/15.

36. See *Policy of Justice and Return Procedures* (March 2002), East Timor Serious Crimes Unit (copy on file with author).

37. Judge Phillip Rapoza, "The Serious Crimes Process in Timor-Leste: Accomplishments, Challenges and Lessons Learned", paper delivered on April 28, 2005, in Dili, Timor-Leste at the "International Symposium on UN

Peacekeeping Operations in Post-Conflict Timor-Leste: Accomplishments and Lessons Learned".

38. The first major investigation was undertaken by the Indonesian Human Rights Commission (KPP-HAM). The second was a special inquiry established by the UN Commission on Human Rights. Both reports were published on the same day, January 31, 2000 (see above, note 13). Notably, the Indonesian Commission declined to find that a state of war existed and found that there was no evidence therefore of war crimes. For a contrary view, see Suzannah Linton, "Cambodia, East Timor and Sierra Leone: Experiments in International Justice", note 5 above at pp. 208–210.

39. See, for example, Matthew Jardine, *East Timor: Genocide in Paradise* (Common Courage Press, 1999); Ben Saul, "Was the Conflict in East Timor 'Genocide' and Why Does It Matter?", (2001) *Melbourne Journal of International Law*, 2, 477.

40. JSMP Submission to the Commission of Experts, April 6, 2005.

41. For further detail see, *Justice for Timor Leste: The Way Forward* (April 14, 2004), AI Index: ASA 21/006/2004 Amnesty International and Judicial System Monitoring Program.

42. Judicial System Monitoring Programme, *The Future of the Serious Crimes Unit* (January 2004); UNMISET, *Strategic Plan for Timor-Leste Justice Sector: Post-UNMISET Continuing Requirements and Suggested Mechanisms* (September 24, 2003).

43. By May 2004, the SCU estimated that it would have completed only 40–50 percent of investigations into the approximately 1,400 murders that occurred during 1999: *Justice for Timor Leste: The Way Forward*, note 41 above, at p. 21.

44. See Special Report of the Secretary-General on the United Nations Mission of Support in East Timor, February 13, 2004, UN Doc S/2004/117, at para. 32.

45. The process of consultation was undertaken by a steering committee of East Timorese and internationals in late 2000–01. See, for example, "Establishing a Commission for Truth, Reception and Reconciliation in East Timor: Operating Principles and Mandate", Concept paper submitted to UNTAET Human Rights Unit, November 2, 2000 (copy on file with author).

46. Interview with General Prosecutor, Dili, September 2003.

47. For further detail on the proposed amnesty law, see *The Draft Law on Amnesty and Pardon* (November 2002), Judicial System Monitoring Programme.

48. Interview with General Prosecutor, Dili, September 2003.

49. In February 2004 this was estimated to number 28,000 former refugees: Special Report of the Secretary-General on the United Nations Mission of Support in East Timor, February 13, 2004, UN Doc. S/2004/117 at para. 9.

50. Law 26/2000.

51. For detailed examinations of the shortcomings of the trials, see David Cohen, *Intended to Fail: The Trials before the Ad Hoc Human Rights Court in Jakarta* (August 2003), International Center for Transitional Justice; also, *Justice for Timor Leste: The Way Forward*, note 41 above.

52. Section 4.2 of UNTAET Regulation 2000/30. See the discussion in *Justice for Timor Leste: The Way Forward*, note 41 above at pp. 8–9 and 58–9.

53. *Memorandum of Understanding Regarding Co-Operation in Legal, Judicial and Human Rights Related Matters* (April 6, 2000), UNTAET and Attorney-General of the Republic of Indonesia.

54. See the discussion in Nehal Bhuta, "Great Expectations – East Timor and the Vicissitudes of Externalised Justice", (2001) *Finnish Yearbook of International Law*, XII, pp. 179–203 at 190.

55. East Timor National Alliance for an International Tribunal, Press Release, February 15, 2004.

56. Jill Joliffe, "UN Accused of Blocking East Timor Warrants", *The Age*, January 14, 2004. The motion, however, was dismissed by the Court: *Prosecutor v. Wiranto and others*, Case No. 05/2003, Decision on the Motion of the Deputy General Prosecutor for a Hearing on the Application for an Arrest Warrant in the case of Wiranto, February 18, 2003. While a warrant has since been issued, the Timorese General Prosecutor (and Attorney-General) has refused to allow its implementation.

57. AP, "Timor Leste's Premier Wants War Crimes Court", *Straits Times*, May 31, 2003, http://straitstimes.asia1.com.sg; Jill Jolliffe, "Timor PM Slams UN on War Criminals", *Asia Times*, May 16, 2003, http://www. atimes. com/atimes/. Although initially more vocal supporters of holding Indonesia accountable, Prime Minister Mari Alkatiri and Foreign Minister Jose Ramos Horta have become increasingly reticent, particularly since the indictment against Wiranto was issued: see, for example, "Dili says relations with Republic of Indonesia more important than justice", *Jakarta Post*, March 5, 2003; "PM Alkatiri wants amnesty for crimes of 1999", *Lusa*, June 12, 2003.

58. JSMP Press Release, "'Commission of Truth and Friendship' Seeks to End the Search for Justice whilst 'Commission of Experts' Keeps it Alive", March 14, 2005.

59. For example, the court failed to apply international jurisprudence on the tests for crimes against humanity and the defenses of superior orders and duress. Suzannah Linton and Caitlin Reiger, "The Evolving Jurisprudence and Practice of East Timor's Special Panels for Serious Crimes on Admissions of Guilt, Duress, and Superior Orders", (2001) *Yearbook of International Humanitarian Law*, 4, 1.

60. David Cohen, "Seeking Justice on the Cheap: Is the East Timor Tribunal Really a Model for the Future?" (2002) *Asia Pacific Issues*, 61, 1.

61. Chris af Jochnick and Roger Normand, "The Legitimation of Violence: A Critical History of the Laws of War", (1994) *Harvard International Law Journal*, 35, 49 at p. 56.

62. Cohen, "Seeking Justice on the Cheap", note 60 above at p. 7, in reference to the proposed Extraordinary Chambers to prosecute the Khmer Rouge in Cambodia.

63. *Special Rapporteurs' Report*, para. 73.

64. The pre-eminent legal and human rights NGO Yayasan HAK was told of the proposal, described as a "back-door international tribunal", only after the

regulation had already been drafted: interview with Joaquim Fonseca (Yayasan HAK advocacy director), November 20, 2002.

65. *Justice in Practice: Human Rights in Court Administration*, note 33 above.

66. See Suzannah Linton, "Prosecuting Atrocities at the District Court of Dili", (2001b) *Melbourne Journal of International Law*, 2, p. 414.

67. Interviews with the following people: SCU Public Information Officer, former Head of UNTAET Human Rights Unit, and General Prosecutor, Dili, September 2003.

68. Kay Rala Xanana Gusmão, *Statement by His Excellency President of the Democratic Republic of Timor-Leste* (February 28, 2003), Dili, http://www.jsmp.minihub.org/Reports/otherresources/ xgonscu28feb03jr01mar03.htm.

69. UNMISET, *Press Release* (February 25, 2003), http://www.un.org/Depts/dpko/missions/unmiset/pr250203b.pdf.

70. UNMISET Strategic Plan for the Justice Sector, note 42 above at para. 8.

71. Jones, *Human Rights and Peacekeeping in East Timor*, note 8 above at p. 11.

72. Frederick Egonde-Ntende, "Building a New Judiciary in East Timor", note 19 above.

73. Within the international politics of peacekeeping operations, nation-building is seen as an inappropriate task for the UN to engage in or at least fund from the mandatory assessed contributions of states: see *A Review of Peace Operations: A Case for Change*, Conflict Security and Development Group, King's College London, April 30, 2003.

74. *Report of the High Commissioner for Human Rights*, note 15 above paras. 17–19. See also Ministry of Justice and United Nations Development Program, *Mission Report Timor Leste: Joint Assessment on the Judiciary System* (November 2002), UNDP, Dili.

75. Mohamed Othman, *East Timor: A "Viable" or "Clumsy" Model of Accountability for Serious Human Rights and International Humanitarian Law Violations* (2002), unpublished paper prepared at the Chr. Michelsen Institute of Development Studies and Human Rights.

76. Letter dated January 11, 2005, from the Secretary-General addressed to the President of the Security Council (Timor Leste, Independent Commission of Experts), UN Doc. S/2005/96, February 18, 2005.

77. UN Security Council, letter dated June 24, 2005, from the Secretary-General to the Security Council, UN Doc. S/2005/458, July 15, 2005, Annex II.

Part II

Levels of justice: Local, national
and international

Introduction to Part II

Naomi Roht-Arriaza

The chapters in this Part focus on the interplay among different spheres or levels on which transitional justice efforts can occur, and the particular challenges and advantages of working at each of these levels. Of course, the question of whether justice should be sought at the local, national or international level is not an either/or question: multiple levels are needed. For example, it is difficult to imagine the *gacaca* process in Rwanda described in Chapter 8 having any legitimacy were it not for simultaneous efforts at the international (ICTR) and national levels to deal with the most serious offenders. But in these cases there is either a new emphasis on local-level efforts, a new conditionality imposed by outside intervention, or a new reopening from outside that intersects with domestic processes.

Chapters 7 and 8 exemplify the local-level approach, in which decentralized fact-finding, justice and, to some extent, reparation, is meted out by local villagers to others who committed crimes (the "little fish") through informal processes based in part on customary law.

Patrick Burgess, principal legal counsel to the East Timor Commission for Reception, Truth and Reconciliation, talks about that Commission's innovative Community Reconciliation Procedures (CRPs). These village-level hearings for low-level offenders exchanged public disclosure, apology and sometimes minimal reparations for legal amnesty and social reintegration into their communities. Burgess finds that the CRPs were a resounding success despite problems with integration into the formal justice system and concerns about potential victim coercion and the inability to get at the major masterminds of the crimes.

Local-level justice is also the centerpiece of Rwanda's attempt to deal with the hundreds of thousands of people accused of participating in the 1994 genocide. Tim Longman explores whether such informal, non-Western based accountability can serve as a basis for justice and at the same time be consistent with human rights norms. He also looks at the interplay of such local-level initiatives with simultaneous national and international trials.

Chapters 9 and 10 turn from the micro to the macro level, focusing on the ways in which national transitional justice processes are shaped – and deformed – by outside intervention. Eric Stover, Hania Mufti and Hanny Magally write in Chapter 9 on the ways in which the US occupation of Iraq during the time of the Coalition Provisional Authority mishandled key decisions regarding transitional justice strategies, resulting in a process lacking in local consultation, ownership and legitimacy while at the same time unable to avail itself of broad-based international support and experience. Combined with the sheer scale of the violations and the continuing political and security problems, the result is an uncertain future for transitional justice initiatives.

In Chapter 10, Patti Gossman explores the possibilities for accountability in the wake of 25 years of war, occupation and invasion in Afghanistan. Here too, US needs in combating Al Qaeda shaped the current policy of non-confrontation with the "warlords" responsible for massive violations, resulting in lost opportunities. On the other hand, the emergence of a still fragile civil society and national human rights institutions provides some cause for hope that a locally supported process for documenting the war's toll and holding to account those responsible will eventually emerge.

Chapters 11 and 12 look at the transnational and temporal dimensions. In both countries examined, Chad and Argentina, early attempts at accountability fell short, and were followed by years of inaction. In both, external processes – transnational investigations and extradition requests – affected local courts, advocacy groups and government officials.

Reed Brody's account of the prosecution(s) of Hissène Habré, the ex-dictator of Chad, shows both the promise and the limits of transnational investigations as a means of jump-starting domestic justice. After Habré was indicted in Senegal and then Belgium, new possibilities opened up for victims, but they were restricted by the limited transformation of the government. The conditions that created the classic "boomerang" effect of the Pinochet case, where an outside stimulus permanently changed the possibilities of justice, are not always present. As Brody put it, "Chad is not Chile."

On the other hand, Kathryn Sikkink and Carrie Walling look at the successful reopening of the issue of justice for past violations in Argentina, the pioneer in both investigative commissions and trials of human rights violators. They find that, rather than a clear boomerang effect, in Argentina domestic legal innovations combined with strategic use of transnational investigations and prosecutions to find cracks in a wall of domestic impunity and break it open. Sikkink and Walling place the Argentine experience within the larger context of an empirically demonstrated "justice cascade" of increasing use of both prosecutions and truth commissions worldwide, a theme that is further explored in the concluding chapter.

7 A new approach to restorative justice – East Timor's Community Reconciliation Processes

Patrick Burgess

Introduction

Like the basic principle of supplying medical aid in emergencies, the primary goal of all transitional justice initiatives must be to first avoid the occurrence of additional violations. While preventing further injury we can also try to heal the wounds which have already been sustained. Punishing those responsible for past violations, preventing them from repeating these in the future, providing a clear deterrent message to others who may be tempted to act in a like manner, and providing some solace to victims by demonstrating that those who caused their suffering will also suffer, are of major importance in this context. They are not, however, the complete picture.

Accountability may be the most essential ingredient to healing the past, but it is the total answer to neither justice nor reconciliation. Punishment will not by itself heal the past wounds, which are so commonly the cause of renewed hostilities and the occurrence of new violations. A serious approach to this challenge needs to be holistic. Despite the overwhelming obstacles, significant advances have been made in recent years towards building mechanisms to provide accountability, but there has been far less progress towards understanding or creating practical mechanisms that promote reconciliation.

Many conflicts take place in societies in which the role of formal policing and legal systems has been negligible or, taken at its best, provided a minimal contribution towards law and order; in others they have been the tools of abuse. This does not mean that there is anarchy. In such cultures the relationships between individuals and groups is the fabric which provides order. It consists of a web of forces, both subtle and strong, which regulate behavior, resolve disputes and maintain a dynamic workable solution between competing demands and priorities. Conflicts and wars rip through this tapestry of relationships, which is responsible for social order, replacing it with frayed emotions, anger, hostility, misunderstanding and suspicion.

The 24-year-long conflict and military occupation of East Timor (now Timor Leste) had this destructive effect on the local culture. Divisions were deep; anger was high, violence very near, whether measured from the past or the future. In this context a number of potential mechanisms for achieving accountability were raised. An international tribunal was recommended but not established. A specific domestic tribunal was set up in Indonesia, which is widely described as a "sham." A mixed tribunal established within Timor Leste has succeeded in prosecuting a significant number of "smaller fish," but cannot touch those most responsible because they reside safely in Indonesia. Into this mix was added the Commission for Reception, Truth and Reconciliation (CAVR).

Through an innovative, grassroots approach to reconciliation which has reached across all areas of the new country, the CAVR has provided fresh stimulation to those seeking workable solutions to ending recurring cycles of violence. Achieving this goal requires that the systemic causes of the violence are uncovered and addressed. This involves not only punishment of perpetrators and the establishment of the truth. It also cries out for a practical method to sew together the frayed edges of torn social fabric, or at least bring them close enough so that time can gradually restore them.

The Community Reconciliation Processes of the CAVR aim to provide a space for perpetrators, victims and communities to seek solutions for reconciliation and reacceptance of those who have committed "harmful acts" to the community. The process involves a mixture of concepts drawn from criminal law, civil procedure, mediation, arbitration, and local traditional and spiritual practices. Although long-term results are as yet unknown, at the close of this program on March 31, 2004, it appears that the target communities view CRPs, in general, to have been a significant success. Much care needs to be taken in drawing lessons from this program for other situations, as it has been very specifically designed for the local context. However, at the very least, the program has refocused attention on the fundamental need for real mechanisms aimed specifically at reconciliation, and the possibility that although total solutions will always be elusive, partial gains can be made. In the dark and hazy post-conflict worlds where each step forward is a major achievement such partial gains should be cause for celebration.

The roots of the problem: decolonization and civil war

East Timor is half an island, with a population of around 800,000. It had been a Portuguese colony for almost 400 years when the Carnation Revolution in Lisbon on April 24, 1974 delivered a policy of immediate release of all colonies. West Timor, the other half of the island, along with the other Dutch colonial holdings in the area, had become part of Indonesia following the struggle for independence in 1945.

The Portuguese decision led to a situation where East Timorese were for the first time faced with the prospect of gaining political power. Two major political parties quickly emerged, dominated by young, inexperienced figures. FRETILIN favoured immediate independence, and the UDT party wanted a further period under Portuguese influence before independence. A third, smaller party, APODETI, favoured integration with Indonesia. The struggle for power led to a relatively short but bloody civil war. FRETILIN declared themselves victors and the legitimate government on November 28, 1975. Ten days later the Indonesian army staged a massive military operation, invading the territory by air, land and sea in the dawn hours of December 7, 1975.

The participating forces in the civil war had little previous experience or discipline. Consequently, during this period East Timorese factions were responsible for significant human rights violations against other East Timorese and an estimated total of 2,000 persons lost their lives. The violations included massacres of civilians, murdering of prisoners, and purges of party members suspected of betrayal.[1]

The Indonesian occupation was to last for twenty-four years, during which time the East Timorese struggle for independence continued, led by the FALINTIL guerrilla force and involving a broad-based clandestine civilian movement.

During the occupation the East Timorese were subjected to many forms of human rights abuses, and little information of what was taking place was able to emerge, as the territory was generally kept closed to outsiders. East Timorese were unable to exercise their right to self-determination, to participate in legitimate political activities, or to travel or speak freely. Many suspected independence supporters were taken away by security forces to be tortured and killed. There was widespread rape and abuse of women. East Timorese children were also taken from the territory by Indonesian military officers. Perhaps most devastating was the tactic of displacing the population from their villages, ostensibly so that they could not provide support to the guerrillas. This led to hundreds of thousands of people being moved to live in areas where there were no means of support. Massive famine and death resulted.

Although no accurate count had been established at the time of writing, it is estimated that one quarter of the East Timorese population, or around 200,000 people died in various ways as a result of the conflict during the Indonesian occupation.[2]

The events and human rights violations of the civil war and those during the Indonesian occupation were intertwined. Murders and massacres by pro-independence forces during the civil war led to some East Timorese becoming sympathizers and agents of the Indonesian military during the occupation, due to the fact that they had common enemies.

Allegiances, however, were often not clear. There was much mixing of loyalties, some of it genuine, some less so. The occupation brought to East Timor the same debilitating and hazy mix of collaboration and resistance that Europeans know so well from the experiences of the Second World War. Some supported the occupiers because they believed integration to be preferable or inevitable or because they could gain materially from it. Others demonstrated support but worked clandestinely for the resistance, or ascribed to the goals of independence but secretly gave information to the Indonesian military. There was much changing of sides, according to the situation. This left the legacy of an extremely blurred historical line and a major challenge to reconciliation. However, it also left an understanding of the mixed history of the conflict which can facilitate understanding and forgiveness by East Timorese, but remains difficult to penetrate and understand for outsiders.

The closure of the territory to the outside world began to change in 1992, when a film showing Indonesian troops massacring East Timorese demonstrators at the Santa Cruz cemetery in Dili was smuggled out of the territory. Pressure to give the East Timorese an opportunity to decide their own future began to escalate. The fall of the Suharto military dictatorship in 1998 brought renewed attention and in January 1999 his temporary replacement, President Habibie, made a unilateral decision to allow a UN-run ballot in the territory.

It appears that following this decision a strategy was devised by the Indonesian military forces to turn the situation to their advantage by implementing a program of intimidating the population to vote to remain part of Indonesia. The operational strategy flowing from such a policy involved the formation of civilian militias, which were armed, trained and paid for by the Indonesian military and civilian administration.[3] Others who voluntarily joined included many who had been opponents of pro-independence politics, or whose family members had been killed by independence supporters during the civil war of 1974–76. Members included groups of mostly young thugs and illiterate youths, looking for thrills, power and money. In addition, thousands of young men were forced to join these groups, although they maintained pro-independence loyalties. The militias were encouraged and forced to attack pro-independence supporters during the ballot process, and to provide a clear threat that if the independence option won, those who had supported it would be killed.[4]

In fact, the belief that the East Timorese population could be intimidated into accepting further Indonesian rule was wrong. On August 30, 1999, more than 99 percent of those registered to vote attended polling booths, despite the presence of militias at many polling sites. Of these 78.5 percent voted for independence. The angry Indonesian military and militias then undertook a massive payback operation. In the weeks following the ballot approximately 1,400 civilians were killed, hundreds of women raped, 60,000 houses and 75 percent of government buildings burned and destroyed. The entire population was displaced. Approximately 250,000 people were forced onto trucks and ships and evacuated to Indonesian West Timor. The rest of the population fled to the forests and mountains.[5]

Eventually INTERFET, the international force led by Australia, landed in Dili and began to restore order as the Indonesian military and East Timorese militias crossed the border to West Timor, taking with them almost all motor vehicles and consumer goods, thousands of head of stolen livestock, and almost anything else that could be carried. The vast majority of these refugees have since returned to live in East Timor.

Justice for those responsible

A comprehensive account of justice mechanisms relating to the human rights violations committed in East Timor is beyond the scope of this chapter, and is considered in greater detail in Chapter 6. The following brief summary is provided as contextual background to the establishment of the CAVR.

Following the 1999 violence, the Report of the United Nations International Commission of Inquiry on East Timor called on the United Nations to "establish an international human rights tribunal consisting of judges appointed by the United Nations."[6] The Secretary-General did not endorse this, but instead recommended that Indonesia be granted the opportunity to first demonstrate its capacity to bring those responsible to justice. On February 18, 2000 the Security Council called upon Indonesia to "institute a swift, comprehensive, effective and transparent legal process, in conformity with international standards of justice and due process of law."[7]

On August 1, 2001, Indonesian President Megawati Sukarnoputri, by presidential decree, established an ad hoc Tribunal in Jakarta, with a mandate to try those responsible for the serious violations committed in East Timor. However, this court was not given a mandate which would realistically allow it to prosecute those responsible, covering only three of the thirteen districts of East Timor, during only two months of the ten-month program of violence. The process has been widely criticized as being a "sham".[8]

On October 25, 1999, the Security Council, through Resolution 1272, created an unprecedented peacekeeping mission, UNTAET, with total administrative responsibility for the territory, including the administration of justice.[9] Resolution 1272 also established a "hybrid court", including the Special Panels for Serious Crimes within the Dili District Court, and a Serious Crimes Investigations Unit, headed up by a Deputy Prosecutor for Serious Crimes. (Every person appointed to this position was a UN international staff member.) These bodies were given exclusive jurisdiction over serious crimes committed throughout East Timor between January 1, 1999 and October 25, 1999. Despite the high level of international outrage, efforts implemented appear to have fallen far short of their goal to achieve justice. Those most responsible, the Indonesian military who planned and executed the operations, remain free and in active military service. Political will for an international Tribunal targeting powerful citizens of the world's largest Muslim nation has waned in the post-September 11 world. The Jakarta ad hoc process has been an evasion rather than a real effort to achieve justice. The Dili Serious Crimes process has succeeded in prosecuting a number of relatively low-level perpetrators. The only East Timorese judge to sit on these panels during the first two years of their operation has stated: "speaking as a Timorese and not as a judge I think this system is not fair. Is it fair to prosecute the small Timorese and not the big ones who gave them orders?"[10]

Practical challenges

During the Indonesian occupation the East Timorese population had little chance to develop skills which might encourage their desire and ability to gain independence. For twenty-four years the Suharto military dictatorship had imported Indonesians as senior government officials, police, high school teachers, health workers and the like, all of whom departed in the trail of smoke left by the military. When UNTAET was established there was only a handful of poorly trained East Timorese lawyers with little or no experience, no laws, no courts, no police force, no national military, no government departments, a few East Timorese doctors, no system for garbage collection, taxation or telephones.

While the Serious Crimes Unit was being established, employing mostly United Nations international staff, a national system of justice was being put together from these scant raw materials. UNTAET decided to select and employ East Timorese judges, prosecutors and defense counsel to undertake roles in the courts, despite their almost total lack of experience. It soon became apparent that this fledgling institution was struggling to deal with new crimes being committed. This gave rise to the question of what should be done with the thousands of lesser criminal offenses which had been committed during the conflict.

The caseload for 1999 alone involved thousands of perpetrators of "less serious crimes". This would impose an overwhelming burden on the already struggling justice system. However, ignoring these cases also presented a significant danger, particularly in the context of so much anger and resentment among local populations. A major challenge threatening the fragile peace was how to reintegrate those who had been involved in the violence and fled to West Timor back into their communities. In East Timor most of the non-Indonesian lesser perpetrators had come from the same villages as their victims. The future would involve them living together and facing each other on a day-to-day basis. Many observers predicted that, as more refugees returned from West Timor, those who earlier had committed these "lesser crimes" while protected by Indonesian military power, would themselves become victims of payback violence. If this eventuated as expected it could destabilize the fragile peace and all efforts and expenses spent on reconstruction would be wasted.

Origins of the Commission for Reception, Truth and Reconciliation (CAVR)

In August 2000 the National Congress of the umbrella group representing all major political parties which had supported independence passed a unanimous resolution supporting the establishment of a "truth and reconciliation commission". Following this, a steering committee was established, consisting of nine representatives of East Timorese groups, assisted primarily by the Human Rights Section of UNTAET.[11]

The steering committee conducted consultations in each of the thirteen districts of East Timor, some at the district level, others meeting with sub-district or village communities. The results of these consultations, in broad terms, were the following:

- Communities wanted an investigation of the truth of what had taken place and who was responsible. This should include not only crimes but also issues such as informers who had harmed their communities by collaboration with the Indonesian military, which had led to disappearances and other violations.
- Those most responsible for the planning and implementation of the programs of violence and perpetrators of the most serious crimes should be arrested and tried in the courts.
- Those involved in lesser crimes need not face a court, but they should face their community members and the victims of their acts.
- Traditional systems of justice should be involved in any proposed program. However, these systems had been greatly weakened by the Indonesian occupation and were not designed to deal with large-scale abuses.
- An investigation of the truth should include 1999, the Indonesian military occupation and the civil war of 1974–76. However, there were significant fears that opening up the events of the civil war might lead to instability and a resurrection of old hostilities.[12]

Following the consultations the steering committee held a number of workshops and meetings over the following months at which the policy and form of a truth and reconciliation commission were discussed and a proposed structure drafted. Regulation 2001/10 established the East Timor Commission for Reception, Truth and Reconciliation or CAVR (from the Portuguese equivalent).[13]

Functions of the CAVR

The Commission was given a two and a half year mandate, later extended later to a total of 39 months, and commenced its operations in April 2002. Its objectives included the following:

1. To inquire into and establish the truth regarding the nature, causes and extent of human rights violations that took place between April 1974 and October 1999.
2. To assist victims, promote human rights and reconciliation.
3. To support the reception and reintegration of individuals who had caused harm to their communities by the commission of minor criminal offences and other harmful acts, through the facilitation of Community Reconciliation Processes (CRPs).
4. To compile a Report which would include its findings, refer matters to the Office of the General Prosecutor where appropriate, and make recommendations to the government.[14]

Community Reconciliation Processes (CRPs)

The innovative system of CRPs was designed to provide an alternative to dealing with the thousands of lesser crimes in the formal justice system. Providing a mechanism for dealing with these crimes at the community level was intended to provide a cheaper, faster, less complicated process focused on repairing community relationships and settling residual anger. The following typical example was envisaged:

A perpetrator who burned houses returns from West Timor, feeling vulnerable and afraid. He approaches the CAVR's local representatives and provides them with a statement including admissions of his actions. This statement is forwarded to the Office of the General Prosecutor (OGP), which decides whether it is appropriate to be dealt with by CRP instead of prosecution. If approved, the CAVR establishes a five-person panel in the community affected by the crimes. The panel conducts a public hearing at which the perpetrator admits his wrongs and apologizes. Community elders and spiritual leaders attend and incorporate traditional practices into the hearing. Victims are able to address and question the perpetrator directly, community members also contribute and a decision is made as to what the perpetrator needs to do to be accepted back by the community. If he accepts this offer, and completes any required acts he will receive full immunity from future prosecution.

The formal mechanisms covering this process were set out in Part IV of the Regulation: The steps set out in this section are:

> *A person responsible for the commission of a criminal or non-criminal act ("A Deponent") must submit a written statement to the Commission*

The statement must include a full description of the acts which the Deponent wishes to be taken into account and an admission of responsibility for these acts. The acts must have been committed in the context of the political conflict. The Deponent must request a CRP hearing, designate which community the procedure should take place in, and renounce the use of violence to achieve political ends. The Deponent will be informed that a copy of the statement will be sent to the Office of the General Prosecutor (OGP) and that its contents might be used against him in a court of law. After providing this statement the Deponent receives a temporary stay of prosecution for the acts declared, so he cannot be arrested while the process is ongoing.

The statement is forwarded to the CAVR national office where it is considered by a Statements Committee

This committee will make a preliminary assessment and recommendation as to whether the acts disclosed are appropriately dealt with by a CRP. In deciding this the Committee will take into account the nature of the crime, the total number of acts, and the Deponent's role in their commission. Those who organized widespread or systematic violence will be excluded at this stage. Schedule 1 of the Regulation cites theft, minor assault, arson, killing of livestock and destruction of crops as examples of appropriate cases for CRPs. It also states that "in principle, serious criminal offences, in particular murder, torture and sexual offences, shall not be dealt with in a CRP."[15] The Statements Committee may decide that a matter is not appropriate to be dealt with by a CRP, and inform the Deponent that the Commission has decided not to proceed. However, all statements received by the CAVR must be forwarded to the Office of the General Prosecutor.

The Deponent's statement is then forwarded to the Office of the General Prosecutor (OGP)

The facts in the statement will be checked with other files, to ensure that he is not wanted for other more serious offences, and that the Deponent's account accords with other records. The OGP may decide to exercise its exclusive jurisdiction over serious criminal offences, and retain the statement of the Deponent. Alternatively, the OGP may return the statement to the CAVR with an indication that there is not an intention to exercise this jurisdiction and the case may proceed by way of CRP.

The CAVR may then organize a CRP hearing in the relevant community

The hearing will be presided over by a Panel, consisting of local leaders and chaired by a Regional Commissioner of the CAVR. The Panel must have appropriate gender and cultural representation. In practice, traditional elders, church leaders, representatives of local women's and youth groups are often chosen to be Panel members. At the hearing the Deponent will read his statement publicly. An opportunity must be given for victims and community members to express their opinions. The Panel should then take the wishes of victims and community members into account when formulating appropriate "acts of reconciliation" for the Deponent to carry out in order to be fully accepted back into the community. If the Deponent agrees this is then recorded as a Community Reconciliation Agreement.

If at any time during the hearing "credible evidence" that the Deponent has been involved in the commission of a "serious criminal offence" is raised, the hearing should be adjourned and referred back to the OGP.[16]

> *The Community Reconciliation Agreement must then be registered with the appropriate District Court*

After the agreement is registered with the appropriate court, and the Deponent completes the required acts of reconciliation he receives full immunity from criminal and civil liability arising out of the actions he has admitted to.[17]

Although the Community Reconciliation Procedures concept was an exciting new idea which held great potential, at the time the Regulation was drafted it was uncertain whether it would be able to be practically implemented. Was this an important step forward, or another "brilliant" idea influenced by foreigners' academic hyperbole, which would find its way into the already overcrowded trash bin for reconstruction programs? The practical task was to formulate a new, untested procedure which had strong connections to both traditional practices and the formal legal system, but would need to be relatively simple, logistically possible and involve entire communities across the territory.

Results of the CRP program

The district programs of the CAVR were completed on March 31, 2004. In general the Commission has been highly commended by international observers, senior government officials, and local leaders for having made an extraordinary contribution to reconciliation in the territory, far exceeding initial expectations. A fundamental aspect of this success was the CRP program. In early 2004 the United Nations Development Program conducted a study of the CRP program, based on over 70 interviews. In his Report of this assessment Piers Pigou concluded:

In terms of impact, there is a widespread feeling that the CRPs have definitely contributed to building social cohesion and relieving tensions in many places . . . There is broad acknowledgement from victims and deponents that the Commission played its neutral role with considerable dexterity. When compared with the formal justice system, the CRP is seen to be relatively quick and a visibly just resolution of the problem. In addition it expedites the possibility of returning to normal life, which is important in a context where violence is regarded by some as a legitimate problem-solving mechanism.[18]

Perhaps the greatest evidence of this success is the level of participation by communities. At the planning stages a goal of 1,000 CRP cases had been established, but this was considered optimistic. At the close of the program the initial goal had been exceeded by more than 50 percent.

The CAVR Final Report, which was made available to the public in March 2006, summarized the results of the CRP program as follows:

- The Commission received a total of 1,541 statements from Deponents requesting to participate in CRP, all of which were forwarded to the OGP.
- Cases involving 1,371 Deponents were successfully completed through CRP hearings.
- The OGP did not grant approval for 85 cases to be proceeded with by way of CRP. These cases were retained by the OGP.
- Thirty-two cases were adjourned during the hearing because credible information came to light, which indicated that the Deponent might have been involved in a "serious criminal offence", or because communities refused to accept the Deponent.
- These figures show that nearly 90 percent of all cases received proceeded to completion. The remaining 10 percent were cases where the Deponent did not attend the scheduled hearing, the hearing was adjourned, or the OGP did not consent to them proceeding by CRP.

More extraordinarily, it is estimated that between 30,000 and 40,000 community members had attended and participated in the hearings.[19]

In March 2004 the government of Timor Leste held a national dialogue on justice. As part of the preparations for this workshop, consultations were held in each district. In almost every district a major demand of communities was that the CRP program should not be ended as planned but be extended and prolonged.

At the time of writing no final assessment of the program had been made. However, the CAVR conducted an interim review in mid-2003, which involved returning to communities several months after hearings and conducting interviews with perpetrators, victims, members of the communities and Panel members. The study revealed the following:

- Over 90 percent of all those interviewed stated that the process had been a positive one and that they had been satisfied with its results.
- Victims interviewed stated that after the CRP hearings they felt more respected within their communities and there had been a change of relationship with the perpetrator.
- Perpetrators interviewed also stated that the CRP process had produced a "significant positive effect" on their day-to-day lives. Every

perpetrator interviewed stated that the process had assisted in repairing the relationship between themselves and their community.

- Many victims answered that the process had helped them to understand the motivation and circumstances surrounding the actions of the perpetrator. An important factor for victims was that the acts had been perpetrated during a time of war, and this made them more understandable and able to be forgiven.
- All of those interviewed stated that the key to forgiveness lay in the strength of the confession of the Deponents. "If it was felt that a person participating had made a full and frank statement covering all of the events they had been involved in, they were in a sense cleansed and could be received again by their communities."[20]
- Victims did not consider that the nature or degree of punishment, or "act of reconciliation" which the perpetrator had to carry out was of crucial importance. If the admissions were full, did not avoid responsibility and the apology was considered to be heartfelt then the major block to acceptance was removed. Acts carried out in furtherance of the agreement were of lesser importance. In fact in many cases victims and communities demanded only a full confession of responsibility and apology, following often extensive and probing questioning on the nature and degree of participation in the relevant events.
- Those interviewed said that they felt that the reconciliation achieved through the CRP process would be lasting. "There was a strong sense that once a decision was reached to reconcile it should not be discarded lightly." Many participants felt that the traditional practices incorporated into the procedures significantly strengthened the agreement to reconcile, and that "both forgiveness and repentance are taken more seriously when made as part of such a ceremony."[21]

Developments in the manner of conducting CRPs

The Regulation had included some specific requirements for CRP hearings, such as the make-up of the Panel, the requirement for victims and community members to speak, the need for public apology by the perpetrator and the goal of the Community Reconciliation Agreement, brokered by the Panel. However, the way in which the hearings were to be conducted was intentionally left open. As the program developed, some relatively uniform practices were created by the CAVR, but cultural traditions from different regions also played a major role. Interesting developments in the manner of proceeding include the following:

The traditional systems of "adat" became more important than had been anticipated at the design stage

The people of East Timor have lived for thousands of years with virtually no reliance on any formal system involving police or courts. Justice systems under both the Portuguese colonial administration and Indonesian military occupation were seen to be so corrupt and politically influenced as to be of little value. According to custom, traditional leaders are responsible for making decisions and resolving disputes "based on both facts and principles set by ancestors of the group." The behavior and activities of members of the society are bound by "collective norms" which are adjudicated by the traditional leaders, who "pronounce these norms, uphold justice and execute justice." These traditional systems are known as *"adat."*[22]

In particular, the traditional dispute-resolution process of *"nahe biti bot"* or "unrolling of the mat" became a fundamental aspect of most hearings, although it was not formally required and some districts used it less than others.[23]

A typical CRP hearing incorporating this practice is commenced with a large, simple woven mat being brought to the site of adjudication of the dispute. The mat is ceremonially unfurled onto the ground, symbolizing the opening of the event. Sacred objects are brought, and elders and spiritual leaders sit on the mat and chew beetle-nut together before commencing. The entrance, unrolling and seating may be accompanied by chanting from traditional spiritual leaders. These leaders will be dressed in traditional attire, which consists of colourful woven textiles, silver breastplates and head-dresses adorned with feathers or beaten silver horns symbolizing a buffalo. A major aspect of the principle of *"biti bot"* is that once the mat has been unfurled it cannot be rolled up until the disputes have been settled.

The CRP Panel is seated at the front, on the ground or at a table. The mat is unfurled in front of the Panel. Deponents are seated to the left of the Panel's table, victims to the right, with the community in front, thus forming a rectangle, with the *"biti bot"* mat in the centre. After the ceremonial unfurling of the mat, the Regional Commissioner chairing the Panel introduces the hearing, often followed by short speeches by the head of the local government or other officials who may be present. Although initially it was felt that the presence of international observers could distort the proceedings, in fact communities welcomed such participation when it did take place, as a sign of the importance of the undertaking. Observers such as Mary Robinson, former UN High Commissioner for Human Rights, and Ian Martin, former Special

Representative of the Secretary-General of the 1999 UNAMET mission attended village hearings and were requested to speak to communities at some point during the hearing.

The requirement that the mat cannot be rolled up until all matters are settled also became an integral part of the process. In many cases matters which had commenced hearing in the morning continued late into the night, sometimes until 2 or 3 a.m. Although a basic lunch was usually provided by the CAVR and community, dinner was not. In one such example the National Commissioner attending reported: "It was incredible. The entire community was there, hundreds of people, almost no-one was at home, and not one person left before the end, at 2.30 a.m."[24]

Importance of the relationship to the formal legal system

As the program developed the value of both tradition and law became apparent. There was no requirement to refer specifically to legislation or sanctions, and yet legal provisions were read with significant solemnity and received well by communities. These included an explanation of the procedures and reading of some relevant sections of the Regulation, particularly those relating to the duty to tell the truth, punishments for not doing so, and the relationship with the Office of the General Prosecutor. The letter from the OGP was read out stating that the particular matter has been considered and a decision made not to proceed. It was also explained that the CAVR is an official organization and that reference to the Commission could be found in the national Constitution.

Many participants interviewed stated that the fact that the CRP proceedings had a formal legal base, connected to the OGP and courts was extremely important. Indeed the Commission's CRP represents the first concrete example of implementing a process that spans aspects of both traditional and formal justice practices, in a new format that accords with constitutional and human rights imperatives, and incorporates a written record of the process and content.[25]

There was one particular unanticipated clash between the legal provisions governing CRPs and traditional *adat* procedures. The Regulation left the power to decide the terms of the Community Reconciliation Agreement in the hands of the Panel. In fact, the design stage had considered whether to require that victims consent to the agreement, and decided to include only a requirement for victims to be heard, not to consent. This was due in part to practical considerations: if there is a formal requirement for victims to consent, how do you ensure that all of those affected by a particular act are present and consent? What happens when eighteen victims of house burnings consent to receiving back a perpetrator and one does not? In addition, the need to provide closure for a large number of people outside the formal legal system supported not giving victims the right to veto an agreement found to be acceptable by the Panel because of residual, albeit perfectly understandable, anger. (Just as victims do not have such a veto right in other more formal legal systems where, unlike CRPs, they also do not usually have any right to be heard or confront perpetrators.)

However, the design had not anticipated that according to the "*biti bot*" tradition the consent of victims is required for any settlement. In some situations, the Panel, Deponent and community recommended that the perpetrator be accepted back into the community, but individual victims did not. That is, the law did not strictly require the victim's consent, but *adat* did.

Although the basis for the CAVR's activities is in fact the law, not *adat*, in these situations it was clear that, despite the legal provisions, the process could not continue to agreement and settlement. The participation of the relevant Deponent in such hearings was halted, and the Deponent's file sent back to the national office to be forwarded to the OGP. In fact, such cases, although few in number, create a legal challenge for the CAVR. Deponents have applied for a CRP in good faith, the hearing has been conducted and an agreement could probably have been reached between the Panel and Deponent, if not for the lack of the consent of victims, a matter which is not required by the law. However, Deponents, too, understand the *adat* principle and have not complained about the lack of result. In hindsight, greater considerations of the interaction between the law and cultural traditions should have taken place at the design stage. The consent, not just the participation, of victims needed to be an integral part of the legal regime, as it was in the traditional practices.

Surveys conducted across the districts of East Timor have indicated that despite much political rhetoric about the plan to implement the formal justice system mechanisms in a practical way across the nation, the "quasi-legal" program of CRPs has been the only visible face of the justice system at village level. Although this is evidence of the resounding success of the Commission, it is a somewhat sad comment on the practical difficulties faced in establishing a workable system of justice in a transitional setting.

CRPs are community events, not individual cases

The CRP provisions in the Regulation were drafted with much reliance on precedents of individualized justice, civil and criminal procedure.

They deal with individual cases, rights, hearings, and the like. However, a major element of the success of the CRPs has been that the CAVR approached them as a community event, not an individual process. The major stakeholder in the process is the larger group, which includes perpetrators and victims. Accordingly, the program focused on communities, not individuals. This wider approach is fundamental to traditional beliefs and was an integral part of the success of the program.

A major factor which must be considered in designing any program is the quality of the identity of each person involved. In East Timor a person's identity is strongly related to a feeling of belonging to a group, and personal feelings and desires are always mixed with those of the common good of the group. From a western viewpoint this may seem like a contradiction or conflict, that an individual must in some way "sacrifice" what they really want in such a situation. However, in the same way as a western parent will not be making any personal sacrifice in making decisions for the good of his or her children, in societies such as East Timor this broader identity relates to a much larger group, without contradiction or conflict. Accordingly, settlement of a dispute according to traditional means is

> not necessarily designed to profit the family or individual who has been wronged, but rather provides an opportunity for a feast or distribution of wealth which creates the public symbolic closure of the issue and amounts to a form of reconciliation . . . the hoped for outcome is a redressive process leading to the mutual recognition of the transgression and a satisfactory final resolution of the conflict it has produced. In many cases, the success of this relies on a collective assessment that adequate recompense has been paid, either in suffering or in suitable goods.[26]

The impact of the CRP process on perpetrators must also be understood in the context of communal life. "Loss of face" and shaming through public humiliation in these communities is a much larger sanction, which continues into the day-to-day relationships with each person the perpetrator meets after the hearing. For example, the morning following a CRP and every morning thereafter, the perpetrator will walk past and look into the eyes of people who he knows well, and to whom he has admitted his wrongs and requested their forgiveness. It makes little sense to equate or try to understand the strength and effect of such a sanction with reference to a similar admission and apology between strangers in a formal system.

Optimally, all Deponents from a particular societal group were dealt with together in a single hearing. In many cases there would be between five and ten perpetrators dealt with at the same time, sometimes more.

The largest hearing, in Oecussi district, involved 55 Deponents and continued over several days. In many cases the focus was not only to reconcile individual Deponents with victims and neighbors, but also to attempt to settle the historical divisions within that particular community. In this way the individual cases of perpetrators became a gateway through which information and opinions on the wider issues of how the conflict had affected the community could flow.

Communities had never spoken publicly about the events and impact of the twenty-four-year period of conflict. Through the CRP hearings, rumours were clarified and information was exchanged publicly from witnesses to various events. Despite the gravity of the subject matter, hearings were sometimes also punctuated by laughter. This might seem to be out of place to an international observer accustomed to the solemnity of a court proceeding. However, it was a natural part of the local manner and traditions. The hearings very often included putting perpetrators through long, extremely uncomfortable rounds of questioning and shaming. However they also symbolized the joyous end to community divisions and suffering. Accordingly, CRPs were often followed by a feast and dancing. The goal of the procedure involved moving through the heavy and dark evidence of what had taken place and who was responsible to a community celebration of the resolution of past divisions. This wider symbolic significance was captured by a community elder at the closing of a CRP hearing attended by the writer in November 2003:

In 1999 we saw the Indonesian soldiers and militia leave. On May 20, 2002 we celebrated our independence as a nation. But it is only today that we as a community can be released from our suffering from this terrible past. Let us roll up the mat, and this will symbolize the end of all of these issues for us. From today we will look only forward. Let us now eat and dance together, and celebrate the future.[27]

Required 'Acts of Reconciliation' were less onerous than expected

Initial concerns that perpetrators would be required to undertake acts of reconciliation beyond their capacity were not realized. In fact the opposite was true. Sanctions required by victims and communities were far more lenient than expected and in many cases there was no additional requirement over the participation in the hearing and a full and heartfelt confession and public apology. Examples of acts which the perpetrators were required to make included payments of money or symbolic valuable items, such as traditional beads, providing the victim with an animal, clothes or other objects, helping to repair the victim's house, and working for specified periods on community projects such as the repair of a school, church or road. The fact that greater compensation and more onerous community service were not demanded is very difficult to understand for international observers who tend to see justice in terms of individual responsibility and concrete and visible forms of punishment. The explanation for this relative leniency is complex and not entirely understood, but interviews with participants indicated that the following factors are involved:

- The desire of communities to settle matters, to delve into the issues deeply, but then leave them behind and not leave hanging threads into the future. They therefore preferred to try to settle the issue of the past, both ceremonially and practically, on the day of the hearing. This was also reinforced by the strict scheduling of the CAVR and the desire of staff to complete as many hearings as possible within the limited time of the mandate.
- A common realization that following the 1999 violence and destruction the vast majority of East Timorese are still acutely poor and lack the ability to pay any substantial compensation.
- Acceptance by all involved that those centrally responsible for all the violence were senior Indonesian military officers and that the East Timorese who became involved were manipulated and promised many things which were not delivered. Victims frequently stated that they forgave the perpetrator because he did things "because of the war" and that everything was different in those times.
- Informal "pressure" felt by victims that they should accept reconciliation with perpetrators for the good of their community. The expectation of a possible resolution of outstanding past issues and the desire of the whole community for settlement on the day of the CRP may have overruled the desires of some victims for greater compensation, or to reject reconciliation with perpetrators.

Shortcomings of the CRP program

Non-participation of all perpetrators

In many hearings community members expressed disappointment that some of those persons most responsible for the violence in their village did not volunteer to participate. The voluntary nature of the program, together with the lack of capacity of the justice system, meant that these persons gained a practical impunity.

The writer attended one hearing at which the call for all those who had not volunteered to participate became so strong that a hearing was adjourned while someone was sent to the houses of five additional persons who had been involved in burning houses but who had not offered statements to the CAVR, with a request for them to attend the hearing. When these young men arrived, the CAVR Commissioner explained that it was too late for them to participate in a formal way, or to gain immunity through the relationship with the formal legal process, but if they wished to speak to the community they could. Each of the five asked to be part of the gathering, admitted their wrongs and asked forgiveness from the victims. The community and victims asked questions of them and finally indicated they too would be accepted back under the authority of the traditional procedures. Although an unusual case, this is an example of the "soft" border between the legal requirements and traditional practices. As in this case, sometimes situations arose in hearings which were dealt with in various ways by the Panel, not always according to the way the Regulation envisaged, but often with positive results.

Due process

At the design stage of the CRPs it was proposed that perpetrators of minor crimes in a community should be compelled to attend a hearing and that decisions of the Panel would be binding on them. However, it was decided that this approach would not provide perpetrators with their fundamental rights. In particular, in reality there was little or no chance that they could receive legal advice before participating. In addition, Panel members had no legal training and therefore should not be given authority to mete out punishments. Accordingly, the procedure was designed on the basis that all participants would do so on a voluntary basis, and that agreement to undertake "acts of reconciliation" would also be voluntary. At that point, however, the agreement became registered as an order of the court and non-compliance with the order is an offence punishable by a maximum of one-year imprisonment and/or a $3,000 fine.

The relationship between the CRP process and the Office of the General Prosecutor (OGP) produced a situation where all Deponents provided statements, each of which was by its nature a confession, without any prior legal advice. These statements may be used in the prosecution of perpetrators, and they are advised of this possibility before providing the statement. In reality, a perpetrator is providing confessional information on the basis of a belief that his case will not be prosecuted, but will be dealt with by CRP. However, in the case of almost 100 Deponents, this belief was mistaken, and their cases were held by the OGP for possible prosecution. Although, in reality, none of these alleged perpetrators were prosecuted by the end of the mandate of the Serious Crimes Unit on May 20, 2005, this failure to protect the rights of participants should be addressed in the development of any similar future mechanisms.

Limited time and scope of CAVR activities

The strategic plan of the CAVR operated on the basis of teams spending a three-month period in each sub-district. Many community representatives felt that this was too short. The flow of statements from the district to the OGP and back took considerable time, which made reaching all villages impossible. The CRP process was a new phenomenon. It was only after communities had experienced a hearing that they realized its potential. Thus many perpetrators became willing to participate only after the hearing had been completed and they had seen the beneficial results. However, by this time it was too late. It is estimated that in excess of 3,000 perpetrators would be prepared to participate in CRP hearings if the program was extended.[28]

Despite pressures to extend the program the CAVR decided that it did not have sufficient human and financial resources to continue to conduct CRPs and successfully complete its mandate by compiling a comprehensive Final Report. (The length of the Final Report was in excess of 2,500 pages.) The Commission did offer to assist any other initiative which could be established to continue to hold CRPs or a similar procedure. Although some initial plans were developed for an international NGO to undertake this task, and discussions for a post-CAVR mechanism to focus on similar work were held, impetus was lost on the formal closure of the program and at the time of writing it appeared that no further CRPs would be conducted. The program had, however, stimulated much interest in the possibility of other forms of alternate dispute resolution which could be implemented at the village level as an extension of the formal justice system.

Lack of progress towards justice for those most responsible

In almost every CRP hearing there were expressions of serious discontent because those involved in the planning and execution of the programs of violence – the Indonesian military commanders and militia leaders – remained free and prosperous in Indonesia. This was the major block for deep healing in communities. There was a feeling that all involved in the CRP procedures had undertaken difficult and serious work to try to settle the past, and this gave rise to resentment towards those who were most responsible for this past suffering and yet had not faced up to the results of their actions in any way.

An integrated approach to reconciliation

Although the CRP process was the only reconciliation program specifically established in the Regulation, the programming of the CAVR has developed an integrated approach to reconciliation in East Timor. The basis of this policy is the belief that reconciliation can only be achieved if practical programs are implemented to achieve each factor required for reconciliation and peace. These factors include:

- Justice for serious perpetrators.
- Mending the social fabric binding communities at a grassroots level.
- Discovering and publicizing the truth surrounding the violations, so that myths and rumours are dissolved, accountability established, and lessons for the future learned.
- Repairing the relationships between national leaders involved in past conflicts.
- Restoring as much as possible the dignity of victims, which will assist in reducing community anger and potential reoccurrence of violence.
- Providing reparations for victims.

The grassroots approach of the CAVR should be understood within the framework of the holistic strategy of the Commission. On March 31, 2004 the district programs of the CAVR were completed. In addition to the 1,371 CRPs, 52 public hearings dedicated to victims had been conducted in most of the sub-districts, and three-day healing workshops had been conducted for the worst affected victims at the national office, also providing them with a small sum as symbolic reparation. Community mapping exercises had produced, through participatory processes, 52 community profiles of human rights abuses in communities which had suffered significant violations, 7,927 victim statements had been collected, and eight major thematic public hearings had been held in the capital, Dili. These results appear to confirm that the CAVR has conducted significantly more grass-roots programs, and of a more varied approach, than any previous truth and reconciliation commission.

Unlike some other commissions, the CAVR public hearings have not closely resembled court proceedings. In the South African TRC, for example, there were many senior lawyers to drive such a process; Timor Leste had no such resources. The goal of the public hearings was more to present to the public information which had not been previously available, to stimulate discussion and provide a basis for healing, rather than to provide a forum for detailed cross-examination of witnesses (although questions were asked by Commissioners, and significant information elicited through the public proceedings.)

The public hearings held in Dili were broadcast throughout Timor Leste via live television and radio, and each public hearing has been repeatedly broadcast following the event, indicating the widespread interest of the population. Themes chosen were: victims of the conflict, political prisoners, massacres, the role of women in the conflict, its impact on children, forced displacement and famine, the political conflict of 1974–76, the right to self-determination and the role of international actors. In addition to East Timorese victims and witnesses, international experts on each theme also gave evidence. These experts represented government, UN and civil society positions, and included representatives from the United Nations, Australia, the United States, Indonesia and Portugal.

The most dramatic public hearing, held in December 2003 in Dili, covered the theme of the political conflict of 1974–76. This was an extremely sensitive issue as this conflict between East Timorese had involved many of the current national leaders. Witnesses at the previous public hearing on massacres had given evidence not only of widespread atrocities committed by the Indonesian military during the occupation, but also massacres by the Timorese factions in the civil war preceding it. These violations had involved not only opponents in the struggle but also suspected traitors within their own ranks.

Although the scale and severity of violations committed during the Indonesian military occupation was far, far greater than similar events during the civil war, the earlier issues were of fundamental importance for national reconciliation. Violations during the civil war produced ongoing divisions within Timorese society, involving unresolved resentment and hatred from many relatives and children of those killed. Information concerning these events had never before been made public in any way.

As a 39-year-old male teacher/villager from Baucau district put it: "Reconciliation is not only for the people on the lower levels, but before that, there must be reconciliation among the elite political leaders because they are the symbols followed by the people. If there is no reconciliation on the level of the elite politicians and they push each other down, then the people will follow their lead." Although initially a number of political leaders indicated that they were hesitant to participate, and predicted that opening up these old wounds would lead to national instability, all major national political figures finally attended and gave evidence to the public hearing. In an extraordinary and unprecedented event, leaders from both sides of the conflict took the stand and gave evidence of their participation in the civil war, accepting responsibility and begging forgiveness from victims. The hearing ended in a gathering of these former allies and enemies, arm in arm, many crying, covered live on national radio and television.

A senior government official who had watched the event at home on television stated: "I have been waiting all my life for this day. People were crying and dancing all over Dili, it was a major personal catharsis for me and thousands of others."[29]

Inconsistency in achievements relating to justice

At the completion of its mandate, on May 20, 2005 the Serious Crimes Unit had been able to investigate less than half the cases of murder and rape committed in 1999. Although the majority of the perpetrators involved remained in West Timor there were still a significant number who had returned to East Timor but not been prosecuted. In addition, no prosecutions of serious crimes committed between 1974 and 1999 had taken place. As only 1,999 cases were dealt with by the Serious Crimes Unit these "old crimes" were within the "Ordinary Crimes" jurisdiction of the Dili District Court. The East Timorese judges of those courts were overwhelmed with current crimes, with a backlog of over 1,600 cases accumulated during the first four years of operations. It appeared unlikely that the older "serious crimes" would ever be prosecuted.

A number of communities had approached the CAVR to request Community Reconciliation hearings for these "old" cases of murder. However, these cases were outside the legal mandate of the CRP procedure, and it was felt that dealing with some instances of murder would confuse communities. As a result a few communities have conducted their own traditional processes to seek settlement for these cases.

The voluntary nature of the CRPs and the scope of the caseload meant that although the program had been much more successful than initial expectations, the perpetrators of thousands of minor crimes had not faced either prosecution for serious crimes or attended CRP hearings. The cumulative result of the various justice initiatives is that:

- All of the "big fish" – those most responsible for the massive human rights violations – remain free in Indonesia. The ad hoc Tribunal has been a "sham" and the Serious Crimes Unit indictments cannot reach these "big fish." Of the eighteen persons indicted and tried by the Indonesian ad hoc Tribunal the sixteen military and police officers were all acquitted. The two East Timorese included were convicted at trial. One of these, the former governor Abilio Soares, was later acquitted on appeal. The only person convicted in Indonesia for the mass violations was East Timorese militia leader Euricco Guterres who received a ten-year sentence for crimes against humanity.
- Most of the "middle-sized fish", East Timorese militia leaders and those who killed, raped or tortured, remain free in Indonesia. As above, Serious Crimes Unit indictments have no practical effect.
- Some of the killers and relatively low-level militia leaders have been tried and received strict sanctions, up to 33 years imprisonment, through the "Serious Crimes" process of the Dili District Court. Many perpetrators, both within and outside East Timor have not yet been investigated.
- The CRP process has produced resolution involving perpetrators, victims and communities for approximately 1,400 cases, but several thousand similar cases are unresolved.

The voices of participants in CRP hearings[30]

I will forgive people who have persecuted me, and that process that should be done by the suspect confessing all he has done, and depends on an agreement between the suspect and victim. For me, personally, I do not have the right to not forgive those involved. (Female ex-political prisoner, Dili)

I think we don't have the right not to forgive, because as a human being I am not beyond mistakes either. (Village head, 41 years old, Maliana district)

I guess everyone has the right not to forgive his or her enemy, but our country will be stagnant as a result because there is no peaceful and harmonious life. (Women's group member, 29 years old, Liquica district)

Reconciliation cannot be forced. If I'm still angry and keep my vengeance, then no one can force me. I need time to make peace with myself. (Women's group member, 29 years old, Liquica district)

If justice, peace, truth and reconciliation existed among the elites then the common people would just have to follow it. (Male villager, 34 years old, Bobonaro district)

I think I still have doubts about reconciliation. My father was murdered; do you think I can reconcile with the person who killed him? I suggest that the offender be punished. (Male villager, 43 years old, Umatolu, Viqueque district)

Reconciliation is a truth for everyone, especially for people discovering their existing differences. (Male villager, 27 years old, Aileu district)

I think sometimes organizations that work for justice in Timor Leste only talk about theories and we never see them realized. (Male ex-political prisoner, 51 years old, Dili)

Traditional leaders play fundamental roles in overcoming any problems in the village based on local tradition or culture. (Male ex-political prisoner, 40 years old, Dili)

What I know is that the Commission works for two years and after that reports the results to the government. My question is: what will the government do about the cases?

Conclusions

Despite significant international attention focused on the issue of gross human rights violations committed in East Timor, it appears that justice for those most responsible is still a distant prospect at best. This represents a serious setback for the worldwide and domestic fight against impunity. The consequences of allowing such powerful figures to commit gross violations without any form of accountability will continue to be felt within and across national borders in years to come.

Inside East Timor the efforts of the Serious Crimes Unit have brought some measure of justice. Despite this, there remain numerous holes in the justice net, and many perpetrators at all levels of responsibility will never be held accountable for their actions. It is in the context of this somewhat sad reality that efforts are being made to heal the divisions in East Timorese society. This goal is of fundamental importance not only because it is the key to breaking the cycle of recurring violence but also because national unity is the most basic foundation for the task of nation-building ahead.

The experience of the East Timor Commission for Reception, Truth and Reconciliation shows that it is vital to recognize that in a post-conflict setting both retributive justice and restorative justice are required. The commanders and serious perpetrators should be in prison; that is not negotiable. But relationships must be restored if peace is to last. It is the tension between individuals and groups, often based on past mistakes, which can readily provide the spark to ignite renewed violence. The tools used to achieve these two interconnected goals must be different if they are to be useful. They must also be based on a thorough consideration of the local environment and a practical plan based on concrete mechanisms. The goals of reconciliation programs are often limited to trying to convince leaders from opposing sides to dialogue. Although this is important, there is an imperative to seek and implement more creative programs tailored to the specific needs of each situation. These approaches need to recognize that the basis of national reconciliation will often be at the grassroots level.

There seems little doubt that the CRPs and other programs of the CAVR have made a significant contribution to maintaining stability and peace in Timor Leste. Perhaps the major contribution of the program is not the relevance it has to individual cases but its role within communities. The CRP is a formal structure under which divided parties and individuals can meet and share their views. The fact that it has a particular goal, the resolution of individual cases, allows this meeting to maintain a focus, and provides some disincentive to the tendency to drift into meaningless or insincere dialogue. Its flexibility, however, and the incorporation of traditional and spiritual practices allows the extension of a process designed for individual perpetrators and victims to have a much wider effect involving the entire community.

The weaknesses of the CRP program include its inability to compel perpetrators to participate, a potential to undermine individual victim desires in the face of community pressures to achieve resolution, legal uncertainties in some aspects of its relationship to the formal justice sector and due process. However, the fact that there has been a widespread request for the continuation of the program in almost all districts is the most compelling evidence of its value to local communities. Its strengths include achieving finality in a large number of criminal cases in a faster, cheaper, community-based manner which has allowed more of the truth to be uncovered and provided the potential for victims and communities to express in a real and practical way their desire to leave the past behind.

It would appear that the CRP experience in Timor Leste could provide valuable assistance for other regions struggling to come to terms with a history of abuses and communal divisions. However, the programs of the CAVR were designed to deal with a very specific context. This is perhaps the most valuable lesson for others – that progress towards reconciliation can be achieved by carefully formulating programs which rely on and draw assistance from all available local tools. The formula which worked in Timor Leste involved significant reliance on the "*adat*" tradition, as well as the nascent formal legal system. Strategies drew upon grass-roots leadership and support from the President and other national leaders. In a staunchly Catholic country, Nobel laureate Bishop Carlos Belo told parishioners that they should "go to the CAVR to confess their sins" and a message of forgiveness based on religious beliefs contributed to a willingness to reconcile. The CAVR ran programs in the refugee camps in West Timor to provide information and answer questions to potential participants. Many other tools with cultural significance were drawn on. Other lessons are more directly transferable. These include:

- the power of providing a safe setting where victims, perpetrators and community members can openly express their emotions;
- the need to incorporate local leaders in the control structures of such processes;
- the value of such opportunities being focused on a specific goal, because working together to achieve a solution has its own cohesive dynamic;
- utilizing the settlement of the caseload of less serious crimes, which exists after all conflicts, as a tool to promote reconciliation as well as fighting impunity; and
- the value of a complementary approach to both serious and less serious crimes.

Other lessons learned from the CRP program will be uncovered slowly with greater opportunity to reflect and analyze its lasting effects and value. Perhaps the most important legacy of this experimental undertaking is the challenge it sets for other similar settings. Justice and reconciliation are not two combatants competing for the same resource pie. They are integrally related and inseparable partners in a common enterprise. Neither accountability nor the healing of historically related divisions between groups and individuals will provide lasting solutions unless they are part of an integrated and coordinated approach. Accordingly, resources, effort and innovative effort need to be directed at providing practical, achievable solutions to both challenges simultaneously and holistically. The success of the CRP program has thrown down a new gauntlet – it challenges us to look for new solutions, to enlist new partners, to formulate individual solutions for highly specific problems, and not to settle for the same tired old language and methods, which do little to achieve real progress towards reconciliation.

NOTES

1. James Dunn, *Timor: A People Betrayed* (Sydney: ABC Books, 1983, 1996); Jill Jolliffe, *East Timor: Nationalism and Colonialism* (St. Lucia: University of Queensland Press, 1978); John G. Taylor, *Indonesia's Forgotten War: The Hidden History of East Timor* (London: Pluto Press, 1991).
2. See references at note 1 above. These historical reports are consistent with witness accounts given publicly and recorded in the East Timor CAVR

booklets on, "Thematic Public Hearing on Political Prisoners", "Massacres, and the Impact of the Conflict on Children", and the "Role of Women in the Conflict."

3. Human Rights Watch, "Justice Denied for East Timor", January 9, 2003; "Report of the International Commission of Inquiry on East Timor to the Secretary-General, January 31, 2000", UN Doc. A/54/26, S/2000/59; *East Timor 1999 Crimes Against Humanity*, Geoffrey Robinson, consultant's report for the United Nations High Commissioner for Human Rights, July 2003.

4. Geoffrey Robinson, *East Timor 1999 Crimes Against Humanity*.

5. Human Rights Watch, *"Justice Denied for East Timor"*; Don Greenless and Robert Garran, *Deliverance: The inside Story of East Timor's Fight for Freedom* (Sydney: Allen and Unwin, 2002).

6. Report of the International Commission of Inquiry on East Timor to the Secretary-General, January 31, 2000, UN Document A/54/26, S/200/59.

7. In his letter which accompanied the Report of the International Commission of Inquiry on East Timor to the Security Council, the Secretary-General stated that he would "closely monitor progress" of the Indonesian domestic efforts to prosecute to ensure that a "credible response in accordance with international human rights principles" was implemented.

8. David Cohen, *Intended to Fail: The Trials before the Ad Hoc Human Rights Court in Jakarta*, International Center for Transitional Justice (August 2003); Amnesty International and Judicial System Monitoring Program, *Justice for Timor Leste: The Way Forward*, AI Index: ASA 21/006/2004.

9. Security Council Resolution 1272 (1999) established UNTAET on October 25, 1999, granting a mandate to "exercise all legislative and executive authority, including the administration of justice."

10. *New York Times*, March 4, 2001.

11. Filenotes of the meetings of the CAVR Steering Committee, July–Dec. 2001.

12. Report on Results of Consultations-CAVR Steering Committee, Sept.–Oct. 2000.

13. The Comissão de Acolhimento, Verdade e Reconciliacão de Timor Leste, established by UNTAET/REG/2001/10, July 13, 2001.

14. *Ibid.* The resulting Regulation in its Chapter 4 refers to Community Reconciliation Procedures. The village hearings are referred to as Community Reconciliation Processes. See Regulation 2001/10, Ch. 4, Section 22.

15. Regulation 2001/10, Schedule 1.

16. Regulation 2001/10, July 13, 2001, Section 27.5.

17. Regulation 2001/10, July 13, 2001, Section 32.

18. Piers Pigou, *CAVR's Community Reconciliation Process*, Report for UNDP, April, 2004. p. 76–77.

19. CAVR, Report of the CAVR, Introduction, p. 33; see also Part 9, Community Reconciliation, which has more detailed statistics. Available at http://www.ictj.org/downloads/CAVR/09-Community-Reconciliation.pdf.

20. *Ibid.*, p. 4.

21. Monitoring and Evaluation of the Community Reconciliation Process (June 2003), Ben Larke, CAVR adviser to CRP program, p. 7.

SOAS Library

Customer ID: 04293C82504A80

Title: Late Ottoman Palestine :the period of
Young Turk rule /Yuval Ben-Bassat and Eyal
Ginio
ID: 1807485518
Due: 16-01-18 23:59
Circulation system messages:
Successfully loanedItem Successfully loaned

Title: Palestinian identity :the construction of
modern national consciousness /Rashid Khalidi
ID: 1807405242
Due: 09-01-18 23:59
Circulation system messages:
Successfully loanedItem Successfully loaned

Title: Rethinking nationalism in the Arab Middle
East /James Jankowski and Israel Gershoni,
editors
ID: 1806561206
Due: 09- :59
Circ

22. D. da C.B. Soares, *A Brief Overview of the Role of Customary Law in East Timor*, paper presented at a symposium on East Timor, Indonesia and the Region organized and sponsored by the Universidade Nova de Lisboa (2000), p. 4.

23. The Regulation allowed for considerable flexibility within the framework required for each hearing and CAVR internal policies encouraged different cultural traditions from different regions being used in the CRPs.

24. Father Juvito, CAVR National Commissioner, speaking of a hearing at Holarua village, January 2004.

25. Piers Pigou, note 18 above, at p. 22.

26. D. Mearns, "Looking Both Ways: Models for Justice in East Timor", (November 2002) *Australian Legal Resources International*, p. 17.

27. Community elder at CRP hearing in Maliana District, November 2003.

28. Interview with Jamito da Costa, Director of Reconciliation procedure, CAVR. This estimate is drawn from information given by district teams on closure of the program.

29. Interview with an East Timorese government Minister, who asked not be named, January 22, 2004.

30. All quotes taken from *"Crying without Tears"*, *In Pursuit of Justice and Reconciliation in Timor-Leste: Community Perspectives and Expectations*, International Center for Transitional Justice, Occasional Paper Series, August 2003.

8 Justice at the grassroots? Gacaca trials in Rwanda

Timothy Longman

On April 6, 1994, a plane carrying the presidents of Rwanda and Burundi was shot down as it approached the airport in the Rwandan capital, Kigali, killing all on board. The assassination of President Juvénal Habyarimana served as a pretext for launching a long-planned program to eliminate political rivals to the president and his supporters. Violence was initially focused in the capital, as the presidential guard and other elite troops targeted opposition politicians and civil society activists of all ethnicities. As the group of military and political leaders who assumed control of Rwanda carried the violence into every corner of the country, however, it quickly assumed the clear characteristics of genocide, since it focused on Rwanda's minority ethnic group, the Tutsi, regardless of their political activity, class, age, or gender. By the time the rebel Rwandan Patriotic Front (RPF) took control of the country in mid-July 1994, more than half a million people had been killed.[1]

In the decade since the 1994 genocide and war, the government of Rwanda has undertaken a variety of programs to attempt to promote reconciliation, combat impunity, and prevent future communal violence. The government has built numerous memorials and established annual commemorations of the genocide, sought to create unity by adopting a new national anthem, flag, and seal, overseen the drafting of a new constitution and various political reforms, and instituted programs, including "solidarity camps" for students, former prisoners, and returned refugees to teach a revised history of the country. In addition, both the international community and the Rwandan government have undertaken trials of alleged perpetrators of genocide and other crimes against humanity as one means of helping to come to terms with the terrible events that overtook Rwanda. Yet classical judicial responses have proven inadequate to the needs of Rwandan society. The enormity of the crimes and the large numbers of people involved have overwhelmed the capacity of the courts. Many Rwandans have also felt that the ability of courts to contribute to reconciliation is limited, since their activity is removed from the general population, they focus on individual

perpetrators rather than social processes, there is little role for victims in
the court process, and there is no attempt to bring restitution to those
who suffered.[2]

In an attempt to meld the desire for justice with the need for reconciliation, the Rwandan government has instituted a novel judicial initiative to try those accused of participation in the genocide that builds upon
traditional Rwandan mechanisms for dispute resolution, known as
"gacaca". The new gacaca courts that have been set up throughout the
country involve popularly elected panels of lay judges who will oversee
open public trials of people accused of lower level crimes. While the
alleged organizers of genocide and those accused of rape will still be
judged in the Western-style national or international courts, the vast
majority of those alleged to have participated in the genocide will be
judged before their neighbors and families and sentenced by a group of
their peers serving as judges. According to the laws establishing it,[3] the
gacaca process will require each community to develop a record of how
the genocide occurred in their community and to determine those responsible for carrying it out and those who were victims, and it will
establish mechanisms for providing reparations to survivors.[4]

The purpose of this paper is to assess the gacaca process as a response
to mass atrocity with particular attention to relevant human rights issues
and logistical and political considerations. To support my analysis,
I draw extensively on research conducted under the auspices of the
Human Rights Center of the University of California, Berkeley. As part
of a wide-ranging study of the process of social reconstruction in
Rwanda, we have conducted an extended qualitative analysis of three
local communities in Butare, Byumba, and Kibuye provinces, including
observation of gacaca trials; a survey of over 2,091 individuals in four
Rwandan communes;[5] and interviews with numerous individuals.[6]
Based upon this research, I contend that despite some human rights,
political, and logistical concerns, gacaca has the potential to make an
important contribution to the fight against impunity and the search for
reconciliation in Rwanda. The ultimate success or failure lies primarily
in the will of the public to make the process work, whatever structural
and political constraints it confronts.

Judicial initiatives in Rwanda

The government that assumed power in July 1994 made a strong initial
commitment to judicial action.[7] Installed by the Rwandan Patriotic
Front, the rebel army composed primarily of Tutsi refugees from previous waves of anti-Tutsi violence in Rwanda, the new government saw

holding accountable those who committed atrocities as an essential means of fighting impunity and establishing order. Shortly after taking office, the government began to arrest thousands of people alleged to have participated in the genocide, but trials would not be possible for several years, since Rwanda's legal system had been devastated by the violence, with the vast majority of judges, lawyers, and magistrates dead or in exile. Furthermore, most of the chief organizers of the genocide were in exile, out of the reach of Rwandan prosecutors. Hence, the government of Rwanda formally requested that the United Nations create a tribunal to try those responsible for the 1994 genocide. On November 8, 1994, the Security Council adopted Resolution 955, creating the International Criminal Tribunal for Rwanda (ICTR), charged with bringing justice to those responsible for "genocide and other systematic, widespread and flagrant violations of international humanitarian law" and with contributing "to the process of national reconciliation and to the restoration and maintenance of peace."[8]

While the Tribunal has been successful at obtaining the arrest and extradition of a large number of suspects, it has worked at an excruciatingly slow pace and at a relatively high cost. The first trial at the ICTR did not begin until January 1997, and by March 2003, only 11 individuals had been judged. By December 2005, the number judged had risen to 26, with an additional 26 accused with cases in progress, and 17 others charged and in detention.[9] Furthermore, as I have argued elsewhere, the Tribunal has made very little attempt to influence the process of reconciliation within Rwanda, despite its being mandated to do so.[10]

Whatever the impact of the ICTR, it will try only a small fraction of those accused of crimes against humanity in Rwanda, focusing primarily on the chief organizers of the genocide, while the Rwandan domestic judicial system will deal with the vast majority of cases. In the months after the RPF took power, they arrested thousands of individuals under accusations of participation in the genocide. When the RPF attacked and closed the Hutu refugee camps in Eastern Zaire (now Congo) in 1996, thousands of additional people were arrested as they returned to their communities, bringing the total number of prisoners to over 120,000 people – nearly 2 percent of the total population. Yet even as thousands languished in poorly equipped prisons, the launch of trials was delayed by a number of factors. Rwanda needed a law to cover the crimes, since although Rwanda was a party to the 1948 Genocide Convention, genocide had never been expressly addressed in Rwanda's penal code. Also, the government needed to train hundreds of new judges, prosecutors, court clerks, police investigators, secretaries, and other judicial officers, to replace those killed, in exile, or in prison.[11]

The first genocide trials began in Rwanda in December 1996, yet even as the pace of trials gradually increased, the sheer numbers of accused overwhelmed the capacity of the system. By June 2001, only 5,310 people had been judged, while thousands of those in prison had yet to have formal charges lodged and dossiers drawn up, even after seven years of incarceration.[12] Yet the slow pace of trials was not the only problem confronting the Rwandan government in regard to its judicial system. The government saw trials as a means not only of bringing justice and combating impunity, but also of helping to heal individual and social wounds, bring reconciliation, and rebuild community.[13] But much of the public has remained skeptical about Rwandan trials. Human rights groups have criticized them for bias, incompetence, and failing to provide defense counsel,[14] though these problems have diminished over time.[15] A more fundamental problem, however, is the nature of trials in Rwanda, which are based on a Western legal system inherited from Rwanda's Belgian colonizers. Although there is a limited role for victims in the Rwandan system, the trials are detached from the communities they are meant to influence. Victims, relatives of the accused, and other observers have little opportunity to attend the trials, and for many people, the legalistic approach of trials is alienating and feels unrelated to local processes of reconciliation. Many Hutu regard the trials as dominated by political concerns, a form of victor's justice, while victims are frustrated at both their limited role in the process and the failure of trials to address such problems as reparations. In our survey, we found that about one third of the population viewed the trials in Rwandan courts negatively, while a slightly smaller proportion viewed them positively.[16] Other research has demonstrated that Rwandans feel only slightly better informed about Rwandan national genocide trials than about the ICTR.[17]

Gacaca as an alternative judicial response

Facing a prison population far beyond the capacity of the established justice system to process and seeking ways to fight impunity while contributing more effectively to reconciliation, the government of Rwanda has turned to a traditional dispute resolution mechanism, known as gacaca, as a basis for developing a new judicial strategy. Dating back to pre-colonial times, gacaca was a public gathering of respected community elders called together whenever necessary to adjudicate disputes between or within families, often involving land and other property, personal injury, or inheritance. Gacaca literally means, "small grass", referring to the lawn where gacaca meetings were traditionally held.[18] Gacaca was a means for Rwandan communities to resolve conflicts without involving political authorities, though when participants were unhappy with the results of gacaca, they could appeal to their chief. Under colonial rule, gacaca continued to occur, but it became less a community and family-based institution, directed instead by chiefs appointed by the colonial administration. The jurisdiction of gacaca also became more limited, as more serious offenses, such as murder, were usually taken to colonial courts.[19] Gacaca continued to be practiced even in the post-colonial era. In 1987, Filip Reyntjens, a Belgian political scientist, spent a month observing gacaca trials and found that gacaca continued to be widely practiced, with informal support from local authorities. Parties unhappy with the gacaca decisions could take their cases to the official courts (as they had previously done with chiefs), while the official judges took account of gacaca decisions in their own deliberations and frequently reaffirmed them.[20] Forms of gacaca have continued to be practiced since the genocide, as local administrators have brought community members together, particularly to regulate disputes over property as refugees have returned to the country.[21]

The proposal for adapting gacaca to deal with genocide cases came out of a series of meetings organized by then-President Pasteur Bizimungu in 1998–99 among leaders of government, business, and civil society to discuss Rwanda's political transition. The meetings, which came to be known as the "Village Urugwiro" consultations, after the presidential residence where they were held, made a variety of proposals for national institutional reform, including reviving gacaca.[22] As part of the Village Urugwiro deliberations, a 13-member ad hoc commission under the leadership of the Minister of Justice came up with a gacaca proposal, which was debated and adopted by the participants. This proposal was circulated for feedback from various Rwandan groups and from the international community before being forwarded to the Transitional National Assembly, where it was adopted October 12, 2000.[23]

The new form of gacaca that is currently being implemented in Rwanda represents a compromise between traditional gacaca and Western legal practices and standards. The new system preserves the popular participation of traditional gacaca and the adjudication by respected community members who are not legal professionals. But unlike the previous system, the gacaca courts organized to deal with crimes linked to the genocide are formally organized and recognized by the government. The rules of the new courts are codified, and their operation was overseen first by a special branch of the Supreme Court, the Sixth Chamber, created specifically for this purpose and later by the National Service of Gacaca Jurisdictions, which provides legal advisors for each district to advise and monitor proceedings.[24] Gacaca judges, known as *Inyangamugayo*, literally "those who detest dishonesty", are formally elected in government-organized elections, and the guidelines for these elections encourage selection of women, who have traditionally been excluded from gacaca, and adults of all ages, rather than simply the most senior men of the community. The new gacaca courts are expected to respect human rights and uphold international standards for fair trials as much as possible, given the structure of gacaca and the economic and social constraints confronting Rwanda. To distinguish the new system from the old, the new courts are called "inkiko gacaca", or gacaca courts, rather than simply gacaca.[25]

The gacaca process consists of two distinct phases. In the first phase, each community in the country will gather in a weekly public meeting to develop a limited record of the genocide in their community and to level charges against those they believe responsible for various genocide crimes. The task of the community meetings is primarily to draw up lists, such as lists of those who were killed in the genocide and those believed to have been responsible for their deaths. The Organic Law of 1996 divides genocide crimes into four categories, and under the gacaca law, each category is treated by a different level of court. It is up to the community meetings to determine the charges against individuals and categorize the crimes for which individuals are accused. In the second phase of the process, the lists of accused are forwarded to the appropriate level of gacaca court where they will be tried in open public trials before the full panel of judges for that court. The judges will have access to any case files that police investigators have developed to date, but the trials will depend primarily upon popular participation and testimony.[26]

As originally set up, there were four levels of gacaca courts, beginning with the smallest political unit, the cell, which groups approximately 100–500 families. Each cell elected 19 inyangamugayo, who were to be individuals of "integrity" at least 21 years of age, who then received a short training in legal procedure. The cell-level panels of judges appointed representatives to the next level, the sector, the sector panel selected members for the district panel, and the district selected members for the province.[27] In a reform in 2004, the province-level gacaca courts were eliminated, and special gacaca appeal panels were created. Crimes in category 4, property crimes, are treated at the cell level, while crimes involving physical injury without death, category 3, are treated at the sector level, and category 2 crimes, people who killed under the orders of others or attempted to kill, are treated at the district level. Those accused of category 1 crimes, organizing the genocide, participating in rape, or being particularly zealous in killing,[28] will continue to be tried in regular courts. Defendants in category 4 crimes have no right to appeal, given the relative leniency of sentences. Those found guilty of category 3 crimes can appeal their cases to an appeals panel of the next level of gacaca court. Appeals for the most serious offenses are to the regular courts.[29] The gacaca law also specifies sentencing guidelines, although gacaca courts have considerable leeway in determining sentences. The law encourages confession by offering those who have confessed reduced sentences and the opportunity to serve half those sentences doing community service.[30] Excluded from consideration in gacaca are the cases of people who were killed in massacres carried out by the RPF or in revenge killings. According to the government, these cases, even if they represent crimes against humanity, are to be taken to the regular courts.[31]

The election of gacaca judges took place quite successfully in October 2001,[32] and training of judges occurred in April and May 2002 and was undertaken again after delays in the gacaca process. After numerous organizations expressed concerns about the ability of Rwanda to successfully implement gacaca nationwide, the Sixth Chamber chose to begin gacaca trials with a pilot phase. On June 19, 2002, gacaca meetings began in one sector in each of Rwanda's provinces. Based upon feedback from these proceedings, the Sixth Chamber made revisions to gacaca procedures, and on November 4, 2002, they launched gacaca trials in one sector in each district in the country.[33] The date to expand the trials to all 9,001 cells, 1,545 sectors, and 106 districts in Rwanda was postponed numerous times until January 15, 2005. In subsequent months, gacaca courts began to function in most communities throughout Rwanda.

Human rights concerns for gacaca trials

Reporting on gacaca was initially quite positive, as observers praised the innovation of the government and spoke in almost romantic terms about gacaca's basis in Rwandan heritage.[34] The initiative has received extensive support from international donors.[35] Further, the gacaca initiative was very popular with the Rwandan public prior to its nationwide launch. In our survey, which was conducted after judges had been elected but before gacaca trials had begun, we found that 90.8 percent of people had a positive attitude toward gacaca.[36] Our qualitative work in the same communities where we conducted our survey suggests that people feel that they have greater control over the gacaca process, that it will speed up the prosecution and release of prisoners, and that gacaca is more linked to the community and local processes of reconciliation.[37]

In contrast to the generally positive popular and journalistic impression of gacaca, human rights groups and international jurists have raised serious concerns about the trials.[38] Human rights experts have raised concerns about the competence of the trial judges, the impartiality and independence of gacaca courts, the susceptibility of the courts to government influence, and the lack of sufficient right to appeal in the original proposal. The sharpest concerns have been raised in reference to the lack of a right to defense counsel and of equality of arms between the prosecution and the defense.

While these human rights concerns deserve serious consideration, gacaca should not be condemned simply because it differs from classical Western courts, since gacaca does have a sound juridical basis. Rather than drawing exclusively on classical Western common law and civil law traditions, gacaca draws in part on customary law. Many countries around the world have plural legal systems, with Western-style courts operating alongside local courts or other institutions, either formal or informal, that settle civil disputes or enforce a (usually unwritten) legal code based on local cultural and religious traditions. Customary courts continue to function in many former colonies, particularly for civil disputes and family issues,[39] but customary law most commonly gains notice when it is invoked in opposition to basic rights, as in attempts to use Islamic law to limit opportunities for women.[40] While the new gacaca courts are not identical to traditional gacaca and have jurisdiction over more serious crimes than customary courts usually address, gacaca should not be rejected simply because it has roots in customary law rather than exclusively Western law. To regard customary law as necessarily inimical to human rights demonstrates a very narrow understanding of both the diversity and the adaptability of customary law and may challenge the very notion of the universality of human rights.

Gacaca also draws on the growing movement for restorative justice, which takes into account community interests as well as the rights and interests of victims of crimes. According to Gordon Brazemore, restorative justice is "a three-dimensional collaborative process" between victims, communities, and offenders, in which offenders are held accountable for their actions before the victims of their crimes and the communities in which they committed offenses and they are provided an opportunity to redeem themselves, generally through community service.[41] In classical retributive judicial systems, crimes are seen as offenses against the state, and little or no consideration is given to the needs of the victims and communities in the aftermath of crimes. Restorative justice is a reaction against the overly formal practices of retributive courts and the exclusion and alienation of victims from the legal process. Neither the principles of customary law nor of restorative justice can be invoked to justify violations of basic human rights, yet the fact that both systems function in countries with comparatively good human rights records, such as the United States, Canada, and New Zealand, suggests that classical retributive judicial practices are not the only judicial approaches capable of providing fair trials. Human rights standards are framed in broad and general terms that, for the most part, do not dictate any particular course of action to be taken to achieve specific standards. Donoho speculates that the openness in human rights doctrines to allow diversity was probably intended by the states negotiating and ratifying treaties in order to preserve their "sovereign prerogatives."[42] The ability to interpret human rights standards in ways that are relevant to specific locales is necessary to protect international diversity without denying the universality of human rights standards.

While the basic principle of limited sovereignty is widely accepted, most international human rights institutions have not developed a juris-prudence to allow for the recognition of diversity in the interpretation of human rights norms.[43] The one exception is in the European human rights system, where the doctrine of the "margin of appreciation" has developed in the jurisprudence of the European Court of Human Rights. The doctrine recognizes the possibility of a number of acceptable alter-natives in relation to the implementation of most rights. The margin of appreciation is an interpretational tool used to differentiate between what can properly be left to the state or community to decide and what is sufficiently fundamental that the same approach is required by all states irrespective of their differing traditions and cultures.[44] The doc-trine of margin of appreciation therefore embraces the protection of diversity and encourages inquiry beyond a single interpretation of human rights norms. If we apply the concept of margin of appreciation to gacaca, we are pushed to look not simply at whether gacaca provides a fair trial in the way that classical Western courts do, but to the more basic question of whether gacaca's structures provide a fair trial.

One major area of concern raised by critics of gacaca is the level of legal competence of gacaca judges, who are not legal professionals and receive only very limited legal training but are being asked to decide on complex legal questions. While there is validity to this concern for competence, there is no basis for assuming that the only way to achieve fairness is to conduct a trial before a highly trained judge. While gacaca judges may lack in legal training, they benefit from an intimate know-ledge of the communities where they are conducting trials, what we might term "contextual competence", as well as from being well-respected members of the community. The immense popularity of the new form of gacaca courts appears to be due in part to a popular sense that gacaca judges will better understand the local communities, their norms, and the events under consideration. This is not to suggest that technical competence is of no significance in Rwanda. Rwandans do recognize that a level of legal knowledge is necessary for the conduct of a fair trial, particularly in classical courts, and some of the negative popular attitudes toward regular Rwandan courts are due to the low level of competence of judicial personnel in these courts in the past.[45]

While there are legitimate concerns about the level of technical training of the gacaca judges, the gacaca process does provide some means to attempt to correct for the problem, such as a system of legal advisors to provide technical assistance. There is one member of the National Jurisdiction of Gacaca Courts assigned to each province in the country, and they oversee a group of legal experts (at least one per district) who are present during gacaca trials – though their numbers are insufficient to be present at every trial every time it meets.[46] Gacaca judges received a short initial training, and they have received refresher courses regularly in the pause between their election and the beginning of most trials. Written booklets explaining the gacaca procedures and the relevant laws have been supplied to gacaca courts and are regularly consulted during the course of hearings. In addition, the most serious cases, and the only ones where the death penalty can be ordered, are referred to the national courts. If the system works well, the combination of legal training, assistance, and contextual competence could be sufficient to guarantee the right to a competent tribunal. In the gacaca general assemblies that my researchers and I have observed, the inyangamugayo judges read aloud relevant rules of procedure before beginning various aspects of the process, and they referred frequently to the gacaca booklet for clarification. On occasion, the gacaca advisers spoke up to clarify a point, while on a few other occasions, the inyangamugayo turned to the advisers for advice.

Concerns are also raised about the independence of gacaca courts, particularly because the judges will not be paid for their extensive service.[47] The judges, the majority of whom are poor farmers, are expected to devote one day per week to the gacaca process, which means leaving their fields or their jobs for the day. Since most judges are poor, there are fears that they may be susceptible to bribery. Furthermore, given traditional deference to authority in Rwandan society, the mostly uneducated inyangamugayo may be unduly influenced by officials or other elite individuals. The official advisors in particular may have undue influence, and government officials may seek to use their influence to dominate proceedings.

Several factors help to protect the independence of the gacaca courts. First, in response to criticism, the original Organic Law was amended to exclude political officials, civil servants, active soldiers, police, and magistrates, and political party leaders from serving as inyangamugayo judges. It was believed that such individuals could have undue influence on the process.[48] Second, the sheer number of judges on each panel helps to make influencing them more difficult. As one informant told us, "They could bribe one or two or even five judges, but nineteen? That would take a lot of money!"[49] This may be an overly optimistic assessment, but the number of judges does militate against an easy attempt to sway the court. Related to this, the sheer number of courts will make it difficult for any individual or group to influence the entire process. Erin Daly argues that, "The sheer number of tribunals operating simultaneously should protect the process as a whole from undue influence by the central government."[50] Third, because the judges live in the communities where the trials are being held and the trials are open to the public, the gacaca judges are more subject to community pressures as well as scrutiny than regular court judges. In fact, Rwanda's regular courts have not been subject to the same level of actual scrutiny, and have been widely and justifiably criticized for their lack of independence.[51] Some witnesses have argued that the accessibility and transparency of the gacaca courts will make them *more* independent than regular courts.[52] Furthermore, there are regulations built into the gacaca law to punish judges caught accepting bribes or otherwise succumbing to outside influences, and the panels of judges themselves can remove members for, among other causes, unethical behavior.[53] The training for gacaca judges has placed significant emphasis on the need for judges to have high integrity and to set an example for the community through their honesty.[54]

The primary concern raised in relation to the impartiality of gacaca is the flip-side of contextual competence and relates to the relationship of the judge to the community, the parties to the case, and possible involvement in the events that they will be asked to judge. Given the localized nature of the gacaca process and the extraordinary impact of the genocide on the entire society, judges are likely to know personally both the accused and their accusers, and they may have intimate, first-hand knowledge of the events described. More seriously, some judges have been accused of having themselves participated in the genocide.[55]

Several safeguards against partiality are included in the gacaca process. The law requires judges to recuse themselves from cases involving family members, and the accused have the right to ask that judges whom they feel will be unfairly biased against them recuse themselves. These rules are to be enforced by the other judges on the panel and by the Sixth

Chamber.[56] The election of the judges by the community on the basis of their "integrity, honesty and good conduct,"[57] and the extremely high level of transparency also provide safeguards against partiality. In the communities where we have conducted research, the elections seem to have been successful at choosing people who are both highly respected by their communities and characterized by a sense of fairness. The communities elected panels of judges that were diverse in terms of ethnicity, gender, and age, which should help to gain confidence from the population and encourage them to participate. Further, judges who prove themselves to be biased or otherwise "acting in a way inconsistent with the qualities of a person of integrity"[58] can be removed by their fellow judges, and community members will be able to raise the issue at various levels.[59] None of this guarantees that Hutu will be willing to convict fellow Hutu, but it does create an environment that encourages fairness.

One other area of concern in terms of impartiality is the lack of distinction between the role of prosecutors and judges.[60] The cell-level inyangamugayo judges are responsible for organizing the initial phase of gacaca trials, the general assemblies, in which charges are registered and alleged crimes categorized. In the cases of category 4 crimes, the judges will then sit in judgment over the accused whose accusations they helped develop, and will also organize the communities in testifying about the alleged crimes. This potential bias is compounded by the lack of defense counsel for the accused (described below). However, it is the president of each gacaca court who is charged with organizing the trials, including the initial phase of laying charges and developing the prosecution. Other judges will not be directly involved in prosecutorial work. This division of responsibilities between the president and the rest of the judges does need to be carefully maintained to reduce concerns of bias in relation to the judges. The official legal advisors as well as monitors of the process must play a role as well in seeing that judges remain unbiased in the process.

A number of concerns for the right to a defense are related to the principle of equality of arms between the prosecution and defense. Where prosecutors appointed by the state investigate and compile the cases, the use of a defense lawyer is seen as restoring equality between the accused and the state/prosecutors. The gacaca process as currently conceived provides no legal representation for defendants. Further, some senior Rwandan government officials have implied that the accused will not be allowed representation by a defense counsel, even if they are able to supply counsel,[61] because permitting defense counsel would distort a popular form of justice.[62] The lack of access by defendants to their case files and questions about the sufficiency of time provided to those accused to prepare their case also raise concerns about equality of arms.[63]

The failure to guarantee a right to defense counsel is certainly a concern. In a highly technical court, an unrepresented accused is at a grave disadvantage compared to the prosecutors, who are trained in the law and in court procedures, and the unrepresented party's ability to put forward an adequate case in defense may be severely undermined without the right to legal counsel. In gacaca, however, the role of professionals in the process is less extensive. Charges are drawn up in the assembly of the community during the first phase of the process. Nonprofessional judges categorize the crimes and forward the charges to the appropriate level of courts, where, in the second phase of the process, the president of the court organizes the trial. Judicial police investigators (IPJs), employees of the office of the prosecutor in the Rwandan system, have been gathering evidence against those accused of participation in the genocide since 1994. The IPJs will supply whatever accusations and evidence they have gathered to the judges for the trial phase of gacaca, but have no further role. The only professionals involved in the process are the representatives of the Sixth Chamber, who are to act in an advisory capacity.[64] As a result, defense counsel is less necessary to provide equality of arms in terms of technical and professional expertise. In fact, with lay judges, the participation in the trials of trained defense lawyers would tip the balance of trials in the favor of the defense.

Furthermore, the involvement of the community in the trial and the transparency of the conduct of the trial will be important factors in reducing the risk to the accused of being without legal counsel. The entire community, including the family and friends of the accused can be in attendance and will have the opportunity to speak in defense, and – contrary to some reports[65] – the accused have a right to call witnesses and to interrogate those who accuse them. As one Supreme Court justice asserted, "The accused will be taken to their own community, so the whole community will be able to testify."[66] The interplay back and forth within the community and with the accused and tribunal may be capable of providing a level of protection for the accused in this context perhaps similar to the protection provided by the use of legally trained counsel in a Western-style court. There is a heightened chance of success with such a system in the Rwandan context where the community is highly structured and organized, members of the community know each other, and many know who did what to whom during the genocide.

Although popular participation can help to correct for the lack of defense counsel during the actual trial, the lack of defense counsel raises serious problems in the pre-trial phase for the ability of the accused to prepare an adequate defense. The inyangamugayo judges have received legal training (albeit quite limited) and have the benefit of legal advisers provided by the Sixth Chamber. No similar resources are available to provide technical assistance to the accused. The most serious problems presented for equality of arms by the lack of defense are in the area of preparation of a case. While the judges will have access to case files, it is not clear that the accused will have similar access. Even with access, the high level of illiteracy among Rwandans means that many will not be able to read their case files. Since the president, vice-president, and secretary of all gacaca courts are required by law to be literate, illiterate accused will be at a disadvantage. Furthermore, the accused, because they are in prison, will not have an opportunity to carry out investigations and locate witnesses who could speak in their defense. Correcting this problem does not require defense lawyers, but could be solved using non-lawyer defense assistants to provide defendants with legal advice and in gathering evidence, locating witnesses, and otherwise preparing their cases.

In brief, there does not appear to be anything inherent to the gacaca process that is prima facie inconsistent with the respect of human rights principles. Of course, whether gacaca tribunals do in fact meet human rights standards will depend on how the trials are conducted on the ground. If the above safeguards are not implemented adequately or if despite the above safeguards judges succumb to external pressure, favor particular parties, or misapply the law, the right of the accused to a fair trial will be compromised. In examining any such failures, it will be important to consider whether the failures were due to an inherent flaw in the gacaca model which is not amenable to improvement by the addition of further appropriate safeguards or the strengthening of existing safeguards, or alternatively, whether the failure was due to factors beyond the design of gacaca which could be improved by strengthening or employing new safeguards. As is demonstrated by the functioning of the national court system in Rwanda, setting up a Western-style court system is no guarantee in itself that the trials conducted in that system will be fair.[67] What is of key importance is how well the system enacts the various safeguards that enable a fair trial, like the provision of a competent, independent and impartial tribunal, and the equality of arms. We must seriously contemplate the possibility that there is more than one acceptable way to do this.

Logistical and political concerns about gacaca

While the organization of the gacaca courts should not be viewed as inherently inimical to the respect of human rights, logistical and political problems do raise serious concerns about how well gacaca will be able to contribute to the process of reconciliation in Rwanda. The effective functioning of gacaca depends on extensive popular participation and its ability to contribute to reconciliation depends in large part on its local autonomy, but several factors threaten both participation and autonomy.

Gacaca is a decentralized system that assumes that most genocide crimes were committed at the local level, where both details of what happened and who was responsible will be known. While this is true in many cases, much of the killing in Rwanda was not, in fact, "intimate violence", where perpetrators and victims knew one another. Many Tutsi fled their communities when violence began and were killed elsewhere, meaning that the details of both who was killed and who did the killing may not be easily ascertained. The majority of victims were killed in major massacre sites, particularly churches, where relatively small groups of killers, mostly local party militia supported by gendarmes or soldiers, systematically killed thousands who had sought sanctuary. Often, killers from one community went to help out in neighboring communities after the slaughter in their own area was finished.

The fact that violence was not contained within local communities creates logistical problems for the decentralized nature of gacaca. In drawing up the lists of those killed, people in one community may know that certain people were killed simply because they were not found after the violence, while those in other communities may know that an individual participated in large-scale massacres without being able to identify most of the victims. Prisoners are generally brought to their home communities to face accusations, and the logistics for this have been relatively well organized, but with gacaca beginning throughout the country, the complexity of transferring accused prisoners to each of the communities where they may have participated in genocide becomes acute. The fact that Rwanda has seen a substantial movement of people since the genocide also creates logistical problems for gacaca. In particular, many genocide survivors, whose evidence is considered essential to the success of gacaca, have moved to urban areas to start a new life. In some parts of the country, particularly in Gikongoro or in northern provinces like Ruhengeri, communities have virtually no genocide survivors left.

The logistical issue of organizing testimony at the local level when potential witnesses are scattered raises a number of broader concerns over the role of witnesses in the gacaca process and the need for extensive popular participation. For gacaca to provide a fair trial it must involve a high level of participation by the population. It is the accessibility and transparency of gacaca that allow it to protect the rights of the defendants. The authors of the gacaca law, recognizing the importance of participation, included requirements for a quorum of community members for gacaca general assemblies.[68] Yet already in the pilot phase there have been problems meeting quorum requirements in some communities. In particular, gacaca's limited focus only on crimes related to genocide and not more broadly on crimes against humanity committed during the war has led to some public frustration and declining participation. In our research in Byumba, in a region where there were extensive massacres by RPF troops, many people expressed anger over the fact that the deaths of their family members were not included in gacaca. As a result, the gacaca assemblies in the communities we studied there had difficulty reaching the required quorum. The years of delay in starting gacaca throughout the country have also led to an increase in frustration and cynicism that may compromise participation. Despite concerns, however, the gacaca process remains popular. In the communities outside Byumba where we carried out observations, participation levels remained high. The statistics gathered by the Sixth Chamber on the test phase show that in general participation drops off after the first few meetings (where novelty encourages high attendance) but that most communities have no difficulty achieving quorum.[69] The level of community participation will need to be monitored to ensure that gacaca is achieving a level of accessibility and transparency sufficient to ensure a fair trial.

In addition to attending gacaca meetings, willingness to testify is essential to the success of gacaca. The testimony of genocide survivors has been considered essential in part because it has been assumed that they will be the most inclined to provide testimony. Relatives will probably be reluctant to testify against their own family members, and many people have assumed that Hutu in general will be under social pressure to show loyalty to their group by not testifying against their own group. Yet survivors generally are not the best sources of information, since they were not involved in the planning and execution of the genocide and most survived because they were in hiding during the violence. Further, survivors risk retraumatization from participating in trials and thus may be reluctant to participate. Where the genocide was most brutal, there may be no survivors. Hence, testimony from Hutu will be essential to the success of gacaca, a fact of which the organizers of gacaca are well aware. They have placed considerable emphasis in their public education surrounding gacaca on the civic duty of all people with knowledge to testify and the importance of this to the future of the country.

A primary means that government officials are using to gain necessary testimony for gacaca is a strong policy encouraging confession. The organic law prescribes substantially reduced sentences for those who confess their crimes, allowing those who plead guilty to serve half of their sentence in their home communities carrying out community service.[70] The government and its supporters have undertaken significant campaigns within the prisons to encourage confession, and thousands have complied, many inspired by a Born Again Christian revival movement that has swept through the prisons and pushed prisoners to repent their sins. In 2003, thousands of prisoners who had confessed were given provisional release into their communities, since many of them had already served more years in prison awaiting trial than their crimes were likely to warrant.

The policy of encouraging confession, while important to the success of gacaca, has certain obvious problems. The fact is that confession is rewarded with reduced sentences and early release creates great incentive to confess, but it does not guarantee the integrity of confessions. Most prisoners have confessed to lesser crimes, while only a limited number have confessed to participating in killings. Those who are innocent of any crime have a strong incentive to confess to something in order to win their release.

The greatest concern related to testimony for gacaca is the possibility of retaliation against those who testify. There have already been reports in a few places of assassinations of people who have testified against individuals in gacaca, and survivors' groups have raised serious concerns about the safety of survivors.[71] Retaliation is a threat not simply for survivors but for anyone who chooses to testify, as a couple of Hutu women at a gacaca hearing that I observed in Kibuye spoke openly about their fear of being punished "for telling the truth". Unfortunately, the decentralized nature of gacaca makes it very difficult to provide protection to witnesses throughout the country. Protection of witnesses will depend upon the support of the general population.

The final major concern for gacaca courts is the susceptibility of the process to political manipulation. The government initially decided to undertake gacaca to speed up the prosecution of genocide trials, but other political considerations (notably the adoption of a new constitution and presidential and parliamentary elections) have delayed the process by several years. The government has promoted gacaca as an important potential source of reconciliation, because it will let communities come to terms with what happened during the genocide,[72] but the decision to completely exclude other crimes, such as massacres carried out by the RPF during the war, means that only a partial accounting of the past will be achieved. Gacaca in part serves the government's interest in highlighting the centrality of the genocide and whitewashing its own crimes.[73] If gacaca in any way challenges these interests, either by insisting on considering RPF offenses or by failing to find sufficient numbers of people guilty of crimes, the government might seek to intervene, which could have severe repercussions for the ability of gacaca to contribute to reconciliation. If the government is too actively engaged in gacaca, then it may appear to be merely a tool for social control and not a fair judicial mechanism.

Conclusions

In this article, I have attempted to assess the potential for gacaca courts in Rwanda. In light of international human rights standards, there are some concerns which must be addressed, but there is nothing inherent to the gacaca process that is inimical to the protection of human rights. Gacaca appears to be a reasonable expression of the Rwandan government's sovereign right to establish courts consistent with the country's own culture and traditions. In addition, the acceptance of customary courts and restorative justice mechanisms in numerous countries around the globe provides important precedent for the acceptance of such mechanisms in a variety of contexts. A review of gacaca highlights the point that the right to a fair trial will not be realized in the same way in each jurisdiction. In fact, there are countless variations in the way states conduct criminal and civil trials, and most variations do not raise concerns for human rights standards. A less culturally bound notion of what constitutes a fair trial than that used by the critics of gacaca must be explored. What is involved in ensuring a fair trial within a community justice mechanism, as opposed to a court system, must be considered, and the cultural, political, social, and economic climate of Rwanda taken into account.

More troubling are some of the logistical and political concerns related to gacaca courts, yet the gacaca process itself is a response to the severe problems facing Rwanda in the aftermath of the genocide. With more than 100,000 people in prison under genocide accusations, Rwanda's court system was simply incapable of treating all of the cases. Whatever logistical problems gacaca may face, the system is certainly an advance over allowing thousands of accused to languish indefinitely in prison without trial. Furthermore, the idea of bringing justice to the people, of involving the population in the process of determining what happened in Rwanda in 1994 and who should be held accountable, is laudable. The involvement of the population in gacaca will, in the end, be what determines gacaca's success or failure. My research indicates that gacaca is highly popular with the general population primarily because it gives the people of Rwanda a rare opportunity to control their own destinies. People are enthusiastic about a judicial system that they hope to be able to see working themselves and over which they expect to have substantial influence. This does not guarantee the success of gacaca, but it does provide hope that gacaca may allow Rwanda to move toward reconciliation. Whatever problems ultimately arise, the popularity within the Rwandan population of the idea of gacaca suggests that other countries recovering from mass atrocity should consider community-based justice mechanisms as a possible alternative.

NOTES

1. The definitive source on the genocide is Alison Des Forges, *Leave None to Tell the Story: Genocide in Rwanda* (New York: Human Rights Watch, 1999). I discuss the genocide elsewhere, including Timothy Longman, "Civil Society and the Rwandan Genocide", in Richard Joseph, ed., *State, Conflict, and Democracy in Africa* (Boulder: Lynne Rienner, 1998).

2. See Gerald Gahima, "Re-establishing the Rule of Law and Encouraging Good Governance", speech given to 55th Annual DPI/NGO Conference, New York, September 9, 2002.

3. The law creating gacaca was adopted in October 2000 as "Organic Law concerning the creation of Gacaca Courts and organization of pursuit of infractions constituting genocide or crimes against humanity, committed between 1 October 1990 and 31 December 1994." In response to criticisms from human rights organizations, and others, a law modifying the original law was adopted in June 2001 as "Organic Law no. 33/2001 of 22/6/2001 modifying and completing Organic Law no. 40/2000 of 26 January 2001 concerning the creation of Gacaca jurisdictions and organization of trials of infractions constituting the crime of genocide or crimes against humanity, committed between October 1, 1990 and December 31, 1994." Both laws are available at www.inkiko-gacaca.gov.rw.

4. Among the tasks laid out in the Organic Law, Article 34, is drawing up lists of those who lived in the cell before the genocide, members of the cell who were victims, "the presumed authors of the crimes covered by the present law," and property damaged or destroyed.

5. The survey was designed and directed by Timothy Longman and Harvey Weinstein of the Human Rights Center of the University of California, Berkeley, Phuong Pham of the Peyson Center of Tulane University, and Alice Karekezi of the Center for Conflict Management at the National University of Rwanda.

6. The research was part of a John D. and Catherine T. MacArthur funded project, "Communities in Crisis: Justice, Accountability and Social Reconstruction in Rwanda and former Yugoslavia," Eric Stover and Harvey Weinstein, Principal Investigators. Longman has conducted fieldwork in Rwanda during two previous periods, 1992–93 and 1995–96.

7. For an overview of judicial initiatives in response to the Rwandan genocide, see Alison Des Forges and Timothy Longman, "Legal Responses to Genocide in Rwanda", in Harvey M. Weinstein and Eric Stover, eds., *My Neighbor, My Enemy: Justice and Community in the Aftermath of Mass Atrocity* (Cambridge: Cambridge University Press, 2004), pp. 49–68.

8. United Nations Security Council Resolution 955, November 8, 1994. Available at www.ictr.org.

9. International Crisis Group, "Tribunal Pénal International pour le Rwanda: Le compte à rebourss", Nairobi and Brussels: ICG, August 1, 2002; and www.ictr.org; letter dated December 5, 2005, from President of the ICTR to President of the Security Council, UN Document, S/2005/782.

10. Timothy Longman, Phuong Pham, and Harvey Weinstein, "Rwandan Attitudes Toward the International Criminal Tribunal for Rwanda", forthcoming paper. See also, Timothy Longman, Phuong Pham, and Harvey Weinstein, "Connecting Justice to Human Experience: Attitudes Toward Justice and Reconciliation in Rwanda", in Weinstein and Stover, *My Neighbor, My Enemy*, pp. 206–225.

11. Lawyers Committee for Human Rights, "Prosecuting Genocide in Rwanda: A Lawyers Commitee Report on the ICTR and National Trials", New York, LCHR, July 1997.

12. Ligue Rwandaise pour la Promotion et la Défense des Droits de l'Homme (LIPRODHOR), *Quatre Ans de Proces de Genocide: Quelle base pour les Juriditions Gacaca* (Kigali: Centre de Documentation et d'Information sur les Procès de Génocide, July 2001), at pp. 4–5.

13. See Gahima, "Reestablishing the Rule of Law", pp. 3–5.

14. LIPRODHOR, *Quatre Ans*, pp. 19–54; Lawyers Committee, "Prosecuting Genocide".

15. Interview with representative of LIPRODHOR, August 28, 2002.

16. See Phuong Pham, Harvey Weinstein, and Timothy Longman, "Rwandan Attitudes Toward the International Criminal Tribunal for Rwanda", *Journal of the American Medical Association*, August 5, 2004, pp. 602–613. Attitudes toward Rwandan trials were slightly more negative than positive among both Hutu and Tutsi, but negative attitudes were strongest among Tutsi.

17. Based on a survey conducted by the author for Internews and the International Center for Transitional Justice in late 2004.

18. Alice Karekezi, "Juridictions Gacaca: Lutte contre l'Impunité et Promotion de la Réconciliation Nationale", *Cahiers du Centre de Gestion des Conflits*, no. 3 (May 2001), pp. 9–96; Filip Reyntjens, "Le *gacaca* ou la justice du gazon au Rwanda", (December 1990) *Politique Africaine*, 40, pp. 31–41.

19. Charles Ntampaka, "Le *gacaca*: une juridiction pénale populaire", in Charles de Lespinay and Emile Mworoha, eds., *Constuire l'Etat de droit: Le Burundi et la région des Grands Lacs* (Paris: Harmattan, 2001). This

limitation was not, however, absolute, as at least some informants in our research remembered gacacas held even for murder during the colonial era.

20. Reyntjens, "Le *Gacaca* ou la justice du gazon".

21. Karekezi, "Juridictions gacaca", p. 36. Participants in the current gacaca process that we observed made considerable reference to disputes over property looted during the genocide already settled through gacaca meetings held since the genocide.

22. Karekezi, "Juridictions gacaca", pp. 17–22.

23. Ibid., pp. 30–37. The law is cited in note 5.

24. Interview with Anastase Balinda, Team Leader of Documents, Production, and Publishing Service, National Service of Gacaca Jurisdictions, in Kigali, January 13, 2005.

25. Alice Karekezi, personal communication.

26. Karekezi, "Juridictions gacaca", and interview with Cyanzayire, August 28, 2002, and interviews in Kigali and Butare, May, June, and August 2002.

27. Districts are similar to American counties.

28. The Organic Law, Article 51, includes in Category 1 not only planners of the genocide and people who used their position of authority to encourage the genocide but also "The murderer of great renown who is distinguished in the location where he resided or wherever he passed, because of the zeal that characterized his killings or the excessive maliciousness with which they were executed." This obviously leaves considerable room for interpretation.

29. The categorization of genocide crimes is spelled out in the Organic Law, Article 51.

30. Karekezi, "Juridictions Gacaca", pp. 37–60. Interviews June 16, 2002, August 28, 2002.

31. Interviews in Kigali, May and June 2002.

32. Stéphanie Maupas, "Gacaca: Une face à face avec le génocide", *Diplomatie Judiciaire*, October 8, 2001; Human Rights Watch, "Rwanda: Elections May Speed Genocide Trials", New York, October 4, 2001.

33. Marco Domeniconi, "Gacaca Takes off Slowly", Foundation Hirondelle, October 14, 2002.

34. See, e.g. Victoria Brittain, "The Unavenged", *Guardian Weekly*, March 21, 1998; Lara Santoro, "Rwanda Attempts Atonement", *Christian Science Monitor*, August 5, 1999.

35. At a meeting with international donors in September 2002, the participants reported that gacaca was at the moment the largest focus for international political assistance to Rwanda.

36. See Pham, Weinstein, and Longman, "Rwandan Attitudes".

37. This information comes from individual interviews and focus groups conducted since June 2001 in Ngoma, Butare; Mabanza, Kibuye, and Buyoga, Bymuba.

38. Amnesty International, "Rwanda: The Troubled Course of Justice", April 26, 2000; Amnesty International, "Rwanda: Gacaca – gambling with justice", June 19, 2002; Amnesty International, "Rwanda: Gacaca: A Question of Justice", December 2002; Human Rights Watch, "Elections May Speed Genocide Trials"; Leach Werchick, "Prospects for Justice in Rwanda's

Citizen Tribunals", *Human Rights Brief*, 8:15 (2000); LIPRODHOR, *Juridictions Gacaca au Rwanda*, pp. 66–68.

39. Jennifer Widner, "Courts and Democracy in Postconflict Transitions: A Social Scientist's Perspective on the African Case", (January 2001) *American Journal of International Law*, 95, pp. 64–75.

40. Ratna Kapur, "The Fundamentalist Face of Secularism and its Impact on Women's Rights", (Fall 1997) *Cleveland State Law Review*, pp. 1279–89.

41. Gordon Brazemore, "Restorative Justice and Earned Redemption: Communities, Victims, and Offender Reintegration", *American Behavioral Scientist* 41, 6 (1998), 768–814.

42. Douglas Lee Donoho, "Autonomy, Self-Governance, and the Margin of Appreciation: Developing a Jurisprudence of Diversity within Universal Human Rights", (2002) *Emory International Law Review*, 15, at p. 427.

43. Ibid., at n. 140.

44. Paul Mahoney, "Marvelous Richness of Diversity or Invidious Cultural Relativism", (1998) *Human Rights Law Journal*, 19, 1, p. 1.

45. Interviews in Butare, Kibuye, and Byumba.

46. Interviews in Kigali, May 31, June 2 and 16, and September 2003; Amnesty 2000, "The Troubled Course of Justice", p. 34; Article 29 of the Organic Law states: "Each time that there is need, the Gacaca Courts can be assured of consultation with judicial councilors designated by the Department of Gacaca Courts of the Supreme Court."

47. Amnesty International, "The Troubled Course of Justice", p. 34; Amnesty International "Gacaca: a question of jusice"; Human Rights Watch, "Elections May Speed Genocide Trials".

48. Organic Law, Article 11; Interview with Supreme Court Judge in Kigali, June 2, 2002.

49. Interview in Kigali, May 31, 2002.

50. Daly, "Between Punitive and Reconstructive Justice", p. 377.

51. See LIPRODHOR, *Juridictions Gacaca au Rwanda*, p. 37.

52. Interviews in Kigali and Butare, June and August, 2002; Organic Law governing gacaca, Article 12.

53. Interviews in Kigali, May 31, 2002, and June 3, 2002.

54. Interviews in Kigali, May 31, 2001, and June 3, 2002. This is also emphasized in the training manuals for gacaca instructors.

55. Interview in Kigali with Antoine Mugesera, President of the survivors' group IBUKA, June 2002.

56. Interviews in Kigali, May, June, and August 2002. Organic Law, Article 16 specifies that judges cannot participate in trials of anyone related to them "up to the 2nd degree," close friends, or former students or teachers. People are expected to recuse themselves, but the law also states that anyone who is aware of such a conflict of interests should bring it up before the court.

57. Integrated Regional Information Networks, "Rwanda: 'Gacaca' Timetable", United Nations Office for the Coordination of Humanitarian Affairs, March 23, 2001. Organic Law Article 10 defines a person of integrity as "being in good conduct, life, and moral; always speaks the truth; is honest; has a willingness to speak; has not been judged and sentenced to more than 6 months of imprisonment; has not participated in the infractions constituting

the crime of genocide or crimes against humanity; is free of the spirit of sectarianism and discrimination."

58. Organic Law Article 12 stipulates the potential reasons for dismissal as a judge.
59. Interviews in Kigali, May, June, and August 2002.
60. Werchick, "Prospects for Justice in Rwanda's Citizen Tribunals".
61. Amnesty International, "The Troubled Course of Justice", p. 33.
62. Human Rights Watch, "Elections May Speed Genocide Trials".
63. *Ibid.*
64. Interviews in Kigali, May, June, and August 2002.
65. Werchick, "Prospects for Justice in Rwanda's Citizen Tribunals".
66. This according to a judge of the Sixth Chamber interviewed on May 31, 2002, in Kigali.
67. Amnesty International, "The Troubled Course of Justice", LIPRODHOR *Juridictions Gacaca au Rwanda.*
68. Organic Law Articles 21 and 23.
69. Interview with Cyanzayire in Kigali, September 2002.
70. See the second revision to the gacaca law, Organic Law No. 16/2004 of June 16, 2004, Chapter II.
71. Interview in Kigali with Antoine Mugesera, President of the survivors' group IBUKA, June 2002; Human Rights Watch, "Rwanda", *World Report 2003*, New York: Human Rights Watch, December 2002.
72. See, for example, Richard Sezibera, "The Only Way to Bring Justice to Rwanda", *Washington Post*, April 7, 2002.
73. See T. Longman and T. Rutagengwa, "Memory, Identity, and Community in Rwanda", in Weinstein and Stover, *My Neighbor My Enemy.*

Eric Stover, Hanny Megally and Hania Mufti

Shortly after the US invasion and occupation of Iraq, L. Paul Bremer III, in his capacity as the chief administrator of the Coalition Provisional Authority (CPA), introduced several transitional justice mechanisms that set the course for how Iraqis would confront the legacy of past crimes for years to come. In developing these mechanisms, Bremer consulted with a select group of Iraqi exiles that had returned to Iraq or were still living abroad. However, he failed to solicit the opinions and attitudes of the Iraqi people as a whole. He also failed to consult many of the governmental and non-governmental entities that could pass on to the CPA and future Iraqi governments the "lessons learned" and "best practices" gleaned from transitional justice processes in other countries. As a result, many of the mechanisms introduced by Bremer either backfired or were hopelessly flawed.

Introduction

In early March 2003, weeks before the US invasion of Iraq, CIA officials and senior military commanders gathered at Camp Doha, Kuwait to plan for the eventual siege of Baghdad by US and coalition forces. Intelligence officials were convinced that Iraqis would rush to the streets to welcome American soldiers as they rode triumphant into the Iraqi capital. One CIA operative suggested that US special forces and Iraqi sympathizers should sneak hundreds of small American flags into the country for Iraqis to wave at their liberators. The agency would capture the spectacle on film and beam it throughout the Middle East. It would be the ultimate photo-op designed to win the "hearts and minds" of doubters back in the United States and throughout the Arab world.

But the idea was quickly quashed by the US commander of allied ground forces, Lt. General David McKiernan, who told those assembled at the meeting that US troops had been instructed not to brandish the flag so as to avoid being perceived as an occupying army. Undeterred,

IA officials continued to press the military officers for some form of ntry to celebrate what they saw as an imminent military victory for the United States and its coalition allies. "At first, it was going to be US flags," a military officer who attended the meeting recalled, "and then it was going to be Iraqi flags. The flags are probably still sitting in a bag somewhere."[1]

The debate in the war room at Camp Doha illustrates the dilemma that the United States faced as coalition forces swept into Baghdad. Having destroyed Saddam's military and security apparatus, the thinking went, American soldiers would be viewed as liberators and not as occupiers. By capitalizing on the good will of the Iraqi people the Americans could quickly scale back their military presence and bring in civilian experts to help a new Iraqi government, headed by expatriates like Ahmed Chalabi, create a new democratic state. "Of course," writes Larry Diamond, a former senior advisor to the Coalition Provisional Authority in Iraq, "these naïve assumptions quickly collapsed, along with overall security, in the immediate aftermath of the war. US troops stood by helplessly, outnumbered and unprepared, as much of Iraq's remaining physical, economic, and institutional infrastructure was systematically looted and sabotaged."[2] Then, as spring turned into summer, a nascent insurgency, comprised of foreign fighters and Saddam loyalists, began to emerge from the rubble, creating a security quagmire that would last for the foreseeable future.

Amid this growing chaos, L. Paul Bremer III, a career diplomat in the US Department of State and an expert on terrorism and homeland security, arrived in Iraq to serve as the chief administrator of the CPA. Bremer's job was to unravel the "Gordian Knot" of a postwar Iraq and to steer it toward a legitimate and viable future. In addition to rebuilding Iraq's overall economy and society, Bremer had to deal with a palpable demand for justice after thirty-five years of despotic rule and massive human rights abuses.[3]

Bremer issued several directives[4] in the first month of his tenure in Iraq that would set the course for how Iraqis would confront the legacy of past crimes for years to come. Most notable (and controversial) was the introduction of a de-Ba'athification program on May 16, 2003 to remove members of the Ba'ath Party from their positions of authority and to ban them from future employment in the public sector. Another decree, issued on December 10, 2003, created the Iraqi Special Tribunal for Crimes Against Humanity ("Special Tribunal")[5] to try Iraqi nationals or residents of Iraq accused of genocide,[6] crimes against humanity, and war crimes. He also mandated a series of administrative and institutional directives, including the establishment of a property claims commission, a central criminal court, and a new Iraqi army and civil defense corps.

In this article, we examine how Bremer's directives affected the process of transitional justice in Iraq and how ordinary Iraqis perceived these processes at the time. Our methods of research included interviews with dozens of Iraqi, US, and British officials, forensic scientists, and representatives of the United Nations and non-governmental organizations. We also conducted on-site visits to mass graves throughout Iraq and to governmental and non-governmental institutions that possess Iraqi state documents obtained during and after the war.[7] Finally, to understand how Iraqis would like to deal with their legacy of human rights violations and political violence, we drew on data obtained from extensive interviews and focus group discussions conducted in July and August 2003 with representatives from a broad cross-section of the Iraqi population by a team of researchers from the International Center for Transitional Justice (ICTJ) and the Human Rights Center of the University of California, Berkeley.[8]

Iraq's confrontation with its violent past presents one of the most complex cases of transitional justice since the end of the World War II. First, there is the sheer magnitude and severity of the crimes Saddam Hussein committed against the Iraqi people. The prior regime left thousands of government opponents executed, more than 300,000 missing and likely dead, thousands of towns and villages across the country destroyed, all dissent crushed, and hundreds of thousands internally displaced or living in exile abroad. This legacy of massive crimes has crippled Iraq and left it vulnerable to internal violence and civil war. Unless a middle ground can be found that brings those responsible for past crimes to justice while not singling out one group at the expense of others, Iraq faces the danger of further bloodshed and turning into a terminally weak state.

Second, deep-seated tensions within Iraqi society over identity, the US occupation, and future political power would determine how effective any transitional justice process will be in Iraq. Having lived under an autocratic state that imposed a single Iraqi identity for decades, Iraqis emerged from the war torn between defending that civic identity and their own ethnic and religious identities. Nowhere was this more evident than in the Kurdish areas to the north and the Shia areas to the south, where both groups had suffered terrible human rights abuses during Ba'athist rule. After the war, many Shia and Kurds were wary of how their groups would be affected by a new central government. Tensions also emerged between those Iraqis who supported the overthrow of Saddam Hussein and the subsequent US occupation and those who opposed it. Meanwhile, many Sunnis, and especially those who openly supported Saddam, feared that a new Iraqi government, and especially one that contained an overwhelming majority of Shia or Kurds, would target Sunnis as a scapegoat for the crimes of the past.

Third, in a post-conflict situation like Iraq in which the state has collapsed, security trumps everything: it is the central pedestal that supports all else. Without some level of security, transitional justice processes are doomed to fail. Court officials cannot guarantee the safety of potential witnesses, let alone the security of their own investigators. Nor can they secure mass graves and other crime scenes. Without security, courthouses and other places where people might gather to provide testimony to truth commissions remain vulnerable to armed attack.

Fourth, by the time of Bremer's arrival in Iraq, insecurity in Baghdad had turned the US occupation into a physical and psychological bunker. Separated from Iraqis by the formidable security around the three-square-mile "Green Zone" (where the CPA was based) and around the CPA's regional and provincial headquarters, the American civilians had little, if any, contact with the Iraqi people.[9] Indeed, the CPA (which ruled Iraq from May 2003 until June 2004) made no significant effort to consult Iraqis about the transitional justice processes that were intended to help them confront a violent past. When consultations did take place they tended to be between CPA officials and Iraqi exiles who had returned to Iraq or with members of the CPA-appointed Iraqi Governing Council (IGC). As a result, Iraq's transitional justice process could potentially be viewed as an American process operating under an Iraqi facade.

Finally, simmering tensions between the United States and the United Nations over the legality and necessity of the war had severely limited the participation of foreign experts in the process of transitional justice in Iraq. By "going it alone" the US had alienated many of the very governmental and non-governmental entities that were best poised to pass on to the Iraqis the "lessons learned" and "best practices" gleaned from similar transitional processes in other countries. Iraqis found they had limited access to international expertise ostensibly because only experts willing to work directly with the CPA, and receiving funding from the US government, were available to provide their knowledge and skills. Meanwhile, other experts, and particularly those working with non-governmental organizations, were left watching or merely critiquing from the sidelines.

Societies emerging from periods of war or political repression can deal with the past in a number of ways. Yet for such mechanisms to be effective in postwar societies they must meet three tests.

First, it is imperative that the wider population view the implementing authorities as both legitimate and impartial. Second, such measures should have been selected through a genuine process of consultation with those most affected by the violence. To the extent possible, all sectors of a war-ravaged society – the individual, community, society, and state – should become *engaged participants in*, and not merely *auxiliaries to*, the processes of transitional justice and social reconstruction – though, undoubtedly, at different periods of time and in different ways. Victims must receive formal acknowledgment and recognition of the grave injustices and loss that they suffered. Families of the disappeared must be able to recover, bury, and memorialize their dead. Bystanders – those who did not actively participate in violence, but who also did not actively intervene to stop abuses – should come to recognize that their passivity contributed to the maintenance of a repressive state. Perpetrators must be held accountable for their crimes so as to validate the pain and suffering of victims and to communicate publicly that the past horrors deserve societal condemnation. At the same time, accountability measures should be implemented in a manner that avoids stigmatizing the communities from which the perpetrators come.

Finally, to work effectively, transitional justice measures must be accompanied by programs that promote political reconstruction of a legitimate and capable state, economic and social reconstruction, freedom of movement, security and the rule of law, access to accurate and unbiased information, educational reform, and cross-ethnic engagement.[10] Critical to the development and implementation of these programs is the recognition that changes in one part of the system can reverberate through the system as a whole. Consequently, those who initiate transitional justice mechanisms must be mindful of how each new intervention or policy affects the aggregate. Such measures must work synergistically, with no single component aspiring to address all the needs of a postwar society. Each decision, each policy, has consequences, both expected and untoward. The challenge is to monitor and respond to these particular elements while at the same time seeing the whole picture.

In the end, the US-led process of developing and implementing mechanisms of transitional justice in Iraq failed on all three accounts. In this chapter, we explain why.

Accountability

At the war's end, it was clear that something had to be done quickly to jump-start a process of transitional justice in Iraq, if only to protect key documentary and physical evidence for future trials. By mid-May 2003,

Iraqis, desperate to find their missing and executed family members, had begun using their own means to exhume mass graves throughout the country. Lacking adequate forensic expertise and international assistance, they began opening graves in a manner that would prevent forensic identification of most—if not, all—of the remains.[11] For example, at two sites located near the Mahawil military base just north of the southern Iraqi city of Hilla, villagers used a backhoe to dig up more than 2,000 sets of remains, gouging and commingling countless skeletons in the process, while some families used their hands to dig for bones and shards of clothing and carted them away in wheelbarrows and buckets.[12]

The grim spectacle at the Hilla burial pits drew protests from international human rights groups which criticized the United States and other coalition authorities for not implementing a plan to help Iraqis recover the remains of their relatives in a dignified manner and to preserve evidence that might convict those responsible for these crimes. In late May 2003, the CPA's predecessor, the US Office of Reconstruction and Humanitarian Assistance, announced that it would take measures to secure grave sites, launch a media campaign to explain to the public the necessity of preserving grave sites, and request governments to send forensic teams to Iraq to exhume graves prioritized for forensic investigation.[13]

In the meantime, hundreds of thousands of Iraqi state documents that could have proven critical in future trials of suspected human rights offenders were lost or destroyed.[14] While US and coalition forces reportedly seized an estimated nine linear miles of documents, many other files were pilfered, looted or otherwise destroyed needlessly, resulting in the loss of potentially vital information. Some of the destruction took place in the context of the widespread looting in Baghdad and elsewhere, carried out within sight of the coalition troops which had apparently received no instructions about securing this material or protecting the premises in which it was found.

Not only was valuable trial evidence being lost, but the failure to protect security archives had the potential of contributing to retaliatory violence and vengeance killings, since the archives could identify thousands of security agents and informers by name. Moreover, a thriving trade in the sale and purchase of Iraqi state archives had emerged in Baghdad and other major cities. The representatives of three Iraqi political parties admitted to us that that they had purchased documents – in some cases on the open market, in other cases when approached by individuals hoping to make a quick sale. One estimated that the number of documents bought through individual sales accounted for as much as forty percent of his party's total collection. Under these conditions, it was likely that a substantial number of faked or forged materials were being injected into the documentation pool.

Amidst this chaos, international human rights groups called on the UN Security Council to appoint a commission of experts, as it had done for the former Yugoslavia and Rwanda, to recommend the best option for moving ahead with a tribunal. While the idea of a commission received the enthusiastic backing of the UN Secretary General's Special Representative to Iraq, Sergio Viera de Mello, it failed to gain traction in the Security Council. In April 2003, the Bush administration announced plans for an "Iraqi-led" trial process and, three months later, the IGC established a judicial commission to set up a special court to investigate and prosecute former government officials.

It was clear from the start that the Iraqi commission and its backers in Washington, DC had little appetite for anything other than an all-Iraqi court, a position that troubled many international human rights groups. "The Iraqi judiciary, weakened and compromised by decades of Ba'ath party rule," wrote Human Rights Watch in December 2003, "lacks the capacity, experience, and independence to provide fair trials for the abuses of the past. Few judges in Iraq, including those who fled into exile, have participated in trials of the complexity that they would face when prosecuting leadership figures for acts of genocide, crimes against humanity, or war crimes."[15]

Yet the prevailing view in Baghdad and Washington was that any future tribunal, with the exception of defense lawyers, had to be purely Iraqi. Some Iraqi jurists said that seeking assistance from international experts would be acceptable, but only for the purposes of sharing expertise with their Iraqi counterparts. Others said that the plethora of evidence of past crimes, in the form of forensic, documentary and testimonial evidence, would make the task of convicting members of Saddam Hussein's government a relatively simple affair. They accepted the notion of seeking international expertise to help in the investigative stage, and especially in the effort to gather forensic evidence from mass graves, but rejected the idea of having foreign jurists involved in any forthcoming trials. Privately, some Iraqi political leaders supported an international tribunal, while others were prepared to consider the option and ensure that it was discussed by the IGC.

Notwithstanding Iraq's strong and legitimate desire to be in charge of its transitional justice process, few if any Iraqi jurists, including those who had returned from exile, were knowledgable about recent developments in the field of international criminal justice. Effectively shut off from the outside world for decades, they knew little about the newly established International Criminal Court (ICC) or the ad hoc international tribunals for Rwanda and the former Yugoslavia. Nor did they have access to the jurisprudence generated by the ad hoc courts on topics like command responsibility, joint criminal enterprise, and complicity doctrine. To compound matters, Iraqi courts had virtually no experience dealing with complex criminal trials involving serious crimes under international law. Iraq's Penal Code, adopted in 1969, made no mention of war crimes, crimes against humanity or genocide.[16]

Much of the antipathy toward international participation in Iraq's transitional justice process was due in large measure to the Bush Administration's opposition to the ICC and any involvement by the United Nations in Iraq's internal affairs.[17] The United States also turned a cold shoulder to the expertise and considerable experience of non-governmental human rights organizations like Amnesty International, Human Rights Watch, and the International Center for Transitional Justice, which were concerned that the flaws of the new tribunal would be locked into place once the first trial began. During the summer and fall of 2003, the CPA and the IGC legal affairs committee consistently denied requests by these groups to comment on drafts of the law establishing the Special Tribunal. In private, some CPA officials said that they supported greater international consultation, and even recognized the merits of a hybrid (national-international) tribunal. But, in the end, they succumbed to the desire of Iraqi jurists and politicians who wanted to manage the process themselves. Some CPA officials felt the drafting process, because of political considerations, was moving too fast, and that consultations had in fact been very limited. In late September 2003, the CPA announced that the consultation process was over and all that remained was some "fine-tuning" of the text before it was to be sent to Paul Bremer.

Bremer signed the order establishing the Special Tribunal on December 10, 2003.[18] In their critique of the court's statute, Human Rights Watch noted that many of its provisions were in accord with international standards of human rights and international humanitarian law and that the definitions of punishable crimes were consistent with those contained in the statutes of the ICC and other international criminal courts. But the organization also criticized the Statute for disregarding essential fair trial guarantees, including the admission as evidence of confessions obtained through coercion. It also said the statute failed to set standards that would insure that judges and prosecutors possessed adequate experience and could function in an independent and impartial manner.[19] The organization called on the United Nations not "to lend its legitimacy and expertise" to what it called a "fundamentally flawed" tribunal[20] that was inherently vulnerable to political manipulation.

One of the most contentious issues surrounding the Special Tribunal's statute was the use of the death penalty.[21] Some UK officials based in Baghdad objected to its inclusion, especially as Paul Bremer had suspended its application for the duration of the occupation. Yet, these same British officials said that there was little they could do given the US government's support of the death penalty[22] and strong Iraqi public opinion in favor of its use against past human rights offenders. For their part, Iraqi political leaders we spoke to, while recognizing the necessity of breaking with a violent past, believed that the desire of Iraqis for retribution through the application of the death penalty far outweighed the financial benefits of gaining international acceptance of future trials. In the meantime, international human rights organizations argued that the Special Tribunal's use of the death penalty would send the message that the court wished to exact vengeance rather than render justice.[23]

By early January 2004, a month after the establishment of the Special Tribunal, it had become clear that neither the Iraqi authorities nor the CPA had taken sufficient steps toward the gathering and preservation of court evidence. Nor had they identified "local talent" that could work with international experts in the preparation of evidence for the trials. As a result, Washington dispatched a team of legal advisers to Baghdad to assess what needed to be done. The team, led by the State Department's Ambassador for War Crimes, Pierre-Richard Prosper, was comprised of legal advisers from the Department of Justice and the Department of Defense. The team had set out four priorities for its visit: (1) to advise the Iraqis on how to launch "a campaign to sell the tribunal to the Iraqi people" as a prelude to the gathering of testimonial evidence by investigators; (2) to find an administrator for the Special Tribunal as a first step towards its institutionalization; (3) to advise the Iraqi officials on appointments of both Iraqi and international investigators for the tribunal; and (4) to make security arrangements for the protection of tribunal personnel, particularly judges, prosecutors and investigators.

Prosper's trip led to significant changes in the US government's backstage handling of the Special Tribunal. In late January 2004, the US Department of Justice, with a budget of US$75 million, took primary responsibility for preparing prosecution cases against Saddam Hussein and other members of his government. In March, a Regime Crimes Liaison Office (RCLO) was established under CPA authority to take responsibility for gathering, organizing, and assessing the evidence to be used in the trials. It also assumed the responsibility of training personnel with the Special Tribunal. In late May, Greg Kehoe, a US attorney with ICTY prosecutorial experience, was appointed as RCLO Adviser and deployed in Baghdad.

US officials in Baghdad told us that they had every desire to "internationalize" the tribunal's team of advisers. Yet this aspiration failed to materialize. Some US officials acknowledged that non-prohibition of the death penalty in the tribunal's statute had discouraged some European experts who opposed capital punishment from coming forward, but that a way had been found around it, such as having the UK and others contribute administrators and advisers to judges, as opposed to prosecutors. The US contribution, by contrast, would consist mainly of analysts, investigators and security personnel. Department of Justice officials reiterated their commitment that it be an Iraqi-led process with an "advisory role" for the United States.

By September 2004, with more than forty of Iraq's most wanted war criminals including Saddam Hussein in custody, the Special Tribunal was in a state of disarray. Salem Chalabi, the American-educated lawyer who had been the court's chief administrator, had resigned and left the country. The court's rules and procedure had not been finalized. Efforts to find suitable jurists and prosecutors had resulted in only eleven appointments, far less than needed to investigate and try suspects charged with serious state crimes.[24] When Saddam Hussein and eleven other co-defendants were arraigned on July 1, 2004, the Special Tribunal was not in a position to take on the task. Instead, the arraignments took place under the jurisdiction of another CPA-established court, the Central Criminal Court of Iraq, applying Iraq's penal code rather than the Special Tribunal's statute. Several of the defendants, including Ali Hassan al-Majid, who is alleged to have led the chemical weapons attacks on Halabja on March 16, 1988 that killed at least 5,000 people, had sought legal counsel from elsewhere in the Arab world, but none had come forward.[25]

The Special Tribunal lacked a comprehensive plan for the collection, preservation, and analysis of physical and documentary evidence of past crimes. Since the overthrow of the Iraq government in April 2003, over 250 mass graves had been located across Iraq. Some are believed to contain the remains of thousands of victims, including entire families. By mid-October 2004, in the face of a deteriorating security situation, only two large-scale forensic investigations of mass graves had begun in Iraq, despite the CPA's initial plan to have several sites completed by the turnover of power to the Iraqis at the end of June. Similarly, the Special Tribunal, through the US-led Regime Special Crimes Office, was still negotiating with Iraqi non-governmental organizations and political parties to gain access to the state archives in their possession. If and when the court took possession of the documents, it would need to verify their authenticity and to link the information contained in them to individual suspects.[26]

In the meantime, interim Prime Minister Ayad Allawi had let it be known that he wanted the Special Tribunal to speed up its investigations so the first high-profile trial, probably against al-Majid, could begin in November 2004. Asked to comment on the prime minister's call to accelerate the trials, Greg Kehoe, an advisor to the special crimes office replied (ironically), "He certainly didn't consult with me first."[27] Kehoe doubted whether the court would be ready to begin its first trial until the first half of 2005. The key in each case was establishing "command responsibility" for systematic and widespread killing that occurred under Hussein's rule, and that, he said, was a very "complex issue."

Aware of the Special Tribunal's shortcomings, the US government sponsored a week-long training program in international humanitarian law for 42 Iraqi judges and prosecutors – almost the entire Special Tribunal – in October 2004. Citing serious doubts that the court could meet "relevant international standards," the UN Secretary General, Kofi Annan barred top prosecutors and judges from the UN war crimes tribunal for the former Yugoslavia from attending the training program. A newspaper correspondent who was allowed to attend the seminar reported that both the Iraqi jurists and their hosts admitted that they had little grasp of what one Iraqi judge called "this whole new body of law." Three Iraqi judges told the correspondent that they felt caught between international public opinion and the opinion of ordinary Iraqis. The judges wanted experienced judges from other nations to sit on the bench with them but feared that many Iraqis would see this as humiliating.[28]

Vetting and de-Ba'athification

Vetting to remove abusive officials from positions of authority, if carried out fairly, properly, and prudently, can be a legitimate part of a larger process of institutional reform in periods of transition. It can also play an important role in ensuring that past abuses are not repeated. History of the last 50 years shows that countries trying to make transitions to democracy must inevitably bring back some members of the ousted regime. After World War II, for example, the American occupiers in Germany implemented a broad de-Nazification program, but came to realize that they lacked the necessary knowledge of German society to rebuild its institutions and that the country would not become a functioning liberal democracy without the cooperation and expertise of many of those tainted by the previous regime.[29] When Paul Bremer arrived in Baghdad in May 2003 he set into motion a vetting and de-Ba'athification process (later adopted by the Iraqi Governing Council) that would have a profoundly destabilizing effect on Iraqi society. Indeed, Bremer and other CPA officials made the same mistakes as their World War II predecessors: they saw the former Ba'ath members only as villains and troublemakers. They did not consider, as difficult as it might be, that the Ba'athists' skills and experience, and their political power, made them indispensable in the effort to rebuild post-war Iraq.

The Ba'ath Party – *ba'ath* means "renaissance" in Arabic – was founded in Syria in 1947, as a political vehicle to promote Pan-Arabism. In the 1950s, Syrian exiles and Iraqi students brought Ba'athism to Iraq, which was then ruled by a military government. The Ba'athists came to power in 1963, in a coup that was followed by a bloodbath during which Ba'athists arrested, tortured, and killed their rivals. In 1968, in another coup, Saddam Hussein's wing of the Ba'ath Party took control of the country, and in 1979 Saddam declared himself president. By the time of the US occupation of Iraq, the Party, which kept its operations secret, was estimated to have had between a million and two and a half million members, most of them Sunnis, like Saddam. The Party had been virtually synonymous with Saddam Hussein's regime and the brutality it unleashed over its thirty-five years in power. Ba'athists were required to inform on their neighbors, their co-workers, and on one another. At the same time, party members filled jobs at every level of society and anchored the middle class.

For many Iraqi Shiites and Kurds, de-Ba'athification was an absolute necessity for a peaceful transition to democracy in Iraq. But the US-led coalition also needed to address the fears of the newly disenfranchised Sunnis, and, on a basic level, to keep the country functioning. In the end, Bremer opted to appease the Shiites and Kurds and issued a sweeping ban of Iraq's Ba'ath Party: all senior party members were barred from public life; lower-level members were also barred, but some could appeal.[30] A week later, he disbanded the Iraqi Army.

Bremer's order removed the top four ranks of Ba'ath party members from their positions and banned them from future employment in state jobs. Other party members, regardless of rank, were sacked from the top three layers of management in all national government ministries, affiliated corporations, and other government institutions. The order, Bremer said, would apply to 15,000 to 25,000 individuals, roughly one percent of the party's 2 million members.[31] Yet, over the next eighteen months, an estimated 30,000 party members, including some 6,000 to 12,000 educators, were summarily sacked from their posts.

Bremer declared from the outset that Iraq's de-Ba'athifciaton program would be Iraqi-led. In late May 2004, he established an Iraqi De-Ba'athification Council (IDC)[32] to investigate the identity and where-abouts of Ba'ath party officials and members involved in violations of human rights.[33] The IDC, whose members were appointed by Bremer, was mandated to investigate and gather information on the "extent, nature, location and current status of all Iraqi Ba'ath Party property."[34] Individuals adversely affected by the decisions of the Council could appeal in writing to Bremer for a reversal and he retained the authority to grant exceptions on a case-by-case basis.

It soon became obvious that the IDC was serving largely at the whim of the CPA.[35] In June, Bremer directed the Commander of Coalition Forces to establish several Accreditation Review Committees (ARCs) composed of two civilians and one military member (one of whom would be an Iraqi nominated by the Council) to undertake the functions previously vested in the Council. Bremer gave the US commander the power to use "military investigative resources" to compile information concerning possible Ba'ath Party affiliations of employees at all minis-tries. In addition, the commander could augment or replace these resources with "US civilian investigators" and, whenever possible, "in-clude professional Iraqis."[36] Bremer noted that as the Council "demon-strates sufficient capability, the Administrator will task [it] to assume increasing and ultimately full responsibility for the process, subject to the authority, direction and control of the administrator. The ARCs shall remain in operation until the people of Iraq adopt a representative form of self-government."[37]

In implementing its de-Ba'athification program, the CPA failed to consult the Iraqi people about the desirability of such a sweeping and often arbitrary process. A survey of a broad cross-section of the Iraqi population conducted by the International Center for Transitio-nal Justice (ICTJ) and the Human Rights Center at the University of California, Berkeley in July and August 2003 found that while the majority of respondents blamed the Ba'ath Party for past crimes and felt that those responsible should be dismissed, they also felt it was unfair to penalize individuals solely on the basis of their party membership and sough to draw distinctions between members of the Party, whom they referred to as Ba'athists, and ardent supporters of Saddam Hussein, whom they termed Saddamists. While respondents in northern Iraq generally supported a purging of the Ba'ath Party from government institutions, many respondents in central or southern regions expressed concern about the impact of wide-scale de-Ba'athification on the need for human resources to rebuild the country.

As the vetting and lustration process got underway in Iraq, Bremer's aim of gradually handing over responsibility to the Council was soon overtaken by events on the ground. In the face of international criticism of Bremer's de-Ba'athification process, the Iraqi Governing Council set up the Higher National De-Ba'athification Commission (HNDC) in August 2003. The following month, Ahmed Chalabi, an extremely vocal proponent of de-Ba'athification and a leading voice in support of the war to topple Saddam, was appointed chairman of the commission. Chalabi, in turn, appointed a protégé, Mithal al-Alusi, as its director. The commission occupied two floors of a concrete office block inside the Green Zone. A poster on one wall bore the message: "Ba'athists=Nazis."

The HNDC established an appeals process (which was retroactively ratified by CPA Memorandum No. 7 of November 14, 2003) to replace the one in place under the occupying authority's Armed Forces Commander. Under the HNDC procedures Director Generals (in the case of Ministries) or their equivalent (in the case of other public institutions) could issue advance notification explaining reasons for dismissals and providing details of the appeals process. Only individuals who held the rank of "group member" (*Udw Firqa*) or below, or officials who held positions in the top three ranks of management in the public sector could appeal. No one of the rank of section member (*Udw Shu'bah*) or above had the right to appeal. In addition, would-be appellants were given the blatantly unenviable choice of receiving their pensions if they accepted their dismissal notice or forgoing their pensions if they appealed.

According to a two-tiered appeals process, appellants could appeal to a local de-Ba'athification committee within two weeks of receiving their notice of dismissal and expect to hear within six weeks of their appeal. If denied, they could then appeal, within two weeks, to the HNDC itself and expect to hear within a further six weeks. The HNDC, acting as a higher appeals board, would include two judges appointed by the Judicial Council sitting alongside it. The signature of one of the two judges would be needed to ratify the decision of the HNDC.[38] At least that was the theory.

On September 14, 2003, Chalabi issued two decisions confirming the removal from public office of all full members who comprised the top four ranks of the Ba'ath Party and banning the nomination to the public sector, the political sphere, organizations of civil society, the media and broadcasting of anyone who had held the rank of group member (*Udw Firqa*) or above.[39] Chalabi's directives made it clear that the appeals process was increasingly more fiction than fact and could backfire by making disgruntled Ba'ath Party officials easy fodder for the insurgency. In response, the IGC sought to undo the damage by establishing central committees within the Ministries, aimed at reviewing individual cases and bringing back officials dismissed through the de-Ba'athification process and, secondly, enabling all those dismissed from the public sphere to apply for retirement pensions.[40] In November, in what seemed like trying to catch a train that had already left the station, the CPA rescinded its original order establishing a de-Ba'athification council and empowered the Iraqi Governing Council, through the HNDC, to carry out the de-Ba'athification process.[41] It also tried to wrest back control by calling on the HNDC to provide monthly reports to Bremer and to the IGC, including the names and positions of Iraqis dismissed from positions of employment, as well as the names of any Iraqi citizens hired to replace a dismissed employee.[42]

But it was too late. By March 2004, Chalabi's aggressive measures had begun to take their toll. Most notable was the dismissal of 12,000 Iraqi teachers who had found their appeals blocked, or endlessly deferred, by the review process. One of Chalabi's aides later criticized the HNDC, calling it a "government within a government" for its wide-ranging mandate and extensive resources.[43] Later that month Bremer intervened, ordering Chalabi to curb what senior American officials were now calling "overzealousness in the post-Saddam purge."[44] In April, the CPA administrator, while still defending his de-Ba'athification program, acknowledged that it had had a negative effect in Iraq, especially in the country's schools and universities:

[M]any Iraqis have complained to me that de-Ba'athification policy has been applied unevenly and unjustly. I have looked into these complaints and they are legitimate. The de-Ba'athification policy was and is sound. It does not need to be changed. It is the right policy for Iraq. But it has been poorly implemented . . . Professors who did not use their posts to intimidate others or commit crimes should be allowed to return to work promptly.[45]

He agreed to speed up appeals and facilitate allowing teachers and professors to return to work or obtain pensions.

By late June 2004, when the CPA dissolved itself, the process of de-Ba'athification had become a model of how not to do it. Initially, members of the Ba'ath Party were dismissed solely on the basis of belonging to the category of senior party member and without any reference to involvement in wrongdoing. However, to appeal successfully the burden of proof lay on the accused to prove no involvement in wrongdoing. Additionally, individuals were essentially blackmailed into choosing between appealing or receiving pensions and power was concentrated in the hands of one entity making an already non-transparent process vulnerable to the influence of individual political agendas. As a result, a significant number of party members were on the streets with no jobs, no way to sustain their families and most importantly no reasonable explanation whatsoever for the situation they found themselves in. Many educated Iraqis were unable to perceive de-Ba'athification policy as anything but "collective punishment."[46] In seeking to rectify the missteps in this process the CPA and the IGC again erred on the side of making sweeping decisions affecting large numbers of Iraqis. The new policies aimed at restoring people, including former members of the Ba'ath Party, to jobs have been more focused on needs for talent and skills than on principle. If an individual is indispensable within a ministry or is highly thought of by the rest of the faculty, they have been reinstated, thus creating a system of favoritism rather than one that upholds due process standards.

By September 2004, Iraq's de-Ba'athification program had emerged as a hotly contested political and security issue. On one side were several Shiite leaders and members of Chalabi's Higher National De-Ba'athification Commission, who argued that while the Commission may have committed errors in the past, former Ba'athists had been returned to their jobs through the appeals process. According to Ali Feisal al-Hamad, director of implementation at the HNDC, by November the Council had reviewed, annulled, and provisionally returned 15,000 of the 35,000 individuals dismissed by the CPA to managerial positions. The Council had retired a further 700 senior members, dismissed 3,000 not included in the original CPA action and was reviewing 8,000 cases.[47] On the other side were Iraqi officials like Prime Minister Ayad Allawi who called for the disbanding of the De-Ba'athification Commission and replacing it with a more lenient judicial system. The Ba'athist purges, Allawi and other IGC members argued, were undermining national unity and unwittingly winning the insurgents new recruits, a position shared by some American military commanders in the field.[48] Other critics charged that the Commission's purpose was being distorted by some of its members who had business interests in blackballing Ba'athist businessmen who had accumulated wealth under the former regime.[49] One day before hastily departing Baghdad, administrator Paul Bremer issued a memorandum paving the way for the disbanding of the HNDC as one of his final acts.[50] Under Memorandum 100, revising many of the CPA orders, regulations and provisions, Bremer withdrew the authority he had given to the HNDC under Memorandum 7 and authorized the interim Iraqi government to abolish the HNDC and establish a new body in its place. Since then, Allawi appointed a number of Ba'athists to senior positions – most significantly, in the military and intelligence apparatus – and moved to disband the HNDC.

Truth-seeking

Long before the onset of war, international human rights organizations and Iraqis in exile had begun discussing the idea of establishing a truth commission in Iraq to confront the massive human rights abuses of the Saddam era.[51] Such a commission could serve several purposes. First, unlike judicial proceedings against a small number of past offenders, an officially sanctioned truth commission could outline the full responsibility of the past regime and its various institutions that carried out or condoned the repression, including not only the military and the police, but also the judiciary itself. Second, a truth commission could provide victims with a forum to have their suffering acknowledged and help explore the possibility of providing reparations. Third, it could gather and analyze a vast amount of evidence from organizations and individuals both in and outside Iraq, with the aim of creating an "official" account of crimes against humanity and genocide, such as the "Anfal" campaign and the killing and displacement of Marsh Arabs. Fourth, a truth commission could help promote tolerance and reconciliation within Iraqi society without sacrificing accountability or ignoring already existing divisions. Finally, an Iraqi commission could explore the role of external actors in preventing or enabling human rights abuse.[52]

For a truth commission to succeed in Iraq, as in any country, it must be regarded by a broad cross-section of society as legitimate and independent from extraneous political factors; otherwise, it risks being marginalized or having a polarizing effect. In their 2003 survey of Iraqis, ICTJ and Berkeley researchers found that legitimacy and public support for a truth-seeking process in Iraq would only emerge through an open, transparent, and inclusive process of public consultation and education. "Among Iraqis in Iraq, there is little knowledge of or exposure to the idea of a truth commission, and not much exposure to other countries' experiences," the researchers said. "Thus, educating the emergent forces of Iraqi civil society, religious and community leaders, representatives of ethnic groups, and a broad cross-section of Iraq's (highly literate) population is an indispensable first step."[53] Respondents in the ICTJ–Berkeley survey were quick to suggest their own version of how a truth-seeking process should be conducted. Among the suggestions were "establishing local committees of reputable individuals to gather testimony and document the names of the dead and missing . . . declaring days of remembrance as national holidays; establishing memorials in every town and region; creating museums and documentation centers, photographic and videographic displays, and artistic works of literature, cinema, and theatre; and preserving detention centers and instruments of torture."[54]

By September 2004, neither the CPA nor the Iraqi Governing Council had consulted the Iraqi people about the need to establish a truth commission. Even so, CPA officials, largely at the urging of Bremer, had debated the merits of creating such a truth-seeking body since the Special Tribunal was established in December 2003. In early 2004, as a split emerged between the British and the Americans on the question of the Special Tribunal's application of the death penalty, the British made clear that they would not be able to play any direct role in supporting the tribunal process. As a result, it was agreed that, within the CPA's office for human rights and transitional justice, an American would oversee the tribunal's work and a British "advisor", working closely with the newly appointed Iraqi Minister for Human Rights, would oversee the process of establishing a truth commission.

In February 2004, one of us (Hanny Megally) met with British and Iraqi officials, including the human rights minister, and representatives of Iraqi civil society to discuss the need for consultation among Iraqis and coordination of the various transitional justice mechanisms being brought into play in Iraq. To their credit the British and the human rights minister accepted that such a process should not be rushed and would be doomed to failure if the CPA failed to consult the Iraqi people. However, in the ensuing months, as US troops sank into the quagmire of Falluja, Bremer, in need of a success story, applied intense pressure on his underlings to draw up plans for a truth commission and to have commissioners appointed to it by the July deadline for the handover of power to an interim Iraqi government. At one point Bremer's office set a ten-day deadline for a blueprint for a commission to be on his desk, but the task was never completed.

At the time of writing, the present Minister of Human Rights, Bakhtiar Amin, has declared the need for a truth commission and expressed his interest in helping set one up. It remains to be seen whether, and, if so, in what way, he will seek wide consultation among the Iraqi people before such a decision is made. In light of the ongoing friction in Iraq regarding the presence of US and coalition forces and the religious, ethnic, and social fault lines that persist, confidence in a non-partisan and impartial truth-seeking process will have to be built from the ground up. And it must involve all sectors of Iraqi society so that it is not perceived as a dialogue only between "elites" or certain political and ethnic groups.

Reparations

History has shown that reparations in the form of material and symbolic compensation are essential for victims of massive violations of human rights. They can be as fundamental as one-time financial payments to individual victims or collective processes, such as public memorials, days of remembrance, parks or other public monuments, renaming of streets or schools, preservation of repressive sites as museums, or other ways of creating public memory. They can encompass education reform, the rewriting of history texts, and education in human rights and tolerance. Yet whatever reparations scheme is pursued, writes Naomi Roht-Arriaza, caution must be taken not to use it "to stigmatize and marginalize those groups whose members perpetrated the abuse. Reparations must be offered in ways that acknowledge the suffering of victims but do not victimize others who did not actively engage in the violence."[55]

According to the 2003 ICTJ–Berkeley survey, while Iraqis overwhelmingly supported material and symbolic compensation for victims of violations of human rights, they did not necessarily support single-instance ex gratia financial payments.[56] Many respondents recognized that the losses suffered were incalculable and that no amount of money could replace a family member (or, in some cases, an entire family) who was killed by the regime. Respondents suggested forms of reparations that included providing physical and mental health services and access to education and employment, meeting basic needs for shelter, food, and clothing; returning confiscated property; and memorials inscribed with victims' names. The vast majority of respondents believed that the financial costs of reparations should be borne by the Iraqi state.[57]

The CPA withdrew from Iraq without paying serious attention to the issue of reparations for abuses committed by either the past regime or the US occupiers. Indeed, it was not until May 26, 2004, five weeks before the handover of power to the Iraqis, that Bremer sought to establish a special task force on reparations for past crimes. "No government or any other institution can erase these past abuses or remove the scars they have left behind," Bremer said. "However, compensation can provide an element of justice to those who suffered under Saddam's brutally oppressive regime."[58]

Bremer appointed Malek Dohan Al-Hassan, then head of the Iraqi Bar Association, as chair of the task force and instructed him "to work with victims, ministries, and others to define the types of injustice for which compensation should be provided." The group was also tasked to decide who would be eligible for compensation, the level of compensation that should be given, and the mechanisms through which it should be delivered. Bremer pledged to provide the task force with $25 million for initial compensation payments to victims and to cover the group's operating costs.

In a telling penultimate paragraph to the press release, the CPA notes that "in order for this to be a fully Iraqi process, the CPA has asked that Dr. Malek's report be concluded by August 1, 2004 so that it can be provided to the Interim Government as soon as possible after the transfer of sovereignty. Iraq's leaders, in the best interests of the Iraqi people, will determine how to act on the recommendations." In essence the task force was given just over two months to learn about the intricacies of reparations, study examples from around the world, conduct its own survey within Iraq, educate victims and families, and present its conclusions and recommendations to the interim authorities. Such a truncated process could hardly do justice to such a complex and potentially explosive issue as reparations. Indeed, soon after Bremer's edict, Malek Dohan was appointed Minister of Justice; a month later, the CPA had ceased to exist and by the end of August the task force had not yet met or begun its work. In December, at the time of writing, the taskforce had held its first meetings and begun to assess the process by which they would study other experiences around the world.

Conclusion

In his study of post-World War II Japan, historian John Dower noted how profoundly the American occupation affected that defeated nation: "Much that lies at the heart of contemporary Japanese society – the nature of its democracy, the intensity of popular feelings about pacifism and remilitarization, the manner in which the war is remembered (and forgotten) – derives from the complexity of the interplay between the victors and the vanquished."[59] How an occupying power interacts with the people of a postwar nation can affect that society for decades to come. Unfortunately, the American occupiers of Iraq never comprehended how Iraqis perceived them. Larry Diamond writes:

The coalition lacked the linguistic and area expertise necessary to understand Iraqi politics and society, and the few long-time experts present were excluded from the inner circle of decision-making in the CPA. Thus the coalition never grasped, for example, the fact that although most Iraqis were grateful for having been liberated from a brutal tyranny, their gratitude was mixed with deep suspicion of the United States' real motives (not to mention those of the United Kingdom, a former colonial ruler of Iraq); humiliation that the Iraqis themselves have proved unable to overthrow Saddam; and unrealistic expectations of the postwar administration, which Iraqis expected to quickly deliver them from their problems. Too many Iraqis viewed the invasion not as an international effort but as an occupation by Western, Christian, essentially Anglo-American powers, and this evoked powerful memories of previous subjugation and of nationalist struggles against Iraq's former overlords.[60]

Lacking an effective political strategy for postwar Iraq, it is easy to understand why the transitional justice mechanisms introduced by the CPA either backfired or were hopelessly flawed. The CPA never understood – or even listened to – the people it was seeking to help. Instead, it adopted an *ex cathedra* approach by which Bremer alone dictated what mechanisms would be adopted. In the case of documentary and physical evidence for future trials, the US-led coalition forces failed to secure the relevant sites at the time of the overthrow of the former government. Nor did they put in place the professional expertise and assistance necessary to ensure proper classification and exhumation procedures, with the result that key physical evidence has been lost or tainted. These failures have also frustrated families of the missing who, after years of silence, wish to know the fate of their loved ones.[61]

Having invaded Iraq without UN Security Council authorization, the United States was unable to convince many countries to take a meaningful role in helping Iraq deal with its violent past, something that could have blunted suspicions of the coalition. Always insisting that it would "go it alone," the CPA implemented accountability measures without properly consulting the United Nations and international human rights organizations, such as Amnesty International, Human Rights Watch, and the International Center for Transitional Justice, all of which possess considerable experience and knowledge of international and national war crimes tribunals. By sidelining these institutions, the CPA deprived Iraqi jurists charged with drafting the statute for the Special Tribunal of a wide range of perspectives on the procedural, evidentiary, and jurisprudential aspects of war crimes trials and the "lessons learned" from vetting and lustration programs in other countries.

It is difficult to measure how the photographs of torture and inhuman and degrading treatment of Iraqi detainees held in Abu Ghraib and other US detention facilities affected the attitudes of ordinary Iraqis toward the CPA and the transitional justice mechanisms it introduced during the occupation simply because no rigorous polling was conducted on that issue at the time. But it stands to reason that the photographs, which were widely circulated in the Iraqi press and repeatedly broadcast by Al-Jazeera and other news outlets in Iraq, must have undermined the legitimacy and authority of the US occupation in the minds of a considerable number of Iraqis. Moreover, the mass arrests of Iraqi men by US and Coalition forces in the second half of 2003 must have further undermined the legitimacy of the US occupation, especially as 70 to 90 percent of those who were taken into custody, according to military intelligence officers with the Coalition forces, "had been arrested by mistake."[62]

Clearly, the US-led coalition faced numerous demands when it took military and administrative control of Iraq in April 2003. It needed to quell a growing insurgency and to give immediate attention to numerous infrastructure, public health, and safety needs. By the same token, public statements by the Bush Administration both before and during the occupation placed a high priority on giving Iraqis back their dignity and a stake in their own future. American officials in Washington and Baghdad repeatedly promised to restore the rule of law in Iraq and to hold past human rights offenders accountable. These were lofty pledges, pledges that many Iraqis across the country, as well as many living abroad, embraced.

Missing, however, was the appreciation that confronting a violent past in a multiethnic society is a complex and inclusive process that involves a wide range of stakeholders including victims, bystanders, and perpetrators. It means consulting widely and broadly on the feasibility and applicability of transitional justice measures and, most of all, giving the Iraqis a voice in the process. For in the end, it is the Iraqi people who must unravel the Gordian Knot of past horrors if they are ever to obtain the justice they so clearly desire.

NOTES

1. See Michael R. Gordon, "Faulty Intelligence Misled Troops at War's Start", *New York Times*, October 20, 2004, at A1.
2. Larry Diamond, *What Went Wrong in Iraq*, (Sept./Oct. 2004) *Foreign Affairs*, 83 at p. 36.
3. For a discussion of the obligations of an "occupying power," see Geoffrey Best, *War and Law Since 1945* (Oxford: Clarendon Press, 1994), at p. 118; see also Caryle Murphy, "Occupation of Territory", in Roy Gutman and David Rieff, eds., 1999, *Crimes of War: What the Public Should Know*, pp. 263–64.
4. See www.cpa.gov/government/governing _council.html. Several orders deal with transitional justice measures, including CPA Order 1, "De-Ba'thification of Iraqi Society", May 16, 2003; CPA Order 2, "Dissolution of Entities", May 23, 2003; CPA Order 7, "Penal Code", June 10, 2003; CPA Order 13 (Revised), "The Central Criminal Court of Iraq", June 18, 2003; CPA Order 15, "Establishment of the Judicial Review Committee", June 23, 2003; CPA Order 35, "Re-establishment of the Council of Judges", September 21, 2003.
5. The jurisdiction of the Iraqi Special Tribunal covers the crimes mentioned above, as well as violations of stipulated Iraqi laws committed from July 17,

1968 to May 1, 2003. (CPA Order 48: "Delegation of Authority Regarding an Iraqi Special Tribunal", http://www.iraqcoalition.org/regulations/20031210_CPAORD_48_IST_and_Appendix_A.pdf). Article 14 of the statute provides: "The Tribunal shall have the power to prosecute persons who have committed the following crimes under Iraqi law: a) For those outside the Judiciary, the attempt to manipulate the judiciary or involvement in the functions of the judiciary, in violation, *inter alia*, of the Iraqi interim constitution of 1970, as amended; b) The wastage of national resources and the squandering of public assets and funds, pursuant to, *inter alia*, Article 2(g) of Law Number 7 of 1958, as amended; and c) The abuse of position and the pursuit of policies that may lead to the threat of war or the use of the armed forces of Iraq against an Arab country, in accordance with Article 1 of Law Number 7 of 1958, as amended.

6. Early in 1959 the government of Iraq, a military dictatorship, signed the Convention on the Prevention and Punishment of the Crime of Genocide.

7. See Human Rights Watch, *Iraq: State of the Evidence*, Vol. 16, No. 7, November 2004, available at www.hrw.org/ reports/2004/iraq1104/.

8. *Iraqi Voices: Attitudes Toward Transitional Justice and Social Reconstruction*, A Report of the International Center for Transitional Justice and the Human Rights Center, University of California, Berkeley, May 2004. A total of 395 people were surveyed through 38 key informant interviews and 49 focus group discussions, between July 18 and August 13, 2003.

9. Diamond, *What Went Wrong in Iraq*, at p. 39.

10. *Ibid.* at pp. 327–39.

11. Eric Stover, William D. Haglund and Margaret Samuels, *Exhumation of Mass Graves in Iraq: Considerations for Forensic Investigations, Humanitarian Needs, and the Demands of Justice*, (August 6, 2003) *Journal of the American Medical Association*, 290, pp. 663–66.

12. Human Rights Watch, *The Mass Graves of Mahawil: The Truth Uncovered* (2003).

13. US Office of Reconstruction and Humanitarian Assistance, Mass Graves Action Plan (2003).

14. See Human Rights Watch, Iraq, "Protect Government Archives from Looting", Press Release), April 10, 2003, letters dated April 9, 2003, addressed to US Secretary of State Colin L. Powell and Secretary of Defense Donald H. Rumsfeld.

15. See Human Rights Watch, Memorandum to the Iraqi Governing Council on "The Statute of the Iraqi Special Tribunal" (Dec. 2003), 1–15.

16. Some Iraqi judges argued that while Iraq's Penal Code does not include genocide in the list of crimes, any defendants facing this charge could be tried under Article 406 of the Code, which deals with murder including mass murder, Law 111 of 1969, Iraq Penal Code and amendments, 6th Edition, 2000 (copy with authors).

17. This position had changed somewhat by March 2004 as terrorist and insurgent violence increased and the Bush Administration realized that certain activities, such as elections, would be best managed by the United Nations.

18. Coalition Provisional Authority Order Number 48: Delegation of authority regarding an Iraqi Special Tribunal with Appendix A, signed into force by

Paul Bremer, December 10, 2003. http:// www.iraqcoalition.org/regulations/ 20031210_CPAORD_48_ IST_and_Appendix_A.pdf

19. Human Rights Watch, Memorandum to the Iraqi Governing Council, see note 15 above, at p. 1.

20. Human Rights Watch, Iraq, "Flawed Tribunal Not Entitled to U. N. Legitimacy", Press Release, January 6, 2004.

21. The death penalty was suspended in Iraq first in April 2003 by General Tommy Franks, the former US Central Command chief, and then by the CPA on June 10, 2003 through Order 7 (Section 3(1). Under Article 24(a) of the statute of the Special Tribunal, penalties for offenses "shall be those prescribed by Iraqi law." The death penalty is permissible under Iraqi law for certain offenses in some circumstances. Under Article 24(a), penalties that "do not have a counterpart under Iraqi law shall be determined by the Trial Chambers taking into account such factors as the gravity of the crime, the individual circumstances of the convicted person and relevant international precedents." See CPA Order 48.

22. Some CPA officials told us privately that the death penalty was slowing down the process of gathering and analyzing forensic evidence. Many medicolegal experts, it seemed, wished to have no part in a judicial process that included the death penalty. Yet other CPA officials said it was a non-issue.

23. Human Rights Watch, Memorandum to the Iraqi Governing Council, see note 15 above.

24. The Iraq Special Tribunal Statute provides for the appointment of one or more trial chambers, each comprising five trial judges, and nine judges to sit on the appeals chamber.

25. See John F. Burns, "For Hussein, a Spartan Life at His Former Palace", *New York Times*, September 19, 2004, at A1.

26. Human Rights Watch, Iraq, "State of the Evidence".

27. John F. Burns, "US Official Says Early Trials of Hussein and Others Are Unlikely, Despite Allawi's Demand", *New York Times*, September 25, 2004, at A6.

28. Marlise Simons, "Iraqis Not Ready for Trials: U.N. to Withhold Training", *New York Times*, October 22, 2004, at A11.

29. See David Cohen, "Transitional Justice in Divided Germany After 1945", in Jon Elster, ed., *Retribution and Reparation* (2005).

30. On May 16, 2003 Ambassador Bremer decreed the de-Ba'athification process in CPA Order No. 1.

31. L. Paul Bremer. CPA Press Briefing, 25 November 2003 (on file with authors).

32. CPA Order 5 of May 25, 2003. Order No. 1 issued by the Commission, September 14, 2004 declared all Ba'ath party members from the rank of *Udw Firqah* (group member) and above as dismissed from their positions and liable to punishment for disobeying this order.

33. CPA Order 5, Establishment of the Iraqi De-Ba'athification Council, May 25, 2003.

34. *Ibid.*

35. CPA Memorandum No. 1, Implementation of De-Ba'athification Order 1, May 16, 2003, issued June 3, 2003.

36. *Ibid.*, § 2.1.
37. *Ibid.*, § 1.2.
38. The official procedures for carrying out de-Ba'athification in the public sector and within government offices and ministries is available at www. debaath.org/page/ajr_h/ajw.htm.
39. Decisions Numbers 1 and 2 of September 14, 2003, issued by the HNDC, and signed by Ahmed Chalabi in his capacity as head of the HNDC are available at http://www.debaath.org/page/ka_h/ index.htm. The decisions banned from nominations anyone who was a member of Special Security, National Security, the special Presidential Protection Unit, military intelligence, Feda'yeen Saddam, and General Security services.
40. Available at www.debaath.org/page/ka_h/52_k.htm. The committees would review individual cases and where they reached a two-thirds majority agree to bring back the dismissed official. One of the criteria to be taken into account by the central committees was the "dire need" for the services of the dismissed person.
41. CPA Memorandum No. 7, November 4, 2003.
42. *Ibid.*
43. Christopher Dickey, "The Master Operator", *Newsweek*, March 2004, see http://msnbc.msn.com/id/4409622/.
44. John F. Burns & Ian Fisher, "US Seeking to Stabilize Iraq Casts Ba'athists in Lead Role", *New York Times*, May 3, 2004, at A1.
45. L. Paul Bremer III, Administrator, Coalition Provisional Authority, Turning the Page, Baghdad, April 23, 2004, available at www.iraqcoalition.org/ transcripts/ 20040423_page_turn.html.
46. Jonathan Steele, "Anti-Baathist Ruling may Force Educated Iraqis Abroad", *The Guardian*, August 30, 2003, at 16.
47. E-mailed memorandum to Hanny Megally dated November 13, 2004, from Ali Feisal al Hamad. He adds that those re-employed underwent a rehabilitation course of several weeks and their employment would be subject to a review by the HNDC after one year, at which point they could be dismissed or permanently re-employed (on file with authors).
48. See Edward Wong and Erik Eckholm, "Allawi Presses Efforts to Bring Back Ba'athists", *New York Times*, October 13, 2004, at A12.
49. Editorial, "Dangers of the Inquisition: How de-Ba'athfication is Helping the Rebels", *Economist*, November 27, 2003, at p. 43.
50. See CPA Order 100 of June 28, 2004, § 6, provisions 7; Revisions of CPA Memoranda Provisions and CPA Memorandum No. 7, "Delegation of Authority Under De-Ba'athification Order Number 1".
51. See, for example, the final report of the Working Group on Transitional Justice in Iraq and the Iraqi Jurists Association (March 2003) (on file with the authors).
52. See "Toward a Truth Commission for Iraq?" A Briefing Paper of the International Center for Transitional Justice, Feb. 2004.
53. *Iraqi Voices*, note 8 above, at pp. 55–57.
54. *Ibid.*, at p. 51.
55. Naomi Roht-Arriaza, "Reparations in the aftermath of repression and political violence", in Eric Stover and Harvey M. Weinstein, *My Neighbor,*

My Enemy: Justice and Community in the Aftermath of Mass Atrocity (Cambridge: Cambridge University Press, 2004), at p. 123.

56. *Iraqi Voices*, note 8 above, at p. 40.
57. *Ibid.*, at pp. 40–43.
58. Coalition Provisional Authority, Press Release, May 26, 2004.
59. John W. Dower, *Embracing Defeat: Japan in the Wake of World War II* (New York: W. W. Norton Inc., 1999).
60. Diamond, *What Went Wrong in Iraq*, at p. 43.
61. See Human Rights Watch, *Iraq: State of the Evidence*, note 7 above, at p. 2.
62. See Report of the International Committee of the Red Cross (ICRC) on the treatment by the coalition forces of prisoners of war and other protected persons by the Geneva Conventions in Iraq during arrest, internment, and interrogation (February 2004), at p. 7.

10 Truth, justice and stability in Afghanistan

Patricia Gossman

Afghanistan differs in important respects from other countries currently struggling with the problem of addressing past abuses. Afghanistan's transition from the repressive Taliban regime was not brought about by a popularly backed revolution, nor by a negotiated power-sharing accord among all parties to the conflict. Since the fall of the Taliban regime in November 2001, there has been no formal national or international agreement on any truth, reconciliation or judicial process to deal with the past – nor that there should be any such process at all. In fact, there has not as yet been any formal peace agreement, and the country is not yet at peace. Continuing conflict throughout broad swathes of the country's southern provinces, as well as in pockets in the north, imperils basic reconstruction efforts and has left civilians vulnerable to continuing abuses – in many cases by the same armed factions responsible for past war crimes.

Afghanistan's demographic indicators also present challenges to political actors who want to pursue a process leading to accountability for past violations. As of mid-2005, Afghanistan had experienced twenty-seven years of conflict, beginning with a bloody revolution, and followed by foreign occupation, civil war and back to international conflict. The endless war has devastated a country that was already at the margins in terms of every indicator of human development. Afghanistan ranks as one of the poorest countries in the world, and among the bottom ten countries in terms of basic human development, measured by infant and child mortality, life expectancy, access to health care and clean water, and general literacy.[1]

It is perhaps the most heavily armed country in the world, measured in per capita quantity of small arms. Its economy is one of the weakest in the world, and its illicit economy far outstrips legal government revenue and foreign aid combined. Its illegal economy is based primarily on the production of opium; it can be said that as of 2005, the afghani, the national currency, was the only opium-backed currency in the world. Control of the country's currently exploitable resources, along with traditional social ties, makes up a large part of the power base of the militarized patronage networks – the leaders of which are frequently referred to as "warlords" – that represent the greatest obstacle to security in Afghanistan.[2] These leaders and the power they wield both within the government and outside it also constitute the greatest challenge to pursuing accountability for past violations as well as curbing ongoing abuses.

A quarter-century of war

There are layers to Afghanistan's wars that also complicate the prospect for addressing past abuses. This was not one war, but a series of wars with the ongoing struggle between US forces and remaining Taliban and Al-Qaeda only the latest phase (along with continuing outbreaks of hostilities among competing factions in other parts of the country). Each time power changed hands in Kabul, the new authorities claimed their right to govern on the grounds that they had vanquished the abusive or corrupt regime that preceded them, and that they would now bring just rule to Afghanistan. The rhetoric of the communist revolution proclaimed an end to the tribal aristocracy, and the promise of land reform, mass literacy and education for women; the Islamic State of Afghanistan took credit for vanquishing an occupying atheistic power and sought to restore Islamic values to the country; the Taliban were initially motivated by a determination to rid the country of predatory warlords and (again) restore Islamic values. But in each phase, the new regime – or in the case of the civil war period, 1992–96, the competing factions – undermined the legitimacy of its own rule by abusing state power against its perceived opponents.[3] And so, the cycles of atrocities and conflict have continued. The US-led Coalition and its allies toppled the rigid and idiosyncratic authoritarian rule of the Taliban, and vowed to build a democratic nation-state. But as Coalition forces continue to engage in abuses, including arbitrary arrest, detention without due process – often in secret facilities – and torture, they have undermined their own authority and that of President Karzai's government.

The historical record of Afghanistan's quarter-century of war is sketchy, with huge gaps in the limited documentation. Although Afghan human rights organizations functioned either inside the country or from Pakistan at different periods of the wars, their efforts were circumscribed by the precarious and repressive conditions under which they had to work. International human rights organizations made a valuable contribution, but their visits to the region were infrequent and also limited in part by the lack of security. Thus, a significant obstacle to pursuing accountability is the absence of an impartial, well-researched and methodologically sound analysis of many of the major incidents of the wars. There is no dearth of witnesses and forensic evidence, but there is an enormous lack of capacity for field research and a need for thorough training in human rights documentation. Even under ideal security conditions, these would present major obstacles. As it is, Afghans engaged in human rights research face serious risks from the ongoing conflict and threats from powerful political actors.[4]

The war began with the communist revolution of April 27, 1978. In the twenty months between the coup that brought to power the Marxist-Leninist People's Democratic Party of Afghanistan (PDPA), and the Soviet invasion of December 24, 1979, Afghans experienced some of the worst atrocities of the entire conflict. The new regime, bent on the eradication of the old order and the elimination of any political or social opposition to its reform policies, rounded up and imprisoned, and then executed, tens of thousands of people.[5] In the countryside, village elders, religious leaders and schoolteachers were executed. Some religious and ethnic minorities were targeted, particularly the Shia Hazaras. In the cities, royalists, Maoists, internal faction members and members of the newly formed Islamist parties were imprisoned or killed. This period is perhaps the least well-documented of the war; few journalists had access to the country, and it was not before several more years that human rights groups began sending investigators to the refugee camps.

Ironically, the PDPA was eager to carry out reforms that nominally promoted fundamental rights, including education for girls and women, and a more equitable distribution of land. However, the regime's approach to implementing these reforms was brutal, and any opposition was crushed. Popular resistance to the regime's atrocities grew into a major military uprising. By late 1979, the army was on the point of collapse, and the regime was faltering. Hundreds of thousands of refugees had taken shelter in Iran and Pakistan, where faction leaders established bases for military resistance and channels for foreign assistance. Fearing imminent chaos on its southern border, the Soviet Union invaded.

Under the Soviet occupation mass executions declined, but the arrests of persons suspected of any ties to the opposition increased. Torture was widespread, and there are a number of documented cases of Soviet officers supervising the use of torture techniques. In the countryside, mass bombing was used to destroy the bases of support for the resistance among the civilian population. The result was catastrophic; hundreds of thousands of civilians were killed, and vast areas of the country laid waste as irrigation systems, orchards and farmland were systematically destroyed.

Despite US rhetoric about human rights violations by Soviet forces as part of its Cold War campaign against the Soviet occupation, the imperative for US policy was to secure a Soviet defeat. There was no discussion of accountability in the negotiations that culminated in the Geneva Accords and the Soviet withdrawal. The last Soviet forces left Afghanistan in February 1989, and on November 28, 1989, the Supreme Soviet adopted an amnesty excluding the possibility of prosecutions of any of its forces for deliberate or indiscriminate attacks against Afghan civilians.[6]

If there was little international interest in accountability for Soviet war crimes in Afghanistan, there was even less concern among the international patrons of Afghanistan's warring factions for what followed in the wake of the Soviet withdrawal. The government of President Najibullah held on to power in the cities for three years.[7] In April 1992, the government collapsed as mujahidin and local militia forces overran the city.

The next phase brought the war to Kabul for the first time. The Islamic State of Afghanistan (ISA) was nominally a coalition government that included many of the mujahidin factions and militias, but its second president, Burhanuddin Rabbani, head of the Jamiat-i Islami party, refused to cede the presidency to anyone else after his four-month term had expired, and thus drove most of the other factions into open revolt as they claimed strategic portions of the city for their own. All of the competing factions had a distinct ethnic base, and they targeted civilians for reprisals or extortion on the basis of ethnicity. The civil war period saw nearly five years of brutal fighting within Kabul. Outside Kabul, rival commanders carved up the country into their own fiefdoms, paying their troops with the spoils of battle and looting the country's limited infrastructure.

It was out of this chaos that the Taliban emerged in late 1994. Their early military successes won them the support of Pakistan as well as that of some Saudi officials and other Saudi sponsors, whose considerable financial and military backing enabled the Taliban to take control over most of the country, including Kabul, in less than two years, and most of the north two years after that. The Taliban quickly acquired international renown for their abusive treatment of women; less well-known was their record of massacres, particularly of minorities. On October 15, 1999, in support of its demand that the Taliban end the use of Afghanistan as a base for international terrorism and hand over Usama bin Laden, the United Nations Security Council imposed limited sanctions on the Taliban through Resolution 1267. The Security Council strengthened its sanctions through the adoption of Resolution 1333 on December 19, 2000. Neither the Taliban, nor any other party to the conflict came under sanctions for war crimes, even though virtually all of Afghanistan's neighboring states were involved in providing materiel support to favored clients.[8]

Even the sanctions against the Taliban were a charade. Through 1999 and 2000, while endless rounds of UN-sponsored negotiations among the so-called Six-plus-Two countries (Afghanistan's neighbors plus the United States and Russia) went nowhere, Pakistan continued to pour in weaponry, advisors and student "volunteers" to help the Taliban take more and more of the country.[9] The only crime the Taliban committed – other than their repressive treatment of women – that ever received international condemnation was the destruction in March 2001 of the ancient Buddhas of Bamiyan in central Afghanistan. The Taliban's long record of massacres and burnings in the very same region went virtually unnoticed.[10]

The Bonn Agreement and the entrenchment of the "warlords"

Afghanistan's transition from the Taliban regime to the current administration came about because of the US response to the attacks that took place on September 11, 2001. The present government of Afghanistan remains in power largely because of that foreign intervention. This distinguishes Afghanistan's transition from many others, though not all, that have taken place in recent years. US policy in Afghanistan has been shaped almost exclusively by this overriding preoccupation with the continuing conflict against Al-Qaeda and the Taliban. The way the military factions opposed to the Taliban – all of whom had the backing of US-led Coalition forces – inserted themselves into positions of power immediately after the Taliban collapsed has impeded efforts to prevent further abuses and pursue justice for past crimes. A significant number of leaders in senior positions of power in Afghanistan today, from provincial governors to police chiefs to members of the administration in Kabul, have been responsible for serious war crimes. Other powerful warlords continue to have inordinate political influence behind the scenes.

In December 2001, a conference bringing together the major military factions that had allied themselves with the US-led Coalition in ousting the Taliban, along with other prominent Afghan political groups – most notably the supporters of the former king, Zahir Shah, who was deposed in a coup in 1973 – was held in Bonn, Germany. The meeting was held under the auspices of the United Nations, and hosted by the government of Germany, with the United States playing a key role to ensure that the outcome suited its interests in its continuing efforts against the Taliban and Al-Qaeda. Indeed, as the negotiators in Bonn hammered out an agreement, the US-led Coalition forces continued to arm, fund and train forces associated with the faction leaders meeting in Bonn, as well as more autonomous armed groups, to fight the Taliban and Al-Qaeda.[11] What came out of the negotiations was a power-sharing agreement, and not an equitable one. It allotted most of the more important ministries to leaders from a single military faction, the Tajik Shura-i Nazar, based in the Panjshir valley in north-eastern Afghanistan. Thus, from the outset, the Bonn Agreement left many Afghans dissatisfied with what they saw as an unrepresentative administration.

International actors involved in shepherding Afghanistan's political transition through first an "interim" and then a "transitional" administration, and on to presidential and parliamentary elections – principally senior US and UN Assistance Mission in Afghanistan (UNAMA) officials – have publicly argued that they could not have prevented these factional leaders from claiming positions of power once the Taliban fell. Off the record, others have acknowledged that the entrenchment of these factional leaders was due to US pressure to include them in positions of power.[12] When the Taliban fled Kabul in November 2001, the ethnic Tajik Shura-i Nazar faction moved into the city first, despite official appeals by the United States and United Nations not to do so until an international agreement on an interim administration could be reached. But the move by the Shura-i Nazar fueled well-founded suspicions among the other factions that it would try to retain power in whatever new power structure took shape. Indeed, the Shura-i Nazar immediately gained control of the ministry of defense, foreign affairs and the ministry of the interior. In an effort to mollify other ethnically based factions, the minister of the interior was later replaced by an ethnic Pashtun, but many Shura-i Nazar loyalists remained within the ministry.

The problem was not isolated to Kabul, nor limited to the Shura-i Nazar. In many other parts of the country, commanders from various factions have become presumptive authorities, in some cases replicating the situation that prevailed after the communist government fell in 1992 and the country was engulfed in civil war. The post-2001 re-entrenchment of local commanders who hold sway over the populations under their control has been exacerbated by the fact that the United States has supported some of these commanders when they have seen them as a useful bulwark against penetration by Al-Qaeda. The entrenchment of the warlords was not inevitable, but a consequence in large part of the Pentagon's policy. While there was no support, understandably, for including any former Taliban leaders in the Bonn negotiations, the failure to identify and include more than a bare handful of credible ethnic Pashtun leaders in the political administration created left many Afghans with the impression that Pashtuns as a whole were to be stigmatized whether or not they had supported the Taliban. This has helped fuel resentment in the southern and eastern "Pashtun belt" of the country, some of which translated into support for a resurgent Taliban.[13]

In late 2004, following the presidential elections, a number of international actors were developing a strategy to persuade former Taliban fighters and other armed factions who had not been represented at the Bonn negotiations to accept a cease-fire with the government, and to identify individuals from these groups who might be acceptable candidates for some governmental positions, or who might form political parties. Such an approach might have defused support for the more extremist elements of these parties. The way the transition took place left little scope for addressing past abuses. During the closed sessions at Bonn, a heated discussion took place over the idea of an amnesty for war crimes. The original draft of the agreement, written by the United Nations, stated that the interim administration could not decree an amnesty for war crimes or crimes against humanity. This paragraph nearly caused the talks to break down after a number of powerful faction leaders told their supporters that the paragraph was aimed at discrediting all Afghans who took up arms, and that foreigners would use the agreement to disarm them. Principal among those making this argument was Abdul Rasul Sayyaf, a former professor of Islamic law at Kabul University and the powerful leader of the Islamist Ittihad-i Islami (Islamic Union), a party responsible for massacres and other war crimes that had amassed enormous support from Saudi sources, and brought many Arab fighters to join the *jihad* (the fight against the Soviet occupation) into Afghanistan in the 1980s.[14] UN Special Representative Lakhdar Brahimi argued forcefully in favor of keeping the paragraph prohibiting an amnesty, but in the end, the paragraph was removed, leaving open the possibility for an amnesty, though none has yet been proclaimed.[15]

While the delegates did not want to include a paragraph they thought could be read as maligning the mujahidin, they were also aware that amnesties have a bad name in Afghanistan's history. When the Islamic State of Afghanistan was formed after the fall of the Najibullah government in 1992, the first president, Sibghatullah Mujaddidi, proclaimed a general amnesty to promote national reconciliation. While it is doubtful that it had much impact, it caused deep resentment among many of the mujahidin factions who objected to what they saw as an attempt at reconciliation with the communists or those who supported them. Despite some fears that the same political leaders would argue for an amnesty during the constitutional convention in December 2003, the constitution does not include it.

Demobilization, disarmament and transitional justice

The passions stirred by the Bonn debate reveal much about the quandary facing Afghanistan's new reformists. Arguably the most serious obstacle to establishing the rule of law in Afghanistan is the ubiquitous presence of armed militias, some of whom answer to recognizable political leaders – when paid – and some of whom operate throughout the country virtually autonomously. How to demobilize these troops is a question with which Afghan authorities, together with the United Nations have been struggling ever since the Bonn Agreement was signed. The agreement calls for all armed forces to be withdrawn from Kabul, but resistance to such efforts has come from some of the country's most powerful leaders.

According to a journalist with long experience in Afghanistan who accompanied Northern Alliance forces into Kabul in November 2001, commanders from various factions anticipated that they would be disarmed immediately after Bonn.[16] That they were not indicated that the United Nations yielded to the United States, who was a reluctant partner in the initial stages of the demobilization effort, preferring to grant discretionary powers to groups they consider useful in the fight against Al-Qaeda. Long after the armed groups were well entrenched, the United Nations and the United States argued that disarmament takes priority over other concerns, including transitional justice.

The UN and Afghan government's Disarmament, Demobilisation and Reintegration (DDR) program, was finally launched in February 2003. DDR has been implemented through the Afghan New Beginnings Program, the main phase of which began in May 2004. Its initial objective had been to demobilize some 60,000 Afghan fighters before the national elections. By the time the elections were held, the numbers fell far short of that goal.[17] The program has continued to make slow progress, with many commanders resisting full demobilization, and some very likely hiding caches of weapons.

Demobilizing thousands of troops involves much more than simply destroying weaponry (all of which can be easily replaced in the arms bazaars of Pakistan). Nor is it realistic to expect thousands of militia forces, many of whom have known no other life than that of battle and the attendant criminal activities that provide the funds to feed and pay them, to take up another livelihood especially where alternatives are scarce.[18] International actors involved in the process have been stymied in their efforts to create alternative employment opportunities as international aid has fallen far short of what had been promised.

The slow demobilization effort is intimately intertwined with efforts to promote accountability for the past. In late 2004, former mujahidin blocked the roads in Panjshir to halt the scheduled handover of heavy weaponry, and *Payam-i Mujahid*, the organ of the Jamiat-i Islami party of former president Rabbani, claimed that the United States and United Nations were planning to use human rights and narcotics charges to prevent mujahidin from running as candidates for parliament after disarming them so they could not resist.[19] As with the amnesty debate in Bonn, some mujahidin leaders – particularly those aligned with Rabbani and Abdul Rasul Sayyaf, whose militia force that had been allied with Rabbani in the 1990s – continue to claim that any effort to address past abuses represents an effort to malign the mujahidin.

In the rhetoric of these leaders, disarming fighters connotes a dishonorable discharge from the *jihad*, and it is seen as a way of shaming those who fought. As one analyst involved in discussions on the demobilization efforts has argued, if the faction leaders convince their fighters that the foreigners want to arrest them for war crimes, they will never agree to demobilize.[20] The presence of thousands of former fighters who have not disarmed remains the greatest single threat to Afghanistan's security.

However, fear of retribution and the lack of other livelihoods are not the most important reasons Afghanistan's former fighters do not want to hand over their weapons. Even for those who might be incorporated into a new national army, the process has been fraught with difficulties. Former defense minister in the transitional government, Muhammad Qasim Fahim, a member of Shura-i Nazar, resisted efforts to demobilize his own militia and instead tried to incorporate most of it into the new national army. Not surprisingly, other commanders and faction leaders saw a Panjshiri Tajik-based national army as a threat to their security, and consequently were reluctant to demobilize their own troops. Some of Sayyaf's commanders in the 10th division have also been incorporated into Kabul's security forces. Progress to create a more ethnically balanced and professional army has been slow.

The power of the "warlords" and their ability to block efforts to transfer power to a more legitimate leadership or ever answer for their own crimes is also linked to the country's war economy. Immediately after the Bonn Agreement was signed, the international actors – the US-led Coalition and the major donors, along with the UN – had more leverage with the promise of badly-needed reconstruction funds to influence the behavior of the interim leaders. It took eighteen months after Bonn for President Karzai to finally get an agreement from the regional governors to hand over hundreds of millions of dollars in tax revenue, only after he threatened to resign if they did not comply. However, how well the governors have adhered to their promise is another question.

In the years since Bonn, many of the most powerful commanders in Afghanistan have come to depend on a more reliable and lucrative income from the country's illicit economy, and are thus far less dependent on foreign assistance to pay their militias, buy their weaponry and otherwise influence events on the ground. The recently rebuilt police cannot possibly compete. During a visit by the UN Office of Drugs and Crime, local opium traffickers had the use of four-by-four vehicles, satellite phones and automatic weapons. The police had bicycles.[21] If the national police cannot interdict drug traffickers, it is not likely they will be able to take action against war criminals either, especially since they are in some cases precisely the same people.

The Emergency Loya Jirga, Constitutional Loya Jirga and presidential elections

The Bonn Agreement established an interim administration and laid out a timetable for the holding of a grand assembly, or Emergency Loya Jirga, to select a transitional administration to govern before elections in 2004. The Loya Jirga took place in June 2002 and ratified the next phase of administration, the Afghan Transitional Administration (ATA).

After it was over, senior UN and US officials argued that the Loya Jirga represented the best that could be done in a country as ethnically divided and lacking in democratic institutions as Afghanistan. This is partly true. The selection of delegates to the assembly was an astounding achievement, as men and women chosen by district representatives from across the country gathered in the first such democratic experiment to take place in the country's history. The delegates arrived fully expecting they would have in their hands the power to make decisions about who would govern the country for the next two years before national elections. But the Loya Jirga was also, in the end, a betrayal of that very achievement. The rules governing the selection of delegates from the districts to attend the Loya Jirga stipulated that persons against whom there exist serious allegations of war crimes or other abuses could not be delegates. Unfortunately the rule was rarely enforced, largely because of pressure within UNAMA not to challenge some powerful commanders. Thus, the Loya Jirga represented another moment when US policy interests, fears within UNAMA about not alienating powerful and dangerous political figures, and simply bad management discredited the political process.

Moreover, contrary to the rules governing the selection of delegates, a number of political delegates were added at the last minute, among them commanders accused of war crimes. And rather than choose their leaders, the assembled delegates, under the watchful eyes of gun-toting commanders and warlords who were supposed to have been banned from the proceedings, found that many of the crucial decisions had already been made in back-room deals involving the United Nations, the United States and Shura-i Nazar.[22]

The delegates had anticipated that they would have a say in the selection of the president and the cabinet. That choice was denied them. The former king, Zahir Shah, was compelled by the United States and the Shura-i Nazar to announce that he would not seek office. The way his stepping aside was orchestrated caused deep resentment among his Pashtun supporters. Nor did the delegates have any say in the selection of the cabinet, which remained largely as it had been before the Loya Jirga, with all the most important ministries in the hands of the Shura-i Nazar. Even UN officials who defended the results of the Loya Jirga at the time acknowledged more than a year later that an opportunity to weaken the grip of the warlords was squandered for the sake of short-term stability.[23] Present at the assembly were a significant number of men and women chosen by their own communities, persons whose presence signaled the possibility of the emergence of new leaders in the country. But they were sidelined because the warlords were what the United States thought it needed at the time.

In December 2003, the Constitutional Loya Jirga was held, and the composition of the administration changed. Despite efforts to manipulate the process, delegates from parties with strong ethnic bases failed to shape the constitution to their purposes. Defense Minister Fahim, who had wanted a single vice-president, lost out: the constitution calls for two vice-presidents. Later in 2004, Fahim was dropped as defense minister and given neither vice-presidential slot on Karzai's ticket in the national presidential elections. Despite fears that he might mount a show of arms in response, nothing of the sort happened. Instead, he has joined the opposition party of former education minister Qanuni (who made a poor showing in the presidential election). As a result, the Constitutional Loya Jirga helped dispel some myths about the presumed legitimacy of the faction leaders as necessarily representing the political interests of ethnic groups. Afghanistan's ethnic groups are not always united in what their political interests might be. The debates on the constitution saw virtually all of the country's ethnic groups divided over key issues, and no "ethnic bloc" emerging around any particular leader. Ethnicity is as much a political variable in Afghanistan as it is anywhere else in the world. Various faction leaders have had the support of their "ethnic constituencies" when those constituencies have been threatened or feared losing out politically against Afghanistan's larger ethnic groups. But support for these ethnic faction leaders is partial, conditional, contested and context-specific.[24]

These would-be ethnic constituents have also been the victims of their very leaders. Many members of Afghanistan's Shia Hazara ethnic minority speak out vehemently against Hizb-i Wahdat, an alliance of principally Hazara parties, and its more notorious commanders, many of whom have been responsible for summary executions, torture and rape. Similarly, the powerful ethnic Uzbek leader Abdul Rashid Dostum is reviled as much as he is feared in his own northern stronghold. During the negotiations over the constitution, other Uzbek leaders keen on weakening Dostum's grip were willing to make compromises on some issues of regional autonomy so long as they could bring back to their constituencies tangible gains on recognition of the Uzbek language and other issues. However, ethnic interests played some part in the proceedings. The ethnic Pashtun delegates too did not initially represent a united front, but organized themselves into three separate groupings: the monarchists supporting a greater role for former king Zahir Shah, Pashtun democrats supporting a parliamentary system, and neo-Taliban Pashtuns along with Sayyaf's supporters who sought a greater emphasis on Islam and predominance given to Islamic sharia law. In the end, they all perceived that their self-interest lay in a strong presidential system, if only because the non-Pashtun delegates opposed it, and because President Karzai himself is a Pashtun.[25]

The passions stirred by the Bonn debate about the legacy of past abuses were revived during the Constitutional Loya Jirga. After Sayyaf had maneuvered to ensure that a mujahidin leader headed all the important working committees, one young delegate boldly called the faction leaders who were present "criminals" and accused them of destroying the country, being vehemently anti-women, and making Afghanistan the nucleus of international war. She called for them to be tried in national or international courts. Her remarks caused an uproar, and Sayyaf tried to have the delegate ousted from the proceedings for criticizing the mujahidin. He failed, but following threats from sources supportive of Sayyaf's position, the delegate has since had the protection of the UN in her home district.

Shortly after the conclusion of the Constitutional Loya Jirga, Kabul Television broadcast footage of a speech Sayyaf made in 1993, during the height of the civil war. In that year, Sayyaf's forces were playing a major part in the massacre of Hazaras and the destruction of the areas in which they lived in west Kabul. The video clip showed him boasting: "We have destroyed much of Kabul, but there are still some buildings left. We will destroy these too, to make way for the City of God." The clip may have had an effect on other leaders as well. Defense Minister Fahim (who at the time had his eye on one of the vice-presidential slots in the upcoming presidential elections), visited west Kabul in February 2004 and acknowledged that his troops were likewise responsible for the destruction of its neighborhoods and for other unspecified "crimes." Citing security concerns, he departed the area without taking questions from residents, some of whom were reportedly gathering to protest his visit.[26]

The reversal of fortunes for some political factions has raised the stakes for the parliamentary elections, where leaders who lost influence and power after the constitution and the presidential elections hope to regain it. In May 2005, *shabnama* (literally, "night letters," pamphlets distributed anonymously at night) began appearing in Kabul urging people to reject the "American-imposed" government and calling on voters to elect mujahidin for parliament. The *Payam-i Mujahid* article appears to represent a growing unease among some mujahidin leaders that their human rights records may be used against them in the parliamentary elections.

Judicial obstacles to justice

Afghanistan's new institutions remain extremely fragile. Its courts are not capable of ensuring due process in handling even ordinary criminal cases. Efforts to reform the judicial system have been slow, and transitional justice is not part of the mandate of the ministry of justice.

The Bonn Agreement stipulated that the Afghan judiciary was to be independent. The new Afghan Constitution, signed on January 4, 2004, also states that the judiciary "is an independent organ of the state of the Islamic Republic of Afghanistan," consisting of the Supreme Court, High Courts, (Appeal Courts), and Primary Courts. After the Bonn negotiations, Italy was asked to spearhead donor and UN efforts to assist the interim and transitional Afghan administrations in the area of judicial reform. But progress has been slow.

The Judicial Commission encountered serious political obstacles from the outset. The first appointees were all linked either to the interim administration's ministries or to the Supreme Court. When it became clear that the commission could not overcome its own internal rivalries nor operate independently, it was disbanded. By the time the next Judicial Commission was appointed in November 2002, the adminis- tration had already adopted several important laws.[27] More important, the Chief Justice of the Supreme Court, Fazl Hadi Shinwari, an Islamist and former head of a religious school in Pakistan, where many Taliban recruits were also educated, had appointed a large number of mullahs (Muslim religious teachers) as judges at district and provincial courts across the country, and had created a "fatwa council" in the Supreme Court to issue religious edicts.[28] Even if Shinwari were to be replaced, he has already left his imprint on the courts. Shinwari's like-minded colleagues made sure that the courts are authorized to rule any law contrary to the "beliefs and provisions" of Islam, potentially under- mining the fundamental rights guaranteed in the 2004 Constitution. Principal among Shinwari's backers has been Abdul Rasul Sayyaf.

As of May 2005, only one case has been tried in Afghanistan in which the defendant was charged with war crimes, and the fact that the case reached the courts at all represented something of a fluke. The defend- ant, who was charged with a range of crimes, only some of which constituted human rights violations or war crimes, had no defense coun- sel, witnesses were not subject to cross-examination and the presiding Chief Justice of the Supreme Court called for the death penalty before the defendant was convicted. Subsequent investigations by human rights organizations indicated that while there appeared to be sufficient evi- dence to convict the defendant on the war crimes charges, other charges brought against him were possibly fabricated.[29] On April 19, 2004, the defendant was executed on the orders of President Karzai, apparently in response to political pressure from Sayyaf, whom the defendant had named as giving orders for a number of massacres that had taken place in Kabul in the early 1990s.[30] Sayyaf holds no official political office but commands authority among Afghanistan's Islamist leaders, and has his own militarized political base west of Kabul. Members of his militia have been granted senior positions in the city's new security apparatus.

The Afghan Independent Human Rights Commission and transitional justice

The Bonn Agreement called for the establishment of independent com- missions to oversee the rebuilding of the judiciary, the monitoring of human rights, drafting the constitution and selection of civil servants. Of these four, the Afghan Independent Human Rights Commission (AIHRC), the only agency charged with addressing past crimes, has been the most successful. Though plagued with many problems common to a new organization operating in an impoverished and under-developed country, including weak management and research skills among its staff, the AIHRC has begun to make its presence felt. In its first year it established seven regional offices and launched a national consultation to survey Afghans about how to address past abuses. It has also issued briefings on specific areas of abuse, launched educational programs, and established a system for monitoring and collecting data on a range of human rights violations. Not surprisingly, some of its staff have already encountered hostility from the administration; some have received threats. Insecurity in many parts of the country has prevented the commission from operating effectively in those areas.

Despite resistance from international and Afghan actors, there are indications that nascent Afghan civil society is beginning to put some pressure on the Afghan government, significant donors and the UN to develop a strategy and mechanisms for addressing the legacy of the past. In November 2003, the AIHRC launched a national consultation process to assess public opinion about whether and how to bring to justice those persons responsible for the most serious crimes of the past. The report was given to President Karzai and made public at a press conference in January 2005.

The exercise alone was a significant achievement in a country completely lacking in any of the modern technological tools for assessing public opinion.[31] Thirty-two of Afghanistan's 34 provinces were visited by teams who conducted a survey of 4,151 individual respondents and separately convened 200 focus groups with over 2,000 participants. Refugee communities were surveyed separately. The report notes that:

In each focus group discussion people were overwhelmingly willing to discuss these issues. There seemed to be a sense of gratitude at the concept of being consulted at all. A man in Salang district of Parwan became quite emotional while responding to the survey questions, saying: "Now I feel that I am a part of this society, nobody ever asked our view on such important decisions." A man in Qandahar said: "So far, no-one has asked us: what do you, victims, want? Do you desire revenge? Do you want housing? Food?" In one of the village focus groups (in Doman), participants said they considered the consultation an extraordinary opportunity for the people of Afghanistan, mentioning that no one since King Amanullah Khan [1919–29] consulted the people on a national level.[32]

The report's findings reveal an understanding among many Afghans about both the difficulties involved in pursuing justice and the need to find an approach that combines some measure of retributive justice with reconciliation. Among the report's recommendations were:

- vetting for official appointments;
- provision for further documentation of war crimes;
- appropriate mechanisms for truth-telling;
- the establishment of a special investigations unit or prosecutor's office to begin investigating past war crimes; and
- symbolic steps to commemorate the victims.

While what the AIHRC's respondents meant by "justice" is not entirely clear, what AIHRC staff and others involved in compiling testimony about past abuses have discovered is that Afghans have expressed a need for the truth about the past to be exposed.

As discussed below, UNAMA's human rights office has begun discussions on some of these recommendations, including vetting procedures. In October 2004, an independent organization, the Afghanistan Justice Project, published a report detailing some of the major war crimes of the war between 1978 and 2001. It made similar recommendations, stressing in particular the need for methodologically sound documentation and getting information into the public domain.[33]

The AIHRC has also had to struggle against US intransigence. In March 2005, at the Human Rights Commission in Geneva, US pressure succeeded in terminating the mandate of the Independent Expert on Human Rights in Afghanistan, who was at the time Cherif Bassiouni, a professor of law who had served as Chairman of the UN Security Council's Commission to Investigate War Crimes in the Former Yugoslavia. The United States argued that because of the progress toward democracy in Afghanistan, the country did not need an independent expert. Bassiouni commented that "without a UN Independent Expert, the Afghan Independent Human Rights Commission as well as civil society in that country will not have that external support to advance human rights."[34]

During Bassiouni's tenure as UN Independent Expert, the United States blocked all of his efforts and those of the AIHRC to inspect detention facilities. Bassiouni had particularly condemned US use of "firebases" to hold detainees, facilities not accessible to the ICRC, in violation of the Geneva Conventions. In explaining why they have denied access to the AIHRC, US military officials have gone so far as to state that they "are not sure the AIHRC are good guys or bad guys."[35]

The United Nations and human rights in Afghanistan: Squandered opportunities

The AIHRC report was to be released together with a 300-page report prepared by the Office of the High Commissioner for Human Rights

mapping major incidents of war crimes and serious human rights violations committed by all parties to the conflict in the course of the war, but
in the weeks before the scheduled release of the UN report, UNAMA
pressed the High Commissioner, Louise Arbour, not to make it public.
UNAMA officials argued that a public release would endanger UN
staff,[36] and complicate negotiations surrounding the planned demobilization of several powerful militias, including one loyal to Sayyaf. They
also argued that as a "shaming exercise," the report raised expectations
that neither the United Nations nor the Afghan government could meet:
namely, that something would be done about the individuals named in
the report.[37]

In authorizing the "mapping" exercise in the first place, the OHCHR
had stated that the undertaking was in support of the AIHRC's consultation, with the explicit understanding that the reports would be released
simultaneously precisely because the UN report did what the AIHRC
report could not do, for security reasons: describe specific incidents, and
identify the perpetrators. Not releasing the report may or may not have
reduced risks to UN staff, but it is likely to have increased them for
the AIHRC. Days after the AIHRC press conference, Burhanuddin
Rabbani, the head of Jamiat-i Islami and the controversial president
of the Islamic State of Afghanistan during the factional fighting in
1992–96, and Sayyaf held a meeting to denounce the AIHRC report as
"anti-mujahidin," even though it named no individuals and discussed
only in general terms the fact that war crimes had been committed in all
phases of the war.

The decision not to release the UN report was only the latest of a series
of backtracks by the United Nations on human rights concerns in Afghanistan. Despite repeated attempts, all efforts by the United Nations
to undertake on-the-ground investigations into serious war crimes since
the mid-1990s have proved fruitless. These failures have left international non-governmental organizations, other international actors
and Afghans cynical about the prospect for the international community
to do anything about the issue.

A short history of this record illuminates some of the reasons behind
those failures, as well as continuing obstacles to investigating the past.
The first effort by the United Nations to undertake a forensic investigation was initiated following the massacre of thousands of Taliban
prisoners in 1997. In May 1997, after the Taliban failed to take control
of the northern city of Mazar-i Sharif, some 3,000 soldiers were taken
prisoner by General Malik, a former commander with the Junbish faction which had tried to seize power. According to witnesses, including
survivors, the prisoners were systematically executed, their bodies left

exposed in the open desert or stuffed into wells.[38] The massacre, unlike so many before it, attracted some press.[39] In addition, the Taliban called for an investigation. Over the course of the next year, the UN Office of the High Commissioner for Human Rights (OHCHR) sent two separate forensic missions to evaluate the sites and determine what would be necessary to undertake a full exhumation. Despite requests by the Taliban leadership, the then special representative of the UN Secretary-General, Lakhdar Brahimi, and the UN Security Council, the full investigation never took place. This failure only confirmed the Taliban's view that the UN and its member states, who were by 1998 very vocal about human rights violations by the Taliban, were partisan.

In August 1998 the Taliban finally took Mazar-i Sharif, and exacted revenge on the community they blamed for betraying them the year before: the ethnic Hazaras. As they swept through the towns and villages west of the city, the Taliban gained new recruits from local Pashtuns who had suffered abuses, including rape, by Wahdat forces. The Hazaras, being Shia, were also apostates in the eyes of the most extreme members of the Taliban movement, and those two factors fueled a second massacre: at least 2,000 people, mostly Hazara civilians were killed. Witnesses claimed that the Taliban official who took over as governor of Mazar-i Sharif incited the killings in public speeches, and that Taliban soldiers demanded that the bodies of those killed be left in the streets "to be eaten by dogs, like you did to us."[40] There is no doubt that revenge was one motivating factor in the second massacre. It could even be said that the UN's failure to properly investigate the first massacre hardened the Taliban's stance toward the rest of the world. From this time on, frustrated officials of humanitarian agencies on the ground began to talk about a cycle of impunity.

Conclusion

International attention to human rights concerns in Afghanistan has been plagued by inconsistency and selectivity. Since the fall of the Taliban, it has been shaped by two overriding preoccupations: fear of rocking the boat and thereby undermining Afghanistan's fragile stability – even if that stability has not translated into security for many Afghans – and the determination on the part of the United States to continue its fight against suspected terrorists on its own terms, in complete disregard of international law. Impunity for US forces responsible for ongoing human rights violations has rendered the prospect of pursuing accountability for past war crimes much more difficult.

Virtually all international and Afghan actors who have supported pursuing some kind of transitional justice process acknowledge that given the precarious security situation in the country, the only way such a process can have an impact is if it is undertaken gradually. Few envision that there will be any possibility of bringing to trial perpetrators of serious violations in Afghanistan any time in the near future; there is no real possibility of doing so within the country's enfeebled judicial system. However, other options both inside and outside the country do exist, and as of mid-2005, there were several initiatives underway.

In recent years, countries that took in Afghan asylum seekers in the early 1990s have begun to look more closely at the war records of those who had held positions as senior military or political figures. In July 2003, Britain arrested Zardad Faryadi Sarwar, a former Hizb-i Islami commander who has been running a pizza franchise in London after obtaining asylum in Britain under a false name. Commander Zardad, as he was known in Afghanistan, was charged with torture and hostage-taking. After an initial trial resulted in a hung jury, Zardad was convicted in July 2005 and sentenced to twenty years in prison, in the first such conviction in the United Kingdom under English law applying the Conventions against Torture and the Taking of Hostages. The response in Afghanistan to the news was resoundingly positive, with many Afghans suggesting other names (including those of commanders still inside the country) of those who ought to face similar charges. In October 2005, a Dutch court convicted two Afghans who had held senior positions within the secret police in the 1980s. Hesamuddin Hesam was sentenced to twelve years and Habibullah Jalalzoy to nine years imprisonment for torture and war crimes. Should other countries bring to trial Afghans charged with war crimes, it could send a powerful signal to others in hiding, or in power, that there will be no safe haven for them.

Despite disappointment among human rights groups and other NGOs over the UN's decision not to release the mapping report and over the perceived lack of support within the UN for any effort that names actual perpetrators or their crimes, there are some positive signs. The recommendations of the AIHRC's report provide the basis for a plan to gradually establish a number of mechanisms that could, if implemented, advance both the discussion of transitional justice in Afghanistan and its acceptance.

In December 2005, President Karzai signed the Transitional Justice Action Plan, a framework for establishing truth-seeking mechanisms, vetting procedures and other steps toward transitional justice. How well it will be implemented remains to be seen.

In the months before the national assembly elections scheduled for September 2005, the principal actors in the disarmament process – the Afghan government, the United Nations, the International Security Assistance force and the US-led Coalition – instituted a vetting process to screen out candidates linked to illegal militias. Under the Electoral Law, no persons could stand as candidates if they "practically command or are members of unofficial military forces or armed groups." The law also prohibited persons who had been "convicted of any crime including a crime against humanity" from standing for election, but in the absence of a functioning judiciary, no one had ever been so convicted. However, even vetting on the grounds of disarmament was fatally flawed. While it compelled some commanders to disarm, the more powerful were not touched, and only a handful of candidates were actually disqualified on these grounds. In some cases the Afghan government agencies involved, as well as the international ones, intervened either to protect clients or to allow a powerful commander to stand out of fear that disqualifying him would actually constitute a greater security risk. As a result, many candidates well-known to be war criminals were elected. Low voter turnout was blamed in part on popular disappointment with the failure to keep out the warlords.

There is no question that there are genuine security concerns in Afghanistan, and as yet no institutions in the country to support the prosecution of major war criminals. Senior UN officials, from Brahimi to his successor as Special Representative, Jean Arnault, have long talked of sequencing: that transitional justice must wait for other institutional transformations before it is possible. But rather than a carefully considered plan of action in which transitional justice finds its place, the security deficit has been used to excuse interminable delays for the sake of political expediency. The argument that accountability will undermine stability is not unique to Afghanistan. Such claims are common in post-conflict situations, though the risks are often exaggerated to suit political ends.[41]

The recent history of wars in Afghanistan makes clear that there is a strong correlation between past abuses and current abuse of power. It is a vicious circle: efforts to bury the past aggravate the very security risks and institutional weaknesses cited as reasons for avoiding addressing the past. In Afghanistan, those who benefit most from the failure to hold those responsible for war crimes to account include many powerful figures with links to criminal or extremist networks (or both). Among their ranks are political leaders who dominate the security and intelligence machinery, profit hugely from increased poppy production, suppress legitimate voices of dissent in the provinces, or incite attacks on foreign aid workers. The power they wield means they pose a genuine threat to every effort aimed at preventing Afghanistan from sliding back into chaos. Confronting the crimes of the past, and those responsible for them, is a process, not an event. It is about many things: restoring dignity to the victims; marginalizing or reducing the power of the war criminals through judicial and non-judicial mechanisms; and building institutions capable of curbing future abuses.

It will be a long time before Afghanistan is ready to initiate any judicial action against the worst offenders. But to the extent that other measures, including vetting, further documentation and symbolic acts acknowledging the victims of abuse move forward, even if slowly, then there is hope that the voices of Afghans who have called for a recognition of the truth as a first step will not be silenced completely. Transitional justice is about setting standards for the use of state power. In Afghanistan, beginning such an exercise would enhance the legitimacy of the current political process and the elected government.

NOTES

1. Barnett R. Rubin, Abby Stoddard, Humayun Hamidzada and Adib Farhadi, *Building a New Afghanistan: The Value of Success, the Cost of Failure* (New York: New York University Center on International Cooperation, in cooperation with CARE, 2004), p. 18.
2. I owe both the comment on the Afghan currency and the term "militarized patronage networks" to Barnett R. Rubin.
3. The interim and transitional administrations that emerged from the negotiations that followed the defeat of the Taliban have been accused of restoring known war criminals to power and failing to act to curb other abuses, but the state as such has not been accused of grave abuses of power.
4. In April 2005, I spoke with an independent human rights researcher who had been accosted by a stranger who warned her against publishing articles critical of the former mujahidin, and who told her that "all it takes is a car accident" to silence her.
5. Aryeh Neier, "What should be done about the guilty?" *New York Review of Books*, February 1, 1990.
6. *Ibid.*
7. Najibullah renamed the PDPA the Watan (Homeland) Party, and called it an Islamic party, claimed Islam as the state religion, abandoned the PDPA's reform policies and promoted "national reconciliation." Rubin et al., *Building a New Afghanistan*, pp. 166–75.
8. Human Rights Watch, *Crisis of Impunity: The Role of Pakistan, Russia and Iran in Fueling the Civil War in Afghanistan* (New York: Human Rights Watch Publications, July 2001), Vol. 13, No. 3 (C).
9. *Ibid.*

10. Afghanistan Justice Project, *Casting Shadows: War Crimes and Crimes against Humanity 1978–2001* (January 2005); Human Rights Watch, *Massacres of Hazaras in Afghanistan* (New York: Human Rights Watch, February 2001), Vol. 13, No. 1(C).

11. J. Alexander Thier, "The Politics of Peace-Building", in Antonio Donini, Norah Niland, and Karin Wermester, eds., *Nation-Building Unraveled? Aid, Peace and Justice in Afghanistan* (Bloomfield, CT: Kumarian Press, 2004), p. 39.

12. A former senior UN official told a number of NGO representatives that the UN Secretary-General's Special Representative to Afghanistan, Lakhdar Brahimi, had later described the Bonn Agreement as the "original sin." Interview with former UN official and with NGO representative, Kabul, 2003.

13. Ahmed Rashid, "The Mess in Afghanistan", *New York Review of Books*, January 29, 2004. Although the Taliban were almost entirely Pashtun, many Pashtuns never supported the Taliban. Some are monarchists and have always backed a stronger role for the former king, Zahir Shah. Others have backed Karzai's demand for a strong presidential system; still others have opposed him and have demanded a parliamentary system.

14. On Ittihad's war crimes, see Afghanistan Justice Project, *Casting Shadows*.

15. Email communication with participant.

16. Interview with journalist in Kabul, April 2005.

17. A pilot program took place in 2003, demobilizing some 6,000 soldiers, according to some reports. Afghan Research and Evaluation Unit, *The A to Z Guide to Afghanistan Assistance* (Kabul: AREU, 2004 3rd edn), p. 25. Others put the figure of those actually demobilized lower.

18. Rubin et al., *Building a New Afghanistan*.

19. Email communication from Barnett Rubin.

20. Email communication with political analyst involved in discussion on the DDR effort.

21. Barnett R. Rubin, "Afghan Dispatch", *Wall Street Journal*, February 10, 2004.

22. Thier, *Politics of Peace-Building*, pp. 55–56.

23. Interview in Afghanistan with former UN official.

24. Analysis of ethnicity as factor in constitutional debates derives from interviews with human rights expert in Afghanistan.

25. Ahmed Rashid, "Lessons from the Loya Jirga", *The Nation* (Lahore, Pakistan), January 12, 2004.

26. Interview with intelligence analyst, Kabul, February 2004.

27. International Crisis Group, *Judicial Reform and Transitional Justice* (Brussels/Kabul: 2003).

28. Another justice on the court with more than 30 years' experience as a judge stated that the "fatwa council", a throwback to the Taliban era, was illegal under Afghan law. J. Alexander Thier, "Attacking Democracy from the Bench", *New York Times*, January 26, 2004.

29. The defendant was a former commander accused of summarily executing civilians during the civil war in Kabul in the early 1990s. In addition he was charged with working for another commander and carrying out orders to

take hostage and torture Afghan men and women. He was initially arrested on charges of trying to murder his wife, and with having murdered three other women. In interviews with human rights researchers he admitted that he had killed civilians when acting under orders, but denied the other charges. Afghanistan Justice Project, *Casting Shadows*.

30. The defendant had offered to show mass grave sites to human rights researchers. Interview with this author, 2004.

31. Afghanistan never had a working telephone service for most of the country before the war; what did exist was destroyed early in the war. Mobile telephones are now common among wealthier Afghans in urban areas, but their range is limited. Internet connections are weak outside major areas as well.

32. Afghan Independent Human Rights Commission, "A Call for Justice", January 2005.

33. Afghanistan Justice Project, *Casting Shadows*.

34. Cherif Bassiouni, email communication made available to this author.

35. James Rupert, "Making enemies instead of friends, Afghans, human rights investigators say killing of civilians undermines support for U. S.", *Newsday*, November 14, 2004.

36. In November 2004, three expatriate UN staff members were kidnapped and held for three weeks in Kabul. A massive manhunt led to the arrest of scores of suspects, many of them former members of the Hizb-i Islami faction. Further investigations pointed to the involvement of forces loyal to Sayyaf and Fahim. All three UN staff members were released unharmed. UN staff and others involved in investigating the incident read it as a warning.

37. The UN report included documentation from a number of incidents from the different periods of the war; the most controversial section named current political leaders.

38. Afghanistan Justice Project, *Addressing the Past*.

39. Barbara Crossette, "UN Investigates Report of Slaying of 2,000 Taliban Fighters", *New York Times*, November 18, 1997.

40. Human Rights Watch, "The Massacre in Mazar-i Sharif", (New York: Human Rights Watch, 1998).

41. Steven R. Ratner and Jason S. Abrams, *Accountability for Human Rights Atrocities in International Law* (Oxford: Oxford University Press, 2001), pp. 156–57.

11 The prosecution of Hissène Habré: International accountability, national impunity[1]

Reed Brody

The regime of Chadian ex-President Hissène Habré, in eight years of repression (1982–90), was responsible for thousands of cases of political killings, torture, "disappearances" and arbitrary detention. After his ouster, the new government led by his former defense chief established a Truth Commission, but then buried its report and ignored its recommendations. Ten years later, Chadian and international activists joined forces to obtain Habré's landmark indictment in his Senegalese exile. Through several twists and turns, the case has survived and Habré now faces extradition to Belgium. The international prosecution had an immediate impact back in Chad, empowering his victims and putting transitional justice issues back on the table for the first time in many years. But Chad remains a repressive society with no tradition of accountability, and Habré's victims continue to wait for the Chadian government to address the suffering that they or their families endured.

Historical background

Chad, a former French colony half covered by the Sahara desert, is as far from the mainstream as any place on earth. Chad routinely makes it onto the list of the world's ten poorest countries. Half of its 8.7 million people can neither read nor write, and three-quarters have no access to clean drinking water. The average person can expect to live just 48 years. N'Djamena, the dusty capital, has no working traffic lights and no working elevators. Almost no one in Chad can afford to connect to the internet.

An artificial state throwing together northern Muslim tribes who have ruled for the last 20 years and southern Christians who were dominant during the French colonial period, Chad has never known democracy. Indeed, Chad has never been of much interest to outsiders, except during the 1980s when France and the United States built up Hissène Habré as a Cold War rampart against Moammar Qadafi of Libya,

Chad's northern neighbor. Recently, again, outsiders have begun to pay attention to Chad because of the discovery of oil in its south, the appearance of Al-Qaeda elements in its barren north and the massive atrocities in Sudan's Darfur province bordering on Chad's east.

The Habré years

Hissène Habré ruled Chad from 1982 until he was deposed in 1990 by current president Idriss Déby and fled to Senegal. On his arrival to power, Habré swiftly established a dictatorship. His one-party regime was marked by widespread atrocities and campaigns against his own people. During his eight years as head of state, he attempted to destroy all forms of opposition to his regime. Habré persecuted different ethnic groups whose leaders he perceived to be posing a threat to his regime, such as the Sara and other southern ethnicities in 1984, the Hadjaraï in 1987, and the Zaghawa in 1989. The exact number of Habré's victims is not known. A 1992 Truth Commission, established by Habré's successor, accused Habré's regime of 40,000 political assassinations and systematic torture.[2] Most predations were carried out by Habré's dreaded political police, the Documentation and Security Directorate (DDS), whose leaders all came from Habré's Gorane ethnic group and who reported directly to Habré.

In 1989, Habré was a local warlord with a reputation for brutality, having kidnapped a French anthropologist and killed the French army officer who came to negotiate her release. Under President Ronald Reagan, however, the United States gave covert CIA paramilitary support to help Habré take power. Later, the United States provided Habré with massive military aid and gave training and support to the DDS.

Today, Chadians still attest to the state of general suspicion that was present throughout the country during Habré's regime. The average citizen explains how he would not dare speak even to his or her spouse, children, or friends without fear that the words might one day be repeated. In certain cases, agents went to children for information, since they could be oblivious of the impact of their words. One DDS intelligence record from April 1988 discovered by Human Rights Watch reports, for example, how a 12-year-old child furnished political information he had overheard his parents discussing during the evening meal.

Hissène Habré's security apparatus was composed of a number of repressive organs. It was the Documentation and Security Directorate (DDS), however, which distinguished itself, according to the Truth Commission, "by its cruelty and contempt for human life." The

DDS was headed by agents who reported directly to the president and who combed national as well as international territory to imprison or eliminate "enemies of the state."

Habré created the DDS by presidential decree on January 26, 1983, as a force that was to be "directly responsible to the Presidency of the Republic, due to the confidential nature of its activities." These activities included primarily "the collection and centralization of all intelligence information . . . that threatens to compromise the national interest . . . and collaboration in suppression through the creation of files concerning individuals, groups, collectivities, suspected of activities contrary to or merely detrimental to the national interest." Very quickly, the DDS was transformed into a ruthless repressive machine. Torture was a common practice in the DDS detention centers. Seven prisons were used in N'Djamena for political prisoners and prisoners of war, one of which was on the grounds of the Presidential compound for "very special" prisoners that Habré wanted to have close at hand. The most sinister of prisons was without a doubt the underground *"Piscine"* (swimming pool). Formerly the Leclerc swimming pool reserved for the families of French soldiers during the colonial period, the *Piscine* was, under Habré's orders, covered by a concrete roof and divided into ten dank cells that were linked to the surface by a single staircase.

In May 2001, Human Rights Watch discovered, in the abandoned former DDS headquarters in N'Djamena, thousands of documents of this sinister political police. Following this discovery, the Chadian government granted the Chadian Association of Victims of Political Repression and Crimes (AVCRP), assisted by Human Rights Watch and by the International Federation of Human Rights Leagues, access to these documents and the right to use them freely. They include death certificates, daily lists of prisoners, intelligence reports, lists of DDS agents, and letters addressed to President Habré. The documents trace in detail the campaign against the ethnic groups that Habré perceived to be threats to his regime.[3] A preliminary analysis of the DDS documents by the Human Rights Data Analysis Group of the Benetech organization[4] shows that the death rate of political detainees was sixteen times greater than the general Chadian population, which includes infant mortality rates.

Habré's regime was marked by several years of war, with government forces facing off against those of the GUNT (Transitional Government of National Unity), which was supported by Libya. Several battles yielded hundreds of prisoners, notably at Faya-Largeau in 1983 and then again in 1986 and 1987. Those who were not executed on the spot were transferred under Habré's orders and imprisoned, in some cases, in N'Djamena prisons under horrible conditions.

After taking power in N'Djamena in 1982, Hissène Habré began planning the "pacification" of the south of the country. Beginning in September 1984, a particularly murderous wave of repression was unleashed with the apparent goal of eliminating the southern elite and replacing them with people loyal to Habré. This period is commonly known among Chadians as "Black September."

Hissène Habré never hesitated to turn on his old comrades-at-arms, nor to take his vengeance on the family or the entire ethnic group of a person or group of people who crossed him. The Hadjeraï and the Zaghawa ethnic groups, for example, were savagely persecuted when some of their members dared to oppose him. Hadjeraï leaders had long backed Habré and they even constituted the principal force that brought him to power in June of 1982. Habré nevertheless began to mistrust the Hadjeraï as early as 1984 when his Minister of Foreign Affairs at the time, Idriss Miskine, a Hadjeraï, became increasingly popular and began to overshadow Habré. In 1987, Habré began attacking Hadjeraï dignitaries who were increasingly voicing their dissent with him, as well as blaming their families and the entire ethnic group in general.

In 1989 Habré suspected Idriss Déby, his advisor on defense and security matters, Mahamat Itno, Minister of the Interior, and Hassan Djamous, Commander in Chief of the Chadian Army and the man who defeated the Libyans, of plotting a coup against him. All three men were ethnic Zaghawa. Habré not only had Itno and Djamous arrested, and killed (Déby managed to escape), but he turned on the rest of the Zaghawa as well, whether or not they were linked to the plotted rebellion. Hundreds were seized in raids, tortured, and imprisoned. Dozens died in detention or were summarily executed.

According to ex-DDS agents, in 1987 and again in 1989, Habré created specific committees within the structure of the DDS that were responsible for arresting and interrogating Hadjeraïs and then Zaghawas. A list dated May 26, 1989, titled "Re: Situation of the traitorous Zaghawa agents arrested for complicity and guarded in our facilities following a plot organized by Hassane Djamous" contains the names of 98 people, including shepherds, drivers, students, businessmen, soldiers, etc. The reason for the arrest of each person on the list is invariably stated as "suspected accomplice of the traitors," with the exception of some people who were related to the rebels.

The Transition

In December 1990, a rebel force led by current President Idriss Déby swept Habré from power. The jail doors swung open and hundreds of political prisoners who were held in various secret detention centers in the capital were freed. As the US State Department reported:

Some released political prisoners presented to the media were unable to walk and bore scars of torture. Chadian television broadcast reports on police detention facilities and featured close-up views of partially covered corpses with bound wrists and feet, as well as of electrical torture instruments.[5]

Habré's fall was followed by a burst of democratic activity. Déby's MPS (Patriotic Front for Salvation) formed a broad-based transitional government with a mandate to draft a new constitution and lead the country towards multi-party democracy. Political parties were legalized. A provisional constitution included guarantees of fundamental rights and freedoms. Déby largely avoided reprisals against Habré supporters. Many who fled the country following the MPS takeover returned, and several were invited to serve as government ministers or presidential advisors.

The Truth Commission

Shortly after taking power, Déby created a "Commission of inquiry into crimes and embezzlement committed by the ex-president and his accomplices," led by a distinguished jurist, Mohamat Hassan Abakar, and put it to work on March 1, 1991.[6] In addition, the government formed a special high court to try Habré, if necessary in absentia, after the Commission concluded its investigations.

The Truth Commission operated under difficult financial and security conditions; it was initially composed of twelve members: two judges, four police officers, two administrators, two archivists and two secretaries.[7] At first, the Commission had to fight to have even a minimal budget, had no headquarters and was obliged to set up shop in the offices of the DDS, which hardly encouraged victims to come and give evidence. In addition, former members of the DDS who had been re-engaged by the new *Centre de Recherches et de Coordination de Renseignements* (CRCR) were accused of intimidating witnesses and carrying out reprisals against some who appeared before the Commission. After six months, the president of the Commission called for the replacement of a number of Commission members, who were apparently too afraid to become really involved, and it was only after they had been replaced that the Commission's real work began. Even then, a shortage of vehicles prevented the Commission from gaining access to many rural areas where massacres had occurred. Other than the advice of Amnesty International, which had documented Habré's atrocities and campaigned for the release of political prisoners,[8] there was no international monetary or technical assistance to or participation in the Truth Commission. The Commission nevertheless heard 1,726 witnesses[9] and conducted three exhumations.

After seventeen months, the Commission published a report, detailing the repressive methods of the Habré government, which it accused of tens of thousands of political assassinations and systematic torture.[10] The Commission also produced a film showing the mass graves it had exhumed, some of Habré's jails and interviews with victims.

The report lamented the reintegration of many DDS agents into key administrative and security posts within the new Chadian government.[11] When the report was published, some of these agents reportedly fled across the river to Cameroon in the misplaced fear that accountability would follow.[12]

The Truth Commission was one of the only ones to date to examine the foreign role in national abuses. The report revealed that the United States was the principal supplier of financial, military, and technical aid to the DDS. The report stated that American advisers regularly visited the Director of the DDS, to give advice or to exchange information.[13] It also accused France, Egypt, Iraq and Zaire of helping to finance, train and equip the DDS.

The Truth Commission included in its report not only the names but the photographs of the principal DDS agents. The Commission stressed the necessity of removing DDS agents who had been reintegrated into the army, the police force, or the new CRCR, which replaced the DDS. The Truth Commission thus called on the government "to relieve of their duties, immediately upon publication of this report, the DDS agents who have been reintegrated and engaged in general activities with the CRCR" as well as "to immediately pursue justice against those participating in this horrible genocide, who are responsible for crimes against humanity."[14]

The Truth Commission also recommended to "construct a monument honoring the memory of the victims of Habré's repression," to "designate a day for prayer and contemplation for the victims," and to "transform the former DDS headquarters and underground prison known as the 'Piscine' into a museum." It also called for the creation of a National Human Rights Commission.

The written report was presented to President Déby and the Chadian government, who also watched the film on a borrowed projector. The Commission's headquarters were then opened to the public for several days to come view the film and see a display of pictures prepared by the commission. According to Maître Abakar, "the public fought to get in."[15] The report was widely covered in the national press.

Although the decree creating the Commission did not mention the report's publication, on the advice of Amnesty's Chad researcher, Jamal Benomar, Maître Abakar pushed to have the report published. When the Chadian government considered this too expensive, Maître Abakar arranged the publication with a French publishing house.

The Chadian Association of Victims of Political Repression and Crime

Also following Habré's fall, former victims of his regime from different ethnic groups created the Chadian Association of Victims of Political Repression and Crime (AVCRP) to locate victims, establish an inventory of unjustly confiscated and stolen goods, pursue the perpetrators of these crimes, demand compensation of victims, inform Chadians and the international community of the repression and "to prevent, denounce and fight against all forms of political crime and repression."[16] The AVCRP helped the Truth Commisison locate victims and encouraged them to give their testimony.

The AVCRP, a rare multi-ethnic group in a country ravaged by north–south divisions, was led by a number of extremely committed and idealistic survivors. Chief among them was Souleymane Guengueng, a modest and deeply religious civil servant who watched hundreds of cell-mates perish from torture and disease during two years in Habré's prisons, and took an oath before God that if he ever got out of jail alive, he would bring his tormentors to justice. As the *New York Times* described him:

He cut the figure of a most ordinary man: the threadbare gray suit of the nondescript style favored by midranking civil servants; the thick, owlish eye-glasses that emphasized his training as an accountant; the slight build that suggested he ate just enough.

But on a continent where ordinary men are tortured, killed and forgotten without a second thought, Mr. Guengueng, 52, has done something extraordinary: fought back. After being unjustly imprisoned and tortured for two years in the late 1980s, he spent the next decade gathering testimony from fellow victims and their families.[17]

Guengueng and his colleagues gathered information and testimonies from 792 of Habré's victims, anticipating their use in actions to win compensation and an eventual case against Habré.

The Government buries the Truth Commission Report

Despite the Truth Commission report, it soon became apparent that the new government would not follow through on its promises of justice. With the exception of the establishment of the National Human Rights Commission, none of the Commission's major recommendations has been implemented. The general opinion of Chadians is that the government no longer saw any advantage from pressing these issues. First and foremost, the Déby government itself began to exhibit authoritarian tendencies, making justice for past crimes a dangerous precedent. Second, many of Habré's henchmen implicated by the report now worked for Déby (and Déby himself had served Habré for many years). As Amnesty International put it, "shortly after [Déby] came to power... the same practices, the same violations and even the same perpetrators reappeared."[18] According to Souleymane Guengueng, the prime minister at the time told him that the Truth Commission report was thus a "double-edged sword."

The National Sovereign Conference of 1993, which brought together all sectors of Chadian society, repeated the call for the "revocation of those DDS members responsible for embezzlement, torture and political crimes who continue to flourish or to work within the CRCR," as well as the implementation of the Truth Commission's recommendations, the paying of damages to Habré's victims and the creation of a special independent criminal court to try violent crimes, expropriations and embezzlements. No action was taken, however.

Chad's international patrons, the United States and France, did not press the matter. No international NGOs were sufficiently invested in Chad to keep the issue alive. The national human rights community was not strong enough, and the AVCRP lacked the political clout. Indeed, without financial resources or the support of the government, the AVCRP was forced to temporarily abandon its work. The evidence gathered by the AVCRP was literally buried away by Souleyamane Guengueng and another AVCRP member, Samuel Togoto, under their houses.

The prosecution of Hissène Habré

Chadian NGOs never lost interest in bringing Hissène Habré to justice in his Senegalese exile, but did not have the resources or the know-how to do so. The Chadian government did institute a successful lawsuit in Senegal to recover the airplane in which Habré fled. In 1998, Chad's then Justice Minister Limane Mahamat publicly said that Chad would seek Habré's extradition from Senegal, but no request was actually made. The Chadian government also commissioned lawyers, including Truth Commission president Mohamat Hassan Abakar, to help recover Habré's ill-gotten gains, but never gave the lawyers any money to begin their work.

Hissène Habré is indicted in Senegal

Then in early 1999, with the "Pinocshet precedent"[19] in mind, Delphine Djiraibe, President of the Chadian Association for the Promotion and Defense of Human Rights, requested Human Rights Watch's assistance in bringing Habré to justice in Senegal. Senegal's democratic tradition, its relatively independent judiciary, and its leadership role on international rights issues[20] made it conceivable that such a prosecution could be successful. The involvement of Human Rights Watch would substantially change the picture, both in the prosecution of Habré and, to a lesser degree, on the justice front in Chad.

Human Rights Watch sent two missions to Chad, where investigators met the remaining faithful of the moribund AVCRP who provided them with the thousands of pages of documentation they had hidden away in 1992. Working in secret, because of fears that someone, including Chadian officials, might tip off Habré who could then flee Senegal for a more protective shelter, the researchers were introduced to victims and potential witnesses and sought documentation of Habré's crimes. Meanwhile, Human Rights Watch quietly organized a coalition of Chadian, Senegalese and international NGOs, including the International Federation of Human Rights Leagues (FIDH) to support the complaint,[21] as well as a group of Senegalese lawyers to represent the victims.

In January 2000, with the assistance of Human Rights Watch and other NGOs, the Chadian victims filed a criminal complaint against Hissène Habré in the Dakar Regional Court in Senegal.[22] In the complaint, the plaintiffs, seven individual Chadians – several of whom came to Senegal – as well as the AVCRP,[23] accused Habré of torture and crimes against humanity. The torture charges were based on the Senegalese statute on torture as well as the 1984 United Nations Convention against Torture, which Senegal ratified in 1986.[24] The groups also cited Senegal's obligations under customary international law to prosecute those accused of crimes against humanity. The case was filed on the eve of Senegal's tightly contested presidential election campaign in the hopes that the ruling party would not want to be seen protecting a brutal dictator.

In the court papers presented to *Juge d'Instruction* (Investigating Judge) Demba Kandji, the groups provided details from the AVCRP files of 97 political killings, 142 cases of torture, 100 "disappearances," and 736 arbitrary arrests, most carried out by the DDS, as well as a 1992 report by a French medical team on torture under Habré, and the Chadian Truth Commission report. The groups also furnished documents describing how Habré placed the DDS under his direct supervision, staffed it with his close friends, and required that it report regularly to him. Over two days, Kandji also heard the testimony of six of Habré's victims.

On February 3, 2000, Kandji indicted Hissène Habré as an accomplice to torture and crimes against humanity and placed him under house arrest. For the first time, a former head of state was prosecuted by the country in which he had taken refuge. The indictment was leading news across the continent. Radio France Internationale, a station listened to throughout francophone Africa, had been carrying stories on the case almost daily. *Jeune Afrique*, the most important weekly magazine for the region, featured a picture of Habré leaving the courthouse on its cover, as well as interviews with the plaintiffs, an editorial and a profile of Judge Kandji.[25] The Senegalese press gave prominent, and almost always positive, coverage to the case during the initial stages.

Unfortunately, politics then entered the picture. The newly elected president of Senegal, Abdoulaye Wade, declared that Habré would not be tried in Senegal. He variously argued that Senegal did not have the resources to bring witnesses and proof to Senegal, that the case had nothing to do with Senegal and that Chad itself did not seem keen to see Habré prosecuted. Wade was said to be under pressure from a number of African heads of state not to prosecute Habré – and create a bad precedent for them. In addition, there were rumors that Habré had used his ill-gotten gains from Chad to win friends and influence the judicial system. Habré was known to enjoy the protection of one of the powerful Muslim *confréries* (brotherhoods).

When Habré's lawyer moved to dismiss the case, asserting that Senegalese courts had no competence over crimes committed in Chad, the prosecutor's office, in a reversal, joined his motion. A state panel transferred Judge Kandji off the case.

The "no safe haven" provisions of the UN Convention against Torture and Other Cruel, Inhuman or Degrading Treatment oblige Senegal to either prosecute or extradite alleged torturers who enter its territory.[26] Under the Senegalese constitution, such international treaties apply automatically.[27] An appeals court nevertheless ruled, on July 4, 2000, that Senegalese courts had no competence to pursue crimes that were not committed in Senegal.[28] The court found that "Senegalese courts do not have competence over acts of torture committed by a foreigner outside of Senegalese territory regardless of the nationality of the victims."[29] The court also rejected charges of crimes against humanity, asserting that Senegalese positive law contained no such crime.

The victims immediately appealed the decision to the Supreme Court of Appeals (*Cour de Cassation*), Senegal's court of final appeals, but the *Cour de Cassation* upheld the ruling on March 20, 2001, saying that "no procedural law gives the Senegalese courts universal jurisdiction to prosecute and to try accused [torturers] who are found on Senegalese territory when the acts were committed outside of Senegal by foreigners; the presence of Hissène Habré in Senegal cannot in and of itself be ground for the prosecution against him."[30]

The case moves to Belgium with United Nations support

Even before the final ruling, the victims, with the support of the same coalition, had quietly filed a case against Habré in Belgium, whose universal jurisdiction law (prior to recent amendments) allowed Belgium's courts to prosecute the worst international crimes no matter where or against whom they were committed. These cases were filed by 21 victims, three of whom have Belgian nationality, and were assigned to Judge Daniel Fransen of the Brussels district court. The victims publicly revealed the Belgian case after the *Cour de Cassation* defeat, and also announced their intention to file a petition against Senegal before the UN Committee Against Torture (CAT), seeking the views of the Committee that Senegal amend its laws to explicitly provide for the prosecution of alleged torturers, and either initiate a state investigation against Habré or compensate the victims.

In April 2001, shortly after the *Cour de Cassation* decision, Senegal's President Abdoulaye Wade declared publicly that he had given Habré one month to leave Senegal. The abrupt decision was a tribute to the victims' efforts, but raised the possibility that Habré would go to a country out of justice's reach. The victims immediately contacted dozens of potential havens to warn that they would pursue Habré wherever he went. A number of governments, including Pakistan, Mauritania and Madagascar, pledged that they would not accept Habré.

The victims also appealed to the UN CAT for provisional measures, and CAT responded by calling on Senegal to "take all necessary measures to prevent Mr. Hissène Habré from leaving the territory of Senegal except pursuant to an extradition demand."[31] Following an appeal by United Nations Secretary-General Kofi Annan, President Wade stated on September 27, 2001, that he had agreed to hold Hissène Habré in Senegal pending an extradition request from a country such as Belgium that was capable of organizing a fair trial.

After months of pressure from the victims and their supporters, the Chadian government gave permission to Judge Fransen to visit Chad.[32] Until news of the Belgian judge's arrival was announced, few Chadians actually believed that the case against Habré would go anywhere. No one was surprised when the Senegalese courts ruled that Habré could not be brought to justice there. Indeed, most Chadians thought the victims were just tilting at windmills.

The actual arrival in February 2002 of seven Belgians – Judge Fransen, a Brussels prosecutor, four strapping police officers, and a court clerk – with their computers, camcorders, cameras and police equipment, however, turned the abstract case against Habré in far-off courts into a concrete reality and touched off a frenzy in a country where Habré's most brutal henchmen still occupy most of the key security posts. Many of Habré's people feared that the judge had come to arrest them, and some left the country as they had when the Truth Commission report was released, while others boldly proclaimed their innocence. Habré's victims, meanwhile, began to line up at the courthouse to tell their stories.

With the full cooperation of the Chadian government, the judge and his team took the testimonies of plaintiffs, victims of Hissène Habré, witnesses to atrocities, and even a number of DDS agents. On a few occasions, the judge allowed victims to confront their tormentors in front of him.[33] The judge also visited massacre sites in and around N'Djaména and detention centers from Habré's regime, including the sinister *Piscine*, the DDS underground prison. Each time, the judge was accompanied by former detainees who described the treatment to which they were subjected and indicated the location of graves. The judge also had access to the DDS archives discovered by Human Rights Watch and consulted and requisitioned thousands of documents.

Judge Fransen's visit came as Belgium's long-arm law was increasingly subject to political and legal attack. In 2001, in a widely acclaimed trial, four Rwandans were convicted by a Belgian jury of involvement in the 1994 genocide in their country. Thereafter, however, Belgian politicians grumbled as cases piled up against leaders such as Ariel Sharon, Yasser Arafat and Fidel Castro. In February, after the Democratic Republic of Congo challenged an arrest warrant against its foreign minister, the International Court of Justice said Belgium had gone too far by not respecting the immunity from criminal jurisdiction of sitting officials of a government, including incumbent heads of state and foreign ministers.[34]

Human rights groups mobilized to defend the Belgian law. With Human Rights Watch's help, Chadian victims came to Belgium and met with government ministers, parliamentary leaders and the press. The Habré case, the victims argued, posed no legal or political problems, because Habré was no longer in office and because both Chad, where the crimes were committed, and Senegal, where Habré resides, seem ready to see him tried in Belgium. Indeed, they argued that the Habré case showed that "universal jurisdiction" laws like Belgium's, properly applied, could be an important tool to curtail impunity for the perpetrators of the worst atrocities and provide a forum for their victims.

Nevertheless, the Habré case almost collapsed in the attacks on the Belgian law. First, dicta in the ICJ case suggested that even former officials enjoyed immunity from jurisdiction for all but "private" acts,[35] creating doubt among Belgian authorities as to whether the Habré case could go forward. In October 2002, again after intense lobbying by Chadian and international groups, the Chadian minister of justice put these doubts to rest when he declared in writing to Judge Fransen that "It is clear that Mr. Hissène Habré cannot claim to have any immunity on the part of the Chadian authorities."[36]

More worryingly, pressure from the United States government was leading the Belgian parliament to repeal the universal jurisdiction law altogether. In meetings with cabinet ministers and legislative leaders, however, the victims and Human Rights Watch won a "grandfather" clause for the Habré prosecution, convincing the authorities that Belgium could not abandon the Chadian victims to whom it had given hope.

The Habré case is thus moving forward, and Judge Fransen in September 2005 issued a warrant for his extradition from Senegal. Habré was arrested in November 2005, but a Dakar court refused to rule on the extradition, leaving the decision up to President Wade. Wade, in turn, brought the matter to the Summit of the African Union, which in January 2006 created a Committee of Eminent African Jurists to consider the appropriate venue for action and report back in June 2006. Among the criteria the Committee is to consider are the need to combat impunity, fair trial standards, efficiency and cost, accessibility to victims, and "priority for an African mechanism."[37] Thus, over six years since the case was filed, it is again in limbo. This slowness has been demoralizing for the chief activists in the case who have struggled to keep the hopes of their constituents alive. It has also created financial problems for the coalition as it tries to maintain its structures in place, ready to engage in the next steps of the fight.

The victims of Hissène Habré still seeking justice in Chad

Just as General Augusto Pinochet's arrest in Great Britain shattered the myth of his impunity in Chile, the indictment of Habré in Senegal had an immediate impact in Chad, opening new channels for justice. The victims and human rights organizations who initiated the case against Habré in Senegal gained a new status in Chadian society, having accomplished something that no one had thought remotely possible.

Chad, of course, is not Chile. While today's situation does not resemble the terror-filled years of Habré's rule, Chad remains an authoritarian country with largely unaccountable rulers. As the most recent State Department country report notes, "Despite the country's multiparty system of government, power remains concentrated in the hands of a northern ethnic oligarchy and its allies, resulting in a culture of impunity for minority ... [T]he judiciary remained ineffective, underfunded, overburdened, and subject to executive interference."[38]

The Chadian government's attitude towards the Habré case has never been fully clear. In a country split along north–south lines, Hissène Habré massacred ethnic groups on both sides. His final victims were the Zaghawas, the group of current president Idriss Déby. At the same time, many high officials of the current government also participated in Habré-era crimes. Déby himself commanded Habré's forces in the south during the "Black September" period.

The Chadian government was clearly caught off-guard by the prosecution in Dakar. It had famously failed to seek Habré's extradition, and probably feared the effects of a full airing of the facts, but it had also built its legitimacy partly on the demonization of the former leader. After a few days of silence, the government announced that the Habré prosecution was a logical continuation of the work it had begun with the Truth Commission. The victims and the human rights groups, through Human Rights Watch, got funding to pursue investigations into Habré's crimes and announced their intention to file criminal charges in Chadian courts against their direct torturers and to seek compensation for their losses. On September 27, 2000, President Idriss Déby met with the AVCRP's leadership to tell them that "the time for justice has come"[39] and that he would "remove all obstacles, from inside Chad or abroad" to their quest for justice.

For several years now, the Chadian government has indeed supported the international cases filed against Habré. This support manifested itself most vividly when the Belgian judge visited N'Djaména from February to March 2002 with the full cooperation and support of the Chadian government. The Chadian government also granted the victims and their supporters unlimited access to the DDS archives, and it lifted Habré's immunity from jurisdiction before Belgian courts in October 2002.

As important as Habré's judgment by a foreign tribunal is, however, it would not guarantee full justice to the victims of his regime nor would it permit Chadian society to confront its past before finally moving on. Unfortunately, the Chadian government has not taken complementary measures at home to ensure such justice.

Habré's accomplices still in positions of power

Despite the Truth Commission's recommendations, Habré's accomplices continue to enjoy impunity for their acts. More than 40 ex-leaders of the DDS today hold key posts in administration or security services of the state, thereby further slowing the possibility of one day achieving real and definitive stability in Chad.

For example, an ex-DDS chief who was accused by his victims of torture is currently the national police chief's secretary. Of the three ex-DDS directors still in Chad, one is the regional delegate of the national police, a second is a regional governor, and a third works for the ministry of communications. One of the "most brutal torturers" of the DDS, to quote the Truth Commission, is now a local police commander. An ex-DDS chief against whom many cases of torture were filed is the current chief of airport security at N'Djamena's international airport. A former director of national security under Habré now occupies the post of national co-ordinator of the country's petroleum zone, and an ex-DDS deputy director of national security is now the director of the judicial police.

During a speech made in N'Djamena in June of 2003, Ismael Hachim, the President of the AVCRP, stated: "Our torturers and killers wander freely among us every day without fear of the justice through which we filed our cases . . . Our tormentors continue to laugh in the face of a justice that remains powerless to punish those responsible and their accomplices."[40]

As decribed by Mr. Hachim, the presence of former Habré henchmen in positions of power within the Chadian administration has a corrosive effect on Chadian society and only serves to encourage intimidations and aggressions against human rights defenders and those fighting for justice in Chad.

Threats against victims and their supporters

The aggression against Jacqueline Moudeïna, the Chadian lawyer for Habré's victims in the Chadian cases against the ex-DDS agents (see below), and its aftermath, is evidence that the power of these former agents stands in the way of justice for Habré's victims. Maître Moudeïna was the victim of a hand-grenade attack on June 11, 2001, while she was participating in a non-violent women's demonstration outside the French embassy to protest the conduct of the Chadian presidential elections. Many believe that she was targeted because she represents the victims of Habré's accomplices. The police squad responsible for the attack was commanded by Mahamat Wakaye, the Deputy Director of National Security under Habré's regime and one of the former agents who was named in a complaint filed by Maître Moudeïna on behalf of Habré's victims. Wakaye is the current Director of the Judicial Police in Chad.

The government did not carry out an investigation into the attack, which also resulted in a number of other injuries. When Maître Moudeïna returned over a year later from France, where she had been hospitalized from her injuries, she filed a complaint against Wakaye. When Wakaye was called in to see the investigating judge, he reportedly tore his convocation up in the judge's face, before he was ordered by the Minister of Justice to appear and give testimony. Only pressure from Chadian and international rights groups forced the case to trial.

Evidence presented at the trial, attended by Human Rights Watch, suggested that Maître Moudeïna was specifically identified by police officers under Wakaye's command before the grenade was thrown, and that after she was injured, the car taking her to the hospital was fired on. Nevertheless, Mahamat Wakaye was acquitted on November 11, 2003 of all charges brought against him.

The simple presence of one of Habré's ex-thugs in a key post such as Director of the Judicial Police, of course, jeopardized hopes for justice and slowed down the end to the intimidation of human rights defenders. In 2005, under intense international pressure, the goverment finally removed Wakaye from his post.

The harassment of Habré's victims intensified with the Belgian judge's visit to Chad in February and March of 2002. The AVCRP offices were broken into, as were the offices of Maître Moudeïna. Souleymane Guengueng, Vice-President of the AVCRP and one of the principal plaintiffs in the case against Habré, was suspended for one month without pay from his job at the intergovernmental Lake Chad Basin Commission. When he refused to quit his AVCRP activities, Mr. Guengueng was dismissed from his position in November 2002. His car was followed by an unregistered vehicle from Cameroon full of uniformed soldiers. An aggressive chase ensued. Two of the victims who went to Belgium to bring charges against Habré were threatened multiple times after they returned to Chad.

The cases against Hissène Habré's accomplices at a standstill

Upon returning from Dakar, Habré's victims announced their intention to file criminal charges in Chadian courts against their direct torturers and those DDS leaders still in the country. According to Ismael Hachim, President of the AVCRP, "We never accepted – and will never accept – the idea that our torturers are escaping justice. After the arrest of Hissène Habré in Senegal, we realized that we can demand that justice be done here, in our own country. Now, it's time for Chad's judicial system to do its duty."

In an unprecedented move for Chad, seventeen victims lodged criminal complaints for torture, murder and "disappearance" on October 26, 2000 against named members of the DDS. The investigating judge in charge of the case – widely seen as frightened and hostile – dismissed the complaints for lack of jurisdiction because a 1993 law had provided for the creation of a special tribunal to judge Habré and his accomplices, a tribunal that was never, in fact, established.[41] The victims took the case to the Constitutional Council of Chad, which boldly ruled that the common law tribunals were able to hear these complaints.[42] The investigation finally began in front of another investigating judge in May 2001. Dozens of other victims then came forward to file complaints and give testimony against their direct torturers. The investigating judge began seeking the testimony of defendants, some of whom appeared, while others refused.

Despite all this, the investigation remains at a standstill. The Chadian investigating judge has repeatedly stated that he needs additional funding and, in particular, security protection if he is to carry out an investigation against these still powerful figures. At a Council of Ministers meeting on May 14, 2003, the Minister of Justice, an ally of human rights groups, informed the Council of the investigating judge's requests for government support. The minister maintained that the procedure concerning the Hissène Habré affair was running into financial, humanitarian, and security problems. At the meeting, the Council of Ministers declared itself "ready to implement any action so as to not impede the path of justice, so that the truth comes out and the case is able to proceed."[43] Despite this commitment, no financial aid or security measures have in fact been forthcoming.

Without enormous political support, which is lacking, it is unfortunately not realistic to think that in a country like Chad a simple investigating judge will have the courage or the resources to go after top-ranking officials for human rights crimes.

The Chadian government has failed to make material or symbolic reparations to the victims

The Truth Commission estimated the losses during Habré's rule at "more than 40,000 victims, more than 80,000 orphans, more than 30,000 widows, and more than 200,000 people who found themselves without moral or material support."[44] Despite these numbers, and despite Chad's legal and moral obligation to repair the damage caused by these agents, no material reparations have been granted to the victims.

The Truth Commission recommended, in 1992, "to construct a monument honoring the memory of the victims of Habré's repression," to "designate a day for prayer and contemplation for said victims," and to "transform the former DDS headquarters and underground prison known as the 'Piscine' into a museum to always remember this horrific regime." Nevertheless, none of these recommendations have been implemented by the Chadian government. There are no ceremonies, monuments or tributes.

While Chadians are certainly aware of the horrors of the Habré regime, little has been done to educate or remind Chadians about that period. The few copies of the Truth Commission's report available in Chadian bookstores are prohibitively expensive and virtually no Chadian consulted by Human Rights Watch had read the report.

South Africa's Robben Island, which during apartheid was used to isolate democratic leaders such as Nelson Mandela, is now a museum which organizes tours to reinforce its motto "never and never again." In Chile, human rights workers, members of social organizations and labor unions, student leaders, ex-prisoners and others participated in the building of the Park of Arts, a memorial built around General Pinochet's infamous torture center, Villa Grimaldi. Tuol Sleng, Cambodia's infamous detention center in which over 20,000 people were brutally murdered, is now a Museum of Genocidal Crimes which houses exhibits and paintings depicting the events that took place there. In Chad, however, the *Piscine*, now in disuse, remains off-limits to ordinary Chadians.

The limits of transitional justice in Chad

The limitations of transitional justice in Chad have been largely determined by the limits of the "transition" itself. Déby's military defeat of

Habré put an end to the most bloody and repressive period of Chad's history, but replaced it with an authoritarian system that has become more and more closed as years go by.

Chad's lack of a rule of law tradition has also made progress difficult. Chad has never had a tradition of official accountability. "Since when has justice come all the way to Chad?" asked a former political prisoner five years ago when a group of torture victims first discussed the idea of prosecuting Habré.[45] The question remains pertinent today.

Chad's transition also came at the early stage of the boom in transitional justice, when accountability was still the exception rather than the norm. Being a francophone country may have also limited Chad's efforts. Most of the great experiments in transitional justice have taken place in English- and Spanish-speaking countries. The literature of transitional justice is largely in these two languages, and there are not that many international transitional justice experts who speak French.

In addition, Chad's transition has been notable for the lack of international involvement, an important factor in the promotion of transitional justice elsewhere. Chad's isolation would also seem to be a factor. Despite his record, Habré was not exactly a household name, and there was no international outcry for bringing him or his henchmen to justice. In many of the lesser-developed countries, such as El Salvador, Guatemala, Timor Leste and Sierra Leone, efforts at transitional justice were guided by international pressure. In Chad, the involvement of Amnesty International, though it did not bring resources, at least generated support for the creation of the Truth Commission.

After years of stagnation, the "Pinochet Precedent" and the subsequent interest in the case of Habré by Human Rights Watch and other international NGOs put the question of transitional justice back on the agenda. Chadian NGOs and the AVCRP were empowered by the international support and the enhanced credibility they gained from arrest. But the inherent weakness of Chad's judiciary and the closed nature of its political system have limited the "bounce" that the Habré prosecution has provided.

Hope for the future

Despite the lack of progress, the fact that the AVCRP's voice is heard and that these transitional issues are even on the table is largely due to the international case against Hissène Habré which, like the international case against Pinochet, focused attention on Chad's unfinished transition.

Now that a database of DDS files has been created in which it is possible to research names and statistics, the AVCRP and Human Rights

Watch plan to transform these documents – copies of which are on CD-ROM – into a public archive so that Chadian victims and their families can discover the fate of those who disappeared, and which can also serve as a memorial to the victims of Habré's regime.

In September 2002, at a skills seminar which Human Rights Watch and the French NGO *Agir Ensemble pour les Droits de l'Homme* organized for AVCRP members, the AVCRP called on the government to establish a compensation fund for victims and their families, and to implement the 1992 Truth Commission recommendations by erecting a monument to the memory of the victims, and purging Habré's accomplices from their key posts in the state security apparatus. With new funding from international donors, it also resolved to campaign on these issues.

In August 2005, following the publication of a Human Rights Watch report, the Chadian government, in a letter to Human Rights Watch, promised to remove all Habré accomplices from government jobs, to introduce a bill granting compensation to victims, and to create a monument to the victims as soon as funds were available to do so. Six leading Habré-era security agents were immediately dismissed.

In 2003 (thirteen years after Habré fell), the AVCRP secured a first grant from the UN Fund for Torture Victims to provide direct assistance for Habré's victims, allowing it to distribute the first 100 sacks of corn meal. The AVCRP is hopeful it can multiply this assistance in the future with UN help.

On the fourth anniversary of Habré's indictment, AVCRP leader Ismaël Hachim summed up the situation when he said that, "Hissène Habré is being prosecuted abroad, but we, his victims, are being forgotten. Four years after Hissène Habré's indictment and fourteen years after he was swept from power, we continue to wait for the Chadian government and society to address the suffering that we and our families endured."[46]

NOTES

1. Parts of this article are drawn from a Human Rights Watch report entitled *Chad: The Victims of Hissène Habré Still Awaiting Justice* (July 2005).
2. *Les crimes et détournements de l'ex-Président Habré et de ses complices*, Commission d'Enquête Nationale du Ministère Tchadien de la Justice (Éditions L'Harmattan, 1993), pp. 69 and 97. The Truth Commission claimed unscientifically the number 40,000 by estimating that the 3,780 victims that it identified represented only 10% of those killed. See also Amnesty International, *Chad – The Habré Legacy* (2001).
3. See Tidiane Dioh, "Tchad: Les archives de l'horreur", *Jeune Afrique l'Intelligent*, March 2, 2003.

4. *Preliminary Statistical Analysis of AVCRP & DDS Documents. A report to Human Rights Watch about Chad under the Government of Hissène Habré,* The Benetech Initiative, November 4, 2003. http://www.hrw.org/justice/pdfs/benetechreport.pdf

5. State Department Country Report on Human Rights Practices in Chad (1991).

6. See "Chad: Decree Creating the Commission of Inquiry into the Crime and Misappropriations Committed by Ex-President Habré, His Accomplices and/or Accessories", United States Institute of Peace Library: Truth Commissions: Charters: Chad, December 29, 1990. www.usip.org/library/tc/doc/charters/ tc_chad.html.

7. See Amnesty International, *Chad – The Habré Legacy* (2001) for a discussion of the Truth Commission.

8. The Truth Commission discovered over 50,000 cards and letters written by members of Amnesty International to Hissène Habré and Chadian officials.

9. The Commission interviewed 662 former political prisoners, 786 families of victims of extrajudicial executions, 236 former prisoners of war, and 30 former members of the DDS.

10. *Les Crimes et Détournements de l'Ex-Président Habré et de ses Complices,* pp. 69 and 97.

11. *Ibid.,* p.29.

12. Interview with Mahamat Hassan Abakar, September 1, 2004.

13. The documents discovered by Human Rights Watch also revealed new information about United States support for the DDS. One DDS document described a "very special" training for Chadian security agents outside of Washington, DC, in 1985. Three of the agents received promotions to the upper echelons of the DDS immediately upon their return from Washington. Two would later be named by the Truth Commission as being among Habré's "most feared torturers." Another document speaks of a Chadian request for truth serum and a "generator for interrogations." Another document referred to a certain "Maurice" who was the "American advisor to the DDS," while other reports discussed in-country US training of Chadian agents.

14. *Ibid.,* pp. 97–99.

15. Interview with Mahamat Hassan Abakar, September 1, 2004.

16. AVCRP By-laws, on file with the author.

17. Onishi, "He Bore Up Under Torture. Now He Bears Witness", *New York Times,* March 31, 2001, p. 3.

18. Amnesty International, *Chad – The Habré Legacy* (2001).

19. See, e.g., Human Rights Watch, "The Pinochet Precedent: How Victims Can Pursue Human Rights Criminals Abroad" (updated, September 2000). Human Rights Watch styled Hissène Habré as the "African Pinochet."

20. Senegal was the first country in the world to ratify the treaty establishing the International Criminal Court, and has ratified the UN Torture Convention (see below) and most other major human rights treaties.

21. The groups supporting the case are RADDHO, the Chadian Association for the Promotion and Defense of Human Rights, the Chadian League for Human Rights (LTDH), the AVCRP, the National Organization for Human

Rights (Senegal), the London-based Interights, the International Federation of Human Rights Leagues (FIDH) and the French organization Agir Ensemble pour les Droits de l'Homme. Upon filing the complaint, the groups formed the International Committee for the Judgment of Hissène Habré.

22. The case, as well as all the legal documents pertaining to the Habré affair, can be found on the following website: http://www.hrw.org/french/themes/habre.htm.

23. In May, another 53 Chadian victims joined the original plaintiffs, as well as a Frenchwoman whose Chadian husband had been murdered in 1984.

24. United Nations Convention against Torture and Other Cruel, Inhuman or Degrading Treatment or Punishment, adopted and opened for signature, ratification and accession by General Assembly Resolution 39/46 of December 10, 1984.

25. "Un Dictateur face a la Justice", *Jeune Afrique l'Intelligent*, February 15–21, 2000.

26. Article 5 section 2 of the Torture Convention, which imposes a legislative duty, states: "Each State Party shall likewise take such measures as may be necessary to establish its jurisdiction over [acts of torture] in cases where the alleged offender is present in any territory under its jurisdiction and it does not extradite him . . ." Article 7, section 1, which establishes the obligation to extradite or prosecute, states: "The State Party in the territory under whose jurisdiction a person alleged to have committed [acts of torture] is found shall . . . if it does not extradite him, submit the case to its competent authorities for the purpose of prosecution."

27. Article 79 of the Senegalese constitution reads, "Les traités ou accords régulièrement ratifiés ou approuvés ont, dès leur publication, une autorité supérieure à celle des lois, sous réserve, pour chaque accord ou traité, de son application par l'autre partie."

28. République du Sénégal, Cour d'Appel de Dakar, Chambre d'accusation, Arrêt no. 135 du 4 juillet 2000. Available at http://www.hrw.org/french/themes/habre-decision.html.

29. The court focused on the Convention's Article 5, which calls on states to adopt legislation establishing competence over extraterritorial torture, rather than on Article 7 which sets forth more clearly the requirement of *aut dedere aut judicare*. The decision was based on the absence of any legislative measure establishing jurisdiction over torture-related offences, as required by Article 5. The court distinguished a previous Supreme Court case involving administrative law, which subordinated national law to an international treaty, on the ground that criminal law operates under more strict rules requiring that crimes formally be set forth. See République du Sénégal, Cour d'Appel de Dakar, note 28 above.

30. République du Sénégal, Cour de Cassation, Première chambre statuant en matière pénale, Arrêt no. 14 du 20-3-2001 Pénal, Souleymane Guengueng et Autres Contre Hissène Habré. Available at http://www.hrw.org/french/themes/habre-cour_de_cass.html.

31. Letter from Chief, Support Services Branch, Office of the High Commissioner for Human Rights, to Reed Brody, http://www.hrw.org/french/themes/images/guengueng_small.jpg.

32. With one week to go before the judge's scheduled visit, final permission had still not been granted. AVCRP President Ismael Hachim, together with the victims' Belgian lawyer George-Henri Beauthier and Human Rights Watch's Olivier Bercault, literally laid siege to the office of the Minister of Justice until permission was granted.

33. Ismael Hachim, the president of the AVCRP, couldn't stop telling his friends the story of how he had confronted the man who had ordered his detention and torture 13 years earlier. Hachim had spent 17 months in the infamous *Piscine*. When he got out of jail upon Habré's overthrow, the three officers who took him into custody told him that it was Touka Haliki, Habré's Director of Intelligence, who had ordered his arrest and torture, but it was only a year later when Hachim got a hold of his DDS files that he could be sure. Haliki, still a police supervisor, was one of those called in by Fransen to testify, and when Haliki denied involvement in the persecution of the Zaghawa, the judge called Hachim to encounter Haliki face-to-face. When Haliki still claimed his innocence, Hachim whipped out the DDS document in which Haliki ordered his arrest and another in which Haliki signed off on Hachim's interrogation. "In that moment, he became very small, and I became very tall," gloated Hachim to all who would listen. "Even if he is never prosecuted, I now feel like some justice has been done. That's what this is really about, isn't it?"

34. Arrest Warrant of April 11, 2000 (*Democratic Republic of the Congo* v. *Belgium*), Judgment of February 14, 2003.

35. *Ibid.*, para. 66.

36. http://www.hrw.org/french/press/2002/tchad1205a.htm.

37. Assembly of the African Union, "Declaration on the Hissène Habré Case and the African Union", January 24, 2006.

38. United States Department of State, *Country Reports on Human Rights* (2004).

39. Communiqué de presse L'AVCRP, les ADH et le Comité International pour le Jugement d'Hissène Habré, October 6, 2000. On file with the author.

40. *Discours du Président de l'association des victimes des crimes et répressions politiques au Tchad à l'occasion de la tenue des états généraux de la justice à N'Djaména*, http://hrw.org/french/press/2003/tchad0619.htm.

41. http://www.hrw.org/french/themes/habre-ordonnance.html.

42. The judge's ruling can be found at http://www.hrw.org/french/themes/habre-decisionduconseil.html.

43. "Engagé à tout mettre en œuvre pour ne pas entraver le cours de la justice, afin que la vérité sorte au grand jour et que le procès aboutisse."

44. *Les crimes et détournements de l'ex-Président Habré et de ses complices*, Rapport de la Commission d'Enquête Nationale du Ministère tchadien de la Justice (Éditions L'Harmattan, 1993), p. 97.

45. Reed Brody, "Justice comes to Chad", March 20, 2002, http://www.hrw.org/editorials/2002/justicetochad.htm.

46. "Tchad: les victimes de Hissène Habré demandent reparation", http://hrw.org/french/docs/2004/01/30/chad7166.htm.

12 Argentina's contribution to global trends in transitional justice

Kathryn Sikkink and Carrie Booth Walling

Introduction

In order to understand the diverse transitional justice mechanisms discussed in this book, we need to look at developments at the international and regional level as well as within individual countries. The doctrine of complementarity built into the statute of the International Criminal Court can be seen as a metaphor for a much broader form of interaction of the international and domestic legal and political spheres in the area of transitional justice. Developments at the international level depend upon processes at the domestic level, and vice versa.

In addition to discussing the case of Argentina, we will also sketch out some broad international and regional trends in the area of transitional justice. These trends make clear that dramatic changes have occurred in the world with regard to accountability for past human rights abuses. This trend is what Lutz and Sikkink[1] have called "The Justice Cascade" – a rapid shift towards new norms and practices of providing more accountability for human rights violations. The case of Argentina is particularly interesting because far from being a passive participant in or recipient of this justice cascade, Argentina was very often an instigator of particular new mechanisms within the cascade. The case illustrates the potential for global human rights protagonism at the periphery of the system. The Argentine case also supports the general thesis of the volume that multiple transitional justice mechanisms are frequently used in a single case.

To discuss this interaction of domestic and international legal and political contexts and processes, we think about transitional justice occurring within a domestic *and* international political and legal opportunity structure.[2] Social movement theorists define political opportunity structures as consistent dimensions of the political environment that provide incentives and constraints for people to undertake collective action by affecting their expectations of success or failure. Political opportunity structures only invite or constrain mobilization if they are perceived by activists.[3] As we will see in the case of Argentina, social movements do not only face existing opportunity structures, but can also help create them at both the domestic and the international level.

History and trends of opportunity structures for transitional justice

We focus on an essential aspect of political opportunity structure at both the domestic and the international level – access to institutions, in other words how open or closed domestic and international institutions are to pressures for accountability for past human rights violations. Internationally, this degree of openness has varied significantly over time, across issues, and across regions. There has been an increase in judicialization or legalization of world politics in the last few decades.[4] Depending on how we count, there are now between seventeen and forty international courts and tribunals. The expansion of the international judiciary has been described by one analyst as "the single most important development of the post-Cold War age."[5]

This expansion of international legalization, however, is uneven, in that it is more pronounced in some issues areas and in some regions than in others. Trade issues have high levels of international legalization in hard treaty law, while regional security regimes display less legalization. In terms of region, Europe is by far the most legalized, but Latin America is also relatively highly legalized in comparative terms. Thus, Latin America has a more propitious regional opportunity structure for human rights activism than Asia, for example, because of the existence and density of the Inter-American human rights norms and institutions, while Asia has no such regional human rights regime.[6]

The mere existence of these domestic and international opportunity structures, however, does not matter unless there are actors poised to take advantage of these opportunity structures. Here domestic and international movements become important. Domestic human rights organizations and transnational human rights networks both operate in existing opportunity structures and either take advantage of them or not. They can also help create new opportunity structures.

Before 1976, domestic, regional, and international opportunity structures were relatively closed for demands for accountability for past human rights violations. Human rights activists in the 1960s and early 1970s in the Soviet Union, Eastern Europe and authoritarian regimes in Latin America initially faced this closed situation. United Nations procedures prohibited the institution from acting in the case of a specific country unless there was a clear threat to international peace and security. Protocol prohibited even the naming aloud of a specific country engaged in human rights violations in the meetings of the Human Rights Commission. The basic human rights treaties, the Covenants on Civil and Political Rights, and on Economic, Social, and Cultural Rights, had been completed and opened for ratification but had not yet entered into force.

After 1976, however, the situation began to change. In that year, the International Covenant on Civil and Political Rights (ICCPR) as well as the International Covenant on Economic, Social, and Cultural Rights received the requisite number of ratifications and entered into force. With the entry into force of the ICCPR, the UN Human Rights Committee was set up to receive government reports and communications on compliance with the Covenant. For countries that ratified the first Optional Protocol to the ICCPR, the Committee was also authorized to receive and consider communications from individuals claiming to be victims of violations. In the UN Human Rights Commission, important changes also began to occur in the 1970s. After 1977, a series of "special procedures" were subsequently developed in the Human Rights Commission to enhance its ability to look into specific human rights situations, including the use of special rapporteurs and working groups.

Before the late 1970s, the Inter-American human rights system was also relatively closed to demands for accountability for human rights violations. The Organization of American States created the Inter-American Commission for Human Rights in 1959, but the Commission was not very active until the 1970s. When the American Convention on Human Rights, which created the Inter-American Court of Human Rights, came into force in 1978, the regional situation began to be more open. Activists began to bring more cases to the Inter-American Commission for Human Rights, and the Commission initiated more on-site investigations of human rights situations in specific countries. The Inter-American Court, however, did not become a more significant structure for accountability until the 1980s.

Activists from countries like Argentina and Chile were not passive beneficiaries of these changes, but active protagonists in helping create the change in opportunity structures. Human rights NGOs and their state allies pushed for the adoption of the special procedures in the Human Rights Commission. These later provided more points of access to the institution, since NGOs could send information to special rapporteurs and working groups, and in some cases, members of NGOs were named as rapporteurs or working group members. Latin American activists also filed more cases with the Inter-American Commission on Human Rights and urged it to conduct on-site visits. Likewise, as states ratified human rights treaties and those treaties went into effect, new mechanisms for access were created in the form of the treaty monitoring bodies that received reports from countries. Human rights activists (inside and outside of states) succeeded in transforming the international opportunity structure from one that was fundamentally closed, to one that offered some important areas of access.

The human rights context in Argentina

The military coup that brought General Jorge Videla to power in 1976 was preceded by an upsurge in activities by right-wing death squads and by left-wing guerrilla movements. Although disappearances surged after the military coup, over 200 people disappeared before the military took power. Once in power, the military government initiated a program of brutal repression of the opposition, including mass kidnappings, imprisonment without charges, torture, and murder. Estimates still vary about the total number of disappearances. The National Commission on Disappearances (CONADEP) documented a total of 8,960 deaths and disappearances in Argentina during the 1975–83 period. Human rights organizations in Argentina have long used much higher estimates of disappearances, based on the assumption that for every reported disappearance, there were many unreported disappearances. While we do not have agreement on an absolute number of deaths, we do know that over 9,000 people were killed, and that the great bulk of these murders took place in a relatively short time period in 1976 and 1977. Most of the "disappeared" were eventually murdered, and their bodies buried in unmarked mass graves, incinerated, or thrown into the sea.[7]

The early period of human rights activity in Chile, Uruguay, and later in Argentina can be seen as a moment where human rights activists, closed off from domestic institutions by authoritarianism and repression, tried to create new international opportunities within existing international and regional human rights organizations. So, for example, Chileans managed to open new international space in the UN Commission on Human Rights and in the General Assembly to work explicitly on human rights in Chile. The Chilean case was the first time the UN responded to a human rights situation that was not seen as a threat to international peace and security, through country-specific resolutions, requests for on-site visits and for a country rapporteur.[8] Uruguayan human rights activists took advantage of the fact that Uruguay had ratified the Covenant on Civil and Political Rights, and its first Optional Protocol, giving Uruguayan citizens the right to bring complaints before the UN Human Rights Committee. In its early years, the Human Rights Committee decided more cases against the Uruguayan government than against any other government in the world.[9] Argentine human rights activists were especially active in the Inter-American Commission on Human Rights (IACHR). The IACHR did its first major country report, based on an on-site visit, on Argentina. Likewise, when the Argentine government with the support of the USSR blocked demands for country-specific actions within the UN Commission on Human Rights, Argentine activists and their allies helped create the Working Group on Disappearances, the first such procedural mechanism that would later become a staple of UN human rights activity.

In the case of Uruguay, the decision of the (democratic) Uruguayan government to ratify the Optional Protocol to the ICCRP before the coup created an international opportunity structure that was not open to the other countries. Chilean human rights activists, on the other hand, taking advantage of the situation in the UN where they had the support of both the Soviet Union and the United States (after Carter took office in 1977) were able to help create international political opportunities within the UN Human Rights Commission and the General Assembly for condemnation of the Chilean regime that were not open to other countries without this broad support. Argentine human rights activists worked closely with the IACHR to provide testimony for its path-breaking country report on Argentina. Essentially, these groups took a situation where both domestic and international institutions were closed to them and converted it into a situation where at least some international and regional political opportunities were more open to their demands.

Not surprisingly, virtually all moves towards accountability for past human rights violations have happened after transitions to democratic or semi-democratic regimes (thus the name transitional justice). Transition to democratic rule would appear to be a necessary condition for establishing accountability for past human rights abuses, but not a sufficient condition. The nature of the transition itself also influenced whether or not activists were able to demand more accountability. Because the Argentine military regime collapsed after its defeat in the Malvinas/Falklands War, the armed forces were not able to negotiate the conditions of their exit from power.

After the elected government of Raul Alfonsín came into office in 1983, one of its early moves was the establishment of a truth commission, the National Commission on the Disappearance of Persons, or CONADEP. This was the first important truth commission in the world, and provided a model for all subsequent truth commissions. The CONADEP report, entitled *Nunca Mas*, was the first published truth commission report. The title has since become a slogan and a symbol of the transitional justice movement. The CONADEP report, now in its fifth edition, has been constantly in print in Argentina since it was issued in 1985 and has been translated into English and published in the United States.[10] The Alfonsín government might have been satisfied with the path-breaking truth commission report, but the human rights movement continued to push for trials. The government first gave the task of trials to the armed forces themselves, but when they failed to make even a minimum good faith attempt at prosecution, the trials were transferred to a civilian court. The trial (*El Juicio a las Juntas*, as it is known in Argentina) of the nine commanders in chief of the armed forces who had been the members of the three military Juntas that ruled Argentina was as path-breaking as the truth commission had been. It lasted almost an entire year in 1985, was attended by large numbers of members of the public and the press, and produced a vast historical record.[11]

No previous trials of the leaders of authoritarian regimes for human rights violations during their governments had ever been held in Latin America. The Bolivian Congress initiated accountability trials against high-ranking members of the military government of General Garcia Meza in 1984, but the proceedings did not begin until 1986, and the decisive phase of the trial occurred from 1989 to 1993.[12] Globally, if we focus on countries holding their own leaders responsible for past human rights violations, the only precedents to the Argentine trials of the Juntas were successor trials after World War II, and the trials of the Greek colonels in 1974 in Greece. In this sense, just as the Argentine truth commission initiated the cascade of truth commissions, the Argentine trials of the Juntas also initiated the modern cascade of transitional justice trials.

It is quite interesting that Argentina should have been the first in initiating both of the major transitional justice mechanisms explored in this book. It also leads us to question the supposition of early work that framed the debate in terms of "truth" *or* "justice." When the Argentine military carried out various coup attempts against the Alfonsín government, it led the government to decree two laws that were essentially amnesty laws, *Punto Final* and *Obediencia Debida* (Full Stop and Due Obedience laws). This experience was also a formative moment for the transitional justice movement, because it led many to what we characterize as a "misreading" of the Argentine "lesson." Analysts concluded that human rights trials were not viable, because they would provoke coups and undermine democracy. But this analysis misinterprets the actual sequence of events in Argentina. In Argentina, the nine Junta members were tried and five were convicted. The two most important leaders of the first Junta, General Videla and Admiral Massera, were sentenced to life in prison. The remaining three were sentenced to between four and a half and seventeen years in prison.[13] The coup attempts did not begin until more far-reaching trials against junior officers were initiated. So to read the Argentine case as an example that trials in and of themselves are not possible is to disregard the successfully completed trial of the Juntas. The amnesty laws did not reverse or overturn the previous trials, they simply blocked the possibility of more trials. The government of Carlos Menem that followed the Alfonsín government then offered a pardon to the convicted military officers in jail. This pardon was again interpreted by some as an indication that the trials had been futile. But pardons did not reverse the trials or the sentences. The Junta members were still (are still) considered guilty of the crimes of which they were accused and for which they were convicted. They had served four years of their prison terms. In the words of some of the most astute observers of the Argentine trials, despite the concessions granted by Alfonsín and Menem, the "high costs and high risks suffered by the armed forces as a result of the investigations and judicial convictions for human rights violations are central reasons for the military's present subordination to constitutional power."[14]

The Argentine case was important for the transitional justice move-ment in multiple ways. It made early use of many important transitional justice mechanisms, including a truth commission, trials, and repar-ations. Few countries, however, could have followed easily in Argentina's footsteps and held near-immediate trials of the top leaders for human rights violations. Argentina's transition was different from the transition in Uruguay, or Chile, or South Africa, for example, and the nature of transition influenced what transitional justice mechanisms were possible, at least in the early transition period.

The transitions literature called our attention to the differences be-tween the so-called negotiated or "pacted" transitions, where the military negotiate the transition, and ensure significant protections and guaran-tees for themselves from prosecution for human rights violations, and the "society-led" transitions, or "rupture transitions" where the military are forced to exit from power without negotiating specific protections.[15] Argentina is an example of a society-led transition after a collapse of the military government in the wake of the failure in the Malvinas War. Chile, Uruguay, and South Africa are classic "pacted" transitions. These differences in transitions help explain why it was more possible for Argentina to hold trials of the Juntas almost immediately following the transition, and why it was more difficult to hold such trials elsewhere. The main previous case of domestic trials prior to the case of Argentina came after a similar type of transition: the Greek trials in 1974 came after the collapse of the Greek authoritarian regime after its failure to effect-ively confront the Cyprus crisis.[16] The case of trials that most closely followed the Argentine case, that against the military dictator García Meza in Bolivia, also occurred after a society-led movement that provoked a collapse of the military rule and a "transition through rupture" rather than a negotiated transition.[17]

Argentina and the justice cascade

Transitional justice norms and practices have diffused rapidly across the Americas and throughout the world, significantly increasing each decade since CONADEP and the trials of the Juntas made their public impact both in and beyond Argentina in the early 1980s. This book illustrates many of those trends. In order to illustrate the reach and significance of this global justice cascade, we identified truth commissions and trials for past human rights violations using existing data sets, human rights organization reports, government documents, and information provided by non-governmental organizations; and analyzed our data in order to ascertain dominant trends.[18] Analysis of our data demonstrates a rapid shift toward new norms and practices providing more accountability for human rights violations – a shift that is regionally concentrated yet internationally diffuse. Specifically, our data demonstrates a significant increase in the judicialization of world politics both regionally and internationally, and illustrates a notable variance in the degree of openness of domestic and international institutions over time and across regions. This is the first effort to present quantitative evidence of the justice cascade, which has previously been described only in qualitative case studies and legal analysis. It may be particularly useful to persuade skeptics who continue to believe that the justice cascade is not occurring, or is less substantial than our data suggests.

As figure 12.1 illustrates, the number of truth commissions worldwide has increased rapidly over the past two decades with the most dramatic increase occurring between 2000 and mid-2004. Uganda inaugurated the first truth commission in 1974, followed by Bolivia in 1982; however, neither truth commission produced a final report of their findings. In this sense, we argue that Argentina's truth commission was the first major commission that would have a more lasting impact regionally and globally. Following the inauguration of Argentina's truth commission in 1983, an additional four truth commissions were established before the end of the decade. During the 1990s, thirteen new truth commissions were established and sixteen truth commissions were inaugurated between the years 2000 and mid-2004, including the first truth commission in the Middle East and North African region (Morocco, 2004). An additional five truth commissions, not included here, were proposed or

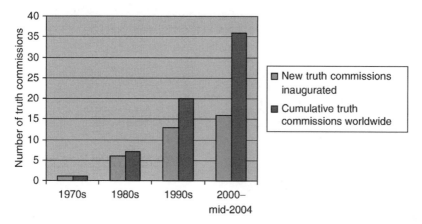

Figure 12.1. Number of truth commissions worldwide.

under development by June 2004, including those in Bosnia-Herzegovina, Burundi, Indonesia, Kenya, and Northern Ireland. Thus, we suspect that this significant growth trend will be much steeper by the end of the decade. Already in 2004, the number of truth commissions newly established at the start of the twenty-first century is only four commissions short of doubling the number of truth commissions inaugurated during the previous decade of the 1990s. In sum, by mid-2004 a cumulative number of thirty-five truth commissions had been established worldwide, the first of which had been established thirty years before.

It is important to note that other forms of transitional justice mechanisms that have been established for the primary purpose of establishing the truth about past human rights violations have been excluded from our data. These include truth commissions or commissions of inquiry reports undertaken by non-governmental organizations (Brazil, 1985), armed resistance groups (African National Congress, 1992 and 1993), special prosecutors (Ethiopia, 1992; Mexico 2002), and commissions that have a mandate limited to a single human rights violation (Côte d'Ivoire, 2000; Peru, 1983).

Our data also shows that truth commissions are regionally concentrated. As figure 12.2 illustrates, truth commissions are more prevalent in Africa and the Americas than in other regions, making up 36 percent and 38 percent of the total respectively. When combined, Africa and the Americas comprise 74 percent of the cumulative total number of truth commissions, whereas 17 percent are found within Asia and the Pacific, followed by only 6 percent in Europe and Central Asia, and 3 percent for the Middle East and North Africa.

Truth commissions by region

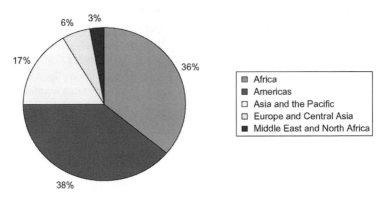

Figure 12.2. Regional distribution of truth commissions.

When analyzed by region, there seems to be a similar upward trend across time, as illustrated in figure 12.1, although the steepness of the upward slope varies by regional grouping. Once a region inaugurates its first truth commission, the number of truth commissions within that region seems to increase each decade. For example, the first truth commission in the Americas region was inaugurated in 1982, followed by an additional two truth commissions during the 1980s. The number of new truth commissions established in the Americas during the 1990s increased to five and already by 2004, only four years into the new decade, five new truth commissions have been established. This upward trend by decade also holds true for Africa, yet it remains to be seen whether or not the trend will hold for both Asia and the Pacific, and Europe and Central Asia as well. Given the overall trend of a justice cascade we anticipate that the pattern will remain consistent.

The data also illustrates that multiple transitional justice mechanisms are frequently used in a single case. In at least eleven of the countries we identified, both truth commissions and domestic trials were implemented.[19] Interestingly, most of these countries were found within the regions of Africa and the Americas and in most cases, truth commissions preceded trials. Thus, it simply does not hold true that countries must choose between trials or truth during democratic transition, although they may indeed choose to do so.

A modern cascade of criminal justice trials is similarly supported by our data. Without an existing comprehensive set of trial data to build upon, we identified our domestic, foreign, international, and hybrid trials through human rights reports, United Nations documents and Security Council Resolutions, government news services, and information gathered by non-governmental organizations.[20] **Domestic trials** are those conducted in a single country for human rights abuses committed in *that* country. **Foreign trials** are those conducted in a single country for human rights abuses committed in *another* country.[21] **International trials** involve international trials for individual criminal responsibility for human rights violations, such as the international ad hoc tribunals for Rwanda and the former Yugoslavia. **Hybrid trials** are third-generation criminal bodies defined by their mixed character of containing a combination of international and national features, typically both in terms of staff as well as compounded international and national substantive and procedural law.

To graph our results we counted each country once for each year in which at least one transitional justice trial was held. As figure 12.3 indicates, domestic trials were largely insignificant until the 1980s, after which there is a significant and uninterrupted increase in the number of domestic trials in countries having undergone democratic transition. Even when domestic transition trials are separated out from the World War II successor trials, the slope remains relatively unchanged. We suspect that our trial data underestimates the actual number of domestic human rights trials in the world today. So many domestic trials are occurring in different countries that it is difficult to count all of them. If we are in error, it is because we have underestimated the magnitude of the trend and the increasing judicialization of human rights is actually steeper.

In the case of foreign trials, nearly all of which have occurred within the European and Central Asian region, we see a mild increase between the 1960s and 1980s followed by a sharp increase until the mid-1990s, after which the number of foreign trials begins to decline yet still remain significant. It is important to note two dominant trends we discovered in our foreign trials data, once World War II successor trials were excluded. The first trend is that many foreign trials are the result of insider–outsider coalition strategies where crimes committed largely in the Americas, and particularly in Argentina and Chile are tried in European courts, regardless of whether or not the victims are citizens of the prosecuting country. The second trend among foreign trials are trials held largely in European countries for war crimes committed abroad, most notably in the former Yugoslavia, Rwanda, or other states in the Great Lakes region of Africa, by individuals who are arrested on the soil of the prosecuting state and who are not under indictment by a domestic or international tribunal.

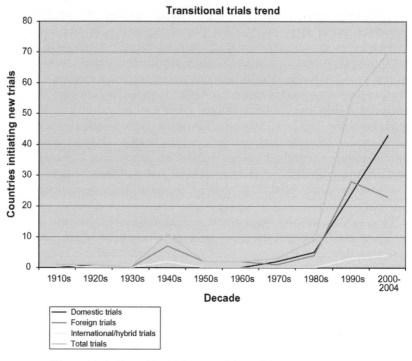

Figure 12.3. Transitional human rights trials.

That foreign trials continue to decrease at the same time that domestic trials continue to increase highlights the interaction between domestic and international legal and political spheres with regard to human rights trials. When domestic opportunity structures are closed, international activism is often used as an alternate option to seek justice. Similarly, as new norms and practices of transitional justice begin to cascade, including putting human rights violators, among them former heads of state, on trial for their domestic crimes, the need to access available international opportunity structures diminishes. As domestic political and legal opportunity structures increasingly open up in the Americas, for example, we can expect the number of foreign trials to decrease. Similarly, as we move further away in time from the wars in the former Yugoslavia and the genocide in Rwanda, the number of cases related to these conflicts will also likely diminish. We can expect that the number of foreign trials may also continue to decrease as European governments begin to revise their judicial practices, and indeed their laws, because of political and economic pressure from powerful states.

In 2003, for example, Belgium modified its universal competence law after the United States threatened to move NATO headquarters from Belgium because of controversial charges brought against members of the US presidential administration and military command.

International trials were instituted following both World War I (Constantinople, 1919) and World War II (Nuremberg, 1945; Tokyo, 1946). International trials for humanitarian law violations and human rights abuses remained closed until the International Criminal Tribunal for the former Yugoslavia (ICTY) was established by Security Council Resolution 827 in 1993, followed shortly thereafter by the International Criminal Tribunal for Rwanda established by Security Council Resolution 955 in 1994. Subsequently, hybrid trials combining international and domestic features were initiated in Kosovo (1999), Timor Leste (2000), and Sierra Leone (2002) and are currently under development for Cambodia (2003). The recent emergence of hybrid trials, described elsewhere in this volume, illustrates what seems to be increasing support for the belief that domestic judicial procedures are preferential to alternate international remedies and that when domestic political and legal structures are not sufficiently developed, hybrid trials containing some national elements are preferable to international trials.

Activists within and beyond borders: Insider–outsider coalitions

Argentina fits nicely into these trends, indeed, has been a trailblazer in creating them. The Argentine case is an example of what can happen in a country in which both international and domestic opportunity structures are relatively open to questions of legal accountability for past violations of human rights. Domestic activists privileged domestic political change, but kept international activism as a complementary and compensatory option. Domestic political change is closer to home and more directly addresses the problems activists face, so they concentrated their attention there. However, activists who learned how to use international institutions in an earlier phase kept this avenue open in case of need. We call this the insider–outsider coalition category.

The insider–outsider model is of particular importance because it is not limited to Argentina but may be a key dynamic in the future as more countries face increasingly open domestic and international opportunity structures for transitional justice.

After the amnesty laws were passed in 1986 and 1987 human rights organizations implemented a two-track strategy. They launched a series of innovative legal challenges to try to make an end run around the amnesty laws, and they cooperated with and initiated some international and regional tactics as well.

The first regional legal opportunity structure that activists turned to was that offered by the Inter-American human rights system (made up of the Commission [IACHR] and the Court [Inter-American Court]. In 1992, the IACHR concluded that the Argentine laws of *Punto Final* and *Obediencia Debida*, and the pardons issued by President Menem for crimes committed during the dictatorship were incompatible with the American Convention.[22] This opened a regional legal option that human rights activists could try to take advantage of by bringing the case of the amnesty laws again to the Inter-American system should they be completely stymied in the domestic legal arena. In 2001, this possibility was heightened when the Inter-American Court adopted the Commission's analysis to declare in the *Barrios Altos* case that two Peruvian amnesty laws were invalid and incompatible with the American Convention on Human Rights.[23]

The innovative domestic legal challenges included efforts by the legal team of the Grandmothers of the Plaza de Mayo to hold military officers responsible for the kidnapping and identity change of the children of the disappeared, who in many cases had been given up for adoption to allies of the military regime. The Grandmothers' lawyers argued that because the crimes of kidnapping of minors and changing their identity had not been covered in the amnesty laws, they were not blocked from pursuing justice for these crimes. The kidnapping of minors exception, along with other exceptions for property theft and for crimes involving civilians, became one of the wedges that domestic groups used to open a breach in the amnesty laws. Their legal strategy began to succeed by the mid-1990s, but initially most of those found guilty were lower level military and the adoptive families.[24]

But on June 9, 1998, Federal Judge Roberto Marquevich ordered preventative prison for ex-president General Rafael Videla for the crimes of kidnapping babies and falsifying public documents. It is often overlooked that when Pinochet was detained in London three months later, Argentine courts had already done the equivalent by ordering the preventative detention of an ex-president for human rights violations. And they had done it using domestic political institutions. But, even in this case, the international sphere was also involved. Videla had been tried for human rights violations during the trials of the Juntas in 1985, convicted, and sentenced to life in prison, but he had been released in 1990 under President Menem's pardon. Why, all of a sudden, was Videla back under arrest?

At the end of May of 1998, President Menem came back from a diplomatic trip to Scandinavian countries. Instead of the economic contacts he had been seeking, both the Finnish and the Swedish governments asked for an investigation of the cases of two disappearances: that of the Swede, Dagmar Hagelin, and the Finn, Hanna Hietala. European human rights activists and family members of the disappeared had made these cases *causes célèbres* in their respective countries and had recruited allies at the highest levels of the relevant European governments. The European press focused its coverage of the Menem visit on these two cases. These two cases in turn are connected to two other cases of disappearances, those of two French nuns, Alice Domon and Leonie Duquet, because all were kidnapped by a Navy group in which the notorious Captain Alfredo Astiz had participated. Menem realized that in his upcoming visit to Paris a week later he would also face demands for the extradition of Astiz to France, where he had been condemned *in absentia* for the kidnapping of the nuns. Menem was scheduled to meet with French President Jacques Chirac, who had publicly stated that he wanted Astiz to be extradited to France. Just a few hours before the Chirac–Menem meeting, Judge Marquevich decided to detain Videla. In his meeting with the French press, instead of facing criticism, Menem was greeted as a human rights hero. Menem told reporters that "this is one more sign that we have one of the best justice systems in the world."[25]

This is an excellent example of an insider–outsider coalition at work. Domestic human rights organizations using innovative legal strategies had done all the preliminary legal and political work to secure Videla's arrest. They still needed some help from their international allies, however, for the final push to put a top-level military leader in jail. The judge who ordered Videla's arrest was not known for his commitment to human rights, but for his intense loyalty to President Menem, who had appointed him. There is strong reason to believe that Judge Marquevich was responding to Menem's political agenda in his trip to France when he ordered the detention.[26]

Four months later, after Pinochet had been detained in London, and the Spanish court had issued arrest warrants for a wide range of Argentine military officers, another Menem loyalist on the bench ordered the preventive detention of Admiral Emilio Massera, ex-head of the Navy and Junta member, and, after Videla, the second most powerful leader in Argentina during the most intense period of repression. The context and timing of Massera's arrest suggests that the decision to imprison Massera was apparently a preemptive measure in response to Spanish international arrest warrants for Argentine military officers.[27] On November 2, 1998, Judge Garzón in Spain issued indictments against 98 members of the Argentine military for genocide and terrorism. Three weeks later, the Argentine judge ordered the preventative imprisonment of Massera for kidnapping babies.

Why would international arrest warrants lead local judges to order arrests in Argentina? International arrest warrants for Argentine military officers created international and domestic pressure to extradite the officers to Spain to stand trial. But the Argentine military was adamantly opposed to extradition, and nationalist sentiment in Argentine political parties resisted the idea. The relevant international legal precept was that a state must either extradite or try the accused domestically. To fend off political pressures to extradite many officers, the Argentine government apparently decided to place under preventative detention a few high profile, but now politically marginalized officers, like Videla and Massera.

Another key legal innovation in Argentina was the concept and practice of "truth trials." After the amnesty law blocked trials for most past human rights violations, the relatives of victims nevertheless encouraged judges to develop trials to learn the truth about the fate and whereabouts of the disappeared. In 1995, family members associated with the Center for Legal and Social Studies (CELS) presented the first petition arguing that although the amnesty laws had blocked criminal proceedings, family members still had the "right to truth" and they could pursue that right through judicial investigations. When a Federal Court of Appeals allowed the petition, it began to establish a judicial process that would come to be called the "truth trials," where Argentine courts solicited and analyzed information and testimony (mainly from members of the Armed Forces) to find out the truth about the disappeared.

In 1998, when truth trials were stalled in Argentina, human rights activists once again sought help outside their borders when they filed a petition with the IACHR. The Commission in turn reached a friendly settlement of the case with the Argentine government that provided a framework for truth trials to proceed in Argentina. Since 1998, truth trials have been underway not only in Buenos Aires, but also in courts in various other cities of Argentina. For the purposes of this volume, the concept of the "truth trial" is particularly interesting because it brings together elements from both truth commission and criminal justice. It also illustrates yet another example of Argentine leadership in developing new human rights tactics and mechanisms.[28]

Perhaps the most challenging of the legal battles was the case led by CELS to have the amnesty laws declared null, or unconstitutional. Once again, using the case of a kidnapped child of the disappeared, CELS argued that the amnesty laws put the Argentine judicial system in the untenable position of being able to find people criminally responsible for kidnapping a child and falsely changing her identity (more minor crimes) but not for the more serious original crime of murder and disappearance of the parents that later gave rise to the crime of kidnapping. Additionally, they argued that the amnesty laws were a violation of international and regional human rights treaties to which Argentina was party, and which were directly incorporated into Argentine law. CELS solicited international groups to write amicus briefs for their cases, and succeeded in establishing for the first time in the Argentine judicial system the practice of using foreign amicus briefs.

A judge of the first instance found the arguments compelling, and wrote a judgment that was a lengthy treatise on the significance of international human rights law in Argentine criminal law.[29] Argentina offered a propitious environment for this kind of decision because the 1994 Constitution gave international human rights treaties constitutional status, and because the courts had earlier found that customary international law could be applied by domestic courts. The Appeals courts supported the decision, but it seemed unlikely that the Supreme Court would follow suit. However, the new President of Argentina, Nestor Kirchner, changed both the composition of the Supreme Court and the political climate for the idea of accountability for past human rights violations. Specifically, Kirchner placed three new judges on the Supreme Court, including Raúl Zaffaroni, a noted legal theorist and expert on criminal law, and Carmen Argibay, a judge on the Ad Hoc Tribunal for the former Yugoslavia. In June 2005 the Supreme Court found the amnesty laws unlawful by a 7–1 vote.[30] The effect of this law was to permit the reopening of the human rights cases that had been closed for the past fifteen years.

Other actions of the executive and legislature have moved in the same direction. In 2003, Kirchner announced that he was revoking the decree of the De La Rua government that denied all extradition requests, and was returning the decision about extradition back to the control of the judiciary.[31] Although no individual has yet been extradited from Argentina to stand trial abroad, Kirchner's announcement signaled a return to a more activist human rights policy on the part of the executive. In August 2003, the Argentine Congress, with the support of the Kirchner administration, passed a law that declared the amnesty laws (*obediencia debida y punto final*) null and void. According to observers, this was an unexpected political and legal development.[32]

Human rights advocates in Argentina had been working for years to get the amnesty law repealed, annulled, or declared unconstitutional.

But it was not until they found greater support from the executive branch that they were able to secure their goal. The political history and orientation of President Kirchner himself and some of his top advisors helps explain this change in executive branch policy. Kirchner is the first president of Argentina to come from the generation most affected by the dictatorship's practice of disappearances. Although he himself did not suffer from repression, Kirchner was a member of the 1970s generation of the Peronist party that was decimated by the repressive apparatus. This generational tone has affected all of his government's policies, but has been most pronounced in the area of human rights.[33]

Although Kirchner's move to have the amnesty laws declared null was mainly the result of his political orientation and that of his closest advisors, it also took place in the context of the international legal opportunity structure discussed above. Just days before the Congress passed the law declaring the amnesty laws null, Judge Canicoba Corral, following the government's new policy on extraditions, had provided for the extradition to Spain of 45 members of the military and one civilian, requested by Judge Garzón. This provided some impetus for reopening domestic trials.

The Kirchner government was also aware of how to use international law as a vehicle to provide support for its chosen policy alternative. The day before the Congressional debate on the law to declare the amnesty laws null, the Kirchner government signed a decree implementing the "Convention on the Non-Applicability of Statutory Limitations to War Crimes and Crimes Against Humanity." In addition to declaring that no statutory limitation shall apply to war crimes and crimes against humanity, the Convention obligates governments to punish these crimes and to adopt all necessary measures to make extradition possible, irrespective of the date the crimes were committed.[34] The Convention essentially prohibits amnesties for these crimes. The Convention entered into force in 1970. The Argentine Congress ratified the Convention in 1995, but the executive had never deposited the ratification instrument. By its decree, the Kirchner government ensured that the treaty would enter into effect in Argentina, and at the same time, it sent to Congress a law that would give the norm constitutional status. Through this move, the government provided additional incentives to the Congress to annul the amnesty laws, but it also provided additional reasons why the amnesty laws should be seen as contrary to international law and to the Argentine constitution. In this we have the case of the government explicitly creating international opportunity structures to support its domestic political moves.

But while pursuing these domestic judicial and political strategies, Argentine activists did not neglect the international realm. Once a case against members of the Argentine military was initiated in the Spanish Audiencia Nacional in 1996, many Argentine family members of the disappeared traveled to Spain to present testimony and to add their cases. Argentine human rights organizations cooperated actively with requests from the Spanish courts and from human rights organizations based in Spain to provide documentation and case material.

One of the most surprising developments came in 2001 when the Mexican government agreed to extradite an Argentine national living in Mexico, Ricardo Miguel Cavallo, to the Audiencia Nacional of Spain, to stand trial for human rights violations he is accused of committing in Argentina during the dictatorship. This is the first case where one country extradited a national of another country to stand trial in yet a third country for human rights abuses committed in his country of origin. The Argentine government did not oppose Cavallo's extradition to Spain, nor did it submit its own extradition request. In other words, Cavallo is the minor official now following the path that Pinochet could have followed, had the Chilean government not secured his return to Chile.[35] Meanwhile, another minor Navy officer, Adolfo Scilingo, was tried and convicted in Spain in early 2005 for his role in murdering prisoners, France continues to request the extradition of Alfredo Astiz, and Germany has issued extradition requests for Argentines accused of human rights violations during the dictatorship.

The Grandmothers of the Plaza de Mayo also pursued an insider–outsider coalition strategy. During the international process of drafting the Convention on the Rights of the Child, the Grandmothers lobbied the Argentine government to include specific provisions in the Convention that they believed would enhance the success of their domestic trials. Specifically, they realized that domestic law did not provide a legal basis for arguing that the kidnapped children had standing in court. So the Grandmothers convinced the Argentine foreign ministry to press for provisions on the "right to identity" in the Convention on the Rights of the Child. In the final Convention they are included as Articles 7 and 8 and are informally called the "Argentine Articles". Because the Argentine constitution incorporates international law directly into domestic law, once Argentina had ratified the Convention, these Articles provided the Grandmothers with the legal basis to argue that children had a right to identity, and thus to permit judges to order blood tests even when opposed by the adoptive parents, to establish whether or not the children were the sons and daughters of the disappeared.[36] In this case, the Grandmothers of the Plaza de Mayo, a domestic Argentine human rights movement, helped to change international opportunity structure by changing the wording of a treaty, and that in turn changed their domestic opportunity structure and made it easier to get convictions.

In other words, domestic groups concentrated primarily on their very active domestic judicial agenda, but they moved with relative ease and fluidity, in foreign, international, and regional institutions as a complement and/or back-up to their domestic work. International and regional activism remains one of the tactics in the repertoires of these groups. At times it is more latent than others, but always there. But it is not a privileged sphere, largely because there has been so much domestic space in which to participate.

The Argentine case also illustrates a point frequently made by social movement theorists that political opportunities are not only perceived and taken advantage of, but are also created by social actors. Argentine political actors faced a more open political opportunity structure for their human rights demands after the transition to democracy in part because the failure of the military in the Malvinas/Falklands War led to an abrupt transition where the military had little bargaining power. This is in contrast to the situation in Chile or Uruguay, where negotiated transitions gave the military more veto power and more control over the agenda. And yet, the tactics groups chose also made a difference. Argentine activists have been unusually active and innovative in this field and have often pursued legal strategies in the face of political opposition.

These social movements and legal strategies are so extensive that we consider Argentine social movement activists, and at times, even members of the Argentine government to be among the most innovative protagonists in the area of domestic human rights. They are not emulating tactics they discovered elsewhere, but are developing new tactics. On a number of occasions, they have then exported or diffused their institutional and tactical innovations abroad. Argentina, which never was a passive recipient of international human rights action, has gone on to become an important international protagonist in the human rights realm, involved in actively modifying the international structure of political opportunities for human rights activism. For example, Argentina was one of the four or five most active countries in the development of the International Criminal Court, and an Argentine attorney and former deputy prosecutor of the Junta Trials, has been named the new prosecutor for the ICC, perhaps the most important position in the Court.[37] This dynamism of the Argentine human rights sector is even more interesting and important in the context of active US hegemonic opposition to the expansion of international human rights law, because it suggests that the advancement of human rights institutions may proceed even in the face of opposition from the United States.

It has now been over twenty years since the transition to democracy in Argentina. We argue that Argentina is more than just another case in a volume on transitional justice. Argentina helped innovate the two main accountability mechanisms that are the topic of this book. Though the actual process of diffusion from Argentina to other countries is not always clear, the Argentine example was very influential for other experiences of transitional justice. The Argentine model suggested that accountability mechanisms like truth commissions and trials need not be mutually exclusive options, but can be beneficially combined. Indeed, Argentina has innovated a type of trial – the truth trial – that actually combines elements of trials and truth commissions. With the recent reopening of blocked human rights trials, however, the pressure for truth trials is likely to decline. The case of Argentina today suggests that it is in the process of innovating yet another mechanism – legislative and judicial strategies for declaring amnesty laws null and void, and permitting blocked human rights trials to proceed. Other countries are beginning to follow suit, as evidenced by efforts underway today in Chile and Uruguay to find judicial strategies to evade amnesty laws. The trends in transitional justice over the last twenty years suggest that Argentina is not an exceptional case or an outlier, but just ahead of its time, and thus a good way to get a glimpse of the future.

NOTES

1. Ellen Lutz and Kathyrn Sikkink, "The Justice Cascade: The Evolution and Impact of Foreign Human Rights Trials in Latin America", (2001) *Chicago Journal of International Law* 2, p. 1.
2. Kathryn Sikkink, "The Transnational Dimension of the Judicialization of Politics in Latin America", in *The Judicialization of Politics in Latin America*, ed. Rachel Sieder and Line Schjolden (New York: Palgrave/Macmillan, forthcoming).
3. Sidney Tarrow, *Power in Movement: Social Movements, Collective Action, and Politics* (New York: Cambridge University Press, 2nd edn, 1998).
4. Alec Stone Sweet, "Judicialization and the Construction of Governance", (1999) *Comparative Political Studies*, 32, pp. 147–84; Judith Goldstein et al., *Legalization and World Politics.* (Cambridge: MIT Press, 2001).
5. Cesare Romano, "The Proliferation of International Judicial Bodies: The Pieces of the Puzzle", (1999) *New York University Journal of International Law and Politics*, 31(4), p. 709.
6. On the low level of legalization in Asia, see Miles Kahler, "Legalization as Strategy: The Asia-Pacific Case", in Goldstein, *Legalization and World Politics.*
7. *Nunca Mas: The Report of the Argentine National Commission on the Disappeared* (New York: Farrar, Straus & Giroux, 1986), pp. 209–234.
8. Menno Kamminga, *Inter-State Accountability for Violations of Human Rights* (Philadelphia: University of Pennsylvania Press, 1992).

9. See Session 1–Session 18, "Decisions and Views of the Human Rights Committee", http://www1.umn.edu/ humanrts/undocs/alldocs.html

10. *Nunca Mas: The Report of the Argentine National Commission of the Disappeared.*

11. See, for example, the *Diario del Juicio*, a weekly newspaper published during the entire period of the trials of the Juntas, with transcripts of testimony, interviews, and legal and political analysis.

12. René Antonion Mayorga, "Democracy Dignified and an End to Impunity: Bolivia's Military Dictatorship on Trial", in *Transitional Justice and the Rule of Law in New Democracies*, ed. A. James McAdams (Notre Dame: University of Notre Dame Press, 1997).

13. "La Sentencia", *El Diario del Juicio*, No. 29, December 11, 1985.

14. Carlos H. Acuña and Catalina Smulovitz, "Guarding the Guardians in Argentina: Some Lessons about the Risks and Benefits of Empowering the Courts", in *Transitional Justice and the Rule of Law in New Democracies*, p. 94.

15. Alfred Stepan, "Paths Toward Redemocratization: Theoretical and Comparative Considerations"' in *Transitions from Authoritarian Rule: Comparative Perspectives*, ed. Guillermo O'Donnell, Philippe C. Schmitter, and Laurence Whitehead (Baltimore: Johns Hopkins University Press, 1986), p. 64–84.

16. Nicos C. Alivizatos and P. Nkikforos Diamandouros, "Politics and the Judiciary in the Greek Transition to Democracy", in McAdams, *Transitional Justice*, pp. 27–60.

17. Mayorga, *Democracy Dignified*, p. 67.

18. The data on truth commissions was gathered using Priscilla Hayner's study of truth commissions, *Unspeakable Truths: Facing the Challenge of Truth Commissions* (New York: Routledge, 2001), and a draft "Afterwards" for a new edition of *Unspeakable Truths* (May 1, 2004), the United States Institute for Peace Truth Commission Digital Collection, and publications of the International Center for Transitional Justice. We want to thank Priscilla Hayner for sharing her draft "Afterwards" with us. The truth commissions identified include: Argentina (1983); Bolivia (1982); Burundi (1995); Central African Republic (2002); Chad (1990); Chile (1990); Democratic Republic of Congo (2003); Ecuador (1996); El Salvador (1992); Federal Republic of Yugoslavia (2001); Germany (1992); Ghana (2002); Grenada (2000); Guatemala (1994); Haiti (1994); Indonesia (1999); Liberia (2003); Morocco (2004); Nepal (1990); Nigeria (1999, 2001); Panama (2001); Paraguay (2003); Peru (2001); Philippines (1986); Sierra Leone (2000); South Africa (1995); South Korea (2000); Sri Lanka (1994); Timor Leste (formerly East Timor, 2001); Uganda (1974, 1986); Uruguay (1985, 2000); and Zimbabwe (1985).

19. The countries we identified as having both truth commissions and domestic trials include Argentina, Bolivia, Burundi, Chile, Federal Republic of Yugoslavia, Germany, Guatemala, Haiti, Indonesia, Peru, and South Africa.

20. The data on transitional justice trials was gathered from Human Rights Watch reports, United Nations Documents and Security Council Resolutions, and information found in the United States Institute for Peace Digital Collections, International Center for Transitional Justice, and the following

non-governmental organizations: Prevent Genocide International, RE-DRESS, Universal Jurisdiction Information Network, Global Policy.org, and Track Impunity Always (TRIAL). Domestic, foreign, international and hybrid trials were included.

The **domestic** data set includes: Argentina (1984, 1985, 2003, 2004); Bosnia-Herzegovina (1993, 2004); Bolivia (1984, 1989–93); Brazil (1998); Burundi (2002); Cambodia (2000–03); Chad (1993, 2001); Chile (2000, 2003); Colombia (2000–01); Croatia (1996, 1999); Denmark (1999); Ethiopia (1992, 1994, 1997, 1999–2000, 2003); France (1945, 1994, 1998); Germany (1921, 1976, 1980, 1990, 1999); Greece (1974); Guatemala (1998, 1999, 2001, 2002, 2004); Haiti (2000); Indonesia (2000–03); Iraq (2003, 2004); Latvia (1999–2002); Lithuania (1999, 2001); Mexico (2001, 2004); Peru (1992, 2001); Poland (1949, 1993, 1999, 2001); Romania (1989, 1990); Russia (2002); Rwanda (1995, 1997–2002); Serbia and Montenegro (2002, 2003); South Africa (2004); Uruguay (1998).

Foreign include: Argentina (France, 1985, 1990; Spain, 1996–1999, 2000, 2003; Netherlands, 2001; Italy 1993, 2001; Germany, 2001; Switzerland, 1977; Sweden, 2001); Austria (France, 1954; Germany 1961, 2001); Belgium (Switzerland, 1948); Belorussia/Belarus (United Kingdom, 1995, 2000); Bosnia-Herzegovina (Austria, 1994; France, 1994; Denmark, 1994; Switzerland, 1995; Belgium, 1995; Sweden, 1995; Netherlands, 1997; Germany 1997, 1999, 2001); Chad (Belgium, 2000; Senegal, 2000); Chile (Belgium, 1998; France 1998; Italy 1995; Spain 1998); Democratic Republic of Congo (Belgium, 2000; Netherlands, 2004); Germany (USSR, 1943, 1947; United Kingdom, 1946; France, 1946, 1952, 1987; Italy, 1947, 1998, 1999; Israel, 1961, 1987; Latvia 2000); Guatemala (Spain, 2000); Honduras (Spain, 1998); Hungary (Canada, 1990); Israel (Belgium, 2001); Iraq (Denmark, 2001); Italy (Germany, 2001); Japan (Russia, 1949); Mauritania (France, 2002); Rwanda (France, 1996; Switzerland, 1998; Belgium, 2001); Soviet Union/Russia (Latvia, 2000); Suriname (Netherlands, 2000); Sudan (United Kingdom, 1997).

International and hybrid trials include: Turkey (Constantinople, 1919); Germany (Nuremberg, 1945); Japan (Tokyo, 1946); former Yugoslavia (ICTY, 1993); Rwanda (ICTR, 1994); Kosovo (1999); Timor Leste/East Timor (2000); Sierra Leone (2002); Cambodia (2003).

21. These are referred to as transnational trials elsewhere in this volume.

22. IACHR reports are generally not seen as binding on member governments. But the opinion of the IACHR may reveal a position that the Court might later adopt, should the case be brought before it. Leonardo Filippini, "La Corte Suprema Argentina y la Convencion Americana sobre Derechos Humanos: Analisis Jurisprudencial", (LLM thesis, Palermo University, 2004).

23. Inter-American Court of Human Rights, Sentence of March 14, 2001, Caso Barrios Altos (*Chumbipuma Aguirre y otros* v. *Peru*) paragraph 41. For more discussion of the case, see Chapter 3 on Peru.

24. Interview with Alcira Rios, Buenos Aires, December 2002.
25. Clarin, December. 22, 2002, "Cuatro historias escandalosas en el legajo del juez Marquevich".
26. Interview with Luis Moreno Ocampo, December 21, 2002, Buenos Aires, Argentina.
27. Interview with Martin Abregu, Buenos Aires, July 1999.
28. These two paragraphs on truth trials draw on an unpublished manuscript by Leonardo Filippini, "Truth Trials in Argentina" (April, 2005).
29. Resolucion del Juez Gabriel Cavallo, Juzgado Federal No. 4, 6 de marzo, 2001, Caso Poblete-Hlaczik. The judge cited the Inter-American Commission and Court jurisprudence extensively. A number of other local and appeals-level courts subsequently came to the same conclusion, as did the government's Prosecutor-General. The Menem-era pardons were also subsequently found unconstitutional.
30. Corte Suprema de Justicia de la Nación, S. 1767, XXXVIII, Recurso de Hecho s./caso Julio Héctor Simon, June 15, 2005.
31. *La Nacion*, June 20, 2003.
32. See, for example, the essays in José Natanson, ed., *El Presidente Inesperado: El gobierno de Kirchner según los intelectuales argentinos.* (Buenos Aires: Homo Sapiens Editorial, 2004).
33. *Ibid.*, p. 53. Kirchner's top advisor on human rights, Secretary of Human Rights Eduardo Luis Duhalde, is a well-known human rights lawyer, who defended political prisoners during the dictatorship, served as a human rights consultant to the UN, and authored an important book on repression in Argentina, *El Estado Terorista Argentina (The Argentine Terrorist State)*.
34. G. A. Res 2391 (XXIII) annex, 23 UN GAOR Supp (No. 18) at 40, UN Doc. A/7218 (1968).
35. The Cavallo case is also discussed in Chapter 4.
36. Abuelas de la Plaza de Mayo, *Juventud e Identidad*, Vol. II (Buenos Aires, Argentina: Espacio Editorial, 2001). Interview with Alcira Rios, December 2, 2002, Buenos Aires.
37. Luis Moreno Ocampo, the new prosecutor of the ICC, after serving as the assistant prosecutor of the trials against the military Juntas in Argentina, resigned from the judicial branch, and founded an important NGO in Argentina called "Poder Ciudadano" (Citizen Power). He was also a member of the board of Transparency International.

13 Transitional justice: Lessons learned and the road ahead

Ellen Lutz

The cases in this volume, which cover a broader spectrum of post-atrocity "accountability" scenarios than any previous study, offer an opportunity to think afresh about what is needed to achieve justice in the aftermath of massive, deliberately inflicted human suffering. All entail deliberate and institutionalized efforts to achieve justice. All were designed and implemented in preparation for, or in the aftermath of, a political transition. All involve some degree of negotiation among parties who were involved in causing abuses and parties who suffered as a result of the crimes. All have both domestic and international components. Moreover, all of the proposed accountability measures were justified in relation to two central, inter-related goals: (1) to respond to the suffering from past abuses; and (2) to prevent similar suffering from happening in the future.

Opportunities for victims and others to tell their stories, and for public acknowledgment of wrongs, accurately told – the most common objectives of truth commissions – are usually justified as measures to ease past suffering. Reparations processes, to the extent that they aim to remedy past harms, are also past-focused. In addition, trials of perpetrators, justified as vehicles for quelling individual or societal needs for justice, fall within the response to past violations goal.

Preventive goals are more numerous. Some, such as preventing past perpetrators from reasserting power or discouraging future perpetrators, are deterrence-driven. Others, such as building a justice system so that people will have a legitimate alternative to violence to which they can bring complaints when abuses occur, are aimed at reconstructing civil society in a form that is more likely to prevent future violations. Still others are aimed at preventing particular types of conduct that could contribute to reopening old wounds or igniting new animosities. These include preventing stigmatization by holding trials that personalize blame and preventing vigilantism through publicly legitimized prosecution and punishment. Steps taken to involve all members of society, regardless of their ethnicity or past affiliations, in the design of accountability processes, the writing of history books that accurately portray the past, or the construction of memorials to victims or courageous leaders who refused to engage in atrocities, are usually justified as efforts to contribute to the goal of future reconciliation.

But while they share the accountability goals of earlier transitional justice efforts, the cases in this volume differ in significant respects. Whereas the first generation transitional justice literature focused on cases involving transitions from military dictatorships, or discriminatory or authoritarian regimes, to democratically elected civilian governments, many of the cases in this volume involve transitions from armed conflict to uneasy peace. In addition, for all their complexity and variability, decision-makers in the early cases had less opportunity to observe how other states managed similar processes over time or garner "best practices" from other states' experiences. Furthermore, decision-makers in the early cases did not have the benefit of the jurisprudence that emerged in the 1990s from the Inter-American Court of Human Rights and the ad hoc Criminal Tribunals for the former Yugoslavia and Rwanda. The early cases also predated the interactive inter-state process of negotiating the norms and procedures for an International Criminal Court (ICC), and the further legitimization of those norms that resulted three years later when the sixtieth nation ratified the ICC statute making the ICC a reality.

More importantly, few of the early cases involved political transitions in the aftermath of civil wars in which large numbers of civilians on both sides were the deliberate victims of war crimes, crimes against humanity, or genocide, and the societal and institutional infra-structure was destroyed. Civilian governments in many first generation transitions had some semblance of a judicial system that could be activated to try cases, and the support of moral leaders who could be enlisted to head up truth commissions. They did not have to contend with circumstances in which those judges and moral leaders present beforehand were casualties of the conflict, or in which a functioning judiciary never existed. Nor did they have to detain thousands of alleged perpetrators of atrocities without adequate penal facilities, courtrooms, lawyers, or capacity to gather evidence. Moreover, in early transitional justice efforts state repression was almost always the main source of violations, and human rights law the explanatory paradigm; in the newer cases, war crimes by organized non-state forces are much more prevalent, and international humanitarian law is increasingly the language in which accountability demands are framed.

Finally, most of the early cases did not involve the kinds of extreme intervention by other states or inter-governmental organizations that characterize many of the cases in this volume. Even where international observers or monitors were present, as was the case in Central America, they were nowhere near as ubiquitous, nor was there as dominant a military or political presence as that of the US forces in Iraq and Afghanistan.

Rephrasing the questions

The cases in this volume reveal some basic truths about transitional justice that were far less evident a decade ago. In an earlier era, scholars and activists debated which was more important: Truth or Justice? Justice or Peace? These cases show the fallacy of such dichotomies. Today, decision-makers designing transitional justice processes increasingly understand that they cannot afford to isolate such fundamental, interdependent interests, and that, in the aftermath of conflict or widespread atrocities, all of the accountability goals must be met. While transitional governments may have some latitude in deciding in what order, when, and how to implement processes to achieve those goals, ignoring any of them risks destabilizing both those governments and the sustainability of peace. Even under the best of circumstances, as the chapters on Argentina and Mexico demonstrate, unmet transitional justice goals will cast a long shadow across the political landscape that will not go away until they are realized.

Grouping transitional justice processes into those involving "truth-telling" and those involving "trials," oversimplifies the complex calculus that states and their international partners must apply to achieve transitional justice objectives. Thus, in some cases decision-makers have afforded victims the opportunity to tell their stories to "truth and reconciliation commissions," while in others they limited them to doing so only in the context of providing evidence for a judicial proceeding. In some cases states have used trials to prevent former perpetrators from reasserting power; in others they achieved that goal by allowing them to "retire" abroad. The cases in this volume, particularly those that examine transitional justice process for atrocities committed many years ago, demonstrate that the most important indicator of the success of transitional justice measures is not *how* they achieve the above goals, but *whether* they do so.

Of course, all transitional justice processes must address multiple goals. Thus to be effective, the process of crafting each transitional justice mechanism must consider and balance all of those goals. In addition, the process must make provision for making adjustments over time to incorporate, adapt, or remove elements to improve its effectiveness and to ensure that whatever product results is actually put into practice. Moreover, transitional justice goals are not the only items on the post-transition agenda. Transitional governments must also address a host of non-transitional justice matters, including security, consolidating democratic practices and institutions, rebuilding neglected or damaged infrastructure, invigorating the economy, reinserting former soldiers into civilian life, and the return or resettlement of refugees or internally displaced persons. In many cases transitional leaders will face challenges from political opponents, including "spoilers" who oppose the transition or felt excluded from negotiations that led to it. Thus, in any transition, those holding power, even when they genuinely want to redress past violations, will feel pressure to balance transitional justice goals with the other urgent societal and political concerns. At the same time, these multiple concerns need at least enough coordination so that they do not run at cross-purposes.

Different post-transition governments have different degrees of interest in realizing transitional justice goals. But unlike two decades ago, they have more constraints operating against them if they lack the political will to undertake meaningful transitional justice measures. International political interest in transitional justice has now solidified, so that simply "brushing the past under the rug" is under most circumstances no longer an option. In part this transformation is the result of the international human rights movement's dogged interest in the issue which began with the trials of the nine Junta members in Argentina in 1985. Over time achieving justice for past violations of human rights assumed a prominent place on the agenda of the leading international human rights organizations, and the foundations that supported their work. Today new pressures, such as the existence of the ICC or the possibility that other states will exercise "universal jurisdiction" over their citizens, are motivating states to strengthen their domestic laws and procedures to ensure that their citizens, no matter how serious their crimes, can be tried at home rather than in an international forum.

But even more interesting, these combined events, along with the continued prodding of the international human rights movement, have led to a degree of international normative consensus that states must hold accountable those responsible for atrocious violations of human rights that approaches the level of consensus that states must respect human rights. As Kathryn Sikkink underscores in her article, the political and legal opportunity structure for accountability has changed. The international justice movement, operating in a dynamic partnership with domestic demands for accountability, has created a new multi-layered political and legal opportunity structure that makes it difficult for states to dismiss demands for accountability for widespread and systematic heinous human rights violations.

Are amnesties dead?

Beginning in the 1980s, civil lawsuits in United States courts and criminal indictments in European countries against perpetrators of human rights violations that were the subject of the first generation transitional justice literature (e.g., Argentina, El Salvador, Guatemala, the Philippines) began to limit the freedom of movement of perpetrators responsible for massive violations of human rights. But the indictment of Augusto Pinochet, former military strongman of Chile, in Spain, and the British House of Lords' subsequent holding that he could be extradited from the United Kingdom to Spain to stand trial for human rights abuses committed in Chile, undermined the long-standing assumption that post-transition, democratically elected governments controlled the transitional justice processes for human rights abuses committed in their territory. The Pinochet case was not the result of UN Security Council decision-making about how to respond to massive atrocities committed in war-torn, failed states. Rather, it was the result of a transnational social movement, backed by international law and other states committed to upholding the rule of law, to fulfill the transitional justice goals that post-Pinochet democratic Chile had failed to perform. Despite their best efforts, governments cannot decree the end of a transition.

The "Pinochet Effect," as Naomi Roht-Arriaza has called it, has made it increasingly difficult for perpetrators of human rights violations to evade accountability measures.[1] Whereas a generation ago, a domestic amnesty pretty well assured any high-level official responsible for massive human rights violations a comfortable retirement anywhere in the world, today travel abroad poses the hazard of arrest, trial, and punishment far from home. The possibility that their citizens might be tried abroad, coupled with establishment of the International Criminal Court, has led some states to sacrifice domestic immunity from prosecution if the alternative is an infringement of sovereignty resulting from having their former political leaders tried elsewhere. As Kathryn Sikkink and I have previously written, governments, and even the armed forces, of countries committed to consolidating democracy, want to foster the perception that their courts possess the competence, capacity, and independence to effectively try their own nationals.[2]

International human rights courts are increasingly declaring that amnesty provisions violate international law. In 1998, an ICTY trial chamber noted that a domestic amnesty covering crimes such as torture that have attained *jus cogens* status "would not be accorded international legal recognition."[3] In the Americas, the Inter-American Court of Human Rights has declared that amnesty measures, to the extent that "they are intended to prevent the investigation and punishment of those responsible for serious human rights violations such as torture, extrajudicial, summary or arbitrary execution and forced disappearance, all of them prohibited because they violate non-derogable rights recognized by international human rights law," violate the American Convention on Human Rights.[4]

These courts do not base their findings on explicit "no amnesty" provisions in international human rights treaties. Indeed, some international law treaties explicitly require states to grant "the broadest possible amnesty to persons who have participated in armed conflict."[5] Rather, the courts imply a duty not to grant amnesty from more general international norms requiring states to provide victims with remedies for human rights violations, or to prosecute perpetrators, as well as from specific provisions in treaties on torture, forced disappearances, genocide and certain war crimes.[6]

There are plausible arguments for amnesties. The Sierra Leone Truth and Reconciliation Commission's Report, for example, cautions that, "those who argue that peace cannot be bartered in exchange for justice, under any circumstances, must be prepared to justify the likely prolongation of an armed conflict."[7] In that case, the Truth and Reconciliation Commission found itself "unable to declare that it considers amnesty too high a price to pay for the delivery of peace to Sierra Leone."[8] Jack Snyder and Leslie Vinjamuri argue elsewhere that amnesties can help entrench the rule of law in a fledgling democracy. They maintain that "norm-governed political order must be based on a political bargain among contending groups and on the creation of robust administrative institutions that can predictably enforce the law." Thus, where restoring peace, security, and order are the paramount concerns, granting amnesties can help accomplish that goal. Once granted, Snyder and Vinjamuri maintain, amnesties must be respected to shore up fragile political and judicial institutions that, in turn, are the best insurance policy against violence breaking out anew. In their view, institution-building is a pragmatic domestic process that is prerequisite to the embedding of norms. Once securely in place, those institutions can help to create a climate of normative consensus for the just norms expressed in international law treaties, but this process never works the other way around.

Both of these arguments are undermined by research conducted by Christine Bell who found that most peace agreements do not deal with past abuses of human rights.[9] Instead, accountability issues are left to the implementation stage. Moreover, when they do appear in the text of settlement agreements, they are vulnerable to post-settlement revision. Thus, in Sierra Leone, both the Truth and Reconciliation Commission and the Special Court's hybrid national-international trials, described in detail in this volume, have been instituted. The government has begun the long, slow process of institution-building necessary to consolidate democratic legitimacy and the rule of law. Neither the offer of amnesty nor the UN caveat of non-support for amnesty had much influence over RUF behavior. Rather, it was the disingenuousness of their leader, who cared more about his own hide and future wealth than peace or prosperity for the country that undermined the Lomé Agreement.

A similar scenario is now being played out in Afghanistan where, instead of being disarmed, former warlords have been selectively welcomed at both the negotiation table and into the transitional government to reduce the likelihood that violence continues. The result is a government that is dominated by heavily armed faction leaders whose power comes from the implied threat of renewed violence rather than true leadership or democratic legitimacy. If there is any lesson to be drawn from these two cases, it is that criminals make untrustworthy negotiating partners, and their inclusion in democratic institution-building is likely to prolong and de-legitimize those processes.

The cases in this volume teach another lesson about amnesties: that no promises to perpetrators of serious human rights and humanitarian law crimes are likely to withstand the test of time. Peru's amnesty laws were overturned as a result of an Inter-American Court decision, and despite problems some prosecutions are going forward.

The indictment in 2004 of former President Luis Echeverría and other Mexican officials on charges of genocide for the massacre of at least 25 student protesters in 1971 is another example. The indictment was brought by the Special Prosecutor named by President Vicente Fox to "discover and reveal past abuses, determine personal and institutional responsibility, and systematize and disseminate the truth about Mexico's dirty war." The hunger for justice for this crime, which human rights activists claim resulted in the deaths of as many as 300 protesters, survived 33 years of tacit agreement among PRI presidents to protect their predecessors from charges for human rights-related crimes.

Argentina is engaged in a similar process of re-examining its amnesty laws. Political interests in Argentina have undergone a sea change between 1987, when President Alfonsín pushed amnesty measures through the Congress, and 2003, when the Argentine Congress, with the support of the newly elected President Néstor Kirchner, passed a law that declared the amnesty laws void. The Supreme Court in June 2005 confirmed this result, and cases against former perpetrators are moving forward in Argentina's courts.

All these developments mean that the political calculus for governments, and for powerful perpetrators of atrocities, has changed. Thus, in Colombia, President Uribe has not granted amnesty to the paramilitary forces with which it is negotiating. Instead, his government has negotiated a nuanced scheme that skirts an outright amnesty but also protects demobilizing paramilitaries from serious penal consequences for past crimes. This suggests that states and perpetrators of atrocities are adapting their behavior to cope with the new normative milieu, and that those who seek to bolster the no-amnesty norm must be vigilant to ensure that negotiated agreements or other processes that pay lip service to accountability are not, in fact, smoke and mirrors tricks.

When others intervene

External intervention has both exacerbated the underlying atrocities that lead to the need for transitional justice, and contributed to the process of achieving that justice. Both such effects occurred in many of the early cases, particularly those in Central America where conservative governments received huge infusions of US military assistance to combat guerrilla movements, but used that aid to commit egregious human rights and humanitarian law crimes. On the other hand, these countries were aided by UN mediators, peacekeeping monitors, and/or international participation in truth and reconciliation activities. In Bosnia and Rwanda, a similar phenomenon occurred, although in those cases it was US, European, and international community inaction that raised the confidence of the parties engaged in genocide, ethnic cleansing, holding siege to civilian strongholds, and committing war crimes and other atrocities.

But nothing from these earlier cases matches the degree to which external intervention skewed transitional justice initiatives in Iraq. No matter when it fell, Saddam Hussein's regime destined itself to leave behind a traumatized and insecure population, aching to know what had happened to hundreds of thousands of disappeared loved ones, and hungering for revenge for ruthless murders and poisonous gassing of thousands of political opponents and genocide victims. But, as the Iraq case study demonstrates, rather than quickly implementing consultation, careful planning, and collaboration with the world's most experienced transitional justice experts, the Bush administration compounded the suffering of the Iraqi people by blindly barreling ahead with its own paradigm of transitional justice. One of the gravest errors made by the United States in Iraq was not planning for meaningful ways to include a broad cross-section of the Iraqi people in decision-making about what transitional justice mechanisms should look like. Instead, determined for its own purposes to capture and condemn Saddam Hussein and his close allies, the United States leaped into action on the accountability front in the same manner that it had proceeded on the liberation front: it ignored local interests and talent, failed to collaborate with its allies and international experts, and, instead of pursuing a carefully mapped-out course, put itself in the position of having constantly to react to ever more severe problems.

Afghanistan is a similar story. While not technically occupied, the US invasion unseated a regime that oppressed an ethnically and politically divided state with few functioning democratic institutions. Civil society efforts to even contemplate transitional justice have been trumped by measures to keep the peace in the most heavily armed country in the world.[10] Both the United States and the United Nations supported including factional leaders responsible for war crimes and worse in positions of power, thereby undermining accountability and putting at risk those who called for those factional leaders to be brought to justice. On the other hand, perhaps because outside interveners have not been all-pervasive in the reconstruction process, national civil-society organizations have found political space in which to become involved.

External intervention has contributed to the standardization of transitional justice goals and methods. As an understanding of what it takes to achieve accountability for past violations permeates the international community, this understanding is transferred to the state domain when international intervention takes place. This is both deliberate and ad hoc. On the one hand, Special Representatives of the UN Secretary-General are now sent on missions with guidelines that prohibit them from sanctioning amnesties and other impediments to the achievement of accountability. On the other, the cadre of civil servants sent by the United Nations from one crisis spot to the next is made up of legal technocrats with shared knowledge, experience, and values who believe that accountability for past violations is an essential component of a transition process. With the support of the UN Office of the High Commissioner for Human Rights, these international agents support and assist local political actors to implement transitional justice mechanisms.

Contextual and cultural appropriateness

The cases in this book also demonstrate that to be effective, transitional justice mechanisms must be both contextually and culturally appropriate. While diffusion from prior experiences of ideas and examples creates the range of examples and potential strategies, each place adapts, develops, and shapes its own transitional justice experience in light of its own context and culture. There are no "off-the-shelf" answers.

There are some essential prerequisites to any accountability process. As the authors of the chapters on Iraq and Afghanistan show, "without some level of security, transitional justice processes are doomed to fail."[11] Moreover, an infrastructure and the requisite political will to create the conditions in which genuine accountability can take place must precede any such measures. There can be no public acknowledgement of wrongs committed in the past if there is no legitimate representative political body able to listen to and acknowledge them. There can be no truth-telling without protection from retaliation for those who desire to do so. There can be no trials without laws, and judges, and lawyers, and courthouses, and the means to gather and protect evidence.

Sometimes justice has to wait. That does not mean it will not happen eventually, or that immediately realizing other goals, such as preventing perpetrators from reasserting power or terrorizing the population, are not essential. One of the lessons of these cases is that even if justice waits, eventually its time will come. Thus immediate action on all aspects of the transitional justice front is not always essential.

Sometimes measures to achieve accountability will conflict with other human rights principles. In such cases, competing rights must be balanced against one another. In Rwanda, for example, the government had to balance the need to detain participants in the genocide so that they could both be held accountable and also prevented from joining antigovernment Hutu militias, with the human rights duty to try criminal defendants within a reasonable time. In that case, while the international community had legitimate concerns about the length and conditions of their detention, the Rwandan government could not be faulted for concluding that "a reasonable time" was many years, or even decades.

Sometimes justice has to come in creative forms. When the Rwandan *gacaca* system was first considered, the international human rights community balked. As the chapter on Rwanda demonstrates, the idea of accused *genocidaires* "sitting on the grass" before elders and other community leaders, facing accusations and defending their conduct in settings other than regularly constituted courts in which the rules of due process applied, did not comport with their understanding of the provisions of international human rights instruments. On the other hand, Rwandans did not see much justice in a dual system in which the planners and promoters of the genocide would be tried under genteel, due process-protecting conditions by well-paid judges, and sentenced to prison terms in comfortable foreign jails, while their followers who did the dirty work faced years in primitive detention centers, because the Rwandan government lacked the resources to bring them to trial, and the death penalty if convicted.

The *gacaca* process was created by Rwandans who looked to their own history and culture to find a culturally acceptable solution to an over-whelming problem. Designed as both a justice and a reconciliation process, *gacaca* trials were meant to overcome inherent problems of the Rwandan justice system, which was widely perceived as detached from the people who suffered and the communities they were meant to influ-ence. Moreover, those who developed the *gacaca* system were mindful of and influenced by international human rights law standards. While some due process problems are of serious human rights concern, such as the failure to provide defendants with adequate mechanisms to assist them in their defense, Rwanda has found alternative ways of satisfying other underlying human rights principles.

In East Timor, local communities increased the level of participation and legitimacy in the Community Reconciliation Process (CRP) by in-corporating attributes of the traditional dispute-resolution process of *nahe biti bot* or "unrolling of the mat" into hearings. The cultural and spiritual underpinnings of *nahe biti bot* had sustained the people of East Timor for thousands of years, including throughout the epoch of Portu-guese and Indonesian rule when the national justice system was corrupt and lacked independence from political powers. While the international community intended traditional and spiritual practices to be elements in the community reconciliation process, Patrick Burgess credits them with heightening CRP success through their incorporation of collective norms that bind communities, and by permitting the conduct of community members to be adjudicated by traditional leaders whose role it is to pronounce on community norms and execute justice.

While these local-level initiatives show great promise as an aspect of transitional justice, caution is in order. Traditional dispute resolution practices may reflect the exclusion of women or other groups, and may privilege the communal over the individual to the degree that they obstruct goals of victim empowerment. They also, by definition, must arise from each society (or even local area), and thus cannot be easily transposed from one place to another. On the other hand, local-level initiatives force international advocates and funders to think in a more nuanced way about the role of formal courts and Western-style legal systems, and to incorporate that new understanding into work at the intersection of transitional justice and rule of law.

Creativity can come in forms other than allowing for adequate expres-sion of cultural traditions or community values. In more legalized societies it can come in the form of identifying novel legal theories that enable justice to take place when more familiar legal theories or procedural barriers appear to block it. In Mexico, Special Prosecutor Carrillo Prieto pressed charges of genocide against former President Luis Echeverria and his co-defendants for the 1968 massacre in Tlatelolco because, under existing laws, there apparently was no other way around the statute of limitations. In Argentina, lawyers for the Grandmothers of the Plaza de Mayo successfully used the innovative legal arguments on the kidnapping of children to persuade that country's courts to find that amnesty provisions did not apply to senior government officials. Creativity can also come in the choice of forum, for example the decision to bring charges against Hissène Habré in Senegal.

Managing multiple mechanisms

If multiple forms of accountability processes are to be undertaken, forethought is needed regarding how to balance and sequence them. Horovitz identifies some of the problems that can arise when that planning is lacking. She concludes that in Sierra Leone it would have been better if the Truth and Reconciliation Commission had finished its operations before the commencement of the Special Court's process. Doing so would have reduced public confusion about the respective roles of the two institutions, and possibly increased public cooperation with the TRC. It would also have enabled the Special Court to make use of the TRC's report to shore up its legitimacy and as a source of evidence. The tensions between truth commission and trial processes recur in many other cases. And the order of sequencing is not foreordained: Burgess suggests that one advantage of setting up the Timorese CAVR after the establishment of a prosecutors' office was that the CAVR could be consciously designed to fill the holes left by the limited mandate of the Special Crimes Unit.

Part of the tension lies in the unique constraints of criminal trials which depend on credible testimony, the presupposition that a defendant is innocent until proven guilty, due process protections that entitle defendants to cross-examine and impeach witnesses, including victims who testify against them, and the possibility that a person that everyone "knows" is responsible for atrocities will be acquitted on account of lack of adequate legally acceptable evidence or procedural error. Truth commissions, which do not have to conform to rules of evidence or worry about the due process rights of perpetrators, are freer to create opportunities for large numbers of survivors to tell their stories without being cross-examined, and to address their reports to posterity rather than to judges or juries. This may explain why Schabas is more encouraging about the simultaneous use of both mechanisms.

Even when truth commissions are designed to contribute to the prosecutorial process, lack of coordination between them and other government agencies can undermine good intentions. In Peru the lack of an agreed strategy by the Truth and Reconciliation Commission and the *Ministerio Público* about how to address the complexities of systemic crimes led to confusion and competition among investigators of the respective institutions. This was aggravated by a disparity of resources in favor of the TRC. The antagonism between the agencies manifested itself in refusals by the *Ministerio Público* to accept into evidence some of the research of the TRC for reasons as absurd as failing to number pages with numbers instead of letters, and even to frivolous, politically motivated criminal indictments against TRC investigators. But the worst consequence was the diminishment of the accountability process as a result of duplicative efforts and the inability to cooperate.

Other cases in this volume also illustrate the importance of careful planning over how to allocate resources among multiple transitional justice processes. For example, in East Timor, the community reconciliation process was predicated on the existence of the Special Panels to try the most serious offenders. But because the Special Crimes Unit had few resources to investigate alleged perpetrators, community reconciliation processes may have been compromised. As was noted earlier, the disparity of resources among the various transitional justice processes for Rwanda, undermined the legitimacy of all of those processes.

Who owns the process?

When outsiders intervene, whether to encourage or to undermine accountability measures, there is an inherent tension over who has ownership of the process. Processes that are largely insider designed and managed, and that are politically popular, such as those that occurred in Argentina and Peru, have the highest levels of legitimacy. Indeed, in Peru the Truth Commission had such high levels of political and popular support that it became politically costly to oppose it or to appear to be obstructing its tasks. On the other extreme, outsider-driven processes like that of Iraq are likely to face significant problems ensuring both continuity and legitimacy.

Even in internally driven processes, insufficient support from both the government and civil society may hamper efforts at accountability. In Mexico, inadequate political support, notwithstanding popular interest in coming to terms with the past, undermined the Special Prosecutor's efforts to move beyond the goal of publicly acknowledging the truth to prosecuting those responsible. The fact that the Special Prosecutor was hindered from operating in an independent and transparent manner undermined his legitimacy and ultimately the legitimacy of the entire accountability endeavor. The lesson seems to be that civil society can keep the issue of accountability alive, but it takes a certain level of government political will to decisively move forward, as the examples of Argentina with the ascent of President Kirchner, Chad, and East Timor illustrate. Furthermore, if the transformation of society is limited, as Schabas points out, transitional justice will also be limited.

Outsider-run processes tend to have less internal legitimacy than those designed and run by insiders, even though they may satisfy the interests of interveners or international human rights advocates to ensure that justice is done. This was apparent in the first generation of transitional justice cases after the Salvadoran Congress immediately negated the efforts of an internationally mandated, funded, and conducted Truth Commission by granting amnesty to those named in the Commission's report. In Sierra Leone, the Truth and Reconciliation Commission encountered some legitimacy problems that arose from its partially external character. In particular, the lack of domestic funding negatively impacted any sense of local ownership. The clear lesson is that even when outsiders intervene, they need to take the necessary steps to ensure that civil society has a genuine sense of ownership of the process, which includes being involved in its design and implementation, and may require that domestic resources be expended in order for it to happen at all.

On the other hand, justice requires that a careful balance be struck between ensuring that a process is "legitimate" in the eyes of internal political elites, or even the populace at large, and that it is "legitimate" to the victims. Transitional justice processes everywhere are plagued by funding shortages, politically mandated short timetables, statutes of limitation, and competing interests that limit their reach and overall effectiveness. Even with such limitations, however, they can achieve justice if they create enough space for those who suffered to feel as though they had a meaningful opportunity to take part in the process.

All of the cases in this volume reveal the influence of resources on decision-making about transitional justice, and ultimately on the legit-imacy of transitional justice processes. In addition to the disparity of resources between international and domestic processes for Rwanda, disparities can occur between different domestic processes. Sometimes the decision to provide greater resources for, say, a truth and reconcili-ation process and be stingy with a prosecution process is made to appease powerful political opponents who might otherwise face trial or other political reasons. But often resource disparities are the result of poor planning or lack of coordination, with different initiatives funded piecemeal rather than as a package. In East Timor, criminal prosecutions were hampered by successive transfers of investigative responsibility from one international agency to another, and by the fact that, for international political reasons unrelated to events in East Timor, none of the international judges participating in the process had any prior experience or training in international criminal law. In Sierra Leone, the mandate of the Special Court had to be scaled back when the international community provided only $56 million to a Voluntary Fund for a process that was originally expected to cost $100 million, and the TRC was similarly scaled back due to funding shortfalls. The disparity in resources between the two institutions also created tensions and resentment.

Conclusion

Since its inception, the transitional justice movement has operated on the principle that transitional justice, and the goals that underlie it, are by definition a good thing. While this may be apparent in the abstract, these cases show how muddy the reality on the ground can be. Comparative case studies, like these, help us to better understand the problems in anecdotal ways, but they are no substitute for more comprehensive evaluation processes designed to measure the effectiveness of accountability mechanisms over time.

Obviously, this is easier to assert than to do. Justice does not lend itself to measurement of improvements in the way that efforts to eradicate disease or improve literacy or increase per capita income do. While we can count the number of alleged perpetrators who are tried or found guilty, it is much harder to calculate victim or societal satisfaction with the process. While we can claim that deterrence is an important transitional justice rationale, where abuses or other violence do not break out anew, it is hard to determine in what way transitional justice processes contributed to non-recurrence. While we might believe that transitional justice processes contribute to the solidification of democratic civil society institutions, there are so many other independent variables that are part of any transition process that it is hard to isolate what role accountability measures played.

Notwithstanding the challenges of measurement, these cases underscore the critical importance of evaluation. As long as we continue to develop transitional justice mechanisms in a reactive, ad hoc, politically biased manner, we will continue to make the mistakes that permeate these cases. Qualitative evaluation processes need to be designed and funded to be carried out not just on a one-time basis or mid-way through or at the end of a particular process, but over a period of many years, even decades. They need to take into account and balance the assessment of a cross-section of stakeholders in accountability processes including victims, perpetrators, participants in the processes, political actors who put the processes in place, a wide sampling of society at large, domestic and international human rights champions, and other relevant international actors. They need to be responsive to all the goals that transitional justice mechanisms purport to achieve. They need to examine the extent of diffusion from one transitional justice process to others.

On the other hand, these cases shed light on some of the problems that arise when the international actors intervened in places where transitional justice measures are needed. Extensive additional evaluation is not needed to begin to craft a set of guidelines that should guide international interveners under such circumstances. Such guidelines should address the importance of creating conditions that allow maximal local control over decision-making about the process, including what mechanisms are established; who can participate; who gets tried; how long the processes should last; and what cultural or contextual factors need to be incorporated. They should address what qualifications international interveners, particularly international investigators, judges, and other participants in the process, should possess, and they should address the urgent need for financial commitments to be clearly made up-front and to be honored once committed. Finally, they should address the question of what legacy international interveners should leave behind. This might include the physical infrastructure of national institutions such as courts, prosecutors' offices, or police departments. It might include leaving behind not only nationals trained to do the jobs required by those institutions, but also the educational systems capable of teaching the next generation of professionals to do those jobs. It might include measures to ensure that other states accurately reflect the outcomes of genuine transitional justice processes in their accounts of history.

As the world relearned when the Berlin wall fell and again on September 11, 2001, seemingly stable political orders can be transformed overnight. The United States' hostility to the International Criminal Court, its post-September 11 acceptance of torture as a means to interrogate or discipline captives, coupled with its single super-power, anti-international law arrogance, has been a blow to the international justice movement. It is too soon to tell how deeply that blow has struck or how long-lasting the consequences will be, but it cannot be ignored. On the other hand, there is reason to hope. In spite of US bombast, 100 nations are now members of the International Criminal Court. Indeed, as Sikkink points out in connection to Argentina, active US hegemonic opposition to the expansion of international human rights law, along with the United States' record in Abu Graib and Guantánamo, may spur worldwide advancement of norms and institutions that strengthen protection for human rights and ensure even greater accountability.

NOTES

1. Naomi Roht-Arriaza, *The Pinochet Effect: Transnational Justice in the Age of Human Rights* (University of Pennsylvania Press, 2005).
2. Ellen Lutz and Kathryn Sikkink, "The Justice Cascade: The Evolution and Impact of Foreign Human Rights Trials in Latin America", (2001) *Chicago Journal of International Law*, 2, p. 1.
3. *Prosecutor* v. *Furundzija*, judgment of December 10, 1998, para. 155.
4. Barrios Altos (*Chumbipuma Aguirre y otros* v. *Peru*), March 14, 2001.
5. Protocol Additional II to the 1949 Geneva Conventions relating to the Protection of Victims of Non-International Armed Conflicts, (1979) 1125 UNTS 609.
6. Convention Against Torture, Art. 5; Genocide Convention, Art. 5; Geneva Conventions "grave breaches" provisions, e.g. Geneva Convention I, Art. 49; II, Art. 50; III, Art. 129; IV, Art. 146; Inter-American Convention on Enforced and Involuntary Disappearances.
7. *Witness to Truth: Report of the Sierra Leone Truth and Reconciliation Commission*, Vol. 3B, Freetown, 2004, Chapter VI, paras. 11–12.
8. *Ibid.*, para. 12.
9. Christine Bell, *Peace Agreements and Human Rights* (Oxford: Oxford University Press, 2000).
10. See Chapter 10.
11. See Chapter 9.

Index